SOMETHING ABOUT THE AUTHOR®

Something about
the Author *was named
an "Outstanding
Reference Source,"*
*the highest honor given
by the American
Library Association
Reference and Adult
Services Division.*

ISSN 0276-816X

SOMETHING ABOUT THE AUTHOR®

**Facts and Pictures about Authors
and Illustrators of Books for Young People**

volume 234

GALE
CENGAGE Learning®

Detroit • New York • San Francisco • New Haven, Conn • Waterville, Maine • London

Something about the Author, Volume 234

Project Editor: Lisa Kumar

Permissions: Leitha Etheridge-Sims

Imaging and Multimedia: Leitha Etheridge-Sims, John Watkins

Composition and Electronic Capture: Amy Darga

Manufacturing: Rhonda Dover

Product Manager: Mary Onorato

For product information and technology assistance, contact us at **Gale Customer Support, 1-800-877-4253.**
For permission to use material from this text or product, submit all requests online at **www.cengage.com/permissions.**
Further permissions questions can be emailed to **permissionrequest@cengage.com**

Gale, Cengage Learning
27500 Drake Rd.
Farmington Hills, MI, 48331-3535

LIBRARY OF CONGRESS CATALOG CARD NUMBER 62-52046

ISBN-13: 978-1-4144-6924-9
ISBN-10: 1-4144-6924-1

ISSN 0276-816X

This title is also available as an e-book.
ISBN-13: 978-1-4144-8236-1
ISBN-10: 1-4144-8236-1Contact your Gale, Cengage Learning sales representative for ordering information.

Printed in Mexico
1 2 3 4 5 6 7 15 14 13 12

Contents

Authors in Forthcoming Volumes

Below are some of the authors and illustrators that will be featured in upcoming volumes of *SATA*. These include new entries on the swiftly rising stars of the field, as well as completely revised and updated entries (indicated with *) on some of the most notable and best-loved creators of books for children.

Simon Basher ▮ Basher, a British artist and designer, has created "Basher Books," a series geared for middle-elementary graders that simplifies science-related topics by personifying key elements and concepts. Noted for an illustration style that has been described as somewhere between manga and "Hello Kitty," Basher also entertains the toddler set with his library of colorful board books featuring counting, the alphabet, and other basic concepts highlighted by his colorful graphics.

*Andrew Clements ▮ Clements is a former teacher who transitioned into publishing and since the mid-1980s has shared his love of books and reading by writing chapter books and middle-grade fiction. His award-winning novel *Frindle* has become something of a classic, and he has continued to earn a wide readership through picture books such as *Temple Cat* and *Dogku*, the middle-grade novel *Things That Are,* and the chapter books in his "Jake Drake" series.

*Susan Middleton Elya ▮ Elya draws on her background as a Spanish teacher to create award-winning books that often contain "Spanglish" texts. While working as an English as a second language (ESL) teacher, she learned the importance of dual English/Spanish texts in helping English-speaking children studying a second language. Elya's books focusing on language-building skills include *F Is for Fiesta*, *Bebé Goes Shopping*, and *Tooth on the Loose*.

*John Green ▮ While Green worked at *Booklist* magazine, he also completed the manuscript that would become his award-winning novel *Looking for Alaska*. In addition to continuing his career in young-adult fiction with novels such as *An Abundance of Katherines* and *Paper Towns*, he has also made his mark in the Web video world; a collaboration with his brother Hank Green, his video blog Brotherhood 2.0 has spawned millions of fans—dubbed Nerdfighters—and also raised money for charities throughout the world.

Nikol Hasler ▮ Hasler wrote her first book, *Sex: A Book for Teens: An Uncensored Guide to Your Body, Sex, and Safety*, while hosting the Web podcast series *The Midwest Teen Sex Show*, which since 2007 has gained a large following and attracted attention from the mainstream media. Suddenly transformed into a media figure and an expert on issues of teen sexuality, she decided to produce a book on the subject that continues her goal of sharing important and sometimes life-saving information with young people.

*David Levithan ▮ An author and editor, Levithan writes for teens and young adults and his novels include *Boy Meets Boy*, *The Realm of Possibility*, and *Are We There Yet?*, as well as collaborative stories with writers John Green and Rachel Cohn. As editorial director and executive editor of Scholastic's Push imprint, he also mentors promising young writers and new authors in the young-adult genre. His accomplishments as an editor include his work on ground-breaking anthologies such as *The Full Spectrum: A New Generation of Writing about Gay, Lesbian, Bisexual, Transgendered, Questioning, and Other Identities*.

Jackson Pearce ▮ Pearce is the author of the young-adult fantasy novels *As You Wish, Sisters Red*, and *Sweetly*. In *As You Wish* a broken-hearted teen winds up in an unusual romance after she inadvertently calls forth a handsome jinn and is offered three wishes. For her more-recent novels, Pearce has mined well-known fairy tales such as "Little Red Riding Hood" and "Hansel and Gretel," recasting her tales with confident young women and settings that reflect Pearces' own Georgia roots.

Polly Shulman ▮ A mathematics major and an editor for magazines such as *Discover* and *Science* magazine, Shulman showcased her literary side in her young-adult novels *Enthusiasm* and *The Grimm Legacy*. An homage to Jane Austen's *Pride and Prejudice*, *Enthusiasm* finds a high-school sophomore drawn into a romantic puzzle by an overly passionate long-time friend. For the heroine of *The Grimm Legacy*, a job at an unusual lending library proves to be the entry to a far more fantastical puzzle, one that weaves together magical as well as malevolent elements.

R.A. Spratt ▮ Born in England and now living in Australia, Spratt wrote for children's television for almost a decade before turning her attention to children's books. Her first book, *The Adventures of Nanny Piggins*, was published in 2009 and was followed by a steady stream of equally humorous elementary-grade chapter books. The "Nanny Piggins" phenomenon quickly made its way to Spratt's native England and from there jumped the Atlantic to win fans in the United States.

Katie Williams ▮ Williams made the decision to become a writer while earning her English degree at the University of Michigan, and she began the manuscript for her first novel, *The Space between Trees*, while completing her M.F.A. program. Highly praised by critics for its sophisticated telling, *The Space between Trees* focuses on a lonely sixteen year old whose penchant for white lies involves her in a local murder and transforms her reality into something far more dangerous than anything her imagination could conjure.

Introduction

Something about the Author (*SATA*) is an ongoing reference series that examines the lives and works of authors and illustrators of books for children. *SATA* includes not only well-known writers and artists but also less prominent individuals whose works are just coming to be recognized. This series is often the only readily available information source on emerging authors and illustrators. You'll find *SATA* informative and entertaining, whether you are a student, a librarian, an English teacher, a parent, or simply an adult who enjoys children's literature.

What's Inside *SATA*

SATA provides detailed information about authors and illustrators who span the full time range of children's literature, from early figures like John Newbery and L. Frank Baum to contemporary figures like Judy Blume and Richard Peck. Authors in the series represent primarily English-speaking countries, particularly the United States, Canada, and the United Kingdom. Also included, however, are authors from around the world whose works are available in English translation. The writings represented in *SATA* include those created intentionally for children and young adults as well as those written for a general audience and known to interest younger readers. These writings cover the entire spectrum of children's literature, including picture books, humor, folk and fairy tales, animal stories, mystery and adventure, science fiction and fantasy, historical fiction, poetry and nonsense verse, drama, biography, and nonfiction. Obituaries are also included in many volumes of *SATA* and are intended not only as death notices but also as concise overviews of people's lives and work. Additionally, each edition features newly revised and updated entries for a selection of *SATA* listees who remain of interest to today's readers and who have been active enough to require extensive revisions of their earlier biographies.

Autobiography Feature

Beginning with Volume 103, many volumes of *SATA* feature one or more specially commissioned autobiographical essays. These unique essays, averaging about ten thousand words in length and illustrated with an abundance of personal photos, present an entertaining and informative first-person perspective on the lives and careers of prominent authors and illustrators profiled in *SATA*.

Two Convenient Indexes

In response to suggestions from librarians, *SATA* indexes no longer appear in every volume but are included in alternate (odd-numbered) volumes of the series, beginning with Volume 57.

SATA continues to include two indexes that cumulate with each alternate volume: the Illustrations Index, arranged by the name of the illustrator, gives the number of the volume and page where the illustrator's work appears in the current volume as well as all preceding volumes in the series; the Author Index gives the number of the volume in which a person's biographical sketch, autobiographical essay, or obituary appears in the current volume as well as all preceding volumes in the series.

These indexes also include references to authors and illustrators who appear in *Gale's Yesterday's Authors of Books for Children, Children's Literature Review,* and *Something about the Author Autobiography Series.*

Easy-to-Use Entry Format

Whether you're already familiar with the *SATA* series or just getting acquainted, you will want to be aware of the kind of information that an entry provides. In every *SATA* entry the editors attempt to give as complete a picture of the person's life and work as possible. A typical entry in *SATA* includes the following clearly labeled information sections:

PERSONAL: date and place of birth and death, parents' names and occupations, name of spouse, date of marriage, names of children, educational institutions attended, degrees received, religious and political affiliations, hobbies and other interests.

ADDRESSES: complete home, office, electronic mail, and agent addresses, whenever available.

CAREER: name of employer, position, and dates for each career post; art exhibitions; military service; memberships and offices held in professional and civic organizations.

MEMBER: professional, civic, and other association memberships and any official posts held.

AWARDS, HONORS: literary and professional awards received.

WRITINGS: title-by-title chronological bibliography of books written and/or illustrated, listed by genre when known; lists of other notable publications, such as plays, screenplays, and periodical contributions.

ADAPTATIONS: a list of films, television programs, plays, CD-ROMs, recordings, and other media presentations that have been adapted from the author's work.

WORK IN PROGRESS: description of projects in progress.

SIDELIGHTS: a biographical portrait of the author or illustrator's development, either directly from the biographee—and often written specifically for the *SATA* entry—or gathered from diaries, letters, interviews, or other published sources.

BIOGRAPHICAL AND CRITICAL SOURCES: cites sources quoted in "Sidelights" along with references for further reading.

EXTENSIVE ILLUSTRATIONS: photographs, movie stills, book illustrations, and other interesting visual materials supplement the text.

How a *SATA* Entry Is Compiled

SATA editors examine a wide variety of published sources to gather information for an entry. Biographical and bibliographic sources are consulted, as are book reviews, feature articles, published interviews, and material sometimes obtained from the biographee's family, publishers, agent, or other associates. Whenever possible, the author or illustrator is sent a copy of the entry to check for accuracy and completeness.

Entries that have not been verified by the biographees or their representatives are marked with an asterisk (*).

Contact the Editor

We encourage our readers to examine the entire *SATA* series. Please write and tell us if we can make *SATA* even more helpful to you. Give your comments and suggestions to the editor:

Editor
Something about the Author
Gale, Cengage Learning
27500 Drake Rd.
Farmington Hills MI 48331-3535

Toll-free: 800-877-GALE
Fax: 248-699-8070

Something about the Author Product Advisory Board

The editors of *Something about the Author* are dedicated to maintaining a high standard of excellence by publishing comprehensive, accurate, and highly readable entries on a wide array of writers for children and young adults. In addition to the quality of the content, the editors take pride in the graphic design of the series, which is intended to be orderly yet inviting, allowing readers to utilize the pages of *SATA* easily and with efficiency. Despite the longevity of the *SATA* print series, and the success of its format, we are mindful that the vitality of a literary reference product is dependent on its ability to serve its users over time. As literature, and attitudes about literature, constantly evolve, so do the reference needs of students, teachers, scholars, journalists, researchers, and book club members. To be certain that we continue to keep pace with the expectations of our customers, the editors of *SATA* listen carefully to their comments regarding the value, utility, and quality of the series. Librarians, who have firsthand knowledge of the needs of library users, are a valuable resource for us. The *Something about the Author* Product Advisory Board, made up of school, public, and academic librarians, is a forum to promote focused feedback about *SATA* on a regular basis. The nine-member advisory board includes the following individuals, whom the editors wish to thank for sharing their expertise:

SOMETHING ABOUT THE AUTHOR

ACKERMAN, Peter

Personal

Born in Pittsburgh, PA; married; children: two sons. *Education:* Yale University, B.A. (English); attended American Conservatory Theater.

Addresses

Home—New York, NY.

Career

Screenwriter and playwright. Voice actor in films, including *Ice Age* and *Ice Age: The Meltdown.*

Awards, Honors

Annie Award nomination for Outstanding Writing in an Animated Feature Production (with Michael Berg and Michael J. Wilson), 2003, for *Ice Age.*

Writings

The Lonely Phonebooth, illustrated by Max Dalton, David R. Godine (Boston, MA), 2010.

SCREENPLAYS

(With Michael Berg and Michael J. Wilson) *Ice Age,* Twentieth Century-Fox, 2002.

(With Michael Berg, Yoni Brenner, and Mike Reiss) *Ice Age: Dawn of the Dinosaurs,* Twentieth Century-Fox, 2009.

OTHER

Also author of play, *Things You Shouldn't Say Past Midnight.*

Sidelights

A playwright and screenwriter, Peter Ackerman is perhaps best known for his work on the popular animated films *Ice Age* and *Ice Age: Dawn of the Dinosaurs,* featuring the voices of Ray Romano, Denis Leary, and John Leguizamo. Ackerman is also the author of *The Lonely Phonebooth,* a picture book that offers an "intimate look at a slice of life in a New York City neighborhood," according to Becca Zerkin in the *New York Times Book Review.*

Ice Age centers on the unlikely friendship between Sid, an obnoxious sloth seeking a protector, and Manny, a neurotic wooly mammoth that is migrating to warmer climes. When the pair stumbles upon Roshan, a human baby separated from his family, they decide to reunite the child with his parents. What Sid and Manny fail to realize, however, is that their new friend, a saber-toothed tiger named Diego, has been assigned to kidnap Roshan. "When the tiger joins Sid and Manny's migration, supposedly to help guide them to the infant's father, *Ice Age* develops a note of ambiguity and complex motivation unexpected in an animated film," Mick La-Salle remarked in his *San Francisco Chronicle* review. "The journey is a real journey. The characters grow. Relationships change." Desson Howe, writing in the *Washington Post,* also praised the efforts of Ackerman and his coauthors, Michael Berg and Michael J. Wilson. *Ice Age* "flows like a dream," Howe concluded. "There's nary a dull moment."

Ackerman has more-recently teamed with Berg, Yoni Brenner, and Mike Reiss on *Ice Age: Dawn of the Dinosaurs,* the third film in the "Ice Age" series. After Sid finds a trio dinosaur eggs, he decides to raise the hatchlings as his own until their mother emerges from her lush subterranean world and comes looking for her offspring. "There is much more of an emphasis on action in this nicely crafted, fast-paced sequel, which at its best shares the antic qualities of classic Warner Bros. cartoons," observed *New York Post* critic Lou Lumenick.

In *The Lonely Phonebooth,* which is illustrated by Max Dalton, Ackerman was inspired by a real-life incident in which an all-but-forgotten piece of technology demonstrated its worth. The story concerns an old-fashioned, coin-operated phone booth located at the intersection of West End Avenue and 100th Street in Manhattan. Thanks to the advent of cell phones, such phone booths had become an anachronism in a world dominated by newer technology. When a fierce storm disrupts the power to cell-phone towers, however, local residents discover that the phone booth's landline is still operational and they flock to the site with a renewed appreciation for the neglected device. "Everything has value," Ackerman told *West Side Spirit* online contributor Reid Spagna. "Even though things are changing, it doesn't mean that something we used to use is valueless. The phone booth is a metaphor for a human being. An older person can't do everything that he or she used to do, but it doesn't mean that they are valueless." Zerkin noted that "Ackerman's story expresses a sentimental connection to an old New York symbol," adding that *The Lonely Phonebooth* "celebrat[es] the fabric of a neighborhood, that intangible quality New Yorkers treasure."

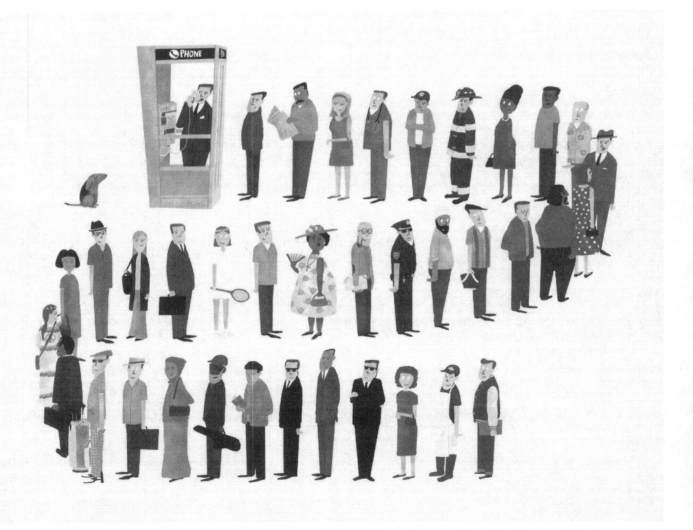

Peter Ackerman's debut children's book, **The Lonely Phone Booth,** *features a story set in New York City and brought to life in retro-inspired artwork by Max Dalton.* (Illustration copyright © 2011 by Max Dalton. Reproduced by permission of David R. Godine, Publisher, Inc.)

Biographical and Critical Sources

PERIODICALS

Chicago Sun-Times, June 29, 2009, Roger Ebert, review of *Ice Age: Dawn of the Dinosaurs.*
Children's Bookwatch, May, 2011, review of *The Lonely Phone Booth.*
New York Post, July 1, 2009, Lou Lumenick, review of *Ice Age: Dawn of the Dinosaurs.*
New York Times Book Review, November 7, 2010, Becca Zerkin, review of *The Lonely Phone Booth,* p. 20.
Publishers Weekly, May 31, 2010, review of *The Lonely Phone Booth,* p. 46.
San Francisco Chronicle, March 15, 2002, Mick LaSalle, review of *Ice Age.*
School Library Journal, September, 2010, Barbara Elleman, review of *The Lonely Phone Booth,* p. 117.
Variety, June 21, 2009, Joe Leydon, review of *Ice Age: Dawn of the Dinosaurs.*
Washington Post, March 15, 2002, Desson Howe, review of *Ice Age.* p. 41.

ONLINE

Lonely Phone Booth Web site, http://lonelyphonebooth. com/ (September 1, 2011).
West Side Spirit Online, http://westsidespirit.com/ (September 1, 2010), Reid Spagna, "Telephone Call from the Past: Writer Pens Ode to 100th Street Phone Booth."*

* * *

ANDERSON, Margaret J. 1931-

Personal

Born December 24, 1931, in Gorebridge, Scotland; immigrated to Canada, 1955; immigrated to United States, 1963; daughter of John A. (a clergyman) and Margaret Hall; married Norman H. Anderson (a professor of entomology), September 15, 1956; children: Richard, Judith, Susan, Karen. *Education:* University of Edinburgh, B.Sc. (genetics; with honors), 1953. *Religion:* Presbyterian.

Addresses

Home—3325 NW 60th St., Corvallis, OR 97330.

Career

Writer. East Malling Research Station, Kent, England, statistician, 1953-55; Canada Department of Agriculture, Summerland, British Columbia, entomologist, 1955-56; Oregon State University, Corvallis, statistician, 1956-57.

Member

Society of Children's Book Writers.

Awards, Honors

Writing competition award, Canadian Entomological Society, 1973, for "Making a Case for the Caddisfly"; Outstanding Science Book for Children selection, National Science Teachers Association/Children's Book Council, 1974, for *Exploring the Insect World;* Outstanding Book of the Year designation, *New York Times Book Review,* 1975, for *To Nowhere and Back;* Charlie Mae Simon Award, Arkansas Young Readers Awards, 1992, for *The Ghost inside the Monitor;* Stevens Prize, 2005, and Oregon Book Award finalist, 2007, both for *Olla-Piska.*

Writings

NONFICTION FOR YOUNG READERS

Exploring the Insect World, McGraw (New York, NY), 1974.
Exploring City Trees, and the Need for Urban Forests, McGraw (New York, NY), 1976.
Food Chains: The Unending Cycle, illustrated by Gretchen Bracher, Enslow (Springfield, NJ), 1991.
Charles Darwin, Naturalist, Enslow (Springfield, NJ), 1994, revised edition, 2008.
(With Nan Field and daughter Karen F. Stephenson) *Ancient Forests,* Dog-Eared Publications (Middleton, WI), 1994.
Bizarre Insects, Enslow (Springfield, NJ), 1996, published as *Bugged-Out Insects,* Enslow (Springfield, NJ), 2011.
Isaac Newton: The Greatest Scientist of All Time, Enslow (Springfield, NJ), 1996, revised edition, 2008.
Carl Linnaeus: Father of Classification, Enslow (Springfield, NJ), 1997, revised edition, 2009.
(With Nan Field and Karen F. Stephenson) *Leapfrogging through Wetlands,* Dog-Eared Publications (Middleton, WI), 1998.
(With Karen F. Stephenson) *Scientists of the Ancient World,* Enslow (Springfield, NJ), 1999.
(With R. Gwinn Vivian) *Chaco Canyon: Digging for the Past,* Oxford University Press (New York, NY), 2002.
(With Karen F. Stephenson) *Aristotle: Philosopher and Scientist,* Enslow (Springfield, NJ), 2004.
(With Pamela J. Cressey) *Alexandria, Virginia: Digging for the Past,* Oxford University Press (New York, NY), 2006.
(With Nan Field and Karen F. Stephenson) *Discovering Black Bears,* Dog-Eared Publications (Middleton, WI), 2007.

FICTION FOR YOUNG READERS

To Nowhere and Back, Knopf (New York, NY), 1975.
Searching for Shona, Knopf (New York, NY), 1978.
The Journey of the Shadow Bairns, Knopf (New York, NY), 1980.
Light in the Mountain, Knopf (New York, NY), 1982.

The Brain on Quartz Mountain, Knopf (New York, NY), 1982.

The Druid's Gift, Knopf (New York, NY), 1989.

The Ghost inside the Monitor, Knopf (New York, NY), 1990.

Children of Summer: Henri Fabre's Insects, illustrated by Marie le Glatin Keis, Farrar, Straus and Giroux (New York, NY), 1997.

Olla-Piska: Tales of David Douglas, Oregon Historical Society Press (Portland, OR), 2006.

"TIME" NOVEL TRILOGY; FOR YOUNG READERS

In the Keep of Time, Knopf (New York, NY), 1977.

In the Circle of Time, Knopf (New York, NY), 1979.

The Mists of Time, Knopf (New York, NY), 1984.

OTHER

Contributor to periodicals, including *ASK, Instructor, Nature & Science,* and *Ranger Rick's.* Contributor to anthologies, including *Medley,* Houghton (Boston, MA), 1976; and *Ranger Rick's Surprise Book,* National Wildlife Federation (Washington, DC), 1976.

Sidelights

Margaret J. Anderson began her writing career creating nonfiction for young readers, and introduced her audience both to insects and the need for green in urban spaces with *Exploring the Insect World* and *Exploring City Trees, and the Need for Urban Forests.* Anderson's husband, Norman Anderson, is a professor of entomology, so writing about insects and producing other articles about nature has been a natural extension of a shared family interest. Although Anderson has continued writing nature articles, she has also penned several novels for children, among them a trilogy. In a review of her novel *The Ghost inside the Monitor,* the tale of a girl whose autobiography project is taken over by a ghost keen on writing her own story, a *Publishers Weekly* contributor commented that Anderson "can start with an improbable idea, explore its possibilities and end up with a credible novel."

Food Chains: The Unending Cycle and *Bizarre Insects* continue Anderson's exploration of nonfiction topics. Walter L. Gojmerac noted in *Science Activities* that, in the latter book the author "describes the advantages and disadvantages" of many qualities of insects in an "interesting" manner. Along with writing about insects,

Margaret J. Anderson and her husband Norm, celebrating their 50th wedding anniversary, 2006. (Photograph by Judith Bender.)

Anderson has also focused on a number of other nature topics, including wetlands and black bears. *Discovering Black Bears* features games, activities, and stickers, as well as stories about these amazing creatures. A critic for *Children's Bookwatch* complimented *Discovering Black Bears* for its "hands-on learning experience."

Anderson has also made several contributions to the "Great Minds of Science" series of biographies, covering such notables as Charles Darwin and Isaac Newton, as well as Carl Linnaeus, who developed the system of binomial nomenclature. Nothing that Anderson's biography of Linnaeus provides "solid information" to students working on reports, Ilene Cooper added in *Booklist* that *Carl Linnaeus: Father of Classification* focuses on Linnaeus's personal life rather than his groundbreaking system. *Aristotle: Philosopher and Scientist* focuses more on the Aristotle's contributions to science, from zoology and logic to drama. Jennifer Ralston wrote in her *School Library Journal* review of the latter biography that Anderson's "clear and concise" writing makes the book "easy-to-understand." *Scientists of the Ancient World* profiles ten early thinkers and the ideas that make them notable. Carolyn Phelan, writing for *Booklist,* deemed the book a "readable book of scientific history/biography."

With *Children of Summer: Henri Fabre's Insects* Anderson merges her interest in science and storytelling into a novel about the French entomologist Jean Henri Fabre. As revealed through the narrative voice of his ten-year-old son, Paul, Fabre is considered strange by his neighbors and is dismissed as a hermit, all due to his passion for learning about insects. Some of his ideas were a little strange—such as shooting a canon to see how well cicadas can hear—particularly in an age when most other scientists studied insects after they were dead rather than studying their behavior. *Children of Summer* describes Fabre and the subjects of his studies in turn, as well as showing how his children were inspired to participate in his experiments. "Fabre's passionate pursuit of science resonates throughout this wondrously multifaceted book," wrote Susan Faust in a review for the *San Francisco Chronicle.* "It's a science text, a family album, a fictionalized biography and travelogue all seamlessly rolled into one." In *Booklist* Karen Morgan suggested that, despite being fiction, *Children of Summer* might "inspire some unusual science projects about insect behavior," and Margaret A. Bush noted in *Horn Book* that the relationship between Fabre and his children in Anderson's story "has much in common with some of today's home-schooling families." A *Children's Digest* reviewer suggested that, for students who want to learn more about the beginning of the field of entomology, *Children of Summer* "is a great place to start."

Anderson once told *SATA:* "When I was young (and maybe even still) it always seemed too bad that when we made one choice we ruled out so many other interesting possibilities. Being one person, living in one place and time, seems so restrictive. I have found that by writing, and to a lesser extent by reading, I can change that. I can explore the 'what might have been' and the 'what might be.' But the fantasy life cannot exist without the emotions and experiences of the real life. It can only be an extension of that."

Biographical and Critical Sources

PERIODICALS

Booklist, March 1, 1997, Karen Morgan, review of *Children of Summer: Henri Fabre's Insects,* p. 1160; December, 1997, Ilene Cooper, review of *Carl Linnaeus: Father of Classification,* p. 625; December 1, 1998, Carolyn Phelan, review of *Scientists of the Ancient World,* p. 674.

Children's Bookwatch, November, 2007, review of *Discovering Black Bears.*

Children's Digest, September, 1997, review of *Children of Summer,* p. 19.

Horn Book, July-August, 1997, Margaret A. Bush, review of *Children of Summer,* p. 448.

Publishers Weekly, July 13, 1990, review of *The Ghost inside the Monitor,* p. 55.

San Francisco Chronicle, August 31, 1997, Susan Faust, "The Frenchman Who Loved Insects," p. 10.

School Library Journal, July, 2004, Jennifer Ralston, review of *Aristotle: Philosopher and Scientist,* p. 115.

Science Activities, spring 1998, Walter L. Gojmerac, review of *Bizarre Insects,* p. 46.

ONLINE

Margaret J. Anderson Home Page, http://members.peak.org/~mja/ (November 22, 2010).

Autobiography Feature

Margaret J. Anderson

Anderson contributed the following autobiographical essay to *Something about the Author:*

I came into the world one Christmas Eve, my eyes dazzled, not by a holy star—but by the beam of a miner's lamp! I was born in Gorebridge, a Scottish mining town, where my father, John Hall, was the Presbyterian minister. That December afternoon, when the doctor's wife heard that the baby was on its way, she thrust a Christmas present into her husband's hand, telling him to open it before he set off for the Halls' house. The package turned out to contain a miner's lamp that he could strap around his head. Now when he delivered a baby in a house without electricity, he wouldn't have to rely on a poorly placed paraffin light.

Naturalists say that when a baby bird hatches from its egg, it is imprinted by the first thing it sets its eyes on. If the nestling sees a person instead of its mother bird, it spends the rest of its life trying to be human. It's lucky people aren't imprinted in the same way—or I'd be a coal miner now. Though I think I was imprinted with a love of books. I grew up surrounded by people who loved reading and storytelling.

By the time I could read to myself, I had a bookcase of favorites: Russian fairy tales, Aesop's fables, and *Gone*

Hall family portrait: Margaret (right) with sister, Ann, parents, John and Margaret, Sr., and baby brother Bill. Older brother, Peter, is not shown.
(Photo courtesy of Margaret J. Anderson. Reproduced by permission.)

is Gone, by Wanda Gág. (For years Wanda Gág was the only author's name I knew.) "Rupert" Books, a series of little yellow books recounting the adventures of a bear (who had obviously been imprinted by a human), took up a whole shelf. These stories were a mixture of fairy tale and high fantasy, with Rupert setting off on a quest and then finding himself in one dire situation after another. I used to lie awake at night worrying about Rupert Bear, though you'd think that by the time I'd read thirty volumes, I'd have learned that he was a survivor! Then, one Christmas, my grandmother gave me a copy of Frances Hodgson's Burnett's *The Secret Garden.* I felt cheated when I saw that it didn't have pictures, and I didn't read it right away, but *The Secret Garden* turned out to be a different kind of magic, where all the ideas were expressed in words.

My grandmother on my mother's side lived in Edinburgh, and so we called her Edinburgh Gran to distinguish her from my father's mother, St. Boswells Gran. Her family, the MacLeans, had moved to Edinburgh from the Scottish Highlands before she was born, exchanging the poverty of the land for poverty in the city. She grew up in the Canongate, a slum neighborhood near the High Street. When she left school, she got a job as a reader for Nelson, the publisher. After she married, she moved a couple of miles or so to a better part of town, and almost never went back to the Canongate. My mother only remembers being taken there once, as a very small child. In recent years, some of the old houses around the High Street have been restored and others rebuilt, so the district has become fashionable, but my grandmother's house is gone.

Visiting Gran in Edinburgh was always a great adventure. She lived in a terraced house on Willowbrae Avenue, close to Holyrood Park, where we were allowed to play on our own. Gran often took us to Princes Street or the Portobello baths or to the zoo, sitting upstairs in the front seat of a rattling tramcar. I once had seven elephant rides in a row at the zoo, because Gran was tired of trailing around after me. One night, long after our usual bedtime, we were taken to a room above one of the shops on Princes Street that overlooked the gardens. Suddenly, floodlights were switched on and there was Edinburgh Castle floating in the night sky.

My grandfather is a rather shadowy figure. He was the sports editor on the *Edinburgh Evening News,* and wrote a column under the name Diogenes, but what I remember best about him was that on Saturday he used to say, "This is the day the ghost walks," and then hand us a penny.

My grandfather on my father's side had been the head gardener for Lord Polworth on Mertoun Estate. By the time we came along, he had retired from gardening and had a sweetie shop in St. Boswells, which was—from our point of view—a very satisfactory occupation, until World War II emptied all the big glass jars of toffees and humbugs and licorice allsorts.

Holidays in St. Boswells brought out the storyteller in my father. He used to take us around Mertoun Estate as if he owned it. In a way he did, because he had grown up there, free to wander all over the acres of grounds. The gardener's house, where he had lived as a boy, was a wonderful place that had been built as the manor house three hundred years before. He showed us the "jogs"—an iron collar chained to the wall of Mertoun Church. In the old days, it was fastened around the neck of any person caught breaking the law. While the offender stood chained to the wall, the good Christians going to church could spit on him and call him names. Standing tiptoe and holding the collar around our necks, we tried to imagine how it must have felt.

At Roxburgh Castle we learned about James II, who was killed by his own cannon while trying to retake the castle from the English, and at Smailholm Tower we heard about Muckle-mouthed Meg. She was so homely that when her father offered to spare the life of a captured English raider on the condition that he marry the girl, the young man took one look at Meg and said he would rather hang. However, at the last moment, he had second thoughts, and Muckle-mouthed Meg made him a good wife. Much later, these stories worked their way into *In the Keep of Time,* though I had no thoughts of being a writer when I first heard them.

My mother's tales were more likely to be colorful episodes from her own past. Once, when she was riding on a tramcar that went past the Edinburgh Royal Infirmary, the she found herself sitting opposite a woman and her young son. The boy had a pot on is head—the kind of chamber pot you kept under your bed in those days of outdoor privies. The most remarkable thing was that the boy was wearing his school uniform, including his school cap, which was perched on top of the pot! The boy and his mother looked neither to the right nor to the left. They got off the tram when it stopped at the infirmary. Perhaps even now, somewhere in Scotland, a child is saying, "Grandpa! Grandpa! Tell us again aboot the time when you were a wee laddie and got your head stuck in the pottie!" I hope so because those tales from the past are the cement that holds the generations together.

*

I don't remember Gorebridge. We moved to Lockerbie in the southwest of Scotland, when I was only two and my brother Peter was five. Ann was born a year later, and then my brother Bill thirteen years after that, so he doesn't figure in my childhood at all. We lived in a big drafty house with lots of rooms—a sitting room, playroom, dining room, study, kitchen, scullery, pantry, hallways, and bedrooms. There was even a room called the boxroom for storing trunks and suitcases. The kitchen had a huge black range against one wall and a row of brass bells up near the ceiling. We used to jerk the bell-pull in each room and then see if we could race back to the kitchen before the bell stopped jangling. The study and the sitting room were off limits, but the playroom was totally our domain. Nobody ever told us to pick up our toys and we scribbled all over the walls as high as we could reach. Peter loved to draw tiny cowboys and Indians. They formed a sort of comic strip all around the room. Looking back, it strikes me as strange that we had so much freedom because my mother is extremely tidy, the sort of person who folds away the newspaper before you've finished reading the headlines.

Our garden had a chestnut tree and apple trees that were good for climbing. The house looked out on pasture fields where we went mushroom gathering on summer mornings. One of our favorite places to play was The Boggy Bit, a stretch of wasteland behind the house that someone had started to drain, but had given up on. It was cored by a great number of parallel ditches, which disappeared into a marsh. Ann and I spent hours there, catching minnows and sticklebacks and tadpoles and picking wildflowers.

Against the garden wall was an old washhouse with a flagstone floor and old sinks and a big boiler with a place underneath to light a fire to heat water. The washhouse was very spidery and hadn't been used for doing laundry for years. We turned it into a museum where we displayed moldering collections of insects and pressed flowers and a sheep's skull we'd found in The Boggy Bit. The sinks were good for rearing tadpoles and keeping snails.

One summer we mapped The Boggy Bit, naming every ditch and plank bridge, and made up involved adventure stories about the imaginary inhabitants of our land. Perhaps that piece of marshy ground provided the crossover between nature study and fiction that eventually led me to write both science books and fantasy. They weren't far removed from one another in The Boggy Bit.

From time to time, the washhouse became a sanctuary for injured animals: flea-ridden hedgehogs or young birds that had fallen from their nests. Most of them didn't last long. (That's why I never thought of being a veterinarian when I grew up!) We also had a pet tortoise that came to a sad end. When we uncovered him after his winter hibernation, there wasn't much there but the shell.

*

When I think back to my early school days, I can practically hear the rhythmic throb of children chanting "times tables" and spelling lists and the names of kings and queens in singsong Scottish voices. That's the way we learned in those days—or didn't learn.

I don't think I cared much for English at school, though grammar and spelling have turned out to be useful. We wrote lots of essays—compositions, we called them—

but I can't remember now what they were about. I do remember that our teachers were never lavish with praise. They thought it was important for us to realize that there was always "room for improvement." I liked math better because you knew where you were with math. Answers were right or wrong. Each morning, after chanting our tables, we were drilled in mental arithmetic. This was back in the days of twelve pennies to a shilling and twenty shillings to a pound, so the teacher would toss problems at us, such as: if coal costs two and sixpence ha'penny a hundredweight, how much do you pay for a ton? You weren't allowed to use a pencil and paper, and if you counted on your fingers, you got your knuckles rapped. You could work your way to the top of the class by answering a question quicker than the person seated above you. It was the closest our teachers ever came to making a game out of learning.

Each year, we seemed to start history back with the Picts and the Scots and the Roman emperor Hadrian, who couldn't subdue them and so he built a wall across the north of England to keep them out. We learned about King Edward, the Hammer of the Scots, and long-ago heroes like William Wallace and Robert the Bruce. We refought ancient battles—Bannockburn and Flodden

Margaret (left) with Peter and Ann, on holiday at Mallaig Mor. (Photo courtesy of Margaret J. Anderson. Reproduced by permission.)

and Culloden. The enemy was always the English, and even though the Scots lost more battles than they won, we were all fiercely proud of being Scottish. The year usually ended before Scotland and England were finally united under King James I in 1603, and then we went back and fought the same battles over again the next year. Along with all that I absorbed from my surroundings, I learned a lot of early Scottish history; but on a wider scale I get a bit fuzzy around the time American history begins—with those troublesome colonies.

*

During my early childhood, in addition to visits to my grandparents, we had an annual holiday by the sea. We spent a month in a rented farmhouse or croft in the Scottish Highlands. The holidays I remember best were at Mallaig Mor. We traveled to Mallaig, a west-coast fishing village, by train and then by rowboat up Loch Nevis to the MacDonalds' croft at Mallaig Mor.

We rented the new house on the bay, and the MacDonalds moved back up the hillside to the old house, where their family had lived for generations. Sometimes, when Peter and I went up to the MacDonalds' to fetch the milk, we were invited in. The byre was next to the house, and so at milking time you could hear the cows gently lowing in their stalls—and smell them, too. Even on the warmest day, old Mrs. MacDonald sat in a rocking chair next to the peat fire, bundled up in woolen cardigans and shawls. She only spoke Gaelic, and so we had no idea what she was saying, but her voice was like music and the words a magic spell.

I learned to swim in the sandy bay at Mallaig Mor. Close to the shore, baby flounders the size of silver dollars wriggled under our bare feet. One afternoon, when the ocean was very calm, we borrowed spears from the MacDonalds and went out in the boat to catch flounders in the shallow water in the bay. My spear seemed to change directions where it went into the water, and the flounders were hard to see because they matched the speckled sand. I didn't want to spear one anyway. It seemed far more cruel than catching silver-blue mackerel on a line behind the boat.

Another afternoon, we rowed across Loch Nevis to Knoydart. On the way home we were escorted by curious seals swimming so close to us that we could look into their round brown eyes and count their whiskers. My mother said that they were selkies: people who had been banished to sea. And she told us that if we ever found a sealskin lying on the beach, we should leave it there, because it belonged to a seal who had become human for a while, and he would die if he couldn't find his skin when it was time to return to the sea.

Farther up Loch Nevis a small island nestled against the shore. Bonny Prince Charlie once escaped from the English soldiers by rowing behind that island. The soldiers went on up the loch, and the prince doubled back to Maillaig.

Our last holiday at Maillag Mor was in August 1939. Even there, beyond the end of the last road, we couldn't ignore what was happening in the rest of the world. Britain was preparing for war. On the way back to Lockerbie, the train from Maillaig was almost empty. Other people had cut their holidays short. As we continued south, the train began to fill up with young men, some in uniform and others in civilian clothes, all of them off to join the armed forces. And after Glasgow, the train was packed with families moving out of the city. When it grew dark outside, the few lights that came on in the carriage had dim blue light bulbs that gave off a ghostly glow. Soldiers, the blackout, evacuees, hushed voices, strained faces. War wasn't something confined to history books. It could happen to us.

And it did.

On Sunday, September 3, 1939, after German chancellor Adolf Hitler and the Nazis invaded Poland, Britain declared war on Germany.

*

I was seven when World War II started, and thirteen by the time it was over, so most of my childhood memories are framed by war; yet it wasn't a bad time to grow up, especially in a small country town. The war united us in a common cause. My mother, along with most of the other women in Lockerbie, worked in a canteen that served tea and sandwiches to soldiers from the nearby army camp. They rolled bandages and made medical dressings out of sphagnum moss. Ann and I gathered rose hips in the hedgerows for syrup containing vitamin C, and we saved tinfoil and knitted khaki scarves and squares for blankets—our part in the war effort. And while we did this, there was "after the war" to look forward to, when everything would be peaceful and plentiful and we'd have oranges and bananas again. (My cousin Ian burst into tears when he tasted his first banana after the war. He'd spent all his life waiting for one. When he finally got it, he didn't like it!)

We grew accustomed to people coming into our lives and then vanishing as suddenly as they'd come. New children turned up in school—evacuees or officers' children from the army camp. Just when we'd made friends with them, they'd be gone. Though we didn't always make friends with those newcomers. To my shame, I remember joining a group of children in the playground who were dancing around some English evacuees, mimicking their accent. Perhaps we'd learned our history lessons too well.

It wasn't only people who came and went. Things did, too. One morning, when Ann and I were on our way home from school, we were astonished to see that a field beside Dumfries Road had sprouted a crop of metal climbing bars. We scrambled over the gate for a closer look, and discovered that the bars were metal frames for supporting the camouflage covers on army trucks: A skeleton of squared-off hoops, with rods connecting each hoop to the next. We began to swing on them, trying to cross the field without touching the grass.

A soldier shouted at us to clear off.

But we didn't stay away for long.

By the next day, everyone had heard about the instant playground. The bars swarmed with swinging, yelling kids.

Another soldier chased us off. Bu the moment he turned his back, we were there again. Even when it grew dark, we couldn't tear ourselves away.

The next morning the giant jungle gym was gone, as if it had never been. A few black-and-white cows were grazing in the field. Nobody could remember whether they'd been there the day before or not. For a long time after that, I held my breath when I turned the corner onto Dumfries Road, wishing that the bars would come back.

They never did.

*

Lockerbie lay beneath the path of German planes on their way to bomb the Glasgow shipyards. The air-raid siren wailed a warning when enemy planes approached, followed by the "all-clear" as they continued north. Then we'd have the warning and the all clear again, when the planes flew south. If the German bombers hadn't found a target around Glasgow, they might unload their bombs wherever they spotted lights beneath them, so the blackout was very strictly enforced. At first, we used to go down to the broom closet under the stairs when the siren sounded, but eventually we grew more confident and stayed in our beds. I became so used to the wailing siren that I could sleep right through it—until the winter I was in the hospital.

When the doctor peered down my throat and announced I had scarlet fever, I felt excited and important. I'd get to ride in an ambulance and to see inside the fever hospital, but the excitement had evaporated by the time I reached the hospital. My throat ached and my head hurt. When the lights were turned out that first night, I tossed and turned in the high, narrow bed. The ward stretched off into the shadowy darkness on either side.

Suddenly, a siren wailed, sounding much more urgent than it ever did at home. Several nurses glided into the ward carrying flashlights that gave off a wavering blue light. They stopped and peered at the chart clipped on the foot of each bed, whispering to one another as they checked off names on a list. They helped people out of bed, wrapping blankets around their shoulders. But when they came to me, they glanced at my chart, shook their heads, and passed on down the ward. They didn't

bother to explain that the air-raid shelter was unheated and they were afraid that with such a high fever, I would come down with pneumonia. Perhaps they thought I was asleep. And maybe I wouldn't have understood if they had told me. I only knew that everyone was taken somewhere safe and I was left alone. Then I heard the planes, throbbing through the night. I held my breath as they flew overhead, heavy with bombs, making a strange unsteady sound, quite different from British planes. I prayed that there weren't chinks of light showing anywhere in town.

The hospital was in Annan, ten miles from Lockerbie. We had no car and traveling was difficult, so my parents were able to visit me only once during the five weeks I was there. Being in a hospital was like the war: I couldn't wait for it to be over, but inside I was afraid it never would be. And when I eventually did go home, I didn't sleep through the sirens anymore. Even the wind sounded like a siren wailing in the night.

*

Food was strictly rationed, both during the war and for years afterwards. We were never actually hungry, but we certainly didn't have to worry about too much cholesterol in our diet when the egg ration was only one egg a week. We could buy dried eggs, which came from America in squat cardboard boxes, decorated with American flags that were red and blue and cardboard colored. Egg powder, mixed with water, produced leathery little omelettes with a greenish tinge around the edge. We wanted eggs boiled in their shells.

The solution was obvious. We could keep hens in the washhouse. So we bought some pullets from a nearby farmer, and when one of them went broody, the farmer gave us a dozen eggs for her to sit on. But only four eggs hatched. When we told the farmer, he said that we children could each help ourselves to a day-old chick from his incubator. Peter and I leaned over the side and caught our cheeping yellow chicks. But Ann was too small to reach into the incubator.

"I want that one," she said, pointing to a little creature that was standing off by itself on one leg, wilting. Its eyes were closed.

We couldn't change Ann's mind and so she carried the droopy chick home, clenched tightly in her fist, imprinting it in more ways than one!

The mother hen took to the foster children quite happily. Peter's chick and mine were soon scratching about with the others, exploring their new world, but Ann's one either hid under the mother hen's feathers or drooped on one foot, its head hanging to the side.

The chicks grew. They soon had pinfeathers instead of yellow fluff. Even Ann's one grew. It was still the smallest, but Ann always made sure it got its share of the hens' mash Mother cooked up each day. Peter and I named our chickens "Red" and "Jenny." Ann's one was still Ann's One, but with capital letters now.

By the time they were grown, Red and Jenny were hard to tell from the other hens—they were all Rhode Island Reds, but Ann's One was white with a ruff of speckled black feathers around her neck. She was now bigger than all the others. And stronger. With a running, flapping start, she could clear the wire fence around the wash green.

One morning, when my mother went to the front door to bring in the milk, she was astonished to find a broken egg on the doorstep. The next day, the same thing happened. And the next. Ann's One had started to lay, and she believed in personal service—a breakfast egg delivered with the milk. In the end, we put a nesting box beside the front door, so that the egg didn't roll off the doorstep and break. And Ann's One had the run of the whole garden. She particularly liked helping herself to the peas, extracting them neatly from the shell, leaving the empty pod hanging on the vine. We could have erected a higher fence around the wash green, but it didn't seem fair to shut Ann's One up with a lot of silly hens when inside herself she knew she was a person.

*

At the beginning of the war, Brooklands, the house next to ours, stood empty. (Most houses in Lockerbie had names. Ours was called St. Cuthberts Manse, or just The Manse, because that's what a minister's house is called in Scotland.) During the war, empty buildings were often taken over by the army, and so for six years Brooklands was occupied by soldiers. Not the same ones, of course. They came and went. But they all had one thing in common. They didn't have time to cut the grass or prune bushes or dig "victory gardens" to provide their own food like the rest of us. They let the shrubs and grass and trees go wild.

Peter and Ann and I used to take a shortcut through Brooklands' garden, ducking under a rhododendron bush, scrambling through a privet hedge, crawling under some shrubs and through the long grass. Making sure no one was watching, we would then dash out between the big stone gateposts, which leaned at drunken angles after having been nudged by so many army trucks. The gate itself was long since gone. This wasn't exactly a shortcut, but it was more interesting than walking down our own driveway.

One Saturday morning, the soldiers loaded everything into trucks and roared away, leaving a glorious silence behind. This was our big chance to look around the house. We walked boldly up to the front door, but it was locked. So was the back door. We separated, trying all the downstairs windows.

"Hey! Come here!"

Peter's voice, sounding strangely hollow, came from around the west side of the house.

"Here!" he yelled again, poking his head out of a green wooden hatch door. From the soot on his face, we could tell that he was in the coal cellar. He pulled us in, and we all crunched our way across the coal scattered on the floor. A door from the cellar opened into a dark passageway. We had found a way in.

"Here's the kitchen," I called to the others. The room smelled of stale cigarettes and boiled cabbage. The big black range was just like ours, and a row of brass bells hung up near the ceiling.

We wandered from room to room. We could see dark patches on the wallpaper where pictures had once hung, and in places the paper was peeling, giving glimpses of old patterns underneath. Brooklands differed from our house in having a back staircase that connected the maids' bedrooms with the kitchen, as well as a main staircase from the front hall to the upstairs landing and bedrooms. We looked down from a front window at our favorite hiding places in the wild garden. The flattened pathway through the grass was as clear as a rabbit's run.

Suddenly, with no warning at all, an army truck careened between the leaning gateposts and came to a stop at the front door, gravel spurting from beneath its wheels. Soldiers spilled out. Soldiers with duffle bags and rifles.

Ann and Peter turned and ran, but I couldn't take my eyes off those soldier swarming toward the house. Their uniforms didn't look right. They had guns. Maybe this was the dreaded German invasion! And even if they were British, soldiers were trained to shoot, not to ask questions. That's what war was all about. My heart was pounding—but at least my legs were working again. I went racing after the others down the backstairs to the kitchen. The soldiers, who were in the front hall by this time, were making so much noise they didn't hear our feet clattering down the hollow wooden steps.

I was never inside Brooklands again—though I did relive that adventure in my imagination when I wrote about Marjorie and Anna going inside Clairmont House in *Searching for Shona*.

*

When I was eleven, instead of continuing at the local school in Lockerbie, I transferred to Dumfries Academy, traveling an hour each way by bus every day. I'd done well on the "eleven-plus," a test that more or less sealed your academic fate in those days. My parents thought that I would benefit from the better teachers in Dumfries, although going there cut me off from my friends in Lockerbie. I did make new friends in Dumfries, but I wasn't able to take part in after-school activities because there was always the bus to catch.

About age fourteen. (Photo courtesy of Margaret J. Anderson. Reproduced by permission.)

By anybody's standards, my teenage years were dull. Dull and unrebellious! School all day, homework every evening, and church twice on Sundays. (My father was a minister, you remember.) But a lot of times when I was off in my room "studying," and thus avoiding helping with the dishes or housework, I was reading. I read my way through my adolescence.

I went to a few school dances, staying overnight in Dumfries with my friend Eleanor. Those dances were agony. All the boys on one side of the hall, and the girls standing in giggling groups on the other side. We were so used to the anonymity of school uniforms that our long, homemade, dance dresses made us feel as self-conscious as if we were wearing nightgowns. It was a relief to get back to Eleanor's house and immerse myself in *Gone with the Wind*. A ball at Tara, enjoyed secondhand, was a lot more exciting than a real dance in our high-school hall!

Another friend, Betty, lived on a sheep farm up in the hills. A group of us sometimes went camping there during the holidays. We spent most of the day trying to light a fire in the rain and the rest of the time flirting with the German prisoners who worked on Betty's farm. They had been released from a prison camp to help with the harvest. They weren't much older than Betty's

brothers, who were still in school, and they seemed to have very little connection with the faceless enemy we'd hated for years. The war may even have been over by then, and they would be awaiting repatriation. Years later, when I saw a news item about a young Catholic girl in Northern Ireland who'd had her head shaved and printer's ink poured over her by an angry mob (a version of tar-and-feathering) for fraternizing with a British soldier, I ached for the poor girl's innocence. I'm sure she wasn't trying to make any political statement when she talked to that soldier. She'd just seen a person and not "the enemy."

At seventeen, I went to Edinburgh University, where I took a degree in genetics. My social life there was only marginally better than at school, though I do remember my roommate, Aileen, and I taking the initiative in getting acquainted with two good-looking men who spent all their time in the student's common room playing bridge. We invested in a copy of *Teach Yourself Bridge*. After we'd read the first three chapters and dealt out a few practise hands, we invited them to our flat for a game.

As my partner fanned out the first hand, he looked up and asked, "What convention do you play?"

I didn't know what he was talking about. The first three chapters hadn't mentioned the word convention. They hadn't gone beyond the opening bid. It was a long evening. To our credit, Aileen and I read the rest of the book and became quite good at bridge, but we had to find ourselves other partners.

Now that we were in college, Eleanor and Aileen and I were eager to see something of the world beyond Scotland. Because we hadn't much money, we hitchhiked, traveling through England and across France with remarkable innocence and good fortune. One spring holiday, we sailed to Dublin and hitchhiked around southern Ireland, mostly staying in youth hostels. People were wonderfully kind, not only giving us rides, but even taking us to their homes for meals. Our most memorable experience was sleeping in a monastery where we'd heard we could get free lodging. This was before the troubles in Northern Ireland divided the Roman Catholics and Protestants, but even so we felt that our Presbyterian heritage was stamped on our faces as we entered the huge quiet building. We wondered if we'd be expected to go to confession, and if we should cross ourselves after grace. However, the brown-clad monks didn't speak to us, and they didn't even say grace before breakfast, which was served on a long scrubbed table in the refectory. We concluded they were under an oath of silence. This was a little opening into a world so totally unlike my own that I was fascinated.

*

After graduating, I got a job as a statistician at East Malling Research Station in Kent in the south of England. I solved mathematical problems on a calculating machine that would be a museum piece in this computer age. While I was working there, I had my first taste of being published. I coauthored a paper called "Some Statistical Aspects of a Recent Series of Fruit Tree Red Spider Mite Control Trials." I didn't get much fan mail on that one!

Now that I had a job, I had my own money (though not much). Even more important, I had more free time than I'd ever had before. My social life picked up. I lived in a hostel, where the ratio of men to women was definitely in my favor. I played a lot of bridge, and was even on the village darts team for a short time—though that was during a flu epidemic when all the regulars were sick.

Although I liked East Malling, I was restless. I was helping design experiments that wouldn't show any results until the trees were grown. Even though (statistically speaking) I had more time ahead of me than most people working there, it depressed me to think of spending ten years waiting to see if we'd grown a better apple tree. In March 1955, I invested my savings in a one-way ticket to Canada on the *Empress of France.*

Years later, when I was writing *The Journey of the Shadow Bairns,* I drew on memories of that voyage. Even though the *Empress of France* was far more luxurious than the boat Elspeth and Robbie traveled on, Elspeth's emotions would be much the same as mine. The feeling of being cut off from the past and not knowing what lay ahead. Instant friendships. Instant romance. The vastness of the ocean. The sense of traveling through space and time. You miss all that nowadays when you tune in to the Theater of the Air as you cross the Atlantic between breakfast and dinner.

There was no romance in our arrival at St. John, New Brunswick. Landing immigrants were herded into the immigration shed, where we waited in wire cages under our initial letter for the customs official to inspect our luggage. When I couldn't find the key to my small steamer trunk, the customs man forced the lock. A long train journey through miles and miles of winter-bleak countryside brought us to Toronto, where a crowd of waving, cheering people met us at the station. Everyone seemed to have someone to take care of them—except for me. I found a taxi, and gave the driver the address of the YWCA hostel. In Britain, cars at that time must all have been black or gray, because I remember that driving through Toronto was like seeing a Technicolor movie for the first time. My other impression of Toronto was of suffocating heat, even though it was March. I had never encountered central heating before. When I walked into my room in the YWCA, I threw open the window. An angry warden followed me into the room and slammed the window shut, asking if I intended to heat all of Toronto.

During my stay at the Y, someone stole things from my unlocked trunk. I still begrudge that thief my coronation mug. In the eyes of Scottish Nationalists, the present queen (Elizabeth II) should really be Elizabeth I, because she's the first Elizabeth to rule both England and Scotland. The other Elizabeth had only been queen of England. (Incidentally, she chopped Mary, Queen of Scots' head off.) When Scotland and England were united under James VI of Scotland in 1603, he became James I of England and Scotland. That coronation mug, inscribed with Elizabeth I, represents one of many lost causes I've supported over the years!

*

I found a job at a biological control lab in Belleville, a small town on Lake Ontario. The work was all right, but I was a total misfit in that male-dominated lab—though not for the reason you might expect. These Canadian men were a very domestic breed! Discussion over coffee always got back to the houses they were building or fixing up. Coming from Britain, with its chronic postwar shortages, I had nothing to say when it came to the merits of different designs of doorknobs.

I was desperately homesick that spring, but I had too much stubbornness to turn around, so I decided to take the long way back to Britain. I'd move on to western Canada, where I'd earn enough money to go to New Zealand, and then I'd work my way across Australia and around the world. In the meantime, I bought a secondhand typewriter in my first tentative step toward being a writer. I didn't get very far with the detective story I was writing, but I must have been serious about it, or I wouldn't have bought the typewriter. Possessions are an encumbrance when you're on the move.

By late summer, I'd saved enough for my train fare to Vancouver, where I managed to land a job as a lab technician in a fruit research station in Summerland, in the Okanagan Valley. Although the landscape in the interior of British Columbia was vastly different from

"Monitoring a spore trap at the Summerland Experimental station," 1956. (Photo courtesy of Margaret J. Anderson. Reproduced by permission.)

"My husband Norm and I, captured by a street photographer," Vancouver, British Colombia, 1956. (Photo courtesy of Margaret J. Anderson. Reproduced by permission.)

Scotland, I felt more at home in Summerland than I had in Bellevile. The apple and peach orchards were on irrigated benches along the narrow lake. Above them, the sagebrush-covered hills were like a setting for a western movie. It was wonderful wild country, and I was fascinated by everything—the new plants, the animals, and the Indian pictographs we found on the rocks.

During the winter, I bought a boat ticket to New Zealand, but by the time the orchards were in bloom, I didn't want to go. It wasn't Canada I minded leaving. I had fallen in love with Norman Anderson, a young entomologist at the lab. In the end, we let a shipping clerk in Vancouver settle our fate. If he would refund my money, I'd throw my lot in with Norm. If not . . . I don't know the outcome of the "if not" because I got the money! We set our wedding date for September 15, 1956.

I knew less about putting on a wedding than I did about building houses. I'd never even been to a wedding. People in Summerland were very kind, but looking back on it now, I'm sure I was a totally unsatisfactory bride-to-be. I didn't know about china patterns and silverware or what to say at showers. Fortunately, Norm's mother,

who had recently married off two daughters, organized the wedding in their family church in Langley in British Columbia.

My wandering lifestyle continued for a while after we were married. We moved south to Oregon State University, where Norm did his master's and I supported us by working in the statistics department. Then we moved to England for Norm to do his Ph.D. at the University of London, though he did his research outside London, near Windsor. I got to see my family again in Scotland and Norm met them for the first time.

Norm had a motorbike while we were in England, but the birth of twins rendered that an impractical method of transportation. Travel became limited to the distance we could push the baby carriage, or pram, as it's called over there. It was, however, a very fine pram—like something out of Mary Poppins. Once when I paused at an open gateway to show Richard and Judith some ponies, I was tooted at by the driver off a sleek Jaguar. I moved quickly out of the way when I saw that it was Prince Philip on his way to play polo! The babies were more interested in the ponies than in the prince.

At that time I was one-hundred-percent immersed in domesticity and motherhood. I didn't have much choice because we had no washing machine or dryer or car, and so shopping and laundry and feeding the babies occupied one hundred and fifty percent of my time. I didn't even have time to read. But I did listen to the radio. I used to feed the babies during "Children's Hour," and it was hearing *Tom's Midnight Garden* by Philippa Pearce that first aroused my interest in children's books. I suddenly couldn't wait for the kids to be old enough to be read to (along with being old enough not to wear diapers!).

Shortly before the twins' second birthday, we returned to Canada. By coincidence, Norm's job was in the same lab in Belleville where I had worked when I first went out to Canada. Even though I now had a family and we

"Our twins, Richard and Judith, in their pram," 1959. (Photo courtesy of Margaret J. Anderson. Reproduced by permission.)

The Anderson children: from left, Susan, Judith, and Richard, with Karen at center, Smailholm Tower, St. Boswells, Scotland, 1969. (Photo courtesy of Margaret J. Anderson. Reproduced by permission.)

bought a house, I still didn't feel settled in Belleville. Maybe if the twins had been old enough to learn to ski, or even to play outdoors, winters wouldn't have seemed so long. Eighteen months later, when Norm was offered a position at Oregon State University in Corvallis, the call of the west was strong and we were both eager to go.

In Corvallis I had various machines to lighten the domestic load—a washer, dryer, dishwasher, and so on—but one job that still piled up was the ironing. I don't much like ironing. But it was worse when Richard and Judith were little, bumping into the ironing board and tripping over the cord—or off in another room being ominously quiet. To keep them in one place, right under my eye, I began to tell "ironing stories." Soon, just the sound of me setting up the board of spitting on a hot iron would bring them running from the farthest corner of the house or yard. They'd plunk themselves down at my feet, and sit there on the floor with shining, upturned faces, as if I were a TV set switched on to their favorite program.

"Tell us a war story," Judith would beg.

"No! Tell us about the boy with the pot on his head," Richard would say quickly.

By never agreeing, they could be sure of at least two stories.

Eventually, Richard and Judith went off to kindergarten, and Susan was born. By the time Susan was in school, little Karen took her place on the floor beside the ironing board. With so many shining, upturned faces, the laundry basket was always full, and ironing stories were a daily ritual that seemed likely to go on forever. But changes were taking place in the outside world. Someone had invented permanent-pressed fabrics. The day came when Norm could rummage in the dryer for a clean shirt, bypassing our whole ironing-story routine, and I suddenly had time to write.

*

Around this time, Norm was doing a survey of the aquatic insects of Oregon. The children and I were enlisted as helpers. We puddled about in streams and ponds all over the state looking for bugs. Oregon, with its mountains and forests and wild rivers, is an ideal place for this. Not many people rate bug protection high in their environmental priorities, but the diversity of insects in streams is a sign of a healthy ecosystem. It occurred to me that insects needed a publicity agent. I knew from watching the twins that kids would be a good target audience. So when I exchanged the ironing board for a desk, and the iron for a typewriter, I decided to write articles on the outdoors for children.

My first attempt was a piece on looking for Native American pictographs which I sent to a magazine called *Nature and Science,* published by the New York Museum of Natural History. I included a cover letter asking the editor to tell me what was wrong with the article if he didn't like it. (Of course, I was hoping he'd say it was great!) The editor didn't like the article, but he did give me some advice. He told me to keep my family out of it and focus on what readers could do. He also sent me a sheet of tips on how to write science articles for young people.

I scrapped the pictograph idea because I couldn't see how to fix it and wrote an article on caddis flies instead, which was accepted. After that I wrote three or four articles a year, mainly for *Nature and Science.* Then in the spring of 1970, the magazine folded. I was very sorry because it was a terrific magazine. It had depended entirely on subscriptions to cover costs and couldn't pay its way. It's too bad you can't tell people about the wonder and diversity of life around them, without subsidizing the message by selling them something they don't really need.

Outside Random Cottage, Dorset, England, 1982. (Photo courtesy of Margaret J. Anderson. Reproduced by permission.)

But for me, there was a positive outcome. I recycled a number of the ideas I'd used in articles and wrote my first book, *Exploring the Insect World,* which was published by McGraw-Hill.

*

We spent the summer of 1969 touring Britain in a Volkswagen bus. With four children ranging in age from not quite two to ten, we didn't visit many art galleries and we were very selective about museums. Concerts and plays were outside our budget. Instead we explored ruined castles and walked on Hadrian's Wall. We camped out for a week in an empty church hall in the Lake District, just a mile or two from Beatrix Potter's house at Hilltop Sawrey. We picnicked at Smailholm Tower, where I found myself retelling the story about Mucklemouthed Meg. We had picked up the key to the tower from a nearby farm. When we let ourselves in through the heavy oak door and our eyes were still adjusting to the dim light, a huge black bird fluttered down from the rafters, landing dead at our feet. The bird must have worked its way through the wire mesh that covered the narrow windows and died of hunger, but such a prosaic explanation didn't occur to me right away. It seemed like some sort of omen—but if it was, it was a good omen. The incident lingered in my thoughts for years, finally providing a starting point for *In the Keep of Time.*

In 1971, we returned to Britain and spent a year living in Dorset in a thatched house called Random Cottage. Susan attended the village school and the twins, outfitted in school uniforms, went to a grammar school that was not much different from the one I had attended. Although the British money system had changed to decimal currency the previous year, the problems in their math textbooks still dealt with the old money. Judith could see no point in figuring out how much change she would get from a pound note if she bought three and a half dozen eggs at two shillings and a sixpence a dozen. I had to agree with her. You don't have to live in the past, even if you are surrounded by history! On weekends we explored the English countryside, both on foot and by car. One afternoon, on the far side of the woods behind Random Cottage, we discovered a tumbledown cottage—the thatch was gone in places and the garden was overgrown with nettles and blackberries. I had feeling that there was a story there—if I could just uncover it.

When we returned to Oregon, I began to write a book about an American family who spent a year in Random Cottage. I was a closet writer in those days. Literally. I had fixed a light in a cupboard under the stairs, where I could hide away and write on my portable typewriter. When I finished the story, which I called *To Nowhere and Back,* I read it to the children. They liked it, but that didn't count for much. The story was about places familiar to them—Random Cottage, Corfe Castle, and the village school. I sent the manuscript to my editor at McGraw-Hill and got it back without much comment. I then set it to Alfred Knopf. Along about the time I was

Getting advice from daughter Karen on a manuscript, 1984. (Photo courtesy of Margaret J. Anderson. Reproduced by permission.)

beginning to blame the U.S. mail for losing the manuscript, a letter arrived from Knopf. I have included pictures of important moments in my life with this essay, but nobody was there with a camera to capture the dazed expression on my face as I read and reread that letter. Knopf was going to publish *To Nowhere and Back!* The letter was signed by Frances Foster. Frances turned out to be a wonderful editor and friend—even if there have been times when she has brought to mind my long-ago English teachers who could always see "room for improvement"!

That first novel led to others. The ironing stories crept into my books—my war stories in *Searching for Shona* and Muckle-mouthed Meg in *In the Keep of Time*. Other peoples' stories became part of my stories, too. Norm's grandfather went out to Saskatchewan, Canada, in 1903, with the Barr colonists. After he'd filed for land and built a house (all in less than six months), he wrote a long letter to relatives in England about his trials and tribulations. He included a list of what everything had cost. Norm's mother gave me a copy of the letter, saying, "You should write a book about this."

My first try sounded like "Little House in Big Saskatchewan. "I knew that wouldn't sell! I started over again. After a number of false starts, the memory of my own journey to Canada when I hadn't known where I was heading gave me the idea of Elspeth and Robbie traveling alone. This time the story worked.

By now, I'd come out of the closet and had a desk in the family room. I talked about my books. Not just to my own children, but to the kids in Corvallis and beyond. I enjoyed talking in schools, though sometimes when I look out across a sea of shining upturned faces, I feel as if I'm back behind the ironing board. Especially when I'm asked where I got the idea for *Search-*

ing for Shona and find myself telling about looking down from the upstairs window in Brooklands as the soldiers spilled out of the truck.

*

I've now lived in Corvallis longer than I've lived anywhere else. It has been a good place to bring up a family. I love the coast and the mountains, and we all enjoy hiking and camping and cross-country skiing. When the children were young, I led a Girl Scout troop and taught Sunday school and was a room mother and carpooled to this and that like lots of other American mothers. But I still didn't totally belong—and I don't think I ever will—because part of me is the child that grew up in Scotland. Yet when I go back to Scotland, it's not home either. My roots are there, but my branches are here, and now there's a new little twig—Judith and Bob's little Alexander Bruce!

Perhaps the feeling of not belonging anywhere is what makes setting so important in my books. Most of my ideas have started from setting. When you write a book "about" a place, you spend so much time there in your mind and make so many discoveries about it that when you've finished the book, you end up owning the place. It's a very convenient ownership—without taxes or upkeep! You also fix the place in time. In 1983, when Karen and I returned to Dorset to see the derelict cottage where Ann had lived in *To Nowhere and Back,* we had trouble finding it. Since we'd last been there, a fire had destroyed the rotting thatch, and the crumbling walls were almost totally hidden by blackberries. But for me, the cottage is still there the way I wrote about it. Smailholm Tower (from *In the Keep of Time*) has changed in the other direction. It has been renovated, with floors rebuilt and the roof repaired. The National Trust for Scotland may own the tower, but I own the old ruined keep!

In 1979, I finally made it to New Zealand with Norm and Susan and Karen. Norm was, as usual, looking for insects, while I was hoping to find inspiration for another book. Schools were on vacation when we got there, so for the first month we toured the countryside, visiting isolated sheep farms and abandoned gold mines. We all caught gold fever. Norm began looking for gold instead of insects in the rivers, but it was soon obvious that insects were a better bet. I thought there might be a story in the gold rush. However, the native forest held even more allure than gold. The New Zealand forest is very different from that of Oregon—a fantasy jungle inhabited by strange flightless birds like the kiwi and the weka. I decided I'd write about the land as it had been when its first settlers—the Maoris—discovered it. This wasn't like writing about Britain, whose history is all recorded in books. Instead I had to figure out the way it must have been from how the Maoris live now, from their crafts and legends, and also from the restrictions of the land itself.

I started writing *Light in the Mountain* while we were still living in Christchurch. Susan and Karen had been

"Norm and I, cross-country skiing," 1986. (Photo courtesy of Margaret J. Anderson. Reproduced by permission.)

in on a lot of the research and took an almost parental interest in my progress. Each afternoon, before I had time to ask them how school had gone, they'd check up on what I'd written that day. Just thinking about the book wasn't good enough for them. They wanted to see words on paper. I might never have finished that book if they hadn't been such hard taskmasters.

My book *The Druid's Gift* is set on the St. Kilda Islands—a group of rocky islands in the north Atlantic, 112 miles west of Scotland. They are sometimes referred to as "the islands on the edge of the world" because they are so remote. Their cliffs, which are the highest in Britain, are the home of hundreds of thousands of seabirds. The St. Kildas were inhabited for more than 1,000 years by people who ate birds harvested from the cliffs. I read everything I could find about the islands. They were first described by Donald Monro, who visted them in 1549, though his book wasn't published until 1774. That must be something of a record in the publishing world.

The story that began to form in my mind was part history and legend and part fantasy. It took me about four years to bring it together. By the time I finished writing the book, I knew St. Kilda better than I knew my own

backyard although I'd never been there. Then in July 1988, I had the chance to take part in an archaeological dig on Hirta, the biggest of the islands. As the boat approached Hirta and the stark cliffs emerged from the thick mist, I felt nervous—as if I were finally meeting someone face-to-face that I'd fallen in love with from a few snapshots and letters! We rounded a headland and anchored in Village Bay. It was exactly as I had pictured it, though I hadn't expected the hills to look so green and inviting. The old pictures I'd pored over had all been in sepia tones or black and white.

The archaeological dig was fascinating. When we were scraping down through the field drains from the fifteenth or sixteenth centuries, we uncovered the complete skeleton of a dog. A dog that had been tossed into the ditch after it died—around 400 years ago. I felt as if I were one of my own characters going through a time slip! We discovered quite a lot of early pottery, so coarse and rough that it was hard to tell from stone. The most important find didn't look like much at all—a piece of shaped soapstone deep in the soil. The nearest place soapstone occurs naturally is Norway, so that fragment of stone was a link with the Vikings.

My stay on St. Kilda was all too short. As I left, I told myself I'd be back—maybe even next year. A few hours later, I was wondering I'd be alive next year! The waves were enormous and our boat, a converted fishing boat, was very small. The crossing took thirty hours instead of twenty-four. Most of the other eleven passengers were violently sick and lay in huddled misery in their bunks. I sat up all night in huddled misery in the cabin. I wasn't seasick, but I was much too scared to go below deck to my bunk. Thirty hours is a long time to be scared. Occasionally, the skipper, a soft-spoken Aberdonian, would look in and tell us how brave we were. (Little did he know!) He added that the real test would be Point of Ardnamurchan, where we'd get the full force of the cross winds. We might have to turn back and lie up in the lee of an island. I felt I could take anything—except turning back. Not only was I short on courage, I was short on time.

Susan and her fiancée, Barry, were going to be married in Portland just two days after I was due back in the States. In order to catch the plane, Richard and his wife, Nancy, were going to meet me in Oban and drive me down to London. Suspense is a necessary ingredient in a story, but it's wearing in real life. However, there was a happy ending. And I learned that when you're really scared your teeth ache from clenching your jaws so tight. Look for that detail in a future story.

*

Anderson with her grandson Alex, 1988. (Photo courtesy of Margaret J. Anderson. Reproduced by permission.)

While writing this essay, I discovered that the ironing stories I used to tell my children were in fact my early autobiography, the story of a Scottish childhood in the thirties and forties. When I do laundry, I don't always separate the whites and colors. Socks from the same pair often lead individual lives for weeks before being reunited in some chance meeting in the bottom of the laundry basket. White underwear turns pink or blue. Sweaters that were too tight shrink, while it's always the ones that were too big to start with that stretch. And that's the way it has been with this essay. When I pulled my memories out of my mind, they were a bit mixed up, so I have tried to sort them into neat piles. In the telling, the colors may have run a little and the stories may have shrunk or stretched—but, at least, they're clean!

*

Anderson contributed the following update to her autobiographical essay in 2010:

On re-reading my earlier essay, I now see that it forms a completed chapter of my life. Not long after I wrote it, we moved from our suburban Corvallis home to a five-acre rural property studded with old oak trees, and it was like turning the page and finding a new chapter heading. The area is a remnant of the oak savannah that

Family portrait taken at Susan's wedding, summer, 1988: center, Norm and Anderson, from left, Susan, Richard, Judith, and Karen. (Photo courtesy of Margaret J. Anderson. Reproduced by permission.)

once covered much of the Willamette Valley. One of the first things we did was cut paths through the long grass and blackberry thickets, and then we gave them names: the High Road, the Low Road, and Boundary Walk. I felt as if I'd found a grown-up version of The Boggy Bit of my childhood.

Most of the land is uncultivated, but nature always seems to need help. I fight a constant battle, trying to keep the blackberries and poison oak at bay. Several intermittent streams rush down the hillside, fed by the winter rains and then run dry in the summer. We've given the streams names, too: Oak Burn, Studio Run, and Outgate Beck. Close to the house, we have rhododendron beds and flower borders planted with sage and rosemary and other herbs that the deer don't eat. We also have a large, fenced vegetable garden. One of our main reasons for moving here was so that Norm could have his bees nearby. He has kept bees for years, but while we lived in town, he had the hives at a friend's place.

A few years after we moved, Norm retired, but like writers, entomologists don't ever really retire. The bugs are still out there, and the streams provide an outdoor lab where he can make new discoveries. The insects that live in streams that run for only part of the year have not been widely studied. Over the years, Norm has found a new species of mayfly and a black fly, and he has written papers on how certain species have adapted to their aquatic home periodically drying up.

Our new place had one great attraction: a small studio close to the house, shaded by spreading oak branches. I pictured myself writing there all day long without interruption, though with the children no longer at home, I don't need my own space as much as I once did. And I soon found that it's just as hard to write a book in pastoral surroundings as it is sitting at a desk in a cupboard under the stairs.

The second big change in my life around that time was that I switched from writing fiction back to writing nonfiction. Perhaps this had to do with the children being grown. I was no longer immersed in kids and their books. Or perhaps the well had run dry. While I was struggling to come up with a new idea, I happened on a notice that Enslow Publishers was looking for children's writers with a science background. I submitted a letter highlighting my writing credentials and my genetics degree from Edinburgh University. (I didn't admit that I'd studied genetics so long ago that Watson and Crick had yet to discover DNA!) I got a quick response, suggesting that I send them a first chapter and an outline for a book on food chains. I'd just finished writing The Druid's Gift, a fantasy based on the lifestyle of the St. Kildan islanders, who subsisted mostly on seabirds. It had been hard to let go of that book, so I wove the St. Kildans into my first chapter, explaining how the seabirds they ate lived on fish far out in the ocean, and

the fish ate plankton—plankton that obtained their nourishment from sunlight. Those self-sufficient St. Kildans were part of a food chain that reached far beyond their island shores.

I wasn't so excited about writing the rest of the book. Then one day I ran into a friend while I was shopping for groceries at Safeway, and she asked (as people tend to do) what I was working on these days. When I answered I was writing a book on food chains, she looked surprised and remarked that that was surely outside my field. I mumbled something about my background in biology. "That kind of food chains!" she exclaimed. "I thought you meant a book on grocery-store chains!" I rushed home and wrote the next chapter, relieved that it had nothing to do with grocery shopping.

After writing Food Chains, I contributed several biographies to Enslow's "Great Minds of Science" series. I enjoyed the time I spent with those famous scientists. Writing those books involved a lot of sitting around reading other people's books, and it also gave a focus to trips to Britain to see my family. I especially loved writing Charles Darwin. Isaac Newton presented a bigger challenge, but the research took us to places that were new to us. If you ever happen to be in Grantham, Lincolnshire, where Isaac Newton attended grammar school, visit the small museum that honors Grantham's famous son. Somewhere in the archives they must still have the 1995 Visitors Book. If you flip the pages over to the end of September, you'll find my name carefully inscribed between the lines on a right-hand page. On the left hand side, flamboyantly written across the entire page is the signature of another Margaret—Prime Minister Margaret Thatcher, Grantham's famous daughter! Margaret Thatcher was born above the chemist's shop on the main street and had apparently visited the museum the day before I did.

Writing fiction tended to be a rather lonely occupation. I never liked to talk about a work in progress. That changed with writing nonfiction. I found that everyone had something they wanted to add to my research. When I told my daughter Karen that Enslow had asked me to write Scientists of the Ancient World, she immediately suggested that I include Hypatia. I could only answer, "Who?" On learning that Hypatia was a fourth-century, female mathematician and philosopher who lived in Alexandria, I asked Karen if she'd like to write that chapter. We ended up collaborating on the entire book and later wrote a biography of Aristotle together.

Another happy collaboration began when a friend invited me to go on a raft trip down the McKenzie River. He had also invited Nan Field. He thought we'd enjoy meeting one another because we were both interested in children's books. He was right! Nan is the owner of Dog-eared Publications and publishes nature activity books. We ended up writing Ancient Forests together, along with Karen. Although we were all well versed on the topic, presenting the material in a logical order and coming up with original activities was challenging. And we found that a three-way collaboration did not mean that the book was written three times faster! The forest book was followed by two more activity books: *Leap-frogging through Wetlands* and *Discovering Black Bears.*

When Nan suggested that we do a book on black bears, I admitted that I knew very little about them, except that they were black. Wrong! The American black bear can be brown, cinnamon, blue-gray, or even white. To remedy my ignorance, Nan proposed that we sign up for a workshop in northern Minnesota run by Lynn Rogers, a scientist who knows bears so intimately that he can put radio collars around their necks without first an-aesthetizing them. He is famous for "walking with bears" to learn their habits.

Lynn offered us a place in his April workshop, the first workshop of the season, when the hungry bears would be fresh out of hibernation. I'm perfectly at ease with spiders and insects and even lizards and snakes, but I sometimes get a bit tense around big dogs, so I was more than a little nervous when I learned that a major part of the workshop involved meeting bears close up

in the wild. On that first morning, after we'd located a bear's radio signal, I was the last to leave the security of the van. We tramped out into the woods, the beeping growing louder with every step. Then we heard a rustling sound and a big, black, female bear emerged from the undergrowth. We spotted her twin cubs up a tree some distance away. Lynn had given each of us a bag of sunflower seeds and said we could feed "June." Again, I was last in line, but I'm proud to say that I let June eat from my hand—and I still have all ten fingers! We learned a great deal about bears that week, but in our book, we DO NOT recommend that you venture into the forest with a bag of sunflower seeds, saying, "Here, bear! Come, bear!"

One change that accompanied my switch to writing nonfiction was that I received less fan mail and I was asked to do fewer school visits. I didn't take this personally. I could see that if you've struggled through writing a report on Isaac Newton, you're not going to sit down and write a fan letter to the author of the book your teacher told you to read! And I did continue to visit schools, or rather, individual classrooms. We have

"Publisher and author Nan Field watching me feed a black bear." (Photo courtesy of Margaret J. Anderson. Reproduced by permission.)

nine grandchildren, so I've talked to kids from pre-school up through middle school all the way from Seattle to Eugene.

After writing *Bizarre Insects* I developed a workshop using bugs as a jumping-off point for a writing exercise. I had a traveling insect zoo that I took along to the classroom and set up stations where the kids could observe the insects or handle them if they wished. When I was doing this fairly regularly, I had cages of insects at home—walking sticks in the studio, hissing cockroaches on top of the water heater, and various water insects in an aquarium. It was quite labor intensive. But it was also rewarding—all those eager, squealing kids. And some of the writing they produced was quite extraordinary. One of my best moments came when I was asked to do a workshop for a remedial writing class. The kids were mostly fourth graders but were writing well below grade level. I approached the assignment with rather low expectations as far as the writing exercise went, but I figured that the kids would enjoy handling the insects. As it turned out, several of them could communicate on paper, just not in a way that would earn them a high grade on a standardized test. One girl wrote about the hissing cockroach and her paragraph read like a poem.

A 3 inch silky animal. A wood like skeliton.
A hiss like the buzz of a bee.
A mild tikeliness. No other insect long wiggley inteni.
A scary creatcher to some, to others a beautiful creatcher.
A small head. A big scaly boady.
6 legs, long pieces of bone for a back.
A soft creamy inside, not for the eyes to see.
Girls screaming, boys scaring.
Some people try to hide pretending not to be scared, but inside, yes.

An unexpected outcome of the insect workshops was that I was invited to give a presentation on "Insects as a Tool for Teaching Creative Writing" at the Pacific Northwest branch of the Entomological Society, followed by an invitation to speak at the national meeting in 2004. So that November, I headed off to Salt Lake City, leaving Norm at home—a reversal of our roles in earlier years.

Over the last few years, I've been given a false sense of productivity. Enslow has published new editions of my biographies of Darwin, Newton, and Linnaeus. This involved updating some of the information in those books, though not much had changed in the lives of those people who died centuries ago! *Bizarre Insects* is going to be published next year under the new title of *Bugged-Out Insects,* so I may have to resurrect my insect zoo.

Although the younger grandchildren don't read my early fiction books with quite the same enthusiasm as they embrace "Harry Potter" and the "Warriors" books by Erin Hunter, they do find them useful when they have to do book reports. You can count on getting extra credit

The cover designed by Fiona for her report. (Photo courtesy of Margaret J. Anderson. Reproduced by permission.)

if you're related to the author! Fiona created a great cover for her book report on *Journey of the Shadow Bairns* posing as Elspeth, while sister Gillian was given the role of Robbie. It was interesting to realize how much background material on the Barr colonists was available to Fiona on the Internet—facts that I had struggled so hard to uncover while I was writing the book back in 1978.

In the spring of 1993, Norm and our daughter Judith and I took the big step of applying for citizenship after living in the United States as resident aliens for thirty years. Judith and Richard came here on green cards when they were three years old. Richard became a citizen while he was in college, but Judith still had a green card with an outdated photo of herself as a round-faced three year old. When we took the citizenship test, Judith had the advantage of having studied U.S. history in school here, whereas my knowledge of the Constitution and so on was a bit sketchy. However, we were given a book to study, and I passed the test, though I still stumble over the words of the "Star-Spangled Banner"—"God Save the Queen" is a lot easier! On a wet day in October we became U.S. citizens at the Portland courthouse. Six weeks later, I was summoned for jury duty. I felt very assimilated!

Until we became citizens, the Fourth of July always seemed like someone else's birthday party—a party to which we hadn't been invited. When the children were young, we used to get around that left-out feeling by going camping over the Fourth, mostly to a state park that didn't allow fireworks. Looking back, I see that this wasn't very fair to Susan and Karen, who were born in Oregon. However, we've made up for it! The Fourth of July is now one of our favorite holidays—partly because it happens in the summer and we have lots of outdoor space for a family gathering. We're lucky in that our children all live in the Pacific Northwest along the I-5 corridor, so we can get together once or twice a year. And when we do, we need a lot of space for all those grandchildren.

People sometimes ask which of my books is my favorite and I usually say somewhat coyly that I don't have a favorite. It's like asking which is my favorite child. But that answer isn't true. I do have favorites. Among them are *Children of Summer* and *The Druid's Gift*. They both took me to enchanted places. For years I'd been fascinated by the eccentric 19th-century French entomologist J. Henry Fabre. He liked to play "tricks" on the insects that visited his two acres of stony soil in Provence so that he could better understand their behavior. His young son, Paul, assisted him in his studies. Fabre was a marvelous writer, and I had read quite a number of his ten volumes of *Souvenirs Entomologiques*—or rather translations of his books. He seemed like a great character for a children's book, but he was too obscure to have a chance as a "Great Mind of Science" candidate. The biographies that sell best are the ones on people who have already been written about.

While I was pondering what to do about Fabre, I got to know Marie le Glatin Keis, a French artist, who had recently moved to Corvallis. We first met in the Oregon State University bookstore. I was autographing a book for Marie's daughter Quena, who volunteered the information that her mother was a very good artist and would like to do the pictures for one of my books. Instead of explaining that most of my books didn't have pictures and if they did, it wasn't up to me to choose the artist, I invited Marie over for coffee and she brought her portfolio with her. I was amazed and excited to find that it was filled with wonderful pictures of Provence and some great line drawings of cicadas and beetles. She had spent the previous two years in the region where Fabre had lived. Pretty soon we were talking about the book we would do together.

Marie told me she was planning to lead a sketching workshop in Provence that summer and she persuaded me to go along. We ended up traveling to France a few days ahead of the other participants so that we could visit Fabre's home in Sérignan, which is now a museum. When we got there, to our utter dismay, we found the museum was closed for several days because the curator was having a family gathering in the grounds, following his father's funeral. Marie managed to find his phone number and explained that we had come all the

way from America to visit the museum because we were working on a book about Fabre. We had only one more day before her workshop. I could never have been so persuasive with my limited French. The curator agreed—somewhat gruffly—that we could come over the next day. He lost his gruffness when he saw the drawings that Marie had already completed, and he gave us a private tour of the house and grounds. I still remember the thrill of walking into Henri Fabre's parlor and seeing his black peasant hat on the table as if he'd just tossed it down and wandered off into another room. And there was his collecting bag hanging on a hook in his study, and the cage where he had trapped the emperor moth. Meanwhile, Marie was busy sketching and taking notes. It was then that I realized an artist has to deal with all sorts of details that the writer can just skip over. I could describe Fabre reading to his children in the parlor without worrying about the pattern on the curtains or the texture of the floorboards.

I still have my sketchbook to remind me of that trip to Provence, but the clearest pictures of the landscape are those etched in my mind—the purple fields of lavender and the warm glow of the sun on the tile roofs. We'd hoped to capture these colors in Marie's illustrations, but we had to settle for black-and-white drawings. Even

Henri Fabre's house in Séringan from Children of Summer. (Courtesy of Marie le Glatin Keis, Reproduced by permission.)

Anderson's grandchildren in 2000; right to left: Jena, Fiona, Casey (holding Gilian), Alex, Cameron (holding Sarah), Christopher, and Connor. (Photo courtesy of Margaret J. Anderson. Reproduced by permission.)

so, we are happy with how it all turned out. It's a Frances Foster book, so I had the pleasure of working once again with the editor of my earlier fiction books. Another happy outcome is all those dinners with Marie and Dick under the grape arbor in their Corvallis back yard. Marie's cooking is like a quick trip back to Provence. I wish I could also say that the sketching workshop was the start of my new career as an illustrator, but I'm definitely still just a word person, though I did learn to sit quietly and absorb a scene rather than take out my camera and shoot and move on.

My most recent novel, *Olla-Piska,* is based on the life of yet another eccentric scientist. David Douglas's passion for plants matched Fabre's passion for insects, but Douglas wasn't content to confine his interest to his own back yard. He traveled from his native Scotland to the Pacific Northwest in the 1820s to find flowers and shrubs and trees that would flourish in English gardens.

When I told people I was writing about David Douglas (in answer to the what-are-you-working-on question), I was often met with a blank stare, so I'd quickly add, "Douglas of the Douglas-fir!" Even though this brought a nod of recognition, I could tell that a biography of

David Douglas would be a hard sell. So I decided to write an historical novel with Douglas as the main character. That was hard, too, because Douglas was a solitary man. He had room for little else in his life beyond botany, though it was his passion and single-mindedness that I admired. My admiration for him grew as we traced some of his routes across Oregon and managed to get lost—even with the help of Mapquest—whereas Douglas covered thousands of miles on foot and by canoe through the roadless wilderness, always finding his way back to the Hudson Bay headquarters at Fort Vancouver.

After writing several drafts of the book, I circled back to my first idea of telling Douglas's story in the voices of various people who knew him—the cabin boy and the ship's doctor on the *William and Ann,* an Indian chief's daughter, and fur trader Edward Ermatinger. Except for the cabin boy, they all figure in Douglas's journal, and Doctor Scouler and Ermatinger kept journals themselves. The manuscript was the winner of the 2005 Stevens Literary Prize and was published by the Oregon Historical Society Press the following year.

The wonderful cover of *Olla-Piska* is by another artist friend—Ellen Beier. Ellen has a great idea for a book that we're going to work on together. But I'm afraid you won't see it on the shelves of your favorite bookstore very soon. Ellen is absorbed in other plans right now, and I am more easily distracted than I used to be. As I sit here at my computer, the bright October sunshine is streaming though the window . . . maybe I should go out and check on the changing colors of the ash trees along Boundary Walk . . . . Then I'll cut back a few blackberries on the Low Road . . . and I really should see if Oak Burn has started to run again after last week's rain. . . .

*　　*　　*

APPELBAUM, Susannah

Personal

Daughter of David Appelbaum (a professor); married; children: two. *Education:* New York University, degree.

Addresses

Home—New Paltz, NY; Cape Breton, Nova Scotia, Canada. *E-mail*—susannah@susannahappelbaum.com.

Career

Author. Formerly worked as a magazine editor.

Writings

"POISONS OF CAUX" NOVEL TRILOGY

The Hollow Bettle, illustrated by Jennifer Taylor, Alfred A. Knopf (New York, NY), 2009.
The Tasters Guild, illustrated by Jennifer Taylor, Alfred A. Knopf (New York, NY), 2010.
The Shepherd of Weeds, illustrated by Andrea Offermann, Alfred A. Knopf (New York, NY), 2011.

Sidelights

Susannah Appelbaum developed an interest in nature's mysteries as a child, and as a writer she melds her knowledge of plant lore into her "Poisons of Caux" trilogy. In *The Hollow Bettle, The Tasters Guild,* and *The Shepherd of Weeds* readers follow a young heroine as she fights against a corrupt world where evil powers may be rooted in the soil rather than embodied in human form. At stake is the ability to harness nature's ancient power through an understanding of the power of plants to either poison or heal, to nourish or destroy.

In *The Hollow Bettle* readers meet Ivy Manx, an eleven year old who lives in the kingdom of Caux. Although Caux had been peacefully ruled by King Verdigris, a coup by the power-hungry King Nightshade has now brought fear into the land. With his knowledge of natural poisons, Nightshade has prompted those who can afford it to employ food tasters and this vocation is now under the control of the Tasters Guild. Those with botanical knowledge, like Ivy's uncle Cecil, once used this knowledge to heal, but healing is fast becoming a lost art; indeed, Ivy herself enjoys concocting deadly substances. Then Cecil mysteriously disappears. When her friend Rowan, a novice taster, fails at his task of detecting poisoned food, he joins Ivy in search of the missing man, and they carry with them a powerful gem (the bettle of the title). When the head of the Taster's Guild, Vidal Verjouce, sends his henchmen in pursuit, Ivy realizes that her uncle, the bettle, and her own special skills may be bound to Caux's destiny.

In praise of Appelbaum's fiction debut, *Booklist* contributor Cindy Welch noted that *The Hollow Bettle* "pulses with imaginatively named characters, gratifying close calls, and a landscape that is vividly alive." "Appelbaum's first novel quickly captures the imagination," asserted *Voice of Youth Advocates* reviewer Etienne Vallee, and her "well-designed fantasy world" contains sufficient "appeal to satisfy younger readers." April Spisak expressed a similar impression, writing in the *Bulletin of the Center for Children's Books* that the "morbid, darkly elegant setting" and "well-developed cast of intriguing and subtle characters add depth and balance to the quick pace and sarcastic tone of" *The Hollow Bettle.*

Praised by *School Library Journal* contributor Sharon Rawlins as an "inventive story . . . full of strange and mysterious characters," *The Tasters Guild* finds Ivy grappling with the knowledge that she is the "Noble Child" that has been prophesied to restore King Verdigris to the throne and return Caux to peace. Along with Tasters Guild leader Verjouce, who is determined to preserve Caux's status quo of fear and death by poisoning, Ivy must also avoid her former taster, one Sorrel Flux, who also wants to do her inquiry. True harm comes from a surprising source, however, when a rare and deadly plant known as scourge bracken invades the region with the intent to grow in power. The "Poisons of Caux" trilogy concludes with *The Shepherd of Weeds,* in which Ivy joins with friends Rue and Lumpen to stop the threat posed by Verjouce, now the unwitting puppet of the toxic sourge bracken. "Appelbaum continues to thrill," asserted Welch in her *Booklist* review of *The Tasters Guild,* the critic praising the novel for its "vivid descriptions and inspired plot twists."

Biographical and Critical Sources

PERIODICALS

Booklist, June 1, 2009, Cindy Welch, review of *The Hollow Bettle,* p. 55; November 15, 2010, Cindy Welch, review of *The Tasters Guild,* p. 47.

Bulletin of the Center for Children's Books, November, 2009, April Spisak, review of *The Hollow Bettle,* p. 100.

Kirkus Reviews, July 15, 2009, review of *The Hollow Bettle;* July 15, 2010, review of *The Tasters Guild.*

Publishers Weekly, August 17, 2009, review of *The Hollow Bettle,* p. 63.

School Library Journal, December, 2009, Tim Wadham, review of *The Hollow Bettle,* p. 105; August, 2010, Sharon Rawlins, review of *The Tasters Guild,* p. 93.

Tribune Books (Chicago, IL), August 15, 2009, Mary Harris Russell, review of *The Hollow Bettle,* p. 17.

Voice of Youth Advocates, October, 2009, Etienne Vallee, review of *The Hollow Bettle,* p. 325.

ONLINE

Chronogram Online, http://www.chronogram.com/ (October 29, 2009), Nina Shengold, "Poison and Polka Dots."

Susannah Appelbaum Home Page, http://poisonsofcaux.com (September 20, 2011).*

B

BARRETT, Robert T. 1949-

Personal
Born May 13, 1949, in Salt Lake City, UT; son of Theodore (an engineer) and Faye (a homemaker) Barrett; married Vicki Noyce, December 13, 1972; children: Elise, Katherine, Blake, Patricia, Anne, Melissa, Brenda, David, Michael, Eric. *Education:* University of Utah, B.F.A. (painting), 1973; University of Iowa, M.A., 1975, M.F.A. (painting), 1976; attended Academy of Arts (Berlin, Germany), 1976-77. *Politics:* Republican. *Religion:* Church of Jesus Christ of Latter-day Saints (Mormon). *Hobbies and other interests:* Traveling, hiking, painting.

Addresses
Home—Provo, UT. *Office*—Brigham Young University, 210 Brmb, Provo, UT 84602.

Career
Fine-art painter, muralist, and illustrator. Brigham Young University, Provo, UT, assistant professor, 1982-89, associate professor, 1991-95, professor of illustration, beginning 1995, chairperson of Department of Design, 1991-95, associate chairperson of Department of Visual Arts, beginning 1995. Kimball Art Center, former artist in residence. *Exhibitions:* Works exhibited widely, including at annual Utah Illustrator's Exhibitions, Salt Lake Art Center, Brigham Young University, College of Eastern Utah, Springville Art Museum, St. George Art Museum, Kimball Art Center, Repartee Gallery, and Busam Gallerie (Berlin, Germany), as well as by Society of Illustrators New York, National Arts Club, and Directors Guild of America. Work included in permanent collections at Southern Baptist Sunday School Board, Nashville, TN; Brigham Young University, Provo, UT; and elsewhere.

Member
Society of Illustrators, Illustrator's Partnership of America, Pastel Society of America, Portrait Society of America, Salmagundi Club, Phi Kappa Phi.

Awards, Honors
German Academic Exchange grant, 1976-77; National Endowment for the Arts/Utah Arts Council grant, 1978-79; Utah Advertising Gold Award, 1991; ADDY Award, 1991; Karl G. Maeser Teaching Award, Brigham Young University, 1995; Karl G. Maeser Research and Creative Arts Award, 2004.

Illustrator
Pamela Kennedy, reteller, *The Other Wise Man* (based on the story by Henry Van Dyke), Ideals Children's Books (Nashville, TN), 1989.

One-Minute Stories of Great Americans, Doubleday (New York, NY), 1990.

Ann Warren Turner, *Dust for Dinner,* HarperCollins (New York, NY), 1995.

(With Jerry Thompson) *Book of Mormon Stories,* Church of Jesus Christ of Latter-day Saints (Salt Lake City, UT), 1997.

Melinda T. Graff, *Gordon B. Hinckley: Fifteenth President of the Church,* Bookcraft (Salt Lake City, UT), 1998.

The New Testament for Latter-day Saint Families: Illustrated King James Version with Helps for Children, Bookcraft (Salt Lake City, UT), 1998.

Don H. Staheli, *The Story of the Walnut Tree,* Bookcraft (Salt Lake City, UT), 2000.

Timothy M. Robinson, *The Nauvoo Temple Stone,* Bookcraft (Salt Lake City, UT), 2002.

Stephen Wunderli, David Warner, and Mack Wilberg, *Silent Night, Holy Night: The Story of the Christmas Truce* (based on a narration by Walter Cronkite), Shadow Mountain and Mormon Tabernacle Choir (Salt Lake City, UT), 2003.

Paul L. Maier, *The Real Story of the Creation,* Concordia Pub. House (St. Louis, MO), 2007.

Paul L. Maier, *The Real Story of the Flood,* Concordia Pub. House (St. Louis, MO), 2008.

Carole Boston Weatherford, *Michelle Obama: First Mom,* Marshall Cavendish Children (Tarrytown, NY), 2010.

Carole Boston Weatherford, *Obama: Only in America,* Marshall Cavendish Children (New York, NY), 2010.

Contributor to periodicals, including *American Artist, International Artists, Ladies' Home Journal, McCalls, Outdoor Life, Redbook,* and *Southwest Art.*

Sidelights

A native of Utah, Robert T. Barrett is a fine artist who has gained wide-ranging recognition for his work. In addition to painting, Barrett also educates future artists as a professor of visual arts at Brigham Young University, where several of his paintings are on permanent display. As an illustrator, he has added a visual element to texts by authors that include Ann Warren Turner, Paul L. Maier, and Carole Boston Weatherford, oftentimes bringing to life Biblical and faith-based themes. The focus turns to history in Weatherford's companion picture books *Obama: Only in America* and *Michelle Obama: First Mom,* both of which were written to commemorate the election of Barack Obama as U.S. president in 2009. "The broad focus and laudatory quality . . . create an overview greatly enhanced by the illustrations," asserted Janet S. Thompson in her *School Library Journal* review of *Michelle Obama,* while Hazel Rochman praised Barrett's "generously sized oil paintings in sepia shades" in her review of the same work for *Booklist.* Appraising *Obama,* a *Children's Bookwatch* critic dubbed it "stunning," adding that Weatherford's "elegant, cadenced" text is matched by "sensitive paintings [that] illustrate the moving story."

"As a child growing up in a small mining town in southern Utah, my exposure to the world of art was somewhat limited," Barrett once told *SATA.* "My parents were, however, both artistic and loved to draw and paint. In addition, my mother was an avid reader and read all of the classics to me and my two brothers. We didn't have a television until I was in junior high school, but I loved to imagine the characters in the books I was exposed to. In addition, my parents subscribed to several magazines which at the time were lavishly illustrated and were printed in large format. I loved looking at the illustrations in those magazines, which included *Life, Post, McCall's, Redbook,* and *Ladies' Home Journal,* and at times copied some of them. I had determined before I entered high school that I would enter some kind of art-related career. I can't say I never wavered from that resolve, but I continued to come back to it over and over again. Many of my teachers in school encouraged me, and I received a variety of recognitions along the way.

"As I entered the university, I chose to study fine art instead of going in more commercial directions. This continued through graduate work and a postgraduate experience in Europe. Though many of my fellow students were intrigued by modern directions, I found myself continually drawn to traditional forms of art and narrative painting. My M.A. and M.F.A. theses involved the subject of figurative painting, and I attempted to communicate to a broader audience with a realistic approach to painting.

"Teaching through the City Colleges of Chicago (European division) in Berlin exposed me to a number of American illustrators and as I returned from Europe, I decided to go that direction with my work. I built a portfolio of figurative work and became successful at securing commissions as a freelance and, later, an inhouse illustrator. I worked for a number of organizations and clients and continued to teach as well. I was invited to join the faculty at Brigham Young University in 1982."

Biographical and Critical Sources

PERIODICALS

Booklist, July, 1995, review of *Dust for Dinner,* p. 1885; October 15, 2010, Hazel Rochman, review of *Michelle Obama: First Mom,* p. 49.
School Library Journal, October, 1995, review of *Dust for Dinner,* p. 121; April, 2010, Stacy Dillon, review of *Obama: Only in America,* p. 183; November, 2010, Janet S. Thompson, review of *Michelle Obama,* p. 95.

ONLINE

Robert T. Barrett Home Page, http://www.roberttbarrett. com (October 15, 2011).*

*   *   *

BEMIS, John Claude

Personal

Born in NC; married; wife's name Amy; children: Rose. *Education:* University of North Carolina at Chapel Hill, M.Ed. *Hobbies and other interests:* Hiking.

Addresses

Home—Hillsborough, NC. *Agent*—Adams Literary, 7845 Colony Rd., C4, No. 215, Charlotte, NC 28226. *E-mail*—john@johnclaudebemis.com.

Career

Writer, musician, and educator. Elementary school teacher in North Carolina for twelve years; teaches workshops on writing children's literature. Songwriter and musician for band Hooverville.

Member

Society of Children's Book Writers and Illustrators, Writers & Illustrators of North Carolina.

Awards, Honors

100 Titles for Reading and Sharing selection, New York Public Library, 2009, and North Carolina Juvenile Literature Award, 2010, both for *The Nine Pound Hammer.*

Writings

"CLOCKWORK DARK" FANTASY NOVEL TRILOGY

The Nine Pound Hammer, Random House (New York, NY), 2009.
The Wolf Tree, Random House (New York, NY), 2010.
The White City, Random House (New York, NY), 2011.

Adaptations

The Nine Pound Hammer, The Wolf Tree, and *The White City* were adapted as audiobooks.

Sidelights

John Claude Bemis offers a fresh take on the legend of John Henry in his "Clockwork Dark" fantasy trilogy, which is set in an alternate, nineteenth-century America. A songwriter, musician, and former elementary-school teacher, Bemis noted that the origins of his first novel, *The Nine Pound Hammer,* evolved from his interest in vintage country, blues, and roots music. As he stated on his home page, "I became fascinated with the way America's myths have been passed down through songs. Drawing on the legend of John Henry's struggle against the steam drill, I thought about how Southern folklore could be turned into epic fantasy."

The debut installment in the "Clockwork Dark" series, *The Nine Pound Hammer* takes place several years after the death of John Henry, the legendary former slave and railroad worker who challenged a steam drill to a tunneling contest, only to perish after his hard-fought victory, hammer still in hand. As Bemis observed, "He's our American Achilles or King Arthur, full of tragic glory. And his instrument, the Nine Pound Hammer, is our Excalibur, a symbol of his enduring heroism." The novel centers on Ray Cobb, an orphaned twelve year old who joins a traveling medicine show whose members include Peg Leg Nel, a root doctor and pitchman; Buck, a blind sharpshooter; Si, a tattooed escape artist; Marisol, a snake charmer; and Conker, a towering muscleman. Ray soon discovers that the performers knew his father, Li'l Bill, a member of the heroic Ramblers. The Ramblers helped John Henry in his battle against the Gog, an evil entity masquerading as a captain of industry. As part of his diabolical plan to enslave human souls, the Gog now seeks the last of the Swamp Sirens, mythical figures protected by the new generation of Ramblers. April Spisak, writing in the *Bulletin of the Center for Children's Books,* applauded Bemis's "rollicking, fast-paced adventure plot," and a critic in *Kirkus Reviews* noted that *The Nine Pound Hammer* "achieves a balance between the tenor of the historical period and the tall-tale tone of the story."

In *The Wolf Tree,* the second work in Bemis's trilogy, Ray and the Ramblers are living in the Smoky Mountains when they learn of a horrible Darkness spreading across America's prairie that transforms human blood

to oil. As Ray and Marisol set out to investigate this plague, Conker (revealed to be John Henry's son) seeks wood from the powerful Wolf Tree to repair the Nine Pound Hammer, restoring the weapon to its former glory. "Fantasy and folklore fashion a subtle ecological nature-versus-machine tale that cautions readers to keep ideals and act thoughtfully," Lucy Schall commented in *Voice of Youth Advocates.* Daniel Kraus, writing in *Booklist,* dubbed *The Wolf Tree* "as peculiar and inventive" as its predecessor.

The White City concludes Bemis's trilogy. The 1893 World's Columbian Exposition in Chicago is the setting for an epic confrontation between the Ramblers and the maniacal Gog. A contributor in *Kirkus Reviews* remarked that "this unique, ambitious American fantasy comes to a satisfying end that would please even John Henry."

Discussing the themes of his "Clockwork Dark" trilogy with online interviewer Beth Revis, Bemis stated: "Our world is an enormously complicated place. Not all that we believe to be good is always good, and not all we assume to be bad is always bad." "My most admirable

Cover of John Claude Bemis's **The Wolf Tree,** *a "Clockwork Dark" novel featuring artwork by Alexander Jansson.* (Illustration copyright © 2010 by Alexander Jansson. Reproduced by permission of Random House Children's Books, a division of Random House, Inc.)

characters are ones who strike a balance between opposing beliefs and stances," he added, "while the characters that are most flawed are obsessively fixated on particular notions."

Biographical and Critical Sources

PERIODICALS

Booklist, May 15, 2009, Daniel Kraus, review of *The Nine Pound Hammer,* p. 52; October 1, 2010, Daniel Kraus, review of *The Wolf Tree,* p. 83.
Bulletin of the Center for Children's Books, February, 2010, April Spisak, review of *The Nine Pound Hammer,* p. 236.
Kirkus Reviews, July 15, 2009, review of *The Nine Pound Hammer;* July 15, 2011, review of *The White City.*
School Library Journal, October, 2009, Connie Tyrrell Burns, review of *The Nine Pound Hammer,* p. 120; December, 2010, Heather M. Campbell, review of *The Wolf Tree,* p. 100.
Voice of Youth Advocates, October, 2010, Lucy Schall, review of *The Wolf Tree,* p. 361; June, 2011, Lucy Schall, review of *The White City,* p. 179.

ONLINE

Beth Revis Web log, http://bethrevis.blogspot.com/ (November 4, 2008), Beth Revis, interview with Bemis.
John Claude Bemis Home Page, http://johnclaudebemis. com (September 21, 2011).
Tor Books Web site, http://www.tor.com/ (February 23, 2010), Mur Lafferty, "American Mythology: *The Nine Pound Hammer* by John Claude Bemis."

*   *   *

BENNETT, Sarah "Pinkie"
See BROWN, Lisa

*   *   *

BRETT, Jan 1949-
(Jan Brett Bowler, Jan Churchill Brett)

Personal

Born December 1, 1949, in Hingham, MA; daughter of George (a sales engineer) and Jean (a teacher) Brett; married Daniel Bowler, February 27, 1970 (divorced, 1979); married Joseph Hearne (a musician), August 18, 1980; children: three. *Education:* Attended Colby Junior College (now Colby-Sawyer College), 1968-69, and Boston Museum of Fine Arts School, 1970. *Hobbies and other interests:* Horses, gliding, raising chickens, traveling.

Addresses

Home—Norwell, MA; and Berkshire County, MA.

Career

Artist and author and illustrator of children's books. Trustee, Boston Symphony Orchestra. *Exhibitions:* Work exhibited at galleries, including Master Eagle Gallery, New York, NY, 1981; Gallery on the Green, Lexington, MA, 1985; Main Street Gallery, Nantucket, MA, 1987; and Society of Illustration show, New York, NY, 1991. Work included in traveling exhibition staged by Oshkosh Public Museum, Oshkosh, WI.

Member

Society of Children's Book Writers and Illustrators, Society of Colonial Dames in America.

Awards, Honors

Parents' Choice award, Parents' Choice Foundation, 1981, for *Fritz and the Beautiful Horses,* 1988, for *Mother's Day Mice;* Children's Choice selection, International Reading Association, 1982, for both *In the Castle of Cats* and *Fritz and the Beautiful Horses;* Ambassador of Honor Book designation, English-Speaking Union of the United States, 1983, for *Some Birds Have Funny Names;* University of Nebraska Children's Book Award, 1984, for *Fritz and the Beautiful Horses;* Outstanding Science Trade Book for Children designation, National Science Teachers Association, 1984, for *Some Plants Have Funny Names;* first prize for juvenile book, New York Book Show, 1987, for *Mother's Day Mice;* certificate of merit, Bookbuilders West Book Show, 1987, for *The Enchanted Book;* Pick of the Lists, *American Bookseller,* 1988, for *The First Dog,* 1989, for *The Mitten,* 1990, for *The Wild Christmas Reindeer,* 1991, for both *The Owl and the Pussycat* and *Berlioz the Bear;* Best Children's Books citation, *New Yorker* magazine, 1988, for *The First Dog,* 1989, for *The Mitten,* 1990, for *The Wild Christmas Reindeer,* 1991, for *Berlioz the Bear; Booklist* Best Children's Book of the 1980s designation, for *The Mitten;* artist award, New England Booksellers' Association, 1990; American Library Association Notable Book designation, 1991, for *The Owl and the Pussycat;* Book of the Year Award, American Booksellers Association, 1998, for *The Hat;* Lifetime Achievement Award, Boston Public Library, 2005.

Writings

SELF-ILLUSTRATED; FOR CHILDREN

Fritz and the Beautiful Horses, Houghton (Boston, MA), 1981.
Good Luck Sneakers, Houghton (Boston, MA), 1981.
Annie and the Wild Animals, Houghton (Boston, MA), 1985.

(Adaptor) *Goldilocks and the Three Bears* (based on the version by Andrew Lang), Dodd (New York, NY), 1987.

The First Dog, [San Diego, CA], 1988.

(Adaptor) *The Mitten: A Ukrainian Folktale,* Putnam (New York, NY), 1989.

(Adaptor) *Beauty and the Beast,* Clarion Books (New York, NY), 1989.

The Wild Christmas Reindeer, Putnam (New York, NY), 1990.

Berlioz the Bear, Putnam (New York, NY), 1991.

The Trouble with Trolls, Putnam (New York, NY), 1992.

Christmas Trolls, Putnam (New York, NY), 1993.

(Adaptor) *Town Mouse, Country Mouse,* Putnam (New York, NY), 1994.

Armadillo Rodeo, Putnam (New York, NY), 1995.

Comet's Nine Lives, Putnam (New York, NY), 1996.

The Hat, Putnam (New York, NY), 1997.

(Adaptor) *Gingerbread Baby,* Putnam (New York, NY), 1999.

Hedgie's Surprise, Putnam (New York, NY), 2000.

Jan Brett's Christmas Treasury, Putnam (New York, NY), 2001.

Daisy Comes Home, Putnam (New York, NY), 2002.

Knockety-Knock, It's Christmas Eve, Putnam (New York, NY), 2002.

Who's That Knocking on Christmas Eve?, Putnam (New York, NY), 2002.

On Noah's Ark, Putnam (New York, NY), 2003.

The Umbrella, Putnam (New York, NY), 2004.

Honey . . . Honey . . . Lion!: A Story from Africa, Putnam (New York, NY), 2005.

Hedgie Blasts Off!, Putnam (New York, NY), 2006.

The Three Snow Bears, Putnam (New York, NY), 2007.

Gingerbread Friends, Putnam (New York, NY), 2008.

Jan Brett's Snowy Treasury, Putnam (New York, NY), 2009.

The Three Little Dassies, Putnam (New York, NY), 2010.

The Easter Egg, Putnam (New York, NY), 2010.

Home for Christmas, Putnam (New York, NY), 2011.

ILLUSTRATOR

(Under name Jan Brett Bowler) Stephen Krensky, *Woodland Crossings,* Atheneum (New York, NY), 1978.

Mary Louise Cuneo, *Inside a Sand Castle and Other Secrets,* Houghton (Boston, MA), 1979.

Simon Seymour, *The Secret Clocks: Time Senses of Living Things,* Viking (New York, NY), 1979.

Eve Bunting, *St. Patrick's Day in the Morning,* Clarion Books (New York, NY), 1980.

Mark Taylor, *Young Melvin and Bulger,* Doubleday (Garden City, NY), 1981.

Betty Boegehold, *In the Castle of Cats,* Dutton (New York, NY), 1981.

Diana Harding Cross, *Some Birds Have Funny Names,* Crown (New York, NY), 1981.

Ruth Krauss, *I Can Fly,* Golden Press (New York, NY), 1981.

Jeanette L. Groth, *Prayer: Learning How to Talk to God,* Concordia (St. Louis, MO), 1983.

Eve Bunting, *The Valentine Bears,* Clarion Books (New York, NY), 1983, reprinted, 2003.

Diana Harding Cross, *Some Plants Have Funny Names,* Crown (New York, NY), 1983.

Mark Taylor, *The Great Rescue* ("Cabbage Patch Kids" series), Parker Brothers (Beverly, MA), 1984.

Annetta Dellinger, *You Are Special to Jesus,* Concordia (St. Louis, MO), 1984.

Dorothy Van Woerkom, *Old Devil Is Waiting: Three Folktales* ("Let Me Read" series), Harcourt (San Diego, CA), 1985.

The Wizard of Oz: A Story to Color, Random House (New York, NY), 1985.

Eve Bunting, *The Mother's Day Mice,* Clarion Books (New York, NY), 1986.

The Twelve Days of Christmas, Dodd (New York, NY), 1986.

Pamela Jane, *Noelle of the Nutcracker,* Houghton (Boston, MA), 1986.

Eve Bunting, *Scary, Scary Halloween,* Clarion Books (New York, NY), 1986.

Janina Porazinska, *The Enchanted Book: A Tale from Krakow,* translated by Bozena Smith, Harcourt (San Diego, CA), 1987.

Eve Bunting, *Happy Birthday, Dear Duck,* Clarion Books (New York, NY), 1988.

Edward Lear, *The Owl and the Pussycat,* Putnam (New York, NY), 1991.

(With others) *For Our Children: A Book to Benefit the Pediatric AIDS Foundation,* Disney Press (Burbank, CA), 1991.

Clement Moore, *The Night before Christmas,* Putnam (New York, NY), 1998.

Also illustrator of a calendar for Sunrise Publications.

Adaptations

Many of Brett's books have been adapted for audiocassette, including *The Great Rescue,* Parker Brothers (Beverly, MA), 1984; *Beauty and the Beast,* Dove Audio (Beverly Hills, CA), 1992; *The Night before Christmas,* Spoken Arts (New Rochelle, NY), 2001; *The Mitten,* Spoken Arts, 2001; *The Hat,* Spoken Arts, 2001; *Gingerbread Baby,* Spoken Arts, 2001; and *The Umbrella* Spoken Arts, 2006.

Sidelights

Jan Brett, a celebrated illustrator of children's books whose works have sold more than thirty-four million copies, has garnered dozens of awards during her long and distinguished career. Praising the artist's efforts on her retelling of *Goldilocks and the Three Bears,* *Horn Book* critic Ellen Fader wrote that Brett's illustrations "burst with action," the reviewer adding that the volume "infuses the old nursery tale with new life."

Brett's artwork, which frequently features animals and nature, often incorporates Old World folklore and motifs. Her books have received attention from critics who are quick to applaud her effective use of illustra-

tion to further the meaning, symbolism, and moral of a story. Her inclusion of detailed borders and side panels to graphically reveal additional aspects not presented in the main story line and pictures has, in fact, become her trademark. Such ornamental peripherals offer "a story around a story, so that the reader instantly becomes an insider," pointed out *New York Times Book Review* contributor Pat Ross in a critique of Brett's illustrations for her original story in *Annie and the Wild Animals.*

The daughter of a sales engineer and a teacher, Brett attended the Boston Museum of Fine Arts School in 1970 to refine her artistic skills. She credits her keen ability to create fantasy through pictures and words to her mother, who encouraged her to be imaginative, and to her own penchant for immersing herself in the stories she read in childhood. "I remember the special quiet of rainy days when I felt that I could enter the pages of my beautiful picture books," Brett once recalled. "Now I try to recreate that feeling of believing that the imagi-

nary place I'm drawing really exists." To elicit such an authentic air, Brett often uses real-life people, settings, and occurrences as the basis for her work. She feels that the beauty and tranquility of her summer home in the mountains, near where her husband plays with the Boston Symphony Orchestra, provides a source of inspiration and new ideas. Brett's travels are also a major influence on her illustrated works. The author/illustrator often incorporates impressions gathered from around the world into her works; for instance, *On Noah's Ark,* which was influenced by a trip to Botswana and *Daisy Comes Homes* was inspired by time spent in China. "Illustrating children's books always seems like a big adventure because as an artist I must explore and give thought to my subject—an artist needs to know everything about their subject," Brett explained on the Scholastic Web site.

Brett began to realize her childhood dream of becoming a professional illustrator of children's books in 1978, rendering the drawings for Stephen Krensky's fable collection *Woodland Crossings*. Her childhood love of horses influenced her 1981 children's story *Fritz and the Beautiful Horses,* the first published book to feature her talents as both writer and illustrator. Centering on the theme that one's inner beauty is more important than ne's outer appearance, *Fritz and the Beautiful Horses* describes how a shy, lanky pony wins the hearts of townspeople through his kindness and good deeds, despite his lack of grandeur and physical stature. Featuring Eastern European motifs and settings, *Fritz and the Beautiful Horses* was widely lauded by critics, many of whom claimed that the book's art evokes the enchantment of a distant era. Several reviewers assessed Brett's paintings as special and magnificent; as a *Publishers Weekly* commentator noted, the text in *Fritz and the Beautiful Horses* is "simple but engaging," and Brett's drawings showcase "the beauty of equines as few pictures do."

Brett has also garnered critical approval with her self-illustrated storybooks, among them *Annie and the Wild Animals* and *The Wild Christmas Reindeer.* In the former title, she draws from her daughter Lia's fascination with undomesticated critters to show what happens when little Annie's pet kitty disappears one winter, leaving the child to search for new friends in the forest. Sad and lonely, she leaves corn cakes in the snow to attract potential playmates and eventually meets a moose, wildcat, bear, and other animals. All are unacceptable replacements for the girl's beloved cat, however: they are too ferocious, too ornery, or too unruly. Annie's desperation is short lived, however; as foreshadowed in the border art of earlier pages, the tabby returns in the spring with three kittens in tow. A number of commentators remarked on the style of clothing and backdrops used in *Annie and the Wild Animals,* pointing out that both are greatly detailed and feature a Scandinavian design. The book's art uses a "treasury of motifs taken from the universal tradition of folk art and crafts," asserted Ross in the *New York Times Book Review*. Brett's depiction of animals was also praised. A *Horn Book* reviewer found the work's creatures "rendered with . . . humor," and praised the artist's "elaborate illustrations" for "adeptly conveying the change from winter to spring."

Like *Annie and the Wild Animals, The Wild Christmas Reindeer* features a young female protagonist and the lessons she learns from her experiences with a group of disobedient beasts. Charting the frustrations of the youngster, who trains Santa Claus's reindeer for the daunting journey on Christmas Eve, Brett shows how uncooperative the feisty reindeer become when scolded by the girl after a lackluster practice session. After the child realizes the ineffectiveness of her harsh instruction and subsequently offers kind words of encouragement to her pupils, the rambunctious creatures respond earnestly and the trainer succeeds in readying the group for their 'round-the-world flight. Brett again uses borders and side panels to disclose additional action: peripheral illustrations feature gift-making elves at work, while intricate borders showcase other holiday paraphernalia. A hit with many critics, *The Wild Christmas Reindeer* was deemed a "sweet Christmas fantasy that shows Brett at her best" by a reviewer in *Publishers Weekly.*

The celebration of the Christmas season is a recurring theme in many of Brett's picture books, such as *The Twelve Days of Christmas, Christmas Trolls, Knockety-Knock, It's Christmas Eve, The Night before Christmas,* and *Who's That Knocking on Christmas Eve?* In *Who's That Knocking on Christmas Eve?* Brett crosses the global landscape to Norway where the title's storyline takes place. She uses her trademark borders to augment her rendition of a Norwegian folktale based on a young boy and his polar bear as they assist a young girl in her effort to chase away the trolls that hope to steal the Christmas treats. A *Kirkus Reviews* critic noted that the inclusion of "authentic cultural details" adds to the "setting, costumes, and food" that Brett depicts in *Who's That Knocking on Christmas Eve?*

Winter is the setting for *The Mitten: A Ukrainian Folktale,* a retelling of a traditional story about several tiny animals that find refuge in a girl's lost piece of outerwear, as well as in *The Hat.* In the latter book, Hedgie the hedgehog finds a red woolen stocking stuck to his prickles after it blows off a clothesline. Pretending that the sock is his new winter hat, Hedgie ignores the other animals as they laugh at his new chapeau. As the sock's owner eventually retrieves her missing item, Hedgie's fellow animal creatures decide that his use of winter clothing is not such a ridiculous idea after all. While the other animals don winter attire, Hedgie laughs at them, finding their new clothing equally humorous. "Brett conveys the season with such loving spirit," according to *Booklist* contributor Susan Dove Lempke, "that children will almost wish for winter." Claiming that "Brett demonstrates an expert eye for color," a *Publishers Weekly* reviewer found the author/illustrator's cast of "animal characters as endearing and expressive" as those in *The Mitten.*

Hedgie is featured again in *Hedgie's Surprise,* and here the hedgehog finds a clever solution to a chicken's problem. Laying eggs every day, Henny loses each of her potential chicks to a hungry troll named Tomten. Hedgie feels sorry for his feathered friend and devises a plan to scare off the greedy troll for good. When substituting round objects such as an acorn, strawberry, mushroom, and potato in Henny's nest does not work, the hedgehog curls up in a ball and uses himself as a egg-shaped decoy. As Tomten tries to steal the prickly fellow, Hedgie's pointed bristles sends the troll away for good. Again, reviewers noted Brett's artwork, and a *Publishers Weekly* critic reported of *Hedgie's Surprise,* that "the author's endearingly expressive animal characters, depicted in meticulous detail, steal the show."

The energetic hedgehog makes yet another return appearance in in *Hedgie Blasts Off!,* a "lighthearted space adventure," observed a contributor in *Kirkus Reviews.* Although he works on the cleanup crew at the Star Lab, Hedgie longs to become an astronaut. When scientists note an unusual occurrence with a volcano on the planet Mikkop, they create a special robot to investigate the problem. A malfunction aboard the craft endangers the mission, until Hedgie heroically mans the controls. "Brett's exquisite artwork will easily draw children's interest," Gillian Engberg noted in *Booklist,* and Kirsten Cutler, writing in *School Library Journal,* maintained that young readers "will cheer for this intrepid hedgehog as he solves the problem of the plugged crater."

Brett's self-illustrated *Daisy Comes Home* was inspired by a trip to China that Brett took with her son and daughter-in-law, as well as by Marjorie Flack's popular children's book *The Story about Ping. Daisy Comes Home* takes place in modern-day China and focuses on Daisy, a hen that is treasured by her owner Mei Mei, but badgered by other hens because she is the smallest of the group. Tired of being harassed by the other hens,

Daisy decides to sleep outside the coop one rainy night. She nests in one of Mei Mei's market baskets, which have been left near the bank of the Li River. When the Li overflows its banks due to a recent rainfall, a market basket carries the sleeping hen downstream, and Daisy awakens to an array of adventures which test her courage and ability to survive. Eventually caught by a fisherman, she is brought to the market to be sold as someone's supper, until she is spotted by her observant owner. Back in the hens' coop Daisy uses her newfound confidence and bravery to move up the established packing order within the group of hens. *Children's Literature* reviewer Claudia Mills commented that *Daisy Comes Home* is a "believable transformation of self-empowerment," while a *Publishers Weekly* acknowledged Brett for her "trademark borders and embellishments [which] intriguingly evoke the timeless setting."

Brett's travels to the Monteverde Cloud Forest in Costa Rica influence the framework of *The Umbrella.* Similar

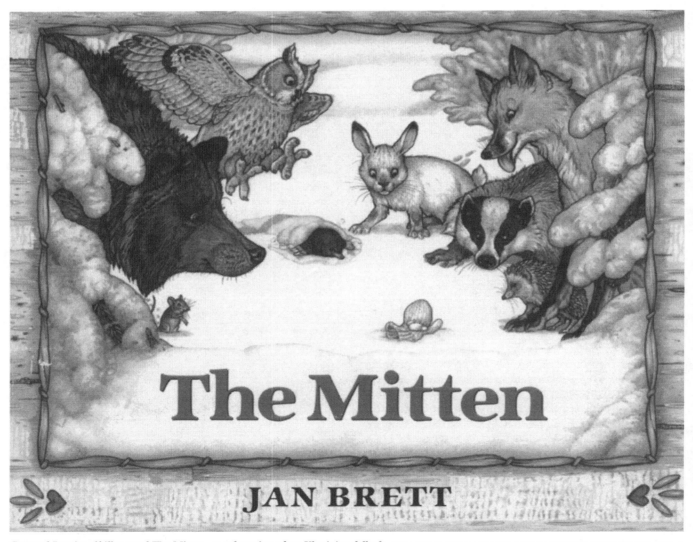

Cover of Brett's self-illustrated **The Mitten,** *an adaptation of an Ukrainian folktale.* (Copyright © 1989 by Jan Brett. Used by permission of G.P. Putnam's Sons, a division of Penguin Young Readers Group, a member of Penguin Group (USA) Inc., 345 Hudson St., New York, NY 10014. All rights reserved.)

to *The Mitten* and *The Hat, The Umbrella* introduces young readers to an array of rain-forest animals. Young Carlos takes a trip to the tropical region with an intent to see some of the forest's animals and brings with him a green umbrella. As the boy enters the forest he is disappointed that there are no animals to see. Carlos decides to climb a tree in order to get a better view, and in the process he drops his green umbrella next to the base of the tree. As the boy watches from the branches above, an assortment of small animals begins collecting inside the green upside-down umbrella, among them a toucan, a jaguar, a tapir, and a monkey. In Brett's text, readers are introduced to snippets of Spanish that add "authenticity to a story with a deeply rooted sense of place," according to *Booklist* reviewer Terry Glover. Characteristically, however, Brett's illustrations captured most critical acclaim. Susan Weitz, writing in *School Library Journal*, for instance, noted that the author/artist's "watercolor-and-gouache illustrations are stunning" and provide an "entertaining visual puzzle for children."

Brett's *Honey . . . Honey . . . Lion!: A Story from Africa* is based on a folktale from Botswana and focuses on the honeyguide, a small African bird that leads stronger creatures to a beehive, hoping to share the spoils after others break open the honeycomb. When Honeyguide's frequent partner-in-crime, Badger, decides to keep the tasty treat to himself one day, the bird decides to seek revenge. After leading Badger on a wild chase, Honeyguide surprises his hungry nemesis with a visit from an even hungrier lion. "Brett has created another lush winner with beautifully detailed illustrations of the animals and a clear, fast-paced story," Kara Schaff Dean reported in *School Library Journal*. A reviewer in *Publishers Weekly* applauded the "meticulous renderings of African animals and vegetation" in *Honey . . . Honey . . . Lion!*, noting that they are "presented against a parchment-like backdrop and framed by striking borders featuring beads and feathers."

In addition to her self-illustrated children's books, Brett has won acclaim for her artistic contributions to other authors' texts, particularly Eve Bunting's *St. Patrick's Day in the Morning* and *Valentine Bears;* Diana Harding Cross's *Some Birds Have Funny Names* and *Some Plants Have Funny Names;* and Betty Boegehold's *In the Castle of Cats.* Her retellings and picture work for classic fairy tales such as *Goldilocks and the Three Bears* and *Beauty and the Beast* have also met with positive critical response. In the last-named title, for example, the book's moral—that appearances can be deceiving—is graphically presented in tapestries adorning the walls depicted in the principal illustrations. In these wall hangings, the beast's servants—who appear in animal guise in the primary story—are depicted as they truly exist: in human form. "Brett shows real finesse in drafting various animals," observed a reviewer in an appraisal of *Beauty and the Beast* for the *Bulletin of the Center for Children's Books.* Calling the same book "lovely" and "carefully made," a *Kirkus Reviews* con-

Brett creates a magical retelling of a time-honored tale in her picture book Beauty and the Beast. (Illustration copyright © 1986 by Jan Brett Studio, Inc. Reproduced by permission of Clarion Books, an imprint of Houghton Mifflin Harcourt Publishing Company. All rights reserved.)

tributor deemed it a "simple, yet graceful retelling." Praising the artist's work on *Beauty and the Beast* as "a brilliant marriage of artwork and text," a *Publishers Weekly* reviewer judged Brett to be "a contemporary illustrator of consummate skill."

Another book featuring animal characters, *Town Mouse, Country Mouse* follows a mouse couple from the city as they exchange residences with a pair of country mice. *Town Mouse, Country Mouse* also adds a twist to the traditional ending: While the mice usually realize that nothing replaces their own home, in Brett's version they are chased by a cat and owl who suggest to each other that they should trade places, potentially starting the cycle all over again. Calling the illustrations "gorgeous," *Booklist* contributor Stephanie Zvirin predicted that Brett's "playful retelling" of *Town Mouse, Country Mouse* is certain to become a favorite."

The biblical story of Noah and his ark is retold in *On Noah's Ark,* which is narrated from the viewpoint of Noah's granddaughter. While a *Publishers Weekly* critic observed that Brett "omits the biblical framework" of the classic tale, a *Kirkus Reviews* contributor acknowledged the book as a "child-friendly, beautifully crafted version" of the familiar story. Brett presents the story in a simplistic manner, but features life-like detail in her illustrations of the animals. Gillian Engberg commented in *Booklist* that Brett uses "precise brushstrokes and vivid colors" to "create . . . incredibly textured feathers and fur." In researching the book's artwork, Brett traveled to Botswana, and her inclusion of vivid details "add to the book's interest for older children, who can find something new to explore."

Brett puts an Arctic spin on a classic tale in *The Three Snow Bears*. While searching for her team of sled dogs, Aloo-ki, an Inuit girl, stumbles upon an igloo belonging to a family of polar bears. After helping herself to their bowls of soup and sampling their warm boots, Aloo-ki settles in for a nap in Baby Bear's bed. When the bears arrive home, a startled Aloo-ki darts out of the igloo, where she discovers a most pleasant surprise, courtesy of the homeowners. "The plot remains true to the progression of the traditional tale and the narrative moves swiftly," remarked Piper Nyman in *School Library Journal.* A contributor in *Publishers Weekly* noted that "the main draw is, as usual, Brett's characteristically detailed art," and a *Kirkus Reviews* critic praised the "strikingly beautiful blue-and-gray-toned world of ice populated with thickly furred creatures and accented with Inuit motifs."

Set in Southern Africa, *The Three Little Dassies* offers a unique variation on the familiar plot of "The Three Little Pigs." After settling down in the desert, Mimbi, Pimbi, and Timbi, three dassies (furry mammals similar to guinea pigs) find themselves harassed by a ravenous eagle. When their hastily and shoddily constructed homes are destroyed, Mimbi and Pimbi are snatched up by the predator and plopped in its nest. Rescued by a friendly agama lizard, the pair now relies on Timbi's stone structure for safety. "Brett invokes the African setting with details of the desert landscape and the animals' colorful, patterned clothing," Andrew Medlar commented in *Booklist,* and Carrie Rogers-Whitehead observed in *School Library Journal* that Brett's tale "will captivate children and introduce a setting and animals unfamiliar to most of them."

In addition to her career as an illustrator, Brett raises Silkie Bantams, Silver Laced Wyandottes, and other breeds of ornamental poultry. The birds have proven to an inspiration to the artist; their portraits line the walls of the hen house and rooster house. Brett once told *SATA:* "My imagination has always run away with me. As a child, this was entertaining but confusing. As an adult, I can direct my ideas toward children's books. Often I put borders in my books to contain the overflow of thoughts."

Cover of* On Noah's Ark, *Brett's self-illustrated version of the well-known biblical tale.

A miniature drama plays out in Jan Brett's original story and detailed art for **The Three Little Dassies,** *which takes place in South Africa.* (Copyright © 2010 by Jan Brett. Reproduced by permission of G.P. Putnam's Sons, a division of Penguin Young Readers, a member of Penguin Group (USA) Inc., 345 Hudson Street, New York, NY 10014. All rights reserved.)

Biographical and Critical Sources

PERIODICALS

Booklist, September 1, 1994, Stephanie Zvirin, review of *Town Mouse, Country Mouse,* p. 45; September 15, 1995, Leone McDermott, review of *Armadillo Rodeo,* p. 174; October 15, 1996, Susan Dove Lempke, review of *Comet's Nine Lives,* p. 430; September 1, 1997, Susan Dove Lempke, review of *The Hat,* p. 116; November 15, 1999, Marta Segal, review of *Gingerbread Baby,* p. 633; September 1, 2000, Denise Wilms, review of *Hedgie's Surprise,* p. 120; October 1, 2003, Gillian Engberg, review of *On Noah's Ark,* p. 333; December 1, 2004, Terry Glover, review of *The Umbrella,* p. 658; August 1, 2006, Gillian Engberg, review of *Hedgie Blasts Off!,* p. 82; September 15, 2007, John Peters, review of *The Three Snow Bears,* p. 71; December 1, 2009, Francisca Goldsmith, review of *The Easter Egg,* p. 49; September 1, 2010, Andrew Medlar, review of *The Three Little Dassies,* p. 110.

Bulletin of the Center for Children's Books, December, 1989, review of *Beauty and the Beast,* p. 79.

Horn Book, July, 1985, review of *Annie and the Wild Animals,* p. 434; February, 1988, Ellen Fader, review of *Goldilocks and the Three Bears,* p. 75; March-April, 1995, Margaret A. Bush, review of *Town Mouse, Country Mouse,* p. 203; January-February, 1996, Elizabeth S. Watson, review of *Armadillo Rodeo,* p. 59.

Kirkus Reviews, August 15, 1989, review of *Beauty and the Beast,* p. 1242; November 1, 2002, review of

Who's That Knocking on Christmas Eve?, p. 1615; August 1, 2003, review of *On Noah's Ark,* p. 1013; August 1, 2005, review of *Honey . . . Honey . . . Lion!: A Story from Africa,* p. 845; August 15, 2006, review of *Hedgie Blasts Off!,* p. 836; August 1, 2007, review of *The Three Snow Bears*; March 1, 2010, review of *The Easter Egg.*

New York Times, September 25, 2009, Julia Lawlor, "Nest for a Children's Author, Her Family, and Her Flock," p. C38.

New York Times Book Review, August 25, 1985, Pat Ross, review of *Annie and the Wild Animals,* p. 25.

Publishers Weekly, January 9, 1981, review of *Fritz and the Beautiful Horses,* p. 76; September 8, 1989, review of *Beauty and the Beast,* p. 69; August 10, 1990, review of *The Wild Christmas Reindeer,* p. 443; July 4, 1994, review of *Town Mouse, Country Mouse,* p. 61; July 17, 1995, review of *Armadillo Rodeo,* p. 229; October 7, 1996, review of *Comet's Nine Lives,* p. 74; June 2, 1997, review of *The Hat,* p. 71; September 20, 1999, review of *Gingerbread Baby,* p. 88; July 17, 2000, review of *Hedgie's Surprise,* p. 192; December 3, 2001, review of *Daisy Comes Home,* p. 60; August 25, 2003, review of *On Noah's Ark,* p. 60; August 8, 2005, review of *Honey . . . Honey . . . Lion!,* p. 233; July 30, 2007, review of *The Three Snow Bears,* p. 81; August 30, 2010, review of *The Three Little Dassies,* p. 49.

School Library Journal, September, 2000, Karen James, review of *Hedgie's Surprise,* p. 184; September, 2003, Kathy Piehl, review of *On Noah's Ark,* p. 175; November, 2004, Susan Weitz, review of *The Umbrella,*

p. 91; September, 2005, Kara Schaff Dean, review of *Honey . . . Honey . . . Lion!,* p. 166; September, 2006, Kirsten Cutler, review of *Hedgie Blasts Off!,* p. 159; December, 2007, Piper Nyman, review of *The Three Snow Bears,* p. 87; February, 2010, Linda L. Walkins, review of *The Easter Egg,* p. 76; October, 2010, Carrie Rogers-Whitehead, review of *The Three Little Dassies,* p. 80.

ONLINE

Jan Brett Home Page, http://www.janbrett.com (September 15, 2011).
Jan Brett Web log, http://janbrettsblog.com (September 15, 2011).
Public Broadcasting Service Web site, http://www.pbs.org/ (September 15, 2011), interview with Brett.
Scholastic Web site, http://www2.scholastic.com/ (September 15, 2011), interview with Brett.*

* * *

BRETT, Jan Churchill
See BRETT, Jan

* * *

BRETT BOWLER, Jan
See BRETT, Jan

* * *

BROMELY, Anne C. 1950-

Personal

Born 1950; father in the military; married; husband's name Rod. *Education:* M.F.A.; M.Ed. *Hobbies and other interests:* Hiking, wildlife.

Addresses

Home—Encinitas, CA. *E-mail*—info@annebromley. com.

Career

Author and teacher. Instructor in business writing. Formerly worked as a library assistant, special-education teacher, substitute teacher, and college professor. Presenter at schools and festivals.

Awards, Honors

Skipping Stones Honor Award for Multicultural Books, and San Diego Book Award finalist in picture-book category, both 2011, both for *The Lunch Thief.*

Writings

(Editor and translator with Anna-Marie Aldaz and Barbara N. Gantt; and author of foreword with Joseph Boles) Rosalía de Castro, *Poems,* introduction by Aldaz and Gantt, State University of New York Press (Albany, NY), 1991.
The Lunch Thief, illustrated by Robert Casilla, Tilbury House (Gardiner, ME), 2010.

Author of poetry collections *Scenes from the Light Years* and *Midwinter Transport,* both published by Carnegie Mellon University Press. Contributor of poems, stories, and reviews to periodicals.

Biographical and Critical Sources

PERIODICALS

School Library Journal, November, 2010, review of *The Lunch Thief,* p. 65.

ONLINE

Anne Bromley Home Page, http://www.annebromley.com (October 1, 2011).
California Readers Online, http://www.californiareaders. org/ (March, 2011), Ann Stalcup, interview with Bromley.*

* * *

BROWN, Lisa
(Sarah "Pinkie" Bennett)

Personal

Married Daniel Handler (an author); children: one son. *Education:* Wesleyan University, B.A., 1993; Pratt Institute, M.S. (communications design), 1998.

Addresses

Home—San Francisco, CA. *Agent*—Charlotte Sheedy, Charlotte Sheedy Literary Agency, 928 Broadway, Ste. 901, New York, NY 10010. *E-mail*—info@ americanchickens.com.

Career

Illustrator, cartoonist, and author of children's books and graphic novels. Presenter at schools.

Member

American Institute of Graphic Artists, Society of Children's Book Writers and Illustrators.

Awards, Honors

Best Books for Children selection, Association of Booksellers for Children, and Recommended selection, Cooperative Children's Book Center, both 2006, and Best Children's Books for Family Literacy selection, Pennsylvania State University/Pennsylvania Center for the Book, 2007, all for *How to Be . . .*; honored by illustration annuals, including *American Illustration* and *Print.*

Writings

FOR CHILDREN; SELF-ILLUSTRATED

How to Be . . ., HarperCollins (New York, NY), 2006.
Vampire Boy's Good Night, Harper (New York, NY), 2010.

ILLUSTRATOR

(Under name Sarah "Pinkie" Bennett) Daniel Handler, *How to Dress for Every Occasion by the Pope,* McSweeney's, 2005.
Daniel Handler, *The Latke Who Couldn't Stop Screaming: A Christmas Story,* McSweeney's (San Francisco, CA), 2007.
Meredith Gary, *Sometimes You Get What You Want,* HarperCollins (New York, NY), 2008.
Susan Rich, editor, *Half-Minute Horrors* (short stories), HarperCollins (New York, NY), 2009.
(And coauthor with Adele Griffin) *Picture the Dead,* Sourcebooks Fire (Napier, IL), 2010.

Illustrator of "Outrageous Women" book series, John Wiley & Sons, 1998-2001.

OTHER

Author/illlustrator of "Baby Be of Use" board-book series published by McSweeney's, including *Baby Make Me Some Breakfast, Baby Mix Me a Drink, Baby Fix My Car, Baby Do My Banking, Baby Get Me Some Lovin',* and *Baby Plan My Wedding,* 2005-09. Author and illustrator of "Three Panel Book Review" cartoon series, *San Francisco Chronicle,* and "Welcome to the Ten-and-One" online comic, www.therumpus.net.

Sidelights

Lisa Brown has channeled her training in communication design into creating unique illustrated books for both children and adults. Brown's illustrations first appeared in a series of board-book parodies in the "Baby Be of Use" series. She also illustrated texts authored by her husband, the pseudonymous Lemony Snicket, that were published as the humor books *How to Dress for Every Occasion by the Pope* and *The Latke Who Couldn't Stop Screaming: A Christmas Story.* Her original self-illustrated picture books include *How to Be*

. . . and *Vampire Boy's Good Night,* and illustration projects include teaming up with writer Adele Griffin to create the illustrated young-adult novel *Picture the Dead.* Reviewing Brown's illustrations for another picture book, educator Meredith Gary's *Sometimes You Get What You Want, Booklist* critic Bina Willams wrote that her "cartoonlike art reflects the story nicely, using sharply outlined figures, minimal props, and bright colors."

Praised by *School Library Journal* contributor Rachel G. Payne as a "striking picture book," *How to Be . . .* finds two children mimicking a menagerie of animals during playtime. Brown divides her story into chapters such as "How to Be a Turtle," or "How to Be a Dog," in which a child adopts the relevant animal actions in a mix of spare text and humorous black-and-white drawings highlighted with splashes of color. While Payne predicted that both toddlers and older children will pick up on the comedy in the book's drawings, *Booklist* critic Jennifer Mattson wrote that readers "will be inspired to think of their own methods of getting in touch with their animal natures." Describing *How to Be . . .* as "elegantly simple," Susan Dove Lempke added in *Horn Book* that Brown "layer[s] enough meaning into text and pictures that children will discover new detail" with each reading.

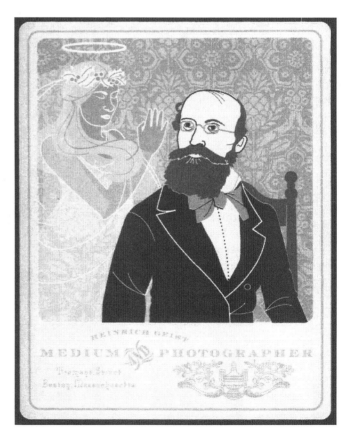

Lisa Brown teams up with author Adele Griffin to present an unusual supernatural tale in Picture the Dead. (Illustration copyright © 2010 by Lisa Brown. Reproduced by permission of Sourcebooks, Inc.)

A Halloween celebration with a twist is the focus of *Vampire Boy's Good Night,* a "friendly story [that] will delight, but not frighten young readers," according to *School Library Journal* contributor Carolyn Janssen. Bela is a young vampire and his best friend, Morgan, is a witch. During their nocturnal search for young humans, which they have heard about but never seen, the two friends discover a house full of surprisingly friendly witches and vampires, as well as assorted ghosts, goblins, and even a pirate or two. In Brown's quirky story, Bela learns that vampires are not always what they seem, and her comics-style art is characterized by "detail-rich scenes" that bring to life her "lyrical, understated prose," according to a *Publishers Weekly* critic.

In *Picture the Dead* readers are taken back in time to Brookline, Massachusetts, during the U.S. Civil War era. Jennie Lovell is mourning the death of her twin brother, Toby, when she learns that her fiancé and cousin, Will, has also been killed. Although the recently returned Quinn, Will's younger brother and also a Union soldier, now informs the distraught young woman that her lover died on the battlefield, Jennie begins to experience choking sensations and strange visions that lead her to question Quinn's story. Certain that these visions are messages from Will, she is aided by a spiritualist photographer named Mr. Geist in bridging the gap between the living and the dead in order to uncover a sinister truth. Jennie's narrative is relayed in an unique fashion; with its integration of Griffin's text and Brown's illustrations, "it combines social and physical history to make the perfect setting," according to *Voice of Youth Advocates* contributor Rachel Wadham. Indeed, the visual backdrop crafted by Brown evokes elements of Victorian culture, such as the penchant for carefully preserving such tokens as hair, cards, flowers, and paper ephemera in scrapbooks, still photographs, or other means, as well as the vogue for spiritualism. In recreating Jennie's scrapbook—a collection of newspaper clippings, pictures, letters, and notes—the artist provides readers with what *School Library Journal* contributor Nora G. Murphy characterized as an "unique perspective" on this "period of American history." In addition to revealing clues to the mystery, her "darkly inked, realistic drawings" effectively capture the late-nineteenth-century aesthetic by incorporating handwriting in "the elaborate cursive style of the era," noted a *Kirkus Reviews* writer. In *Booklist* Carolyn Phelan dubbed *Picture the Dead* "a Civil War ghost story with gothic overtones," and a *Publishers Weekly* contributor praised the way in which Jennie's "stark yet beautiful narration" is given added dimension through illustrations that add "to the unease."

Biographical and Critical Sources

PERIODICALS

Booklist, July 1, 2006, Jennifer Mattson, review of *How to Be . . . ,* p. 64; May 15, 2008, Bina Williams, review of *Sometimes You Get What You Want,* p. 50; May, 2010, Carolyn Phelan, review of *Picture the Dead,* p. 49.

Horn Book, July-August, 2006, Susan Dove Lempke, review of *How to Be . . . ,* p. 422; May-June, 2008, Christine M. Heppermann, review of *Sometimes You Get What You Want,* p. 293.

Kirkus Reviews, April 15, 2010, Adele Griffin, review of *Picture the Dead.*

Publishers Weekly, May 29, 2006, review of *How to Be . . . ,* p. 57; October 29, 2007, review of *The Latke Who Couldn't Stop Screaming: A Christmas Story,* p. 56; May 17, 2010, review of *Picture the Dead,* p. 52; August 16, 2010, review of *Vampire Boy's Good Night,* p. 52.

School Library Journal, June, 2006, Rachel Payne, review of *How to Be . . . ,* p. 107; April, 2008, Anne Parker, review of *Sometimes You Get What You Want,* p. 108; January, 2010, Caitlin Augusta, review of *Half-Minute Horrors,* p. 112; October, 2010, Nora G. Murphy, review of *Picture the Dead,* p. 116; November, 2010, Carolyn Janssen, review of *Vampire Boy's Good Night,* p. 65.

Voice of Youth Advocates, August, 2010, Rachel Wadham, review of *Picture the Dead,* p. 266.

ONLINE

American Chickens Web site, http://www.americanchickens.com (October 1, 2011), "Lisa Brown."

HarperCollins Web site, http://www.harpercollins.com/ (September 21, 2011), "Lisa Brown."

Lisa Brown Home Page, http://www.americanchickens.com (September 21, 2011).

Picture the Dead Web site, http://www.picturethedead.com/ (October 1, 2011), "Lisa Brown."

*　　*　　*

BUCHANAN, Lang
See LANG, Diane

*　　*　　*

BURNS, T.R.
See RAYBURN, Tricia

C

CAPOZZOLA, Michael

Personal

Born in New Rochelle, NY. *Education:* Ithaca College, degree (comedy studies). *Hobbies and other interests:* Sports.

Addresses

Home—San Francisco, CA. *E-mail*—michael_c@mindspring.com.

Career

Comedian and cartoonist. Performer at comedy clubs throughout the United States, beginning 1990. Actor on television. Founder and host of annual Comics for Comix fundraiser at Cartoon Art Museum.

Writings

Nikol Hasler, *Sex: A Book for Teens: An Uncensored Guide to Your Body, Sex, and Safety,* Zest/Orange Avenue, 2010.

Creator of comic strips, including "Chubby Browne" and "Surveillance Caricatures," for *San Francisco Chronicle.* Contributor to periodicals, including *Mad, National Lampoon,* and the *New York Times.*

Biographical and Critical Sources

PERIODICALS

Booklist, July 1, 2010, Gillian Engberg, review of *Sex: A Book for Teens: An Uncensored Guide to Your Body, Sex, and Safety,* p. 47.

Kirkus Reviews, May 15, 2010, review of *Sex.*
School Library Journal, February, 2011, Traci Glass, review of *Sex,* p. 128.

ONLINE

Michael Capozzola Home Page, http://www.capozzola.com (October 15, 2011).*

* * *

CAVE, Patrick 1965-

Personal

Born October, 1965, in Bath, England; children: three. *Education:* College degree; teaching certification.

Addresses

Home—Bath, England. *Agent*—A.P. Watt, 20 John St., London WC1N 2DR, England.

Career

Writer and educator. Taught English in France, Greece, and England for ten years; currently manager of a pub in England.

Awards, Honors

London *Guardian* Children's Fiction Prize shortlist, 2006, for *Blown Away.*

Writings

Number 99, Oxford University Press (New York, NY), 2001.
Last Chance, Oxford University Press (Oxford, England), 2002.

Sharp North, Simon & Schuster (London, England), 2004, Atheneum Books for Young Readers (New York, NY), 2006.

Blown Away (sequel to *Sharp North*), Simon & Schuster (London, England), 2005, published as *The Selected,* Atheneum Books for Young Readers (New York, NY), 2010.

Sidelights

Educator-turned-writer Patrick Cave has garnered critical acclaim for his young-adult novels, among them the dystopian thriller *Sharp North* and its sequel, *Blown Away,* which was shortlisted for the London *Guardian* Children's Fiction Prize. "The teen years have a magical selection of ingredients that make them, in this author's humble opinion, an unparalleled time of possibility and adventure," Cave noted on his home page in discussing his choice of audience.

Born in 1965 in Bath, England, Cave taught in Greece and France, among other places, for ten years. In 1998, tired of teaching and living in rural France, he decided to try his hand at writing. "I estimated that my savings

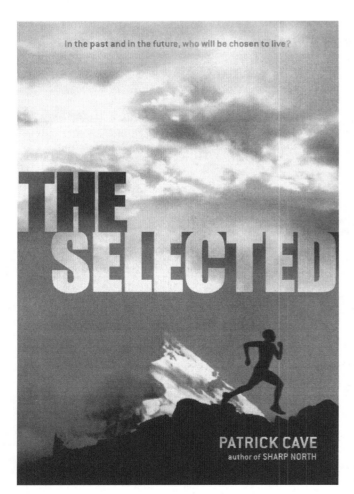

Cover of Patrick Cave's young-adult novel The Selected, *a sequel to his dystopian thriller* Sharp North. (Photograph copyright © 2010 by Bobby Model/Getty Images; illustration by iStock. Reproduced by permission of Simon & Schuster, Inc.)

would last for a year, but as it transpired it took longer than that to get published, and even longer to make any money out of it," he remarked in a *Just Image Story Centre* online interview. "The third novel, *Number 99,* was accepted in 2000 and published in 2001." *Number 99,* which the author described as "an issue-based thriller," centers on a teen's search for her free-spirited mother, who disappeared under mysterious circumstances. In the work, Cave "perceptively considers . . . the choices we make about how we want to live," according to Lyn Gardner in her review of the novel for the London *Guardian.*

In *Sharp North* Cave examines the dangers of cloning and genetic engineering. Set 200 years into the future, amid a world ravaged by disease, war, and climate change, the novel concerns Mira, a young girl living in a remote Scottish village. After she witnesses the brutal murder of a woman who appeared in the woods near her home, Mira begins investigating the stranger's death, uncovering a plot involving clones, called "spares," and their "watchers." According to *Horn Book* reviewer Susan P. Bloom, the author "plays a skillful game of cat and mouse with readers," and Hephzibah Anderson stated in the London *Observer* that "an atmospheric backdrop lends Cave's world a completeness that keeps [the narrative] on track."

The struggle for survival is at the heart of *Blown Away* (published in the United State as *The Selected*), which is told through the alternating narratives of Adeline, a flawed clone, and her ancestor, Dominic. Battling a heart condition, Adeline discovers Dom's centuries-old diaries, in which he describes the origins of a super race that threatens human existence. Realizing it is her destiny to save the world, Adeline enters a televised survival contest, hoping to bring the truth to light. *Blown Away,* Cave remarked in his *Just Image Story Centre* interview, "is about the individual being subject to many different forces, pressures and influences, seen and unseen. It's about not providing too much resistance because if you try to control events too much you get trapped." Reviewing the novel in the *Guardian,* Julia Eccleshare remarked that "Cave's chillingly realised dystopia raises questions and offers no easy solutions," while a *Kirkus Reviews* contributor found the work to be "constantly gripping, always fascinating and completely compelling."

The ethics of scientific and technological advancements are of prime importance to Cave. "Artificial intelligence and genetic research are the two main things that particularly bother me," he stated in his *Just Image Story Centre* online interview. "Often researchers develop a pure fascination with solving a problem or exploring uncharted territory. They may become so absorbed by the problem that they cease to be interested in the external uses."

Biographical and Critical Sources

PERIODICALS

Guardian (London, England), April 24, 2002, Lyn Gardner, review of *Number 99*; June 3, 2006, Julia Eccleshare, review of *Blown Away*.
Horn Book, July-August, 2006, Susan P. Bloom, review of *Sharp North*, p. 436.
Kirkus Reviews, June 1, 2010, review of *The Selected*.
Observer (London, England), October 24, 2004, Hephzibah Anderson, review of *Sharp North*.
School Library Journal, December, 2010, Leah J. Sparks, review of *The Selected*, p. 106.
Voice of Youth Advocates, October, 2010, Gina Bowling, review of *The Selected*, p. 364.

ONLINE

A.P. Watt Web site, http://www.apwatt.co.uk/ (September 15, 2011), "Patrick Cave."
Just Image Story Centre Web site, http://www.justimaginestorycentre.co.uk/ (September 15, 2011), interview with Cave.
Patrick Cave Home Page, http://www.patrickcave.com (September 15, 2011).*

*   *   *

CERVANTES, Jennifer

Personal

Born in San Diego, CA; married Joseph Cervantes (an attorney and state legislator); children: Alex; Bella, Jules (daughters). *Education:* University of New Mexico, B.A. (communication studies); New Mexico State University, M.A. (rhetoric and communication studies). *Hobbies and other interests:* Travel, spending time with family, reading.

Addresses

Home—Las Cruces, NM. *Office*—Department of English, New Mexico State University, P.O. Box 30001, MSC 3E, Las Cruces, NM 88003. *Agent*—Holly Root, Waxman Literary Agency, 80 5th Ave., Ste. 1101, New York, NY 10011. *E-mail*—jcervant@nmsu.edu.

Career

Writer and educator. New Mexico State University, Las Cruces, assistant dean for advancement and alumni relations in College of Health and Social Services.

Member

Society of Children's Book Writers and Illustrators.

Awards, Honors

New Voice selection, Association of Children's Booksellers, Best Book selection, and Bank Street College of Education, both 2010, and New Mexico Book Award finalist, 2011, all for *Tortilla Sun.*

Jennifer Cervantes (Reproduced by permission.)

Writings

Tortilla Sun, Chronicle Books (San Francisco, CA), 2010.

Sidelights

In *Tortilla Sun,* the debut novel of New Mexico-based author Jennifer Cervantes, a curious and sensitive twelve year old searches for clues to the mystery surrounding her father's death. The novel introduces Isadora "Izzy" Roybal, who is spending the summer with her maternal grandmother in New Mexico while her widowed and still-grieving mother completes a research project. When she arrives at Nana's village, Izzy finds herself drawn to the beauty of the New Mexico landscape as well as to her grandmother's traditional lifestyle, which includes an amazing array of unusual home-cooked meals. With the help of Socorro, a local storyteller, Mateo, an adventurous neighbor, and Maggie, an orphaned youngster, Izzy begins to unlock the secrets of her family's complicated past.

Tortilla Sun garnered solid reviews from critics, some of whom applauded the author's use of magical realism to advance the narrative. "Cervantes fills her story with mystical possibilities," noted a *Publishers Weekly* contributor, the critic describing the work as an "imaginative yet grounded novel." According to *School Library Journal* reviewer Marilyn Taniguchi, "Cervantes's prose is lean and lightly spiced with evocative metaphor," and a critic in *Kirkus Reviews* observed that the author "develops a memorable cast of characters, brought to life through Izzy's heartfelt narration."

"My road to publication was long and sometimes quiet," Cervantes told *SATA.* "I didn't set out to write a novel (I'd never written a word of fiction), but when my youngest daughter Juliana asked me to write her a story one day, I picked up a pen and was hooked! As I got to know the characters one idea led to the next and I had to see what happened to them, so I wrote until I had completed the manuscript. After joining a critique group and editing over and over, I sent out queries to agents and the rest is history.

"People will often ask me what has changed for me since publication: the one element that has changed significantly is that I now have a larger stage to discuss education, literacy, and books. I have been fortunate to travel all over the United States to various events and conferences sharing my love of books and learning from teachers, authors, and students. Oftentimes, others will ask me if I have any advice for a new writer and I always have the same answer: Read, read, read. Study the style, plotting, word choice, and literary elements used by authors you like and admire. Believe in yourself, be passionate, and join a supportive writing group whose members can share the journey with you."

Biographical and Critical Sources

PERIODICALS

Albuquerque Journal, August 8, 2010, David Steinberg, "A Little Magic, and Anything's Possible under *Sun*."
Kirkus Reviews, June 1, 2010, review of *Tortilla Sun*.
Publishers Weekly, May 24, 2010, review of *Tortilla Sun*, p. 52.
School Library Journal, June, 2010, Marilyn Taniguchi, review of *Tortilla Sun*, p. 98.

ONLINE

Desert Exposure Web site, http://www.desertexposure.com/ (February, 2011), Jeff Berg, "Las Cruces Author Jennifer Cervantes Is a Rising Star in Young-Adult Fiction."
Jennifer Cervantes Home Page, http://www.jennifer cervantes.com (September 1, 2011).

* * *

COOPER, Elisha 1971-

Personal

Born February 22, 1971, in New Haven, CT; son of Peter (a lawyer and farmer) and Diana (a writer and farmer) Cooper; married; children: Zoë, Mia. *Education:* Yale University, B.A., 1993.

Addresses

Home and office—New York, NY. *Agent*—Darhansoff & Verrill Literary Agency, 236 W. 26th St., Ste. 802, New York, NY 10001.

Elisha Cooper (Photograph by Elise Cappella. Courtesy of Elisha Cooper.)

Career

Illustrator, graphic artist, and author. *New Yorker* magazine, New York, NY, messenger and member of art department, 1993-95; writer and artist, 1995—.

Awards, Honors

Highly Commended citation, Charlotte Zolotow Award, 1998, for *Country Fair;* honorable mention, Bologna Ragazzi Award, 2000, for *Building;* gold medal, Society of Illustrators New York, 2006, for *Beach*.

Writings

FOR CHILDREN; SELF-ILLUSTRATED

Country Fair, Greenwillow (New York, NY), 1997.
Ballpark, Greenwillow (New York, NY), 1998.
Building, Greenwillow (New York, NY), 1999.
Henry, Chronicle Books (San Francisco, CA), 1999.
Dance!, Greenwillow (New York, NY), 2001.
Ice Cream, Greenwillow (New York, NY), 2002.
Magic Thinks Big, Greenwillow (New York, NY), 2004.
A Good Night Walk, Orchard Books (New York, NY), 2005.
Beach, Orchard Books (New York, NY), 2006.
Bear Dreams, Greenwillow Books (New York, NY), 2006.
Beaver Is Lost, Schwartz & Wade Books (New York, NY), 2010.

Farm, Orchard Books (New York, NY), 2010.

OTHER; SELF-ILLUSTRATED

(Self-illustrated) *A Year in New York,* City and Company (New York, NY), 1995.

Off the Road: An American Sketchbook, Villard (New York, NY), 1997.

A Day at Yale, Yale Bookstore (New Haven, CT), 1998.

California: A Sketchbook, Chronicle Books (San Francisco, CA), 2000.

Paris Night and Day: From the Marais to the Café, Impressions from the City of Lights, Artisan (New York, NY), 2002.

Crawling: A Father's First Year (memoir), Pantheon Books (New York, NY), 2006.

ridiculous/hilarious/terrible/cool: A Year in an American High School, Dial Books (New York, NY), 2008.

Sidelights

Author and illustrator Elisha Cooper has garnered recognition for his contemplative and entertaining picture books, including *A Good Night Walk, Beach,* and *Farm.* Additionally, Cooper has paired an original text with his signature loose-lined sketches in *Crawling: A Father's First Year,* a memoir, and *ridiculous/hilarious/terrible/cool: A Year in An American High School,* a nonfiction work. "I love all parts of making books," he stated in a *Chicago Public Library* online interview. "I love the sketching, painting, writing, design, and the crafting of a book. But if there's one part I love most, it's probably that raw, initial moment when it's just me and my sketchbook and I'm standing in a field, or in a dance studio, and it comes together."

Cooper took an early interest in the arts, once telling *SATA:* "I grew up drawing cows. In the fields below our house there was a herd of Jerseys, and when I was three or four I sat on our porch with pencils and paper

Cooper takes young readers on a tour through rural America in his self-illustrated picture book **Farm.** (Copyright © 2010 by Elisha Cooper. Reproduced by permission of Orchard Books, an imprint of Scholastic, Inc.)

Cooper captures the excitement and dedication of a group of dance students in his energetic watercolor-and-ink illustrations for **Dance!** (Copyright © 2001 by Elisha Cooper. Reproduced by permission of HarperCollins Children's, a division of HarperCollins Publishers.)

and tried to sketch them. The results were pretty lousy, or so I thought at the time, and I remember having tantrums and ripping up the drawings when they didn't look exactly right.

"When I got older, my best friend and I started a lawn-mowing business; we took the money we made and went on trips. I disliked cameras—more accurately, I disliked the loud, splashy tourists who used them—so I kept notebooks and wrote down things we saw, what we ate, smells. My mother gave me a tin of watercolors (the same one I use now) and I took that on my trips, too. At home I read a lot, especially the comic books *Tintin* and *Asterix*. I took books and newspapers on walks with my goats.

"When I was at Yale and playing football, I brought sketch books with me on road trips. I also wrote for the *New Journal,* a magazine, usually about things I had done, like bottling beer at a factory or playing in a game. I spent the summer before my senior year in Idaho working for the Forest Service—inspired by Norman Maclean's short stories—and wrote in a notebook and missed my friends.

"When I graduated and came to New York City, I took a sketchbook along on the subway when I made deliveries as a messenger for the *New Yorker* magazine. That became my first book, *A Year in New York.* I think at this time I fell in love with books, and with New York.

They both have a richness to them. Then I quit my job and drove around the country, sleeping in the front seat, showering in rivers, and seeing what I could find. That book was called *Off the Road: An American Sketchbook.*

"I think most kids' books are stories. I like reading stories, but can't write them. I write what I see. For my first two kids' books, I spent a fall hanging out at country fairs and ballparks. I like nosing around and looking for the weird, something that hits me, a goofy gesture."

Cooper's penchant for "nosing around" paid off for readers of *Country Fair,* his self-illustrated look at the popular rural event. *Booklist* reviewer Susan Dove Lempke called the work "as removed from big, splashy preschool books as it can be. It is brimming with tiny, precisely described moments." Lolly Robinson wrote in *Horn Book:* "The small size of this book and the quiet honesty of text and art indicate a book that will be shared one-on-one and frequently revisited by children who enjoy an amiable ramble." A *Kirkus Reviews* critic called Cooper's work "a quirky, engaging look at the sights, sounds, and scents of a country fair."

Cooper next turned his gaze to baseball for his book *Ballpark.* A *Kirkus Reviews* critic noted the author/illustrator's attention to detail and his ability to evoke the baseball experience and share it with everyone, writing that, "Sports fan or not, spectators or athletes, children will be engaged for the full nine innings."

Elizabeth Bush, reviewing the book for the *Bulletin of the Center for Children's Books,* noted Cooper's "tidy phrasing . . . and restrained humor" in recommending *Ballpark* as "an elegant visual presentation."

In *Building* Cooper depicts a vacant lot's transformation into a building. He combines simple illustrations of construction workers and equipment with text that at times reads sideways or upside down. A *Publishers Weekly* reviewer praised Cooper's "signature pleasing balance between the factual and the whimsical," describing the book as a "cheerful tribute" to building construction. *Horn Book* contributor Lolly Robinson characterized the "measured pace and detail-oriented approach" as akin to that of the author/illustrator's previous works, but added that, "occasionally, Cooper's loose style makes it difficult to decipher objects." While Lauren Peterson concluded in *Booklist* that *Building* is well written and presents the information in easily understood language, she added that the book's small text makes it more appropriate for older children.

Critics embraced *Dance!* for its expressive illustrations, simple text, and introduction to the process of rehearsal and training. The book focuses not on the performance and the costumes, but instead on the dancers as they learn new steps and practice new routines. K.C. Patrick commented in *Dance* magazine that the illustrations "almost move," and *Horn Book* critic Robinson wrote: "With an economy of line and color, Cooper conjures up pain and grace, hard work and camaraderie, stillness and velocity." While applauding Cooper's delightful illustrations, Kelly Milner Halls added in *Booklist* that this "sensitive" treatment of dance is more than the

"usual dreams of pink tutus and toe shoes," and Catherine Threadgill concluded in *School Library Journal* that *Dance!* "successfully provides inquisitive children with a believable vicarious experience." In *Publishers Weekly,* a reviewer noted Cooper's "spontaneous, lyrical narrative," adding that the portrayal of "the many steps leading up to the grand event are deserving of enthusiastic applause."

With *Ice Cream* Cooper offers a step-by-step look at how ice cream is made, starting with a field of grazing cows and finishing with a delivery of the frozen concoction. In *Publishers Weekly,* a reviewer commented that, not only is the book informative as it relates "specifics that may surprise even the most ardent aficionados," but Cooper's text is also fun to read. The reviewer observed that "readers can hear the sounds in the barn at milking time" and that the "small-scale art precisely follows each step." Blair Christolon, writing in *School Library Journal,* praised both the appearance of the book and its content, noting that the author's "sense of humor finds its way into the pages" and makes "an excellent vocabulary enhancer." In *Horn Book,* Robinson wrote that "Cooper balances the relevant facts with his folksy, child-centered descriptions of minutiae," and *Booklist* reviewer Diane Foote noted of the "appealing" drawings that Cooper's "creative type placement in spirals, loops, and curves adds interest."

A bedtime tale, *A Good Night Walk* was inspired by Cooper's memories of his soothing strolls near the San Francisco Bay with his infant daughter. In the words of *Horn Book* critic Jennifer M. Brabander, the work offers the author/illustrator's trademark "leisurely pace

Magic the cat may be a little overweight, but that does not stop him from aspiring to acts of cat-greatness in Cooper's sly and engaging picture book **Magic Thinks Big.** (Illustration copyright © 2004 by Elisha Cooper. Reproduced by permission of HarperCollins Children's, a division of HarperCollins Publishers.)

and quiet observations." In *Beach* Cooper invites readers to consider the simple pleasures of a day at the shore. A *Publishers Weekly* reviewer praised the story, noting that it "combines a prosaic text with loose, cartoon-like figures." *Horn Book* contributor Lolly Robinson also complimented Cooper's illustrations, remarking that "the body positions and gestures of his people provide all the visual information we need for complete character studies."

Cooper drew on a number of experiences—including his own childhood—in crafting *Farm,* a "subtle, handsome view of modern, rural life," as Gillian Engberg noted in *Booklist.* "I was [also] inspired by the huge, great Midwestern farms I saw when I was living in Chicago," the author/illustrator remarked in a *Publishers Weekly* interview with Sally Lodge. "I'd get in my car and drive out past these farms with their monster John Deere tractors and huge, open fields and I realized that that was the real American farm. I knew then what kind of farm I really wanted to write about and draw." *Farm* follows one year in the life of a working farm, from planting to harvesting. "The graceful text and serenely stunning illustrations create a portrait both reverent and realistic," maintained a *Publishers Weekly* critic, and Brabander called the work "as thorough and pleasing an introduction to a farm as one could ask of a picture book."

Offering a completely different look and feel from Cooper's standard picture-book fare, *Magic Thinks Big* is about a large housecat whose imagination takes him on adventures he is too contented to pursue. Praising the book's fun story, *Horn Book* reviewer Susan Dove Lempke also commented that, "in contrast to Elisha Cooper's previous picture books, with their tiny pictures and copious white space, the pictures here fill each page almost to the edges." In a review for *School Library Journal,* Julie Roach cited the strength of the book's story and illustrations: "The simple text is full of dry humor and whimsy," she noted. "The dreamy pencil-and-watercolor illustrations are a pleasing mixture of soft colors and thick lines." In *Publishers Weekly,* a reviewer described the illustrations in *Magic Thinks Big* as "spare [and] wryly understated," while also praising the artist's "clever use of the hypothetical and his story's fittingly languid tone." "Cooper has captured feline behavior and attitude to a T in both story and art," declared a *Kirkus Reviews* contributor, the critic going on to dub *Magic Thinks Big* "totally charming."

Animals star in several other picture books by Cooper. In *Bear Dreams* a young cub has trouble settling down to hibernate. Convinced that his fellow creatures are still enjoying the outdoors, Bear ventures from his cave to play. A contributor in *Publishers Weekly* noted that Cooper's illustrations are a highlight of the work, stating that the "bright, entertain-me-now gleam in Bear's eye will likely strike a chord with even the most sedentary youngsters." Another nearly wordless picture book, *Beaver Is Lost* follows the exploits of a forest dweller who accidentally finds himself transported to an urban environments. After hitching a ride aboard a log that ends up in a lumberyard, Beaver must navigate the hazards of the city streets before finding his way home with an assist from a friendly mouse. "The finely detailed, watercolor-and-pencil pictures are always true to the small creature's viewpoint," Hazel Rochman commented in *Booklist,* and a *Publishers Weekly* reviewer stated that "Cooper's artwork has a placidity that never allows the city to feel too overwhelming—or frightening."

In another change of pace, Cooper released *ridiculous/ hilarious/terrible/cool: A Year in an American High School,* which documents the lives of eight students at Walter Payton College Preparatory High School. "Payton is . . . a magnet school, drawing students from all over Chicago, and I knew I wanted to look at a diversity of students," Cooper remarked in his *Chicago Public Library* online interview. "This felt important to me, since I wanted readers of the book to be able to see themselves, and also to see people who were not like themselves at all." Readers are introduced to Diana, a shy senior from a bilingual home; Zef, whose passion for music exceeds his academic prowess; and Aisha, the school's only Muslim student. "Sewing together visits with the main subjects over the course of the academic year, Cooper's anonymous, omniscient narrator drifts freely along intersecting narrative paths, including funny vignettes set in the school's see-and-be-seen atrium, overheard conversations, and descriptions of the larger Chicago landscape," Jennifer Mattson commented in *Booklist.* "Far from the straightforward reportage that most readers expect of journalistic writing, the impressionistic quality of Cooper's style lends the book an aura of fiction."

Biographical and Critical Sources

PERIODICALS

Cooper, Elisha, *Crawling: A Father's First Year,* Pantheon Books (New York, NY), 2006.

PERIODICALS

Booklist, September 1, 1997, Susan Dove Lempke, review of *Country Fair,* p. 240; June 1, 1999, Lauren Peterson, review of *Building,* p. 1832; September 15, 2001, Kelly Milner Halls, review of *Dance!,* p. 217; May 15, 2002, Diane Foote, review of *Ice Cream,* p. 1598; May 1, 2008, Jennifer Mattson, review of *ridiculous/ hilarious/terrible/cool: A Year in an American High School,* p. 79; February 1, 2010, Gillian Engberg, review of *Farm,* p. 49; June 1, 2010, Hazel Rochman, review of *Beaver Is Lost,* p. 90.
Bulletin of the Center for Children's Books, March 1998, Elizabeth Bush, review of *Ballpark,* p. 239.

Dance, December, 2001, K.C. Patrick, review of *Dance!,* p. 77.

Horn Book, September-October, 1997, Lolly Robinson, review of *Country Fair,* p. 554; May 1999, Lolly Robinson, review of *Building,* p. 312; November-December, 2001, Lolly Robinson, review of *Dance!,* pp. 733-734; May-June, 2002, Lolly Robinson, review of *Ice Cream,* p. 343; May-June, 2004, Susan Dove Lempke, review of *Magic Thinks Big,* p. 309; November-December, 2005, review of *A Good Night Walk,* p. 703; July-August, 2006, Lolly Robinson, review of *Beach,* p. 422; May-June, 2010, Jennifer Brabander, review of *Farm,* p. 63; July-August, 2010, Roger Sutton, review of *Beaver Is Lost,* p. 88.

Kirkus Reviews, June 15, 1997, review of *Country Fair,* pp. 947-948; February 15, 1998, review of *Ballpark,* p. 265; April 1, 2004, review of *Magic Thinks Big,* p. 326.

New York Times, October 8, 2006, Liesl Schillinger, review of *Crawling: A Father's First Year,* p. ST8.

Publishers Weekly, March 15, 1999, review of *Building,* p. 57; July 30, 2001, review of *Dance!,* p. 84; February 18, 2002, review of *Ice Cream,* p. 96; April 12, 2004, review of *Magic Thinks Big,* p. 64; April 24, 2006, review of *Beach,* p. 59; July 17, 2006, reviews of *Crawling,* p. 148, and *Bear Dreams,* p. 155; February 25, 2008, review of *ridiculous/hilarious/terrible/cool,* p. 81; July 21, 2008, "Self-description Is the Ultimate Writing Challenge," p. 164; February 15, 2010, review of *Farm,* p. 128; May 17, 2010, review of *Beaver Is Lost,* p. 47.

School Library Journal, September, 2001, Catherine Threadgill, review of *Dance!,* p. 212; May, 2002, Blair Christolon, review of *Ice Cream,* p. 136; April, 2004, Julie Roach, review of *Magic Thinks Big,* pp. 103-104.

USA Today, July 20, 2006, Bob Minzesheimer, review of *Beach,* p. 5D; April 8, 2010, review of *Farm,* p. 4D.

ONLINE

Chicago Public Library Web site, http://www.chipublib.org/forteens/ (April, 2008), Karen Feng, interview with Cooper.

Elisha Cooper Home Page, http://www.elishacooper.com (September 15, 2011).

Publishers Weekly Online, http://www.publishersweekly.com/ (March 4, 2010), Sally Lodge, "Q & A with Elisha Cooper."

Seven Impossible Things before Breakfast Web log, http://blaine.org/sevenimpossiblethings/ (September 22, 2008), "Elisha Cooper."*

*   *   *

CREAGH, Kelly

Personal

Female. *Education:* University of Louisville, B.S. (theater arts); Spalding University, M.F.A. (writing for children and young adults). *Hobbies and other interests:* Bellydancing.

Addresses

Home—Louisville, KY. *Agent*—Adams Literary, 7845 Colony Rd., C4 No. 215, Charlotte, NC 28226. *E-mail*—klcreagh@yahoo.com.

Career

Writer. Has worked variously as a bookmobile driver/service provider, waitress, library assistant, computer lab supervisor, and bellydancing instructor.

Writings

Nevermore, Atheneum Books for Young Readers (New York, NY), 2010.

Sidelights

The works of nineteenth-century American author and poet Edgar Allan Poe play a pivotal role in *Nevermore,* Kelly Creagh's debut novel for young adults. Creagh's paranormal romance centers on the unlikely relationship

Cover of Kelly Creagh's young-adult mystery Nevermore, *a mix of romance, humor, and something far more creepy.* (Photography copyright © 2010 by Michael Frost. Reproduced by permission of Michael Frost Inc.)

between high-school cheerleader Isobel Lanley and Varen Nethers, her brooding Goth classmate, as they enter a terrifying otherworld where Poe's surreal stories become real. Interestingly, Poe's career was only of secondary concern to Creagh when she began researching her novel. "At the time, I was more concerned about the drama developing between my lead characters," the author stated on her home page. "Then the weirdness set in. I was startled by all of the strangeness and mystery surrounding Poe's death. I began to notice a trend in his writing—that he mentioned dreams and dreaming constantly in his works. His poetry began to read like riddles to me, and I started to develop my own otherworldly 'what if?' scenarios about his fate. Isobel and Varen's story began to change and morph."

In *Nevermore* Isobel is aghast after being paired with Varen for a literature project on Poe, yet she soon finds herself drawn to the secretive classmate despite her boyfriend's objections. When Isobel discovers Varen's private notebook, which contains dark and eerie tales, she begins having strange visions and learns that his writings have opened a portal to a dream world inhabited by spirits who hold her new love captive. "This page-turner intertwines ghoulish confrontations with Poe's works, in-group/out-group conflicts, and possessive love-angst," remarked *Voice of Youth Advocates* critic Lucy Shall. A contributor in *Kirkus Reviews* also offered praise for *Nevermore,* citing its "creepy, otherworldly climax."

Biographical and Critical Sources

PERIODICALS

Bulletin of the Center for Children's Books, September, 2010, Karen Coats, review of *Nevermore,* p. 11.
Kirkus Reviews, July 15, 2010, review of *Nevermore.*
School Library Journal, December, 2010, Corinne Henning-Sachs, review of *Nevermore,* p. 110.
Voice of Youth Advocates, August, 2010, Lucy Shall, review of *Nevermore,* p. 263.

ONLINE

Adams Literary Web site, http://www.adamsliterary.com/ (September 15, 2011), "Kelly Creagh."
Kelly Creagh Home Page, http://www.kellycreagh.com (September 15, 2011).
Kelly Creagh Web log, http://blog.kellycreagh.com (September 15, 2011).
Simon & Schuster Web site, http://www.simonandschuster. com/ (September 15, 2011), "Kelly Creagh."*

D

DALTON, Max

Personal
Male. *Hobbies and other interests:* Writing, taking photographs, playing music, reading about animal behavior.

Addresses
Home—Buenos Aires, Argentina. *E-mail*—maximdalton @gmail.com.

Career
Artist, illustrator, and animator. *Exhibitions:* Work exhibited at group shows, including at Spoke Art Gallery, San Francisco, CA, 2011, and Gallery 1988, Los Angeles, CA, 2011.

Illustrator
Peter Ackerman, *The Lonely Phone Booth,* David R. Godine (Boston, MA), 2010.

Sidelights
An illustrator and animator based in Buenos Aires, Argentina, Max Dalton provided the artwork for *The Lonely Phone Booth,* Peter Ackerman's story "celebrating the fabric of a neighborhood, that intangible quality New Yorkers treasure," in the words of *New York Times Book Review* critic Becca Zerkin. Dalton, a self-taught artist who is noted for his retro style, told a contributor for the London *Times* online that he is "very influenced by the cartoons from the fifties. I am a huge fan of *The Pink Panther* and *The Inspector,* mostly because of their de-saturated colours. Many beloved mid-[twentieth-]century children's books have accompanied me during my life and I can't help being influenced by those too, like the 'This is' series by Miroslav Sasek."

Max Dalton (Photograph by Andres Onna. Reproduced by permission.)

Ackerman's *The Lonely Phone Booth* is based on a real-life incident. The work focuses on a glass-enclosed, coin-operated phone booth at 100th Street and West End Avenue in New York City that had become an anachronism in a world filled with cell phones. When an electrical storm knocks out power to the city, rendering cell phones useless, locals discover that the booth's landline is still operational and customers flock to the site, drawing attention to the all-but-forgotten device and saving it from demolition. Dalton's "scene-stealing illustrations . . . convey the story's nostalgic sensibility," Zerkin noted, and a contributor in *Children's Bookwatch* remarked that *The Lonely Phone Booth* "is filled with nostalgic, colorful illustrations that bring back the era of '60's children's book illustrations, which harmonizes well with the story."

Dalton contributed the stylized artwork that captures the sense of community in Peter Ackerman's **The Lonely Phone Booth.** (Illustration copyright © 2010 by Max Dalton. Reproduced by permission of David R. Godine.)

Biographical and Critical Sources

PERIODICALS

Children's Bookwatch, May, 2011, review of *The Lonely Phone Booth.*

New York Times Book Review, November 7, 2010, Becca Zerkin, "When a City Feels like Home," review of *The Lonely Phone Booth,* p. 20.

Publishers Weekly, May 31, 2010, review of *The Lonely Phone Booth,* p. 46.

School Library Journal, September, 2010, Barbara Elleman, review of *The Lonely Phone Booth,* p. 117.

ONLINE

Diskursdisko Web site, http://www.diskursdisko.de/ (August 14, 2009), interview with Dalton.

Lonely Phone Booth Web site, http://lonelyPhone Booth.com/ (September 21, 2011).

Max Dalton Home Page, http://www.maximdalton.com (September 21, 2011).

Max Dalton Web log, http://maxdalton.wordpress.com (September 21, 2011).

Poster Shizzle Web site, http://www.postershizzle.com/ (October 1, 2011), interview with Dalton.

Times Online, http://www.timesonline.co.uk/ (May 22, 2010), "Max Dalton on His Guitar Lessons."

*   *   *

DEGMAN, Lori

Personal

Born in Wilmette, IL; married; husband's name John; children: Sean, Brian. *Education:* MacMurray College, B.S. (deaf education), 1979; National-Louis University, M.A.T. (early childhood education), 2002.

Addresses

Home—Vernon Hills, IL. *Agent*—Jamie Weiss Chilton, Andrea Brown Literary Agency; jamie@andreabrownlit.com. *E-mail*—lori@loridegman.com.

Career

Educator and writer. Special Education District of Lake County, Gages Lake, IL, itinerant teacher of deaf and hard of hearing, beginning 1995.

Member

Society of Children's Book Writers and Illustrators.

Awards, Honors

Grand prize, Cheerios Spoonfuls of Stories New Author Contest, 2008, for *One Zany Zoo.*

Writings

One Zany Zoo, illustrated by Colin Jack, Simon & Schuster Books for Young Readers (New York, NY), 2010.

Sidelights

Lori Degman's debut picture book, *One Zany Zoo,* was the grand prize winner in the second annual Cheerios Spoonfuls of Stories New Author Contest, earning her a cash prize as well as a publishing contract with Simon & Schuster. In addition, more than two million paperback copies of the book were included in boxes of the popular cereal in 2010, helping Degman's work find a large audience. "When I think about 2.2 million children reading and hearing my story, I realize how lucky I am that the judges of the contest saw something in my book that made them choose it," the author commented in a *Prairie Wind* essay, referencing the story which she began writing almost twenty years earlier. "If there's one thing I've learned from this crazy journey, it is how subjective this business is and how dedicated and thick-skinned we writers must be to make it."

A counting book told in rhyming couplets, *One Zany Zoo* follows the adventures of a young boy who sneaks into the zoo early one day and witnesses a host of animal shenanigans staged by blues-singing hyenas and dancing hippos, among others. "Degman's giggle-inducing rhymes move this read-aloud story along," Richelle Roth commented in *School Library Journal.* Citing the colorful cartoon art by Colin Jack, a *Kirkus Reviews* contributor added that the author's "verse is bright" and described *One Zany Zoo* as "crackling good fun."

Biographical and Critical Sources

PERIODICALS

Jacksonville Journal-Courier (Jacksonville, IL), March 23, 2010, Jake Russell, "Mac Alum's Face on Cheerios Box."
Kirkus Reviews, June 1, 2010, review of *One Zany Zoo.*
Prairie Wind (publication of SCBWI-Illinois), spring, 2010, Lori Degman, "Tales from the Front: One Peculiar Path to Publication."
School Library Journal, July 20, 2010, Richelle Roth, review of *One Zany Zoo,* p. 58.

ONLINE

Lori Degman Home Page, http://www.loridegman.com (September 21, 2011).

Lori Degman's entertaining story for **One Zany Zoo** *comes to life in colorful, quirky art by Colin Jack.* (Illustration copyright © 2010 by Colin Jack. Reproduced by permission of Simon & Schuster Books for Young Readers, an imprint Simon & Schuster Children's Publishing Division.)

Lori Degman Web log, http://www.loridegman.blogspot. com (September 21, 2011).

Simon & Schuster Web site, http://www.simonandschuster. com/ (September 21, 2011), "Lori Degman."*

*   *   *

DUNNING, John Harris 1974-

Personal

Born 1974, in South Africa. *Education:* College degree (film and screenwriting).

Addresses

Home—London, England.

Career

Journalist and comic-book writer. Film editor for *Sleazenation* magazine.

Writings

Salem Brownstone: All Along the Watchtowers (graphic novel; originally serialized in *Sturgeon White Moss*), illustrated by Nikhil Singh, Walker Books (London, England), 2009, Candlewick Press (Somerville, MA), 2010.

Also author of *Lolajean Riddle* (comic book), illustrated by Sacha Mardou. Contributor to anthology *Sturgeon White Moss,* and to periodicals, including London *Guardian, Metro, Esquire, Arena, i-D,* and *Dazed and Confused.*

Sidelights

A native of South Africa, John Harris Dunning is the author of *Salem Brownstone: All Along the Watchtowers,* a graphic novel that has drawn comparisons to the works of H.P. Lovecraft and Edgar Allan Poe. With its purple fabric cover and eerie, black-and-white illustration by Nikhil Singh, another South African native, *Salem Brownstone* "looks and feels unlike anything else out there," Jesse Karp noted in *Booklist.* The graphicnovel format suits Dunning, a former journalist. As he told *Interview* reporter Katie Mendelson, "My first love has always been comic books—to the point that when I was ten I was dreaming in comic book frames with captions and word bubbles!"

Born in 1974, Dunning grew up in South Africa "during the height of Apartheid, so it was a very culturally isolated place," as he remarked to Mendelson. "There was what was called 'a state of emergency,' and that meant that everything was censored, from TV to newspapers." Feeling stifled creatively, Dunning left for England immediately after graduating from college, where he had studied film and screenwriting. A a journalist, he has written for the London *Guardian* and *Metro* newspapers and has contributed to such magazines as *Esquire, Arena,* and *i-D,* although comic books remain his first love. "My central drive is to tell stories," Dunning told Mendelson. "I love narratives. I love words, sure, but journalism doesn't fulfill that need to tell a story."

Salem Brownstone began as part of another comic-book project, a realistic story about three teenagers. As Dunning related to interviewer Paul Gravett, the original

John Harris Dunning's graphic novel Salem Brownstone: All along the Watchtowers *comes to life in Nikhil Singh's unique high-contrast art.* (Illustration copyright © 2010 by Nikhil Singh. Reproduced by permission of Candlewick Press, Somerville, MA on behalf of Walker Books, London.)

work "was going to be a much more stylized one-pager that the characters in the comic were reading. The other comic project dropped away, but work had started on *Salem Brownstone,* and we kept going." First serialized in *Sturgeon White Moss,* a comics anthology, *Salem Brownstone* developed a cult following, prompting Dunning and Singh to expand the work, and the resulting graphic novel was published several years later. "I think the extended time period makes for a very rich variety of styles in the pictures—and they hang together very well," Dunning told Gravett.

Salem Brownstone opens as the eponymous protagonist, the owner of the Sit & Spin Laundromat, receives a telegraph containing the news that his father, Jedediah Brownstone, has died. Arriving at the gothic mansion he has inherited, Salem discovers that Jedediah led a secret life as a mystic protector of the world, guarding against otherworldly diabolical spirits, and Salem must now take up his cause. Aided by the members of Dr. Kinoshita's Circus of Unearthly Delights, Salem joins the fight against the Dark Elders of Mu'bric, who seek to control the world's innocents. "Salem's world is a haunting one, made only more so by the mysterious and enthralling images that accompany the storyline," according to *Voice of Youth Advocates* reviewer Courtney Huse Wika. Further praise came from London *Guardian* critic S.F. Said, who noted that "Salem's otherworldly foes resemble the sinister extraterrestrials of Lovecraft's classic *The Call of Cthulhu,* and Dunning serves up some genuinely chilling moments that are in the best traditions of Lovecraftian horror."

Biographical and Critical Sources

PERIODICALS

Booklist, July 1, 2010, Jesse Karp, review of *Salem Brownstone: All Along the Watchtowers,* p. 63.
Bulletin of the Center for Children's Books, October, 2010, April Spisak, review of *Salem Brownstone,* p. 72.
Guardian (London, England), November 28, 2009, S.F. Said, review of *Salem Brownstone,* p. 20.
School Library Journal, July, 2010, Lisa Gieskes, review of *Salem Brownstone,* p. 105.
Voice of Youth Advocates, August, 2010, Courtney Huse Wika, review of *Salem Brownstone,* p. 264.

ONLINE

Interview Online, http://www.interviewmagazine.com/ (July 22, 2010), Katie Mendelson, "John Harris Dunning's Haunted House."
Paul Gravett Web site, http://www.paulgravett.com/ (October 18, 2009), Paul Gravett, interview with Dunning and Nikhil Singh.
Walker Books Web site, http://www.walker.co.uk/ (September 15, 2011), "John Harris Dunning."*

E-F

ELIO
See ELIOPOULOS, Chris

*   *   *

ELIOPOULOS, Chris
(Elio)

Personal

Male. *Education:* Columbia College Chicago, B.F.A.

Addresses

Home—Chicago, IL. *E-mail*—elio@eliohouse.com.

Career

Illustrator and cartoonist. Columbia College Chicago, adjunct professor of sequential art.

Writings

SELF-ILLUSTRATED GRAPHIC NOVELS

Yo Gabba Gabba!: Gabba Ball! (board book; based on the television series *Yo Gabba Gabba!*), Oni, 2010.
Okie Dokie Donuts: Open for Business, Top Shelf Comics (Maretta, GA), 2011.

Creator of comic-book series, including "Monster Party!," published by Koyama Press; and "Mr. Puzzle," published by Top Shelf Comics. Creator of Web comic "Misery Loves Sherman."

ILLUSTRATOR

Peter Mandel, *Bun, Onion, Burger,* Simon & Schuster Books for Young Readers (New York, NY), 2010.

Sidelights

Chris "Elio" Eliopoulos is a sequential artist whose comic-book creations include the "Monster Party!," "Mr. Puzzle," and "Okie Dokie Donuts" comics, which combine anime-style graphic art with lighthearted stories. A graduate of Columbia College Chicago, where he continues to work as an adjunct professor, Eliopoulos is inspired by mid-twentieth-century graphic design as well as by the U.F.O. craze. In addition to his work

Chris Eliopoulos makes his picture-book debut as the illustrator of Peter Mandel's toddler-friendly Bun, Onion, Burger. (Illustration copyright © 2010 by Chris Eliopoulos. Reproduced by permission of Simon & Schuster, Inc.)

in comics, he has also created the cleanly drawn cartoon art for Peter Mandel's *Bun, Onion, Burger,* a picture-book ode to the family backyard barbecue.

In his graphic novel *Okie Dokie Donuts: Open for Business* series, which is published by Georgia-based Top Shelf Comics, Eliopoulos's colorful and clearly drawn panels radiate humor and energy as he follows the exploits of master pastry-maker Big Mama as she sets out to make her donut shop, Okie Dokie Donuts, the top source for sweets. Another project, the board book *Yo Gabba Gabba: Gabba Ball!,* finds the author/illustrator casting characters from a Nick Jr. television series in a sequential-art story that *Booklist* contributor Kat Kan dubbed "an ideal choice for toddlers" wishing for "their very own 'comic books,' just like their older brothers and sisters."

Biographical and Critical Sources

PERIODICALS

Booklist, March 15, 2011, Kat Kan, review of *Yo Gabba Gabba!: Gabba Ball!,* p. 44.
Kirkus Reviews, May 15, 2010, review of *Bun, Onion, Burger.*
Publishers Weekly, June 14, 2010, review of *Bun, Onion, Burger,* p. 50.

ONLINE

Chris Eliopoulos Home Page, http://www.elihouse.com (October 1, 2011).
Chris Eliopoulos Web log, http://eliohouse.blogspot.com (September 21, 2011).*

* * *

EMBER, Kathi

Personal

Born in September. *Education:* Kutztown University, B.F.A., 1976.

Addresses

Home and office—Fleetwood, PA. *Agent*—Mela Bolinao, MB Artists, 775 6th Ave., No. 6, New York, NY 10001. *E-mail*—katember@enter.net.

Career

Illustrator and graphic designer. Rodale Press, Emmaus, PA, assistant art director, 1979-81; Kutztown University, Kutztown, PA, instructor in illustration, 1990-92, 2003, 2010; freelance illustrator, beginning 1981. Designer of greeting cards, puzzles, wallpaper, and packaging.

Member

Kutztown Area Democratic Club.

Illustrator

Margaret Wise Brown, *The Color Kittens,* Western Publishing (Racine, WI), 1994.
Old MacDonald Had a Farm, Golden Books (Racine, WI), 1997.
Penelope J. Neri, *The Wind in the Willows,* LeapFrog (Everyville, CA), 2000.
Lissa Rovetech, *Shoofly Pie,* Kindermusic International (Greensboro, NC), 2003.
Jenette Donovan Guntly, *I Can Show Respect,* Gareth Stevens (Milwaukee, WI), 2005.
Allia Nolan, *The Secret Fairy Garden,* Reader's Digest Children's Books (Pleasantville, NY), 2005.
There's a Dragon in My Castle, Reader's Digest Children's Books (Pleasantville, NY), 2005.
Pat Miller, *Substitute Groundhog,* Albert Whitman (Morton Grove, IL), 2006.
Janet Nolan, *A Father's Day Thank You,* Albert Whitman (Morton Grove, IL), 2007.
Christine Mehlhaff, *Don't Talk to Strangers,* Scholastic (New York, NY), 2007.
Steve Metzger, *Easter Eggs Everywhere,* Scholastic (New York, NY), 2008.
Stephen Krensky, *Mother's Day Surprise,* Marshall Cavendish Children (Tarrytown, NY), 2010.
Pat Miller, *Squirrel's New Year's Resolution,* Albert Whitman (Chicago, IL), 2010.

Contributor to periodicals, including *Bicycling, Graphis, Highlights for Children, New Shelter,* and *Prevention.*

Sidelights

An artist with more than three decades of experience, Kathi Ember lives in rural Pennsylvania surrounded by cats, sheep, and horses, creature companions that have served as unwitting models in her artwork. In addition to creating artwork for greeting cards and designing gift packaging, puzzles, and wall coverings, Ember also works as a children's book illustrator, contributing artwork to stories by Janet Nolan, Pat Miller, and Stephen Krensky. "I try to bring my animal characters to life," she told *Reading Eagle* contributor Ron Devlin. "I have one major rule—the art should appeal to kids."

According to a *Children's Bookwatch* critic, Ember's "warm drawings enhance" *Substitute Groundhog,* a picture book featuring a text by Miller. In the story, a sickly groundhog attempts to find another animal to take its place on Groundhog Day, only to discover its own unique attributes. Citing the book's "whimsical" storyline, Susan E. Murray added in a *School Library Journal* of *Substitute Groundhog* that Ember's "pictures add much life to the various animals as well as to the humor of the search" at the center of Miller's tale.

Nolan's picture book *A Father's Day Thank You* focuses on the efforts of a bear cub to select just the right present for Father Bear. While his older siblings suggest

Kathi Ember's illustration projects include creating the child-friendly artwork for Stephen Krensky's **Mother's Day Surprise.** (Illustration copyright © 2010 by Kathi Ember. Reproduced by permission of Marshall Cavendish Children.)

such tried-and-true gifts as ties and golf balls, Harvey the cub wants to give his dad something unique and original. After a busy day during which Father Bear comes to the cub's aid several times, the toddler stand-in devises a clever solution to his problem. Reviewing *A Father's Day Thank You,* Todd Morning wrote in *Booklist* that Ember's artwork "elevates the cuddly factor" through her decision to cast the story with a family of brown bears while preserving "settings and situations kids will recognize." Predicting that Nolan's book will be an "enduring" storytime favorite, *School Library Journal* critic Kathleen Pavin added that *A Father's Day Thank You* features art that is "bright and expressive, and . . . filled with homey details."

In *Mother's Day Surprise,* a story by Stephen Krensky, a spotted snake named Violet grows concerned after she spots her woodland friends preparing gifts for their moms. Since Violet does not have arms, legs, or teeth, she cannot gather acorns like her squirrel companion or carve a statue like Beaver. The snake does possess a sharp mind and a flexible body, however, and she uses these assets to present her mother with a wonderfully creative offering on her special day. Martha Simpson, writing in *Booklist,* described Ember's illustrations as "endearing," and a contributor in *Publishers Weekly* applauded the artist's forest scenes, "where the woodsier animals look . . . at home."

Ember and Miller have also joined forces on *Squirrel's New Year's Resolution,* a holiday tale. When the New Year rolls around, Squirrel decides to make a resolution, although she does not know exactly what doing so entails. After friend Bear helpfully explains the concept of making personal commitments, Squirrel decides to

seek advice from neighbors Skunk, Mole, and Turtle, all of whom need some assistance solving their own dilemmas. Squirrel's involvement in her friend's lives finally helps her settle on a resolution that suits her own generous nature. According to Kristine M. Casper in *School Library Journal,* Ember's "brightly colored, acrylic cartoons are full of fun details and expression, giving the woodland creatures anthropomorphic characteristics." A *Publishers Weekly* critic noted that the artist's "thoughtfully detailed . . . paintings create a friendly woodland setting for this largely conflict-free story."

Biographical and Critical Sources

PERIODICALS

Booklist, April 1, 2007, Todd Morning, review of *A Father's Day Thank You,* p. 58; October 15, 2010, Ilene Cooper, review of *Squirrel's New Year's Resolution,* p. 58.

Children's Bookwatch, January, 2007, review of *Substitute Groundhog.*

Kirkus Reviews, January 15, 2007, review of *A Father's Day Thank You,* p. 78.

Library Media Connection, November-December, 2010, Spencer Korson, review of *Squirrel's New Year Resolution,* p. 72.

Publishers Weekly, March 22, 2010, review of *Mother's Day Surprise,* p. 68; September 13, 2010, review of *Squirrel's New Year's Resolution,* p. 44.

Reading Eagle (Reading, PA), May 9, 2010, Ron Devlin, "Local Artist Illustrates Children's Book."

School Library Journal, December, 2006, Susan E. Murray, review of *Substitute Groundhog,* p. 110; March, 2007, Kathleen Pavin, review of *A Father's Day Thank You,* p. 182; April, 2010, Martha Simpson, review of *Mother's Day Surprise,* p. 133; October, 2010, Kristine M. Casper, review of *Squirrel's New Year's Resolution,* p. 90.

ONLINE

MB Artists Web site, http://www.mbartists.com/ (September 21, 2011), "Kathi Ember."

*   *   *

FERGUSON, Pamela
See FERGUSON, Pamela Ellen

*   *   *

FERGUSON, Pamela Ellen
(Pamela Ferguson)

Personal

Born in Chihuahua, Mexico. *Hobbies and other interests:* Gardening, cycling.

Addresses

Home—Austin, TX.

Career

Massage therapist, educator, journalist, and author. Worked as a journalist in London, England, beginning c. 1960s; Academy of Oriental Medicine at Austin, Austin, TX, former dean of graduate program in Asian Bodywork Therapy. Teacher of Zen Shiatsu; presenter at workshops.

Member

Author's League, American Organization for Bodywork Therapies of Asia (member of board and director of council of schools and programs), Breast Cancer Action Group (former president).

Writings

FOR CHILDREN

Sunshine Picklelime, illustrated by Christian Slade, Random House (New York, NY), 2010.

FOR ADULTS

The Palestine Problem (nonfiction), Martin Brian & O'Keeffe (London, England), 1973.
(Under name Pamela Ferguson) *Dominion* (novel), Atheneum (New York, NY), 1978.
(Under name Pamela Ferguson) *The Sacrifice* (novel), Atheneum (New York, NY), 1981.
(Under name Pamela Ferguson) *Decoration and Design for the 80's,* Excalibur Books, 1983.
(Under name Pamela Ferguson) *The Self-Shiatsu Handbook,* photographs by Alison Russell, Berkley (New York, NY), 1995.
(Under name Pamela Ferguson) *Take Five: The Five Elements Guide to Health and Harmony,* Newleaf (Dublin, Ireland), 2000.
(Editor with Debra Duncan Persinger) *Sand to Sky: Conversations with Teachers of Asian Medicine,* iUniverse, 2008.

Columnist for *Acupuncture Today.* Contributor to online journals and periodicals, including *Adweek, Dallas Morning News, Design Financial Mail* (Johannesburg, South Africa), *International Herald Tribune, International Journal of Therapeutic Massage and Bodywork, Marketing, Massage Today, North American Journal of Oriental Medicine,* and London *Times.*

Author's books have been translated into several languages, including German.

Sidelights

Pamela Ellen Ferguson has a diverse background that includes both writing and work as a massage therapist. Born in Mexico and now making her home in Texas,

Ferguson worked as a business journalist in London, England, for several years, and this investigative work sparked her interest in smoking-related and stress-induced diseases. It also inspired her first published writing, the adult novels *Dominion* and *The Sacrifice,* which feature political themes and were released in the late 1970s and early 1980s under the name Pamela Ferguson. Her more-recent writings—*The Self-Shiatsu Handbook* and *Take Five: The Five Elements Guide to Health and Harmony*—reflect her deep interest in Asian medicine, particularly Zen Shiatsu, which she now teaches in the United States as well as in northern Europe. In *Sunshine Picklelime* Ferguson entertains preteen readers with a story that was sparked by a conversation with a friend and inspired by childhood memories and her enjoyment in telling stories to children.

Featuring artwork by Christian Slade, *Sunshine Picklelime* introduces a young girl named P.J. Picklelime, who lives in a vibrant multicultural, multi-faith community where the adults work for a local computer

Pamela Ellen Ferguson creates a gentle story with New-Age appeal in **Sunshine Picklelime,** *featuring artwork by Christian Slade.* (Illustration copyright © 2010 by Christian Slade. Reproduced by permission of Random House Children's Books, a division Random House, Inc.)

company. P.J. sports thick, curly black hair, and it so resembles a bird's nest that her hair becomes home to a yellow warbler learning to sing. Despite her growing friendship with this bird living atop her head, which she names Lemon Pie, it eventually flies away, migrating back to Africa. The girl now also develops her gift of communicating with birds, even coming to their aid in the wake of an oil spill that dirties the nearby coastline. While P.J. is a giving girl, she also learns to ask help from others when problems surface in her own family.

"Earnest lessons on multiculturalism . . . are interspersed with lessons highlighting the value of counseling, composting, and not trashing the planet," observed a *Kirkus Reviews* writer in reviewing *Sunshine Picklelime,* while Richelle Roth noted in *School Library Journal* that the author's "celebration of diversity rings true, delivering a subtle, poignant message." Noting the story's "dreamy" setting and "touches of magic realism," *Booklist* contributor Kathleen Isaacs concluded that *Sunshine Picklelime* "will appeal to families who share [Ferguson's] . . . alternative values of conscious living."

Biographical and Critical Sources

PERIODICALS

Booklist, June 1, 2010, Kathleen Isaacs, review of *Sunshine Picklelime,* p. 80.
Kirkus Reviews, May 15, 2010, review of *Sunshine Picklelime.*
School Library Journal, August, 2010, Richelle Roth, review of *Sunshine Picklelime,* p. 99.

ONLINE

Cynsations Web log, http://cynthialeitichsmith.blogspot.com/ (September 13, 2010), Cynthia Leitich Smith, interview with Ferguson.
Pamela Ellen Ferguson Home Page, http://www.pamelaferguson.net (October 21, 2011).*

*   *   *

FRAZIER, Angie

Personal

Married; children: three. *Education:* College degree.

Addresses

Home—NH. *Agent*—Ted Malawer, Upstart Crow Literary, P.O. Box 25404, Brooklyn, NY 11202. *E-mail*—angie@angiefrazier.com.

Career

Author.

Member

Society of Children's Book Writers and Illustrators.

Writings

YOUNG-ADULT NOVELS

Everlasting, Scholastic Press (New York, NY), 2010.
The Eternal Sea (sequel to *Everlasting*), Scholastic Press (New York, NY), 2011.

"SUZANNA SNOW" NOVEL SERIES

The Midnight Tunnel, Scholastic Press (New York, NY), 2011.
Suzanna Snow, Scholastic Press (New York, NY), 2012.

Sidelights

New Hampshire-based writer Angie Frazier has had a life-long love affair with history, and as an author she is able to create characters whose lives play out during her favorite historical epochs: the nineteenth and early twentieth centuries. Frazier's first novel, *Everlasting,* required years of research to make its 1855 setting authentic, and her middle-grade mystery *The Midnight Tunnel* also gave her an excuse to study the past: in this case, life as it would have been lived by an eleven-year-old Canadian who dreams of becoming a detective.

In *Everlasting* readers are transported to Australia, where seventeen-year-old Camille Rowen faces the prospect of leaving the company of her widowed, sea-captain father and landing in San Francisco, where her arranged marriage to a wealthy man will save her father's livelihood. While sailing home to port in Australia—Camille's last trip prior to marriage—a terrible storm sinks the ship and kills her father, but not before he reveals that Camille's mother is still alive but infirm and living in South Australia. With the help of Oscar, the ship's first mate and another surviver of the storm, Camille determines to locate her mother, a task that is transformed into a hunt for a magical stone containing a power that may not be benign. In a sequel, *The Eternal Sea,* Frazier continues the saga of Camille and Oscar, as events conspire to keep them in Australia, where an ancient curse may determine their ultimate destiny.

Praising *Everlasting* as a "strong and charming" fiction debut, Geri Diorio added in her *School Library Journal* review that Frazier's novel is energized by "terrific, if slightly anachronistic, characters" that "are feisty, strong, caring, smarmy, slick, dashing, and dastardly." "Camille is a nicely realized character—vulnerable yet determined," asserted a *Kirkus Reviews* writer, and a *Publishers Weekly* critic predicted that "readers whose dreams of adventure and true love mirror Camille's will find her an easy heroine with whom to identify."

Cover of Angie Frazier's young-adult novel **Everlasting,** *a mix of seafaring adventure and romance.* (Photographs copyright © 2010 Dennis Hallinan/ Getty Images (silhouette of couple on boat); Romilly Lockyer/Getty Images (old world map of eastern hemisphere); Somos Photography/Veer (calm ocean).)

Readers meet eleven-year-old junior sleuth Suzanna "Zanna" Snow in *The Midnight Tunnel,* as she narrates her experience solving her first crime. Because her Uncle Bruce is a famous detective, Zanna is certain that she must share his investigative prowess, but nothing even the slightest bit suspicious seems to happen in her small coastal town. Instead, her life is directed by her job at her parents' resort hotel, the Rosemount, which caters to a wealthy clientele. When a guest's daughter disappears from the Rosemount one stormy night, Zanna observes a mysterious figure lurking outside in the moonlight, but only her friends Lucy and Isaac believe her. Although Uncle Bruce is hired to investigate the case, he disregards the girl's evidence and theories, leaving Zanna to follow her own leads to an uncertain and possibly dangerous conclusion. "What Zanna lacks in grace and composure, she makes up for in pluck, persistence and cleverness," noted a *Kirkus Reviews* writer, the critic likening Frazier's heroine to "a likely and likable Edwardian Nancy Drew." In *Booklist* Ilene Cooper praised *The Midnight Tunnel* as "a solid mystery" that keeps readers guessing and advised that "more Suzanna Snow mysteries will be quite welcome." In *School Library Journal* Shannon Seglin recommended

Frazier's novel to "fans of the 'American Girl' series," noting that *The Midnight Tunnel* "gives a bird's eye view" of a girl's life as it was lived at the turn of the twentieth century.

Biographical and Critical Sources

PERIODICALS

Booklist, February 15, 2011, Ilene Cooper, review of *The Midnight Tunnel,* p. 75.
Bulletin of the Center for Children's Books, March, 2011, Kate Quealy-Gainer, review of *The Midnight Tunnel,* p. 328.
Kirkus Reviews, May 15, 2010, review of *Everlasting;* February 1, 2011, review of *The Midnight Tunnel.*
Publishers Weekly, June 21, 2010, review of *Everlasting,* p. 50.
School Library Journal, September, 2010, Geri Diorio, review of *Everlasting,* p. 153; April, 2011, Shannon Seglin, review of *The Midnight Tunnel,* p. 172.
Voice of Youth Advocates, June, 2010, Robyn Gurdel, review of *Everlasting,* p. 164.

ONLINE

Angie Frazier Home Page, http://www.angiefrazier.com (September 21, 2011).
Angie Frazier Web log, http://angie-frazier.livejournal.com (September 21, 2011).*

*   *   *

FRENCH, Wendy 1972-
(W.C. Mack, Winnie Mack, Wendy Smith)

Personal

Born 1972, in Vancouver, British Columbia, Canada; daughter of teachers; married; husband's name Mike. *Education:* University of Victoria, B.A. (writing and English).

Addresses

Home—Portland, OR. *Agent*—Cooke Agency, 278 Bloor St. E., Ste. 305, Toronto, Ontario M4W 3M4, Canada. *E-mail*—info@winnie-mack.com.

Career

Author.

Awards, Honors

Oregon Spirit Book Awards Honor Book selection, Bank Street Best Children's Book of the Year nomination, and Maryland Black-Eyed Susan Award nomination, all

2010, and New Hampshire Great Stone Face Children's Book Award nomination, and Diamond Willow Award nomination, both 2011, all for *After All, You're Callie Boone*.

Writings

ADULT NOVELS

sMothering (adult novel), Forge Books (New York, NY), 2003.
Going Coastal, Tom Doherty (New York, NY), 2005.
After the Rice, Forge Books (New York, NY), 2006.
Full of It, Tom Doherty (New York, NY), 2008.

JUVENILE NOVELS

(Under name Winnie Mack) *After All, You're Callie Boone*, Feiwel & Friends (New York, NY), 2010.
(Under name W.C. Mack) *Hat Trick*, Scholastic Canada Toronto, Ontario, Canada), 2010.
(Under name W.C. Mack) *Line Change*, Scholastic Canada Toronto, Ontario, Canada), 2011.

Sidelights

While she began her writing career focusing on humorous relationship novels for twenty-somethings, Canadian author Wendy French has gained a preteen following through her middle-grade novel *After All, You're Callie Boone*, which was published under her pen name, Winnie Mack. French has also written two middle-grade novels that are geared toward boys using the pen name W.C. Mack. Titled *Hat Trick* and *Line Change*, these novels feature a pint-sized hockey player named J.T. "Nugget" McDonald.

French was raised in Vancouver, British Columbia, and attended the University of Victoria where she earned a degree in English and creative writing. After a move to Portland, Oregon, she began channeling her humor and observations regarding her generation into fiction and published her first novel, *sMothering*, in 2003.

For Lauren Peterson, star of French's adult novel *Full of It*, the problem is loss, first of a boyfriend and then of a best friend. *Going Coastal* follows Jody Rogers after she quits her waitressing job and wallows in the wake of a disastrous romance while rooming with a supportive friend. In *After the Rice* French tells the story of Megan, a newlywed whose future with new hubbie Matt is threatened by the intrusions and demands of various family members, including an uncle who takes up residence in the basement of the young couple's home.

A switch in focus from college graduates to middle schoolers resulted in *After All, You're Callie Boone*, which earned the pseudonymous Winnie Mack kudos from several awards committees. In French's novel, eleven-year-old Callie is enduring a terrible summer. Not only has her bff resigned from the job, but Callie has been restricted from swimming at the town pool, a tragedy given that her dream is to swim for the U.S.A. in the Olympic Games. Facing a summer brimming with boring chores and annoying family members, the girl finds a much-needed friend in a new neighbor named Hoot. Although she first worries about appearances (will people think that she is the girlfriend of a skater?), Callie eventually learns to look deeper, and a family tragedy helps her move beyond her adolescent self-absorption as well. "Callie's process of self-discovery is realistic and appealing," noted Shelle Rosenfeld in *Booklist*, and *After All, You're Callie Boone* resonates with "themes about the importance and rewards of compassion and support." "Mack's well-drawn personalities and lighthearted touch keep the narrative lively and engaging," observed Marilyn Taniguchi in *School Library Journal*, and a *Publishers Weekly* contributor predicted of the novel that "young female readers should be attracted to Mack's earnest characters and hopeful message."

Biographical and Critical Sources

PERIODICALS

Booklist, April 15, 2010, Shelle Rosenfeld, review of *After All, You're Callie Boone*, p. 46.
Publishers Weekly, June 21, 2010, review of *After All, You're Callie Boone*, p. 46.
School Library Journal, August, 2010, Marilyn Taniguchi, review of *After All, You're Callie Boone*, p. 106.

ONLINE

Winnie Mack Home Page, http://www.winnie-mack.com (September 29, 2011).

*   *   *

FUSSELL, Sandy 1960-

Personal

Born 1960, in Australia; married; children: two sons. *Education:* Attended university in Australia. *Hobbies and other interests:* Sudoku, collecting toy Yowies.

Addresses

Home—Wollongong, New South Wales, Australia.

Career

Writer and information technology specialist. Webmaster for *Reading Stack* Web log and Children's Book Council of Australia Ilawarraù South Coast Branch Web site.

Member

Children's Book Council of Australia, Australian Society of Authors, Society of Children's Book Writers and Illustrators.

Awards, Honors

Younger Readers Book of the Year shortlist, Children's Book Council of Australia (CBCA), 2009, for *Polar Boy;* Outstanding Book for Children with Disabilities designation, International Board on Books for Young People, 2010, for *White Crane;* Book of the Year shortlist, Speech Pathology Australia, 2010, for *Shaolin Tiger;* CBCA Notable Book designation, 2011, for both *Fire Lizard* and *Jaguar Warrior.*

Writings

Ratbags, illustrated by Peter Viska, Aussie School Books (Mt. Waverley, Victoria, Australia), 2007.

The Smart Shopper (nonfiction), Harcourt Education (Australia), 2007.

Polar Boy, Walker Books Australia (Newtown, New South Wales, Australia), 2008.

Jaguar Warrior, Walker Books Australia (Newtown, New South Wales, Australia), 2010.

"SAMURAI KIDS" MIDDLE-GRADE NOVEL SERIES

White Crane, illustrated by Rhian Nest James, Walker Books Australia (Newtown, New South Wales, Australia), 2008, Candlewick Press (Somerville, MA), 2010.

Owl Ninja, illustrated by Rhian Nest James, Walker Books Australia (Newtown, New South Wales, Australia), 2008, Candlewick Press (Somerville, MA), 2011.

Shaolin Tiger, illustrated by Rhian Nest James, Walker Books Australia (Newtown, New South Wales, Australia), 2009, Candlewick Press (Somerville, MA), 2011.

Monkey Fist, illustrated by Rhian Nest James, Walker Books Australia (Newtown, New South Wales, Australia), 2009.

Fire Lizard, illustrated by Rhian Nest James, Walker Books Australia (Newtown, New South Wales, Australia), 2010.

Golden Bat, illustrated by Rhian Nest James, Walker Books Australia (Newtown, New South Wales, Australia), 2011.

Adaptations

Some of Fussell's novels have been adapted as audio books.

Sidelights

Sandy Fussell, a writer and computer programmer who lives in Australia, takes readers on a journey to feudal Japan in her well-received "Samurai Kids" series of middle-grade novels. The works follow the adventures of a group of disabled children who band together under the guidance of a legendary warrior. Describing the series for *Australian Literature Review* online, Fussell explained that "*Samurai Kids* is an exciting action adventure with lots of sword waving and shuriken star throwing. But it's also an historical novel with interesting facts woven into the story such as how a samurai sword is made and the importance of the bushido code."

Fussell began her career as an author after one of her sons suddenly and surprisingly lost interest in reading when he was ten years old, claiming that books were dull. Seeking an innovative method to rekindle the boy's love of literature, she convinced her son to write his own story. The tactic backfired, however: when she insisted on offering suggestions, Fussell's son fired back, exclaiming that she might as well pen her own tale. "So I . . . took his advice," she recalled in her *Australian Literature Review* online interview. "I found I loved writing and haven't stopped since."

Set in the thirteenth century, *Polar Boy* was Fussell's first work of historical fiction. "I have always been fas-

Sandy Fussell introduces the adventures of a young samurai in White Crane, *the first part of her "Samurai Kids" series featuring artwork by Rhian Nest James.* (Illustration copyright © 2010 by Rhian Nest James. Reproduced by permission of Candlewick Press, Somerville, MA on behalf of Walker Books Australia.)

cinated by history and I think that shows in the stories I tell," she noted in her *Australian Literature Review* interview. "I choose slivers of time that are not necessarily well known but are still accessible to my readers." *Polar Boy* concerns Iluak, a thirteen-year-old Thule Inuit whose mystic grandmother has foretold his terrifying destiny: Iluak will face a polar bear that threatens his people. As the Inuit begin their annual migration across the ice to their summer camp, they encounter "Northmen"—intruders from Greenland—and Iluak must make a courageous decision when a Viking child comes under attack from a polar bear. The author's "descriptions . . . of this bleak, bitter, icy world is flawless and makes utterly compelling reading," observed *Magpies* critic Russ Merrin.

In *White Crane,* the first installment in her "Samurai Kids" series, Fussell introduces Niya Moto, a one-legged boy who is determined to become a formidable warrior. Although a number of samurai schools reject him, Niya eventually receives an offer from Ki-Yaga, sensei of the Cockroach Ryu. There the youngster meets his fellow students, including Taji, who is blind, and Kyoko, an albino girl. Led by their wise and strong-willed sensei, the Cockroaches enter the prestigious Samurai Trainee Games, where they do battle with the pugnacious members of the Dragon Ryu. "Filled with Zen-sounding aphorisms, the book has moments of sheer cleverness," Alana Joli Abbott commented in *School Library Journal,* and in *Booklist* John Peters observed that *White Crane* "is threaded with information about traditional samurai values."

An impending war is the focus of *Owl Ninja,* the second title in the "Samurai Kids" series. Hoping to avert conflict between the samurai ryus, the Cockroaches set out to persuade their emperor to quell the hostilities. After learning that the powerful leader has threatened the life of Ki-Yaga, however, the children seek additional training from the Owl Ninja Clan, their rivals. "As before, there's plenty of horseplay," Peters noted, and Allison Tran wrote in *School Library Journal* that Fussell's "adventure is sprinkled with gentle humor, adding to its general appeal."

The exploits of the Cockroaches continue in works such as *Shaolin Tiger* and *Golden Bat.* "*Samurai Kids* contains a strong theme that disabilities, physical or otherwise, should not define who we are or what opportunities we are offered. But it's not said like that," Fussell maintained in *Australian Literature Review* online. "The Samurai Kids each have a disability and they just get on with the job of learning to be samurai and have some marvelous adventures along the way. They find strengths in spite of, and sometimes as a direct result of, their so-called weaknesses."

Biographical and Critical Sources

PERIODICALS

Booklist, June 1, 2010, John Peters, review of *White Crane,* p. 80; February 1, 2011, John Peters, review of *Owl Ninja,* p. 78.
Bulletin of the Center for Children's Books, September, 2010, April Spisak, review of *White Crane,* p. 18.
Magpies, August, 2008, Russ Merrin, review of *Polar Boy.*
Reading Time, October, 2008, review of *Polar Boy.*
School Library Journal, September, 2010, Alana Joli Abbott, review of *White Crane,* p. 154; April, 2011, Allison Tran, review of *Owl Ninja,* p. 172.

ONLINE

Australian Literature Review Online, http://auslit.net/ (July 19, 2010), interview with Fussell.
Samurai Kids Web site, http://www.samuraikids.com.au/ (September 15, 2011).
Sandy Fussell Home Page, http://www.sandyfussell.com (September 15, 2011).
Sandy Fussell Web log, http://www.sandyfussell.blogspot. com (September 15, 2011).*

G-H

GLEITZMAN, Morris 1953-

Personal

First syllable of surname rhymes with "light"; born January 9, 1953, in Sleaford, Lincolnshire, England; immigrated to Australia, 1969; son of Phillip (a real-estate agent) and Pamela Gleitzman; married Christine McCaul (a film editor), February 9, 1978 (separated January, 1994); children: Sophie, Ben. *Education:* Canberra College of Advanced Education, B.A. (professional writing), 1974. *Hobbies and other interests:* Travel, reading, making lists.

Addresses

Home—Victoria, Australia. *Agent*—Anthony Williams Agency, P.O. Box. 1379, Darlinghurst, Sydney, New South Wales 1300, Australia. *E-mail*—morris@ morrisgleitzman.com.

Career

Australian Broadcasting Corporation, Sydney, New South Wales, television promotions director, 1973-75, television entertainment script editor and producer, 1975-76, and writer for *The Norman Gunston Show,* 1976-78; Seven Network, Sydney, writer for *The Norman Gunston Show,* 1978-81; freelance writer, beginning 1981.

Awards, Honors

AWGIE Award, Australian Writers Guild, 1985, for television film *The Other Facts of Life;* Family Award, 1990, for *Two Weeks with the Queen,* 2002, for *Boy Overboard;* Book of the Year Younger Honour, Children's Book Council of Australia, 1992, for *Misery Guts,* and 1993, for *Blabber Mouth; Guardian* Children's Fiction Award shortlist, 1999, for *Bumface,* 2009, for *Then,* and 2010, for *Now;* Queensland Premier's Literary Award, 2000, for *Toad Rage;* Children's Peace Lit Award, 2003, for *Teacher's Pet;* Animal Welfare Award, 2004, for *Toad Away;* Aurealis Award, 2005, for *Worm Story;* Speech Pathology Australia award, 2007, for *Doubting Thomas,* 2011, for *Now;* ANTO Cole Award, 2008, for *Toad Rage;* German Youth Literature Prize, 2010, and U.S. Board on Books for Young People honor, and Sydney Taylor Award, American Association of Jewish Libraries, both 2011, all for *Once;* Kate Greenaway Award, and Prime Minister's Literary Award, both 2011, for *Now;* Australian Book Industry Award, 2011, for *Once, Then,* and *Now;* numerous Australian child-selected awards, including COOL (Australia Capital Territory), BILBY (Queensland), YABBA (Victoria), and KOALA (New South Wales) awards.

Writings

NOVELS; FOR CHILDREN

The Other Facts of Life (adapted from author's television screenplay of the same title; also see below), Penguin (Ringwood, Victoria, Australia), 1985, reprinted, 2004.

Second Childhood (adapted from author's television screenplay), Puffin (Ringwood, Victoria, Australia), 1990.

Misery Guts, Piper (Sydney, New South Wales, Australia), 1991, Harcourt (San Diego, CA), 1993.

Worry Warts, Pan Macmillan (Sydney, New South Wales, Australia), 1992, Harcourt (San Diego, CA), 1993.

Puppy Fat, Pan Macmillan (Sydney, New South Wales, Australia), 1992, Harcourt (San Diego, CA), 1995.

Blabber Mouth (also see below), Pan Macmillan (Sydney, New South Wales, Australia), 1992, Harcourt (San Diego, CA), 1995.

Sticky Beak (also see below), Pan Macmillan (Sydney, New South Wales, Australia), 1993, Harcourt (San Diego, CA), 1995.

Belly Flop, Pan Macmillan (Sydney, New South Wales, Australia), 1996, published with *Water Wings,* Macmillan (London, England), 2006.

Water Wings, Pan Macmillan (Sydney, New South Wales, Australia), 1996, published with *Belly Flop,* Macmillan (London, England), 2006.

Bumface, Puffin (Ringwood, Victoria, Australia), 1998.

Gift of the Gab (also see below), Puffin (Ringwood, Victoria, Australia), 1999.

Adults Only, Puffin (Ringwood, Victoria, Australia), 2001.

Boy Overboard, Puffin (Camberwell, Victoria, Australia), 2002.

Teacher's Pet, Puffin (Camberwell, Victoria, Australia), 2003.

Girl Underground, Puffin (Camberwell, Victoria, Australia), 2004.

Worm Story, Puffin (Camberwell, Victoria, Australia), 2004.

Aristotle's Nostril, Penguin (Melbourne, Victoria, Australia), 2005.

Doubting Thomas, Puffin (London, England), 2007.

Give Peas a Chance, Puffin (London, England), 2008.

The Blabber Mouth Collection (includes *Blabber Mouth, Sticky Beak,* and *Gift of the Gab*), Macmillan Children's (London, England), 2008.

Grace, Puffin (Melbourne, Victoria, Australia), 2009.

Pizza Cake, and Other Funny Stories, Puffin (Melbourne, Victoria, Australia), 2011.

Too Small to Fail, Puffin (Melbourne, Victoria, Australia), 2011.

Gleitzman's books have been translated into Catalan, Czech, Dutch, French, German, Icelandic, Indonesian, Italian, Japanese, Mandarin, Portuguese, Russian, Scandinavian, Spanish, and Welsh.

"WICKED!" NOVEL SERIES; WITH PAUL JENNINGS

The Slobberers, Puffin (Ringwood, Victoria, Australia), 1997.

Battering Rams, Puffin (Ringwood, Victoria, Australia), 1997.

Croaked, Puffin (Ringwood, Victoria, Australia), 1997.

Dead Ringer, Puffin (Ringwood, Victoria, Australia), 1997.

The Creeper, Puffin (Ringwood, Victoria, Australia), 1997.

Till Death Us Do Part, Puffin (Ringwood, Victoria, Australia), 1997.

Wicked! (includes six volumes), Puffin (Ringwood, Victoria, Australia), 1998.

"TOAD!" BEGINNING READER SERIES

Toad Rage, Puffin (Ringwood, Victoria, Australia), 1999, Random House (New York, NY), 2004.

Toad Heaven, Puffin (Ringwood, Victoria, Australia), 2001, Random House (New York, NY), 2005.

Toad Away, Puffin (Camberwell, Victoria, Australia), 2003, Yearling (New York, NY), 2003.

Toad Surprise, Puffin (Camberwell, Victoria, Australia), 2009.

"DEADLY!" NOVEL SERIES; WITH PAUL JENNINGS

Nude, Puffin (Ringwood, Victoria, Australia), 2000.

Brats, Puffin (Ringwood, Victoria, Australia), 2000.

Stiff, Puffin (Ringwood, Victoria, Australia), 2000.

Hunt, Puffin (Ringwood, Victoria, Australia), 2001.

Grope, Puffin (Ringwood, Victoria, Australia), 2001.

Pluck, Puffin (Ringwood, Victoria, Australia), 2001.

Deadly! (includes all six volumes), Puffin (Ringwood, Victoria, Australia), 2002.

"REAL LIFE STORIES" NOVEL SERIES

Then (also see below), Viking (Camberwell, Victoria, Australia), 2008, Henry Holt (New York, NY), 2010.

Once and Then (includes *Once* and *Then*), Penguin (Harmondsworth, England), 2009.

Once (also see below), Henry Holt (New York, NY), 2010.

Now, Puffin (London, England), 2010.

OTHER

Doctors and Nurses (screenplay), Universal Entertainment, 1981.

Melvin Son of Alvin (screenplay), Roadshow, 1984.

The Other Facts of Life (teleplay), Ten Network, 1985.

Skin Free (two-act play), produced in Sydney, New South Wales, Australia, 1986.

(With Trevor Farrant) *Not a Papal Tour* (stage show), produced in Canberra, Australian Capital Territory, Australia, 1987.

Two Weeks with the Queen (adult novel), illustrated by Moira Millman, Blackie & Son, 1989, Putnam (New York, NY), 1991.

Harbour Beat (screenplay), Palm Beach Pictures/Zenith Productions, 1990.

Just Looking: Gleitzman on Television (collected columns), Sun Books (Chippendale, New South Wales, Australia), 1992.

Gleitzman on Saturday (collected columns), Macmillan, 1993.

SelfHelpLess: Fifty-seven Pieces of Crucial Advice for People Who Need a Bit More Time to Get It Right, Penguin (Ringwood, Victoria, Australia), 2000.

Writer of scripts for television series, including *Second Childhood, Crossroads, Bust, Instant TV, The Norman Gunston Show,* and *The Daryl Somers Show.* Author of weekly television column in *Sydney Morning Herald,* 1987-92; columnist for *Good Weekend* (magazine supplement to *Sydney Morning Herald* and *Melbourne Age*), beginning 1990.

Adaptations

Gleitzman's novel *Two Weeks with the Queen* was adapted as a play by Mary Morris, Piper, 1994. Many of his books have been adapted as audiobooks, including *Bumface,* BBC Audiobooks, 2007.

Sidelights

Although he started out his writing career as a television scriptwriter, Morris Gleitzman has earned a reputation in his adopted country of Australia for creating humorous, evocative young-adult novels as well as teaming up with fellow writer Paul Jennings to pen the entertaining stories in the "Wicked!" and "Deadly!" series. The "cheeky brand of humor" and "sensible, tolerant attitude" toward family life that a *Publishers Weekly* reviewer noticed in Gleitzman's early novels has been honed sharp by the author, and his dry wit continues to find an appreciative audience with children and critics alike. "One looks forward to a Gleitzman title," wrote Trevor Carey in *Magpies;* and according to *Horn Book* critic Karen Jameyson, the award-winning writer's name "has been steadily edging its way into cult territory." By 1999 Gleitzman was considered one of the most popular children's writers in Australia, and the majority of his books have been translated into several languages.

The secret of Gleitzman's success, according to some critics, is his ability to couch highly sensitive topics and conflicts in chaotic situations peppered with amusing dialogue. Readers may find themselves laughing through stories about divorce, alienation, and physical challenges as these crises are encountered by the author's young protagonists. In his book *Boy Overboard* he addresses a broader concern facing young people while still employing his trademark humor, creating a likeable protagonist who lives in Afghanistan and must deal daily with intolerance and the problems faced by refugees after he and his family are forced to flee to Australia. Gleitzman once explained that, when writing for a young audience, he uses "humor to explore the big subjects. I like characters who find themselves face to face with The Biggies unequipped with the adult armory of evasion, rationalization, and red wine."

Born and raised in the south of London, Gleitzman immigrated to Australia with his family at age sixteen and quickly decided to become a writer. "I thought I'd better do some of those colorful jobs writers always seem to have done," he once commented. "I worked for a bit as a frozen chicken-thawer, a department store Santa Claus, an assistant to a fashion designer, and a rolling-stock unhooker in a sugar mill. I applied for whaling, but they rejected me because I said I'd only do it if I could throw the whales back." After enrolling in a college program in professional writing, Gleitzman established a career in Australia's film and television industry. He worked as a promotions director and script editor and producer for the Australian Broadcasting Corporation and wrote for *The Norman Gunston Show* for several years before becoming a freelance writer.

Gleitzman's first two books were adapted from his screenplays, and these projects gave him the confidence to make the career move from playwright to novelist. His most widely known novel, the award-winning *Two Weeks with the Queen,* was conceived "in a flash," as the writer once explained. "As I was writing it, I realized it was, in part, a story about the tendency of loving parents to overprotect their kids from difficult realities, both domestic and global. I was pleased to discover this, as I do it all the time myself."

"The things that happen in my books are almost all made up," Gleitzman admitted in a question-and-answer on his home page. "For me, imagination makes much better stories than memory. Specially as my memory isn't very good. I can't remember many of the adventures of my childhood, so it's easier for me to make them up. Occasionally, though, a bit of my real life creeps into a story. I emigrated from England with my folks when I was 16, and that experience helped me write *Misery Guts.*"

In *Misery Guts* and its sequel, *Worry Warts,* Gleitzman focuses on a nervous teen named Keith Shipley. The novels describe the unintended condequences of parents' efforts to protect their children, and also of children's efforts to protect their parents. Keith is troubled by his worried Mom and Dad, a pair of "misery guts." His attempt to pick up their business—as well as their spirits—by painting their fish-and-chips shop in the south of London a glossy mango color fails. Keith's parents show no interest in his plans for a tropical vacation or a move to Australia. When Keith finally persuades them to take a day trip to the beach, he forgets to turn the deep-fryer at the shop off. As a result, the building burns down and the family's business is ruined. To Keith's delight, his parents decide to begin another business in sunny Australia. As *Misery Guts* closes, readers find Keith content and the misery guts hopeful.

The Shipley family drama continues in *Worry Warts,* as money problems provoke Keith's parents into quarreling. Ever ready with a paint brush, Keith paints their car to cheer them up but it does not help; they announce that they want to divorce. Thinking that money will keep his parents together, Keith runs away to the opal fields. Although he manages to find an opal, he becomes trapped in a mine and his parents are forced into a costly rescue effort to bring their son home safely. While Keith eventually convinces his parents to stay together for the good of the family, he ultimately puts his own desires aside for the good of all. While Ilene Cooper noted in *Booklist* that the conclusion of *Worry Warts* may be "unsatisfying" for those who applaude the boy's "efforts to keep his family together," a *Kirkus Reviews* critic found the same conclusion "surprising but appropriate."

Keith and his family return in several more novels by Gleitzman, including *Puppy Fat,* which finds Keith still at work solving his separated and now-single parents' problems for them. Worried that, in their mid-thirties, they have both become overweight and doddery and need to find new romantic partners, he channels his artistic talents into finding ways to advertise their availability for dating. However, painting them in skimpy bathing suits on a wall in his South London neighborhood proves unsuccessful, so he calls in help, with predictably humorous results. A *Publishers Weekly* contributor wrote that Gleitzman's "punchy narrative, droll characters, and original plot" make *Puppy Fat* a "real page-turner," while in *Booklist* Ilene Cooper noted that the author characteristically "turns everyday situations upside down with his humor and off-the-wall take on life."

Blabber Mouth, Sticky Beak, and *Gift of the Gab* all feature Rowena Batts, a girl who was born without the ability to speak. Despite her impairment, Rowena manages to express her opinion with signs, written words, and actions. While in *Blabber Mouth* the central problems revolve around Rowena's relationship with her flamboyant father, his decision to remarry causes new problems in *Sticky Beak,* In this novel Rowena expands her communication tools by throwing a Jelly Custard Surprise during a party for her teacher, who has married Rowena's father and is now pregnant with Rowena's half-sibling. Despite Rowena's speech problem and sometimes-outlandish behavior, she is a resilient protagonist. By the end of *Sticky Beak,* for example, she has learned new ways of coping with her outrageous yet loving father, her new stepmother, the new baby, and even the class bully. *Gift of the Gab* finds Rowena reconciling with her father while attempting to

Cover of Morris Gleitzman's **Toad Rage**, *the humorous saga of a cane toad named Limpy that features cover art by Rod Clement.* (Illustration by Rod Clement, copyright © 1999 by Random House Children's Books. Reproduced by permission of Random House Children's Books, a division of Random House, Inc. All rights reserved.)

uncover the reason for her speech problem, which takes the family to France in search of answers. According to *Magpies* contributor Cathryn Crowe, in *Sticky Beak* Gleitzman "wraps" themes involving rejection and insecurity into "a tight bundle with plenty of zany humour."

In an unusual step, Gleitzman takes on an animal protagonist in his elementary-grade novel *Toad Rage* and its sequels *Toad Heaven, Toad Away,* and *Toad Surprise.* In *Toad Rage* readers meet Limpy, an Australian cane toad that is angered over the number of relatives who have ended up as road kill. In an effort to end the needless slaughter of amphibians, Limpy begins a public relations campaign, trying to sell humans on the notion that cane toads are truly man's best friend and ultimately hoping to become the next Olympic mascot. *Toad Away* finds Limpy still searching for a safe haven for cane toads, and joining with friends Charm and Goliath to travel to the mythical Amazon, which is rumored to be such a place, while in *Toad Surprise* the three cane toads try to work toad imagery into the traditions of the Christmas Season.

Praising *Toad Rage* as a "hilarious dark comedy," a *Publishers Weekly* writer revealed that Gleitzman originally wrote the novel for the 2000 Sydney Olympics as a tongue-in-cheek commentary on the country's animal-mascot selection process. Whatever its origins, *Toad Rage* works on its own merits; as Ed Sullivan wrote in *Booklist,* Gleitzman's saga of "one toad's bold quest to reach out to another species will give readers plenty of laughs." "This toad's-eye view of human society provides both solid entertainment and a barbed commentary on the importance of looks," added a *Kirkus Reviews* contributor. In *School Library Journal* Elaine E. Knight pegged the appeal of *Toad Heaven* to boys: Gleitzman's "often-raucous dialogue includes lots of body humor and gross-out descriptions of toad diet and personal habits." Limpy and Charm's "loving sibling relationship" adds depth to the plot of *Toad Away,* according to *School Library Journal* contributor Quinby Frank, the critic predicting that "there is enough kooky humor" in Gleitzman's story "to hold children's interest."

While Gleitzman is perhaps best known for his humorous stories, he has also touched on more complex topics, earning critical praise in the process. *Two Weeks with the Queen,* for example, focuses on a child coping with a fatal disease, while *Boy Overboard* finds two young soccer players determined to escape the war-torn Middle East and play their favorite sport in Australia. In his young-adult novel *Grace* a teen raised in a strict Christian community finds the strength to reexamine the sometimes intolerant tenets of her faith. Most notable among Gleitzman's more-sophisticated works are his "Real Life Stories," which are set during World War II and include *Once, Then,* and *Now.* "Gleitzman . . . has made a specialty of handling challenging issues in an engaging way," asserted Nicolette Jones in the London *Times.*

In writing *Once* and its sequels, Gleitzman was inspired by his own family history; several of his distant rela-

Limpy's adventures continue in Gleitzman's Toad Heaven, *an amphibian-centered saga featuring artwork by Rod Clement.* (Cover illustration copyright © 2006 by Yearling. Reproduced by permission of Yearling, an imprint of Random House Children's Book, a division of Random House, Inc.)

tives were Polish Jews who died during the Holocaust. The story of heroic Janusz Korczak was also inspirational: Korczak was a Polish Jew and physician who bravely gave up his life rather than abandon the hundreds of Jewish orphans under his care when they were captured by the Nazis in 1942. In *Once* Gleitzman introduces ten-year-old Felix, a Jewish boy who is warehoused in a Catholic orphanage in Poland by his busy parents. When dark-suited soldiers arrive, Felix escapes and makes the journey to his home town, but finds no one there any more. Told that the Jews have gone to the city, the boy sets out again, encountering vestiges of Nazi brutality along the way. At one burnt-out home surrounded by corpses he finds a survivor: a little girl named Zelda who he takes with him, calming her with stories. Ultimately, Felix and Zelda find themselves among the many Jews being gathered together in the city, there to be sorted by age or health, and sometimes killed by brutal Nazi soldiers. Their adventures continue to play out in a "gripping novel" that captures "the horror of the Holocaust" in a way that will inspire young readers with an interest in researching the period's history, according to *Booklist* critic Hazel Rochman. While noting Felix's ability to spin the horrors he wit-

nesses into stories that suffuse the horror, Claire E. Gross added in her *Horn Book* review that *Once* "is the rare Holocaust book for young readers that doesn't alleviate its dark themes with a comforting ending." Instead, the novel "taps gut-punching power by contrasting the way in which children would like to imagine their world with the tragic way that life sometimes unfolds," according to *School Library Journal* contributor Jeffrey Hastings.

The story of Felix and Zelda continues in *Then,* as they find themselves free of the Nazis but now on their own in a harsh world where noone can be trusted. Although the children find temporary shelter with a kindly farm woman named Genia, Felix knows that he can not disguise his Jewish lineage for long. Unwilling to bring danger to Zelda or his benefactor, the boy makes a brave decision in a novel that "captures horrors through the lens of childhood," according to a *Publishers Weekly* critic. The boy's poignant narration in *Then* resonates a mix of "innocence and maturity . . . [that] conveys human resilience when faced with the impossible," the critic added. In the London *Guardian,* Meg Rosoff described Felix's narrative voice as "filled alternately with tenderness and the desperation of fathomless loss"; readers of *Then* "will leave this book sadder and wiser about the race of men," the critic added.

Gleitzman fast forwards to the present in *Now,* as an elderly and accomplished Felix lives in Australia. He reflects on his own youth while spending time with his granddaughter, an eleven year old who has been honored with the name of Zelda. While helping the girl deal with difficulties at school as well as the loneliness caused by her absent parents, Felix has the chance to resolve the survivor's guilt he has carried throughout his life when a tragic fire threatens to destroy his home and community. "Once again Gleitzman proves that he is a brilliant storyteller," asserted Marzena Currie in her review of *Now* for *School Librarian,* the critic praising the book as "a beautiful ending to an extraordinary and heartwarming tale." While noting that parts of the novel are "not easy to read," Jones hailed its author for shouldering "the difficult task of enabling us to think about unthinkable episodes of history."

Biographical and Critical Sources

PERIODICALS

Booklist, July, 1993, Ilene Cooper, review of *Worry Warts,* p. 1958; May 1, 1995, Mary Harris Veeder, review of *Blabber Mouth,* p. 1561; June 1, 1995, Mary Harris Veeder, review of *Sticky Beak,* p. 1770; June 1, 1996, Ilene Cooper, review of *Puppy Fat,* p. 171; March 1, 2004, Ed Sullivan, review of *Toad Rage,* p. 1188; February 15, 2010, Hazel Rochman, review of *Once,* p. 71.

Horn Book, July, 1993, Karen Jameyson, "News from down Under," pp. 496-498; July-August, 1995, Elizabeth S. Watson, review of *Blabber Mouth,* p. 458; March-April, 2010, Claire E. Gross, review of *Once,* p. 55.

Guardian (London, England), February 21, 2009, Meg Rosoff, review of *Then,* p. 14; August 22, 2009, review of *Once and Then,* p. 13.

Journal of Adolescent and Adult Literacy, April, 2011, Emily Ventura, review of *Once,* p. 546.

Junior Bookshelf, November, 1993, review of *Sticky Beak,* pp. 65-66.

Kirkus Reviews, February 1, 1993, review of *Misery Guts,* p. 146; April 1, 2004, review of *Toad Rage,* p. 329; December 15, 2004, review of *Toad Heaven,* p. 1202; January 15, 2006, review of *Toad Away,* p. 84.

Magpies, November, 1992, Trevor Carey, review of *Blabber Mouth,* p. 30; November, 1993, Cathryn Crowe, review of *Sticky Beak,* p. 32.

Observer (London, England), August 23, 2009, Alexandra Masters, review of *Once and Then,* p. 23.

Publishers Weekly, January 11, 1991, review of *Two Weeks with the Queen,* p. 105; February 8, 1993, reviews of both *Misery Guts* and *Worry Warts,* p. 87; May 6, 1996, review of *Puppy Fat,* p. 8; March 22, 2004, review of *Toad Rage,* p. 86; March 8, 2010, review of *Once,* p. 58; March 28, 2011, review of *Then,* p. 58.

School Librarian, autumn, 2010, Marzena Currie, review of *Now,* p. 164.

School Library Journal, January, 2005, Elaine E. Knight, review of *Toad Heaven,* p. 130; April, 2006, Quinby Frank, review of *Toad Away,* p. 139; April, 2010, Jeffrey Hastings, review of *Once,* p. 156.

Sunday Times (London, England), February 26, 2006, Nicolette Jones, review of *Once,* p. 56; May 23, 2010, Nicolette Jones, review of *Now,* p. 50; January 9, 2011, Nicolette Jones, review of *Grace,* p. 42.

ONLINE

Morris Gleitzman Home Page, http://www.morrisgleitzman .com (September 29, 2011).

Penguin Books Australia Web site, http://www.penguin. com.au/ (September 29, 2011), "Morris Gleitzman."

*   *   *

HANKE, Karen

Personal

Married; husband's name Bob. *Education:* University of California, Santa Barbara, B.F.A., 1985. *Hobbies and other interests:* Ultramarathon running, her dogs.

Addresses

Home—Santa Rosa, CA. *E-mail*—pinklime@sonic.net.

Career

Illustrator and graphic designer. Former newspaper layout artist in San Francisco, CA; designer and illustrator of toys, games, and gift products.

Awards, Honors

Benjamin Franklin Award for children's book/audio book, and *Writer's Digest* National Self-Published Book Award, both c. 2000, both for *The Jazz Fly* by Matthew Gollub.

Illustrator

Matthew Gollub, *The Jazz Fly* (includes audio CD), Tortuga Press (Santa Rosa, CA), 2000.

Matthew Gollub, *Jazz Fly Two: The Jungle Pachanga* (includes audio CD), Tortuga Press (Santa Rosa, CA), 2010.

Illustrator of *Five Little Monkeys* and *Monkey in the Story Tree,* both adapted by Dr. Jean Feldman, Creative Teaching Press (Huntington Beach, CA).

Sidelights

An illustrator and graphic designer, Karen Hanke contributed the artwork to Matthew Gollub's award-winning picture book *The Jazz Fly* and its sequel, *Jazz Fly Two: The Jungle Pachanga,* which follow the exploits of a music-loving insect. Both works include audio CD's featuring performances by the author, an accomplished drummer. "To research *The Jazz Fly,*" Hanke remarked in a Tortuga Press Web site interview, "I studied many jazz magazines and listened to a variety of jazz music. Also, I did extensive research on insects. I collected gnats and flies, bought books and made lots of sketches. Drawing clothes on bugs was fun. I also made lots of sketches of . . . Gollub playing on his drum set."

In *The Jazz Fly* the drummer for a jazz quartet gets lost while heading to a gig. As he attempts to get directions from a frog, a hog, and a donkey, none can understand the insect's snappy patter. Finally arriving at the club, the fly incorporates the rhythms of these animals' sounds into his drumming, giving his band a freshness and vitality that energizes the crowd. Hanke's "unique . . . gray-toned pictures with contrasting hints of pastel colors," drew praise from *School Library Journal* reviewer Tim Wadham. According to a *Publishers Weekly* critic, the illustrator's computer-enhanced artwork "emulates 1960s animated cartoons, especially in close-up scenes of the club performers."

Jazz Fly Two concerns the band's troubled gig in a tropical rainforest. Hanke's art again complements Gollub's text, "delivering swarming details from diaphanous wings to pools of ambient lighting to bug eyes extraordinaire," according to a *Kirkus Reviews* contributor.

Biographical and Critical Sources

PERIODICALS

Booklist, August, 2000, Susan Dove Lempke, review of *The Jazz Fly,* p. 2146.

Karen Hanke's illustration projects include Matthew Gollub's upbeat picture book **The Jazz Fly.** (Illustration copyright © 2000 by Karen Hanke. Reproduced by permission of Tortuga Press.)

Kirkus Reviews, May 15, 2010, review of *Jazz Fly Two: The Jungle Pachanga.*

Publishers Weekly, March 20, 2000, review of *The Jazz Fly,* p. 90.

School Library Journal, August, 2000, Tim Wadham, review of *The Jazz Fly,* p. 155; August, 2010, Mary Landrum, review of *Jazz Fly Two,* p. 76.

ONLINE

Karen Hanke Home Page, http://www.karenhanke.com (September 21, 2011).

Tortuga Press Web site, http://tortugapress.com/ (August 15, 2011), interview with Hanke.

*   *   *

HART, Alison
See LEONHARDT, Alice

*   *   *

HAUGE, Lesley

Personal

Born in England; immigrated to Zimbabwe, then United States; married; children: sons. *Hobbies and other interests:* Dancing.

Addresses

Home—Brooklyn, NY. *Agent*—Ann Tobias, 520 E. 84th St., Apt. 4L, New York, NY 10028.

Career

Author

Writings

Nomansland, Henry Holt (New York, NY), 2010.

Sidelights

Born in England and spending her childhood in Zimbabwe before immigrating to the United States, author Lesley Hauge draws on her experience living in diverse cultural settings in her first novel, *Nomansland.* Set in a future dystopia—an anti-utopia where the government has morphed from empowering to all-powerful—Hague's story also tackles the evolution of feminism, a movement that the author believes has been coopted and distorted by the media to the disadvantage of today's girls and teens. Discussing her novel with an interviewer for *Mangamania Café* online, she expressed the hope that *Nomansland* will make readers "unsettled in some way, turning ideas about feminism and oppressive ways of ruling over in their minds, as well as asking themselves: What kinds of things might doom a society to failure? The girls in *Nomansland* look back at the objects of a failed society and wonder about it. They also look at their own society, and begin to question it."

Keller is a novice tracker when readers meet her in *Nomansland,* which she narrates. Together with her fellow teen novices, Keller's job is to patrol the coastline of Foundland, an island society. Foundland is governed through the political machinations of cliques of women, and the incursions of the hated and inferior human males are guarded against. Life there is harsh and rigorous: since the time of the Tribulation the land has produced little, and much technology has been lost since the demise of humans from the Time Before. Now the female community of Foundland farms the barren earth during a shortened growing season and builds its population through artificial insemination. While on patrol, Keller and her team stumble upon a hidden structure from the Time Before. After digging their way in, the teens find themselves in a time capsule: a home full of strange objects that reveal a different way of life: make-up and breath mints, glossy magazines, colorful clothing and fashion accessories, and press-on fingernails. As they attempt to fathom a way of life that would allow such things, Keller and her fellow trackers also begin to question their own society, although such questioning is rewarded with brutal harshness.

"Secrets revealed make for a compelling emotional journey," concluded a *Kirkus Reviews* contributor in appraising *Nomansland,* while a *New York Times Book Review* contributor dubbed Hauge's novel "vividly imagined." An "artfully crafted tale," according to *Voice of Youth Advocates* critic Cynthia Winfield, *Nomansland* "reveals a complex society in decline that is compelling for its possibilities and failures," and in *Horn Book* Deirdre F. Baker praised Hauge's futuristic tale for encouraging teen readers "to look afresh at the strangeness of contemporary cultural artifacts we take for granted."

Biographical and Critical Sources

PERIODICALS

Booklist, May 15, 2010, Ian Chipman, review of *Nomansland,* p. 50.
Horn Book, July-August, 2010, Deirdre F. Baker, review of *Nomansland,* p. 109.
Kirkus Reviews, May 15, 2010, review of *Nomansland.*
New York Times Book Review, August 15, 2010, review of *Nomansland,* p. 13.
Publishers Weekly, July 5, 2010, review of *Nomansland,* p. 45.
School Library Journal, August, 2010, Johanna Lewis, review of *Nomansland,* p. 102.
Voice of Youth Advocates, October, 2010, Cynthia Winfield, review of *Nomansland,* p. 366.

ONLINE

Lesley Hauge Home Page, http://www.lesleyhauge.com (October 21, 2011).
Mangamania Café Web site, http://www.mangamaniacafe.com/ (June 17, 2010), interview with Hauge.
SFSite.com, http://www.sfsite.com/ (October 15, 2011), Dan Shade, review of *Nomansland.**

*   *   *

HIMLER, Ronald 1937-
(Ronald Norbert Himler)

Personal

Born October 16, 1937, in Cleveland, OH; son of Norbert and Grace Himler; married Ann Danowitz, June 18, 1972 (divorced); children: Daniel, Anna, Peer. *Education:* Cleveland Institute of Art, diploma, 1960; graduate study in painting at Cranbrook Academy of Art (Bloomfield Hills, MI), 1960-61, and New York University and Hunter College, 1968-70.

Addresses

Home—Tucson, AZ. *E-mail*—ron@ronhimler.com.

Career

Illustrator and author of children's books. General Motors Technical Center, Warren, MI, technical sculptor (styling), 1961-63; artist and illustrator, 1963—. Toy designer and sculptor for Transogram Co., New York, NY, 1968, and Remco Industries, Newark, NJ, 1969. Cofounder and headmaster, Blue Rock School, NC, 1982-84. *Exhibitions:* Work exhibited at Wolfe Galleries, Tucson, AZ, 1990; Chemers Gallery, Tustin, CA, 2009; and Agora Gallery, Chelsea, NY, 2010. *Best Town in the World* exhibited at Bratislava Biennale of Illustration, 1985.

Ronald Himler (Reproduced by permission.)

Awards, Honors

Award for Graphic Excellence, American Institute of Graphic Arts (AIGA), and citation of merit, Society of Illustrators, both 1972, both for *Baby;* Printing Industries of America citation, 1972, for *Rocket in My Pocket;* Children's Book Showcase selection, Children's Book Council (CBC), 1975, for *Indian Harvests* by Carl A. Withers; New Jersey Institute of Technology Award, 1976, for *Little Owl, Keeper of the Trees* by Ann Himler; AIGA Best of Bias-free Illustration citation, 1976, for *Make a Circle, Keep Us In* by Arnold Adoff; Children's Choice selection, International Reading Association/CBC, 1979, for *Bus Ride* by Nancy Jewell; Children's Books of the Year selection, Child Study Children's Book Committee at Bank Street College, 1982, for both *Moon Song* Byrd Baylor and *Jem's Island* by Katherine Lasky, and 1992, for *Fly Away Home* by Eve Bunting; Best Books designation, New York Public Library, 1985, and Notable Book designation, American Library Association (ALA), 1986, both for *Dakota Dugout* by Ann Taylor; Pick of the Lists selection, American Booksellers Association, 1987, for *Nettie's Trip South* by Ann Turner, 1990, for *The Wall* by Bunting, 1991, for *I'm Going to Pet a Worm Today* by Constance Levy, and 1992, for both *Fly Away Home* and *Katie's Trunk* by Turner; Notable Book selection, ALA, 1990, for *The Wall;* One Hundred Titles for Reading and Sharing selection, New York Public Library, 1990, for *The Wall,* and 1992, for *The Lily Cupboard*

by Shulamith Levey Oppenheim; Notable Book designation, ALA, 1991, for *Fly away Home;* Silver Medal, Society of Illustrators, 1992; Christopher Award; Golden Sower Award nomination; Black-eyed Susan Picture-Book Award; Colorado Children's Book Award nomination; numerous other awards.

Writings

FOR CHILDREN; SELF-ILLUSTRATED

(Compiler) *Glad Day, and Other Classical Poems for Children,* Putnam (New York, NY), 1972.
(With first wife, Ann Himler) *Little Owl, Keeper of the Trees,* Harper (New York, NY), 1974.
The Girl on the Yellow Giraffe, Harper (New York, NY), 1976, reprinted, Star Bright Books (New York, NY), 2004.
Wake Up, Jeremiah, Harper (New York, NY), 1979.
Six Is So Much Less than Seven, Star Bright Books (New York, NY), 2002.
Dancing Boy, Star Bright (New York, NY), 2005.

ILLUSTRATOR

Robert Burgess, *Exploring a Coral Reef,* Macmillan (New York, NY), 1972.
Carl A. Withers, compiler, *Rocket in My Pocket* (poetry anthology), revised edition, Western Publishing (New York, NY), 1972.
Fran Manushkin, *Baby,* Harper (New York, NY), 1972.
Elizabeth Winthrop, *Bunk Beds,* Harper (New York, NY), 1972.
Millicent Brower, *I Am Going Nowhere,* Putnam (New York, NY), 1972.
Charlotte Zolotow, *Janey,* Harper (New York, NY), 1973.
Marjorie Weinman Sharmat, *Morris Brookside, a Dog,* Holiday House (New York, NY), 1973.
Tom Glazer, *Eye Winker, Tom Tinker, Chin Chopper,* Doubleday (New York, NY), 1973.
Fran Manushkin, *Bubblebath,* Harper (New York, NY), 1974.
William C. Grimm, *Indian Harvests,* McGraw-Hill (New York, NY), 1974.
Robert Burch, *Hut School and the Wartime Homefront Heroes,* Viking (New York, NY), 1974.
Marjorie Weinman Sharmat, *Morris Brookside Is Missing,* Holiday House (New York, NY), 1974.
Betsy Byars, *After the Goat Man,* Viking (New York, NY), 1974.
Polly Curran, *A Patch of Peas,* Golden Press (New York, NY), 1975.
Arnold Adoff, *Make a Circle, Keep Us In,* Delacorte (New York, NY), 1975.
Achim Broger, *Bruno,* Morrow (New York, NY), 1975.
Marty Kelly, *The House on Deer-Track Trail,* Harper (New York, NY), 1976.
Crescent Dragonwagon, *Windrose,* Harper (New York, NY), 1976.

Betty Boegehold, *Alone in the Cabin,* Harcourt (San Diego, CA), 1976.

Yoshiko Uchida, *Another Goodbye,* Allyn & Bacon (Newton, MA), 1976.

Richard Kennedy, *The Blue Stone,* Holiday House (New York, NY), 1976.

Jeanette Caines, *Daddy,* Harper (New York, NY), 1977.

Johanna Johnston, *Harriet and the Runaway Book: The Story of Harriet Beecher Stowe and Uncle Tom's Cabin,* Harper (New York, NY), 1977.

Arnold Adoff, *Tornado,* Delacorte (New York, NY), 1977.

Louise Dickerson, *Good Wife, Good Wife,* McGraw-Hill (New York, NY), 1977.

Arnold Adoff, *Under the Early Morning Trees,* Dutton (New York, NY), 1978.

Clyde Bulla and Michael Dyson, *Conquista,* Crowell (New York, NY), 1978.

Nancy Jewell, *Bus Ride,* Harper (New York, NY), 1978.

Fred Gipson, *Little Arliss,* Harper (New York, NY), 1978.

Fred Gipson, *Curly and the Wild Boar,* Harper (New York, NY), 1979.

Richard Kennedy, *Inside My Feet: The Story of a Giant,* Harper (New York, NY), 1979.

Carla Stevens, *Trouble for Lucy,* Houghton (Boston, MA), 1979.

Arnold Adoff, *I Am the Running Girl,* Harper (New York, NY), 1979.

Douglas Davis, *The Lion's Tail,* Atheneum (New York, NY), 1980.

Elizabeth Parsons, *The Upside-Down Cat,* Atheneum (New York, NY), 1981.

Linda Peavy, *Allison's Grandfather,* Scribner (New York, NY), 1981.

Byrd Baylor, *Moon Song,* Scribner (New York, NY), 1982.

Katherine Lasky, *Jem's Island,* Scribner (New York, NY), 1982.

Byrd Baylor, *Best Town in the World,* Scribner (New York, NY), 1983.

Thor Heyerdahl, *Kon Tiki: A True Adventure of Survival at Sea,* Random House (New York, NY), 1984.

Ann Turner, *Dakota Dugout,* Macmillan (New York, NY), 1985.

Ellen Howard, *Edith Herself,* Atheneum (New York, NY), 1987.

Ann Turner, *Nettie's Trip South,* Macmillan (New York, NY), 1987.

Susan Pearson, *Happy Birthday, Grampie,* Dial (New York, NY), 1987.

Emily Cheney Neville, *The Bridge,* Harper (New York, NY), 1988.

Alice Fleming, *The King of Prussia and a Peanut Butter Sandwich,* Scribner (New York, NY), 1988.

Susan Nunes, *Coyote Dreams,* Atheneum (New York, NY), 1988.

Ann Herbert Scott, *Someday Rider,* Clarion (New York, NY), 1989.

(With John Gurney) Della Rowland, *A World of Cats,* Contemporary Books (Chicago, IL), 1989.

Crescent Dragonwagon, *Winter Holding Spring,* Macmillan (New York, NY), 1990.

Eve Bunting, *The Wall,* Clarion (New York, NY), 1990.

Dorothy and Thomas Hoobler, *George Washington and Presidents' Day,* Silver Press (Englewood Cliffs, NJ), 1990.

Merry Banks, *Animals of the Night,* Scribner (New York, NY), 1990.

Liza Ketchum Murrow, *Dancing on the Table,* Holiday House (New York, NY), 1990.

Patricia Hubbell, *A Grass Green Gallop,* Atheneum (New York, NY), 1990.

Eve Bunting, *Fly Away Home,* Clarion (New York, NY), 1991.

Constance Levy, *I'm Going to Pet a Worm Today, and Other Poems,* McElderry Books (New York, NY), 1991.

Virginia T. Gross, *The Day It Rained Forever: A Story of the Johnstown Flood,* Viking (New York, NY), 1991.

Kathleen V. Kudlinski, *Pearl Harbor Is Burning,* Viking (New York, NY), 1991.

Shulamith Levey Oppenheim, *The Lily Cupboard,* HarperCollins (New York, NY), 1992.

Byrd Baylor, *One Small Blue Bead,* Scribner (New York, NY), 1992.

Ann Turner, *Katie's Trunk,* Macmillan (New York, NY), 1992.

Kate Aver, *Joey's Way,* McElderry Books (New York, NY), 1992.

Ann Herbert Scott, *A Brand Is Forever,* Clarion (New York, NY), 1993.

Eve Bunting, *Someday a Tree,* Clarion (New York, NY), 1993.

Kathleen V. Kudlinski, *Lone Star,* Viking (New York, NY), 1994.

Kathleen V. Kudlinski, *Earthquake,* Viking (New York, NY), 1994.

Eve Bunting, *A Day's Work,* Clarion (New York, NY), 1994.

Nancy Luenn, *SQUISH! A Wetland Walk,* Atheneum (New York, NY), 1994.

Wendy Kesselman, *Sand in My Shoes,* Hyperion (New York, NY), 1995.

D. Anne Love, *Bess's Log Cabin Quilt,* Holiday House (New York, NY), 1995.

D. Anne Love, *Dakota Spring,* Holiday House (New York, NY), 1995.

Sue Alexander, *Sara's City,* Clarion (New York, NY), 1995.

Eve Bunting, *Train to Somewhere,* Clarion (New York, NY), 1996.

Barbara A. Steiner, *Desert Trip,* Sierra Club Books (San Francisco, CA), 1996.

Ellen Howard, *The Log Cabin Quilt,* Holiday House (New York, NY), 1996.

Linda Oatman High, *A Christmas Star,* Holiday House (New York, NY), 1997.

Faye Gibbons, *Hook Moon Night: Spooky Tales from the Georgia Mountains,* Morrow Junior Books (New York, NY), 1997.

Rukhsana Khan, *The Roses in My Carpets,* Holiday House (New York, NY), 1998.

Eve Bunting, *Rudi's Pond,* Clarion Books (New York, NY), 1999.

Eleanor Coerr, *Sadako and the Thousand Paper Cranes,* Putnam (New York, NY), 1999.

Jean Fritz, *Why Not, Lafayette?,* G.P. Putnam's Sons (New York, NY), 1999.

Katherine Kirkpatrick, *Redcoats and Petticoats,* Holiday House (New York, NY), 1999.

Stewart Ross, *Mark Twain and Huckleberry Finn,* Viking (New York, NY), 1999.

Jane Resh Thomas, *The Snoop,* Clarion Books (New York, NY), 1999.

Sherry Garland, *Voices of the Alamo,* Scholastic (New York, NY), 2000.

Steven Kroll, *William Penn: Founder of Pennsylvania,* Holiday House (New York, NY), 2000.

Ellen Howard, *The Log Cabin Christmas,* Holiday House (New York, NY), 2000.

Frederick Lipp, *The Caged Birds of Phnom Penh,* Holiday House (New York, NY), 2001.

Julian Scheer, *By the Light of the Captured Moon,* Holiday House (New York, NY), 2001.

Julian Scheer, *A Thanksgiving Turkey,* Holiday House (New York, NY), 2001.

Ellen Howard, *The Log Cabin Church,* Holiday House (New York, NY), 2002.

Fran Manushkin, *Baby, Come Out!,* Star Bright Books (New York, NY), 2002.

Mike Spradlin, *The Legend of Blue Jacket,* HarperCollins (New York, NY), 2002.

David A. Adler, *A Picture Book of Lewis and Clark,* Holiday House (New York, NY), 2003.

Betty Ren Wright, *The Blizzard,* Holiday House (New York, NY), 2003.

Gwenyth Swain, *I Wonder as I Wander,* Eerdman's (Grand Rapids, MI), 2003.

Leslea Newman, *The Best Cat in the World,* Eerdmans (Grand Rapids, MI), 2004.

Laurie Lawlor, *The School at Crooked Creek,* Holiday House (New York, NY), 2004.

Barbara H. Cole, *Wash Day,* Star Bright Books (New York, NY), 2004.

Miriam Cohen, *My Big Brother,* Star Bright Books (New York, NY), 2005.

David A. Adler and Michael S. Adler, *A Picture Book of Samuel Adams,* Holiday House (New York, NY), 2005.

Elizabeth van Steenwyk, *Prairie Christmas,* Eerdman's (Grand Rapids, MI), 2006.

Ellen Howard, *The Log Cabin Wedding,* Holiday House (New York, NY), 2006.

Sherry Garland, *The Buffalo Soldier,* Pelican (Gretna, LA), 2006.

Miriam Cohen, *First Grade Takes a Test,* Star Bright Books (New York, NY), 2006.

David A. Adler and Michael S. Adler, *A Picture Book of John Hancock,* Holiday House (New York, NY), 2007.

Barbara H. Cole, *Anna and Natalie,* Star Bright Books (New York, NY), 2007.

Ruth Vander Zee, *Always with You,* Eerdman's (Grand Rapids, MI), 2008.

Miriam Cohen, *Jim's Dog, Muffins,* Star Bright Books (New York, NY), 2008.

Miriam Cohen, *Liar, Liar, Pants on Fire!,* Star Bright Books (New York, NY), 2008.

Miriam Cohen, *Tough Jim,* Star Bright Books (New York, NY), 2008.

David A. Adler and Michael S. Adler, *A Picture Book of Dolley and James Madison,* Holiday House (New York, NY), 2009.

Miriam Cohen, *Bee My Valentine,* Star Bright Books (Long Island City, NY), 2009.

Miriam Cohen, *Layla's Head Scarf,* Star Bright Books (Long Island City, NY), 2009.

Miriam Cohen, *Will I Have a Friend?,* Star Bright Books (Long Island City, NY), 2009.

Alice DeLaCroix, *The Best Horse Ever,* Holiday House (New York, NY), 2010.

David A. Adler and Michael S. Adler, *A Picture Book of John and Abigail Adams,* Holiday House (New York, NY), 2010.

Works featuring Himler's art have been translated into other languages, including Dutch and Japanese.

ILLUSTRATOR; "FIRST AMERICANS" SERIES BY VIRGINIA DRIVING HAWK SNEVE

The Sioux, Holiday House (New York, NY), 1993.
The Navajos, Holiday House (New York, NY), 1993.
The Seminoles, Holiday House (New York, NY), 1994.
The Nez Perce, Holiday House (New York, NY), 1994.
The Hopis, Holiday House (New York, NY), 1995.
The Iroquois, Holiday House (New York, NY), 1995.
The Cherokees, Holiday House (New York, NY), 1996.
The Cheyenne, Holiday House (New York, NY), 1996.
The Apaches, Holiday House (New York, NY), 1997.

Sidelights

An award-winning artist, Ronald Himler has earned recognition for crafting beautifully executed illustrations that appear in more than 150 children's books. In addition to his self-illustrated titles and the works he has illustrated for writers such as Eve Bunting, Jean Fritz, Ellen Howard, and David A. Adler, Himler has also created cover art for dozens of young-adult books. In creating his images, he employs a variety of artistic media, including watercolor, oils, gouache, and pencil. His characteristically gentle and sensitive depictions of the characters that populate these works have earned Himler critical praise as well as a wide and appreciative readership.

Raised in Cleveland, Ohio, Himler spent many childhood hours immersed in drawing, especially during the weekly trips he took to his grandmother's house where he spent his time sketching at the dining-room table. According to the artist, drawing has been such a constant part of his life that it has almost seemed as though art chose him rather than vice versa. After graduating from high school, he studied painting at the Cleveland Institute of Art, and went on to graduate school at the Cranbrook Academy of Art in Bloomfield Hills,

Himler captures the joy of a young boy exploring his culture in his art-work for Eleanor Coerr's **Sadako and the Thousand Paper Crane.** (Il-lustration copyright © 1979 by Ronald Himler. Reproduced in the U.K. by permission of the artist from Carol Bancroft & Friends, in the rest of the world by permission of G.P. Putnam's Sons, an imprint of Penguin Putnam Books for Young Readers, a division of Penguin Young Readers Group, a member of Penguin Group (USA) Inc., 345 Hudson Street, New York, NY 10014. All rights reserved.)

Michigan. Thereafter, Himler worked in various positions as a commercial artist, including a stint as a technical sculptor at the General Motors Technical Center and also as a toy designer and sculptor for two companies.

Early in his career, Himler decided to travel throughout Europe and Scandinavia, doing independent research at the Louvre in Paris, at the Uffizi Galleries in Florence, and at Amsterdam's Rijksmuseum. His tours through some of the world's finest collections of fine art broadened the scope of Himler's own painting, while the contacts he made with people of so many different cultures increased his sensitivity to the diversity of the world's peoples. Upon returning to the United States, Himler was determined to pursue a career as an illustrator of children's books. His first project was creating art for a verse anthology titled *Glad Day, and Other Classical Poems for Children,* which was published in 1972, the same year the artist married Ann Danowitz. This illustration project was quickly followed by others, in-

cluding drawings to accompany a work of nonfiction titled *Exploring a Coral Reef.* Requests for illustrations for other books continued to come his way, and Himler was soon bringing to life texts by a wide variety of popular children's writers, among them Betsy Byars, Tom Glazer, Marjorie Weinman Sharmat, and Charlotte Zolotow.

In 1974 Himler and his wife collaborated on the children's book *Little Owl, Keeper of the Trees,* with Himler also providing the illustrations. Comprising three tales that center on a young owl living high up in a sycamore tree, *Little Owl, Keeper of the Trees* weaves magic into the world of forest-dwelling animals through the character of Jonas, a small, friendly monster that possesses special powers. Himler went on to write two other books, including his self-illustrated *The Girl on the Yellow Giraffe.* Calling the book "an affectionate celebration of a child's imaginative powers," *Booklist* reviewer Denise M. Wilms praised *The Girl on the Yellow Giraffe* as an effective portrayal of a child's imaginary world. Himler wrote *The Girl on the Yellow Giraffe* for his daughter, Anna; four years later, he produced *Wake up, Jeremiah* for his son, Peer. Accompanied by a minimal text, Himler's impressionist-style, full-color illustrations depict a young boy's excitement at the start of a new day. Getting up extra early to watch the sunrise from the top of a hill near his home, Jeremiah then rushes home to share this fresh new day with his drowsy parents. "The evolution of dawn—from early murk to resplendent full light—in Mr. Himler's illustrations represent his best, most colorful performance to date," remarked *New York Times Book Review* contributor George A. Woods.

Reviewing Himler's next self-illustrated title, *Six Is So Much Less than Seven,* a *Kirkus Reviews* writer called the picture book a "touching tribute to pets and how they enrich our lives." The work tells of an elderly farmer who goes about his daily activities, all the while accompanied by six cats. However, there is an underlying feeling of sadness in the scenes, and the reader learns why toward the end of the day when the man goes to visit the grave of a seventh feline. The somber tone brightens, however, during the last activity of the day: the man then goes to visit a cat and her four new kittens. The *Kirkus Reviews* critic, in addition to praising Himler's gentle illustrations and "trademark soft watercolors," described *Six Is So Much Less than Seven* "soothing" for anyone getting over the loss of a pet.

An original book by Himler, *Dancing Boy* is a wordless tale that follows a youngster who, dancing through a small town without any clothes on, inspires all the children who see him to follow his happy and carefree example. In Himler's pen-and-watercolor art, the nudity of the young figures is depicted in an innocent fashion, and no objectionable body parts are exposed. Although *School Library Journal* contributor Rachel G. Payne noted that Himler's story is more a "nostalgia for the innocence of childhood lost" than a story for children, *Dancing Boy* is nonetheless successful as a "provocative and artful reverie."

In illustrating the works of other authors, Himler must sometimes deal with complex, emotional-laden subjects. In Eve Bunting's *Fly Away Home,* for example, a homeless young boy and his out-of-work dad are depicted by Himler in muted shades of brown and blue, and he places father and son at the edge of the page to symbolize their existence on the fringes of society. "Himler matches Bunting's understated text with gentle sensibility," noted a *Kirkus Reviews* contributor. Zena Sutherland, writing in the *Bulletin of the Center for Children's Books,* similarly noted that "Himler's quiet paintings echo the economy and the touching quality of the story," and *Horn Book* critic Ann A. Flowers commented that "the yearning sadness" of Bunting's tale "is reflected in the subtle, expressive watercolors."

Other collaborations between Himler and Bunting include *The Wall, Someday a Tree, A Day's Work,* and *A Train to Somewhere.* In a review of *The Wall,* which sensitively presents a boy's impressions of a visit to Washington, DC's Vietnam War Memorial, Wilms maintained that "Himler's intense, quiet watercolors capture the dignity of the setting as Bunting's story reaches right to the heart of deep emotions." In her *Booklist* review of *Someday a Tree,* Hazel Rochman noted that "Himler's watercolors express the quiet harmony" of the ecological fable's setting, and a *Publishers Weekly* critic maintained that "nostalgia and timelessness merge seamlessly in this uncommonly evocative picture book." The *Publishers Weekly* contributor also lauded Himler's "delicate paintings," noting that they "movingly reinforce" Bunting's message.

In *A Day's Work* a Mexican-American boy finds work for his Mexican-born grandfather. A story of integrity and honesty, Bunting's story is aided by Himler's "expressive, gestural watercolors," according to a reviewer for *Publishers Weekly,* the critic adding that the artwork "invokes both the harsh and the tender landscapes" of

Himler's illustrations capture the texture of pioneering life in Ellen Howard's **The Log Cabin Quilt.** (Illustration copyright © 1996 by Ronald Himler. Reproduced by permission of Holiday House, Inc.)

the young boy's world. In *Train to Somewhere,* Bunting's story of an orphan train that carried New York children to the Midwest in the late nineteenth century, readers meet Marianne, a girl nobody wants. "Himler's paintings in watercolor and gouache set the story against a bleak Midwestern fall landscape," Rochman remarked, while a *Publishers Weekly* reviewer deemed the book a "characteristically incisive collaboration" featuring artwork that is "at once sobering and uplifting—and assuredly memorable."

Himler is particularly noted for his depiction of the life and history of the American West and of the Native Americans who made that region their home. Praised by critics are the illustrations he created for the "First Americans" series, books written by Virginia Driving Hawk Sneve that focus on Native-American tribal culture. Series titles include *The Nez Perce, The Sioux,* and *The Seminoles,* the last which *School Library Journal* contributor M. Colleen McDougall noted: "Himler's illustrations are the book's high point" and his "figures and landscapes are both aesthetically pleasing and pertinent to the discussion." A *Publishers Weekly* reviewer praised the "striking oil paintings" Himler contributed to both *The Sioux* and *The Navajos,* while *School Library Journal* contributor Jacqueline Elsner remarked in a review of *The Cherokees* that the artist's "familiar watercolors, rich, warm, and serene, grace the text." Reviewing *The Cherokees,* Elizabeth S. Watson commented in *Horn Book* that any book that opens with "a wonderfully clear, cleanly drawn map starts out on the right foot." Writing in *Booklist,* Rochman maintained that in *The Apaches* Himler provides young readers with "a handsomely illustrated overview" of tribal traditions via "warm watercolors" full of detail about clothing and daily life.

Other books featuring Himler's art that focus on life along America's western frontier include the ranch stories of Ann Herbert Scott—*Someday Rider* and *A Brand Is Forever*—as well as Byrd Baylor's story collection *Moon Song.* His art also brings to life Barbara A. Steiner's *Desert Trip* and D. Anne Love's *Bess's Log Cabin Quilt* and *Dakota Spring,* the last two which focus on a family making a home on the Dakota prairie. According to Rochman, Himler's watercolors for *Desert Trip* "show the wide open spaces, the astonishing rock formations," and even the amazing detail when viewing a single flower close up.

In *The Buffalo Soldier* Sherry Garland offers a fictional retelling of the creation of six African-American military units in 1866. Nicknamed "buffalo soldiers" by Cheyenne warriors, the troops gained notice for their courage, loyalty, and fighting ability. "Himler's vibrant illustrations capture the broad vistas of western landscape," Kay Weisman noted in *Booklist.* Set in Nebraska in 1880, Elizabeth van Steenwyk's *Prairie Christmas* centers on a youngster who must accompany her mother, a doctor, when she is called to deliver a baby on Christmas Eve. Here "Himler's pencil-and-

watercolor illustrations bring the setting . . . to life and include many details of pioneer existence," remarked Weisman. Nancy Menaldi-Scanlan, writing in *School Library Journal,* maintained that the combination of van Steenwyk's text and Himler's art help "contrast the poverty of the setting with the richness of the characters' feelings."

More tales of America's pioneering days are brought to life through Himler's collaboration with author Ellen Howard. *The Log Cabin Quilt* deals with the Freshwater family as they move from Carolina to Michigan via wagon train, building a log cabin for their new home. In *Booklist* Phelan described the book as "sensitively written and illustrated," and praised Himler's "impressionistic paintings [which] have a rather muted palette." The family saga progresses in *Log Cabin Christmas,* in which Himler "capture[s] the cramped, rustic, hard-lived conditions in a log cabin," according to a *School Library Journal* contributor. Other installments include *The Log Cabin Church* and *The Log Cabin Wedding.* Himler's illustrations for *The Log Cabin Church* "accurately show the life led by pioneers," noted a *Kirkus Reviews* critic, the writer concluding that the book is "an effort doubly blessed." Reviewing *The Log Cabin Wedding,* Rochman noted that the book's pencil illustrations "express the intense feelings and connections among the people in the small cabin." Reviewing Himler's illustrations for Sherry Garland's *Voices of the*

Himler and Howard continue their collaboration in their history-themed chapter book The Log Cabin Wedding. (Illustration copyright © 2006 by Ronald Himler. Reproduced by permission of Holiday House, Inc.)

Alamo, Ruth Semrau wrote in *School Library Journal* that the book's "outstanding double-page watercolors depict characters, sweeping landscapes, [and] battle scenes" that figure in a crucial moment in Texas history.

Expanding his focus on U.S. history, Himler has also created art for picture-book biographies such as Steven Kroll's *William Penn: Founder of Pennsylvania,* and a series of works by the father-and-son team of David A. Alder and Michael S. Alder that includes *A Picture Book of John Hancock* and *A Picture Book of Samuel Adams.* Reviewing *A Picture Book of John Hancock,* Jody Kopple noted in *School Library Journal* that the artist's "muted" images "offer visual clues to historical events." A timely work for younger children, David A. Adler's *A Picture Book of Lewis and Clark,* which celebrates the 200th anniversary of Meriwether Lewis and William Clark's famed expedition to the Pacific, also benefits from the Himler touch. According to Phelan, "Himler's impressionistic paintings include . . . dramatic scenes from their adventures."

Himler also collaborated with the Adlers on *A Picture Book of John and Abigail Adams,* a look at the second president of the United States and his wife, an early advocate of women's rights. Phelan applauded Himler's "graceful and well-composed drawings," and in *School Library Journal,* Lucinda Snyder Whitehurst commented that the illustrations "provide a sense of the time period for young readers." *A Picture Book of Dolley and James Madison,* another work by the Adlers, focuses on the man known as the "Father of the Constitution" and his spouse, one of the most popular First Ladies in American history. "Himler's soft watercolors and wispy lines suit the historical setting and balance the substantial text," observed a contributor in *Kirkus Reviews.* A critic in *Publishers Weekly* also praised Himler's paintings, noting that "their strength lies in evoking the dress, furnishings and architecture of the period."

Himler moves forward in time to the Great Depression of the early twentieth century in his work for Linda Oatman High's *A Christmas Star,* in which a congregation's faith as well as a bit of Yuletide magic come to play in making the season a merry one for a little girl. A contributor to *Publishers Weekly* praised the book's art, which "creates a sparse, snowy countryside and a cast of characters," according to the reviewer. Rochman noted in *Booklist* that Himler's pictures of snow in "blue-toned moonlight" contrast with the interior of the church, depicted as "cozy" due to the artist's use of "warm shades of brown." Another work that hails from the same era and season, Betty Ren Wright's *The Blizzard* tells an "evocative" story of rural neighborliness in which Himler depicts the travails of a group of stranded students with a "golden glow" that reflects the story's good will, according to *Booklist* critic Ilene Cooper.

Reflecting his versatility, Himler imbues his work for picture books such as Rukhsana Khan's *The Roses in My Carpets* and Eleanor Coerr's *Sadako and the Thou-*sand *Paper Cranes* with an appropriately international flavor. Khan's story follows a day in the life of a young Afghani refugee who has survived the aerial bombing that killed his father, while Coerr's tale tells the true story of a Japanese girl whose promise is cut short when she falls ill with leukemia as a result of the Hiroshima bombing. In *The Roses in My Carpets* "Himler paints the family with dignity and warmth," a reviewer declared in *Publishers Weekly,* "enveloping them in earth-colored, rosy tones and the details of daily life." Also praising the work, *Booklist* critic Linda Perkins deemed *The Roses in My Carpets* "a rare and welcome glimpse into a culture children usually don't see."

Reviewing Himler's illustrations for Frederick Lipp's *The Caged Birds of Phnom Penh,* which tells the story of a girl living in the Cambodian capital who dreams of a place where birds can fly free, Anne Parker lauded Himler's "outstanding" artwork" in her *School Library Journal* review. The illustrator is able to "capture many different kinds of light," Parker explained, adding of *The Caged Birds of Phnom Penh* that the writing and art "work well together, providing an excellent window into another culture."

While Himler has won praise for capturing historical and cultural settings, many of his illustrations are paired with stories that focus on the everyday. In Julian Scheer's *By the Light of the Captured Moon,* for example, he depicts a group of young children as they gather fireflies, while his work for Lesléa Newman's *The Best Cat in the World* captures the poignancy of a child dealing with an elderly and infirm pet. Himler's art also breathes new life into a new edition of Miriam Cohen's *First Grade Takes a Test,* a story originally published in 1980 that is transformed into a multicultural picture book through the artist's "loose-lined, pencil-and-watercolor pictures," according to Stephanie Zvirin in *Booklist.* In another book by Cohen, *My Big Brother,* a story of brotherly love benefits from "Himler's artwork," which "sensitively depicts each character's emotions through body language and facial expressions," in Phelan's opinion. Noting the illustrator's ability to evoke the love within the close-knit African-American family at the heart of Cohen's tale, *School Library Journal* reviewer Jane Marino added that Himler's "soft, watercolor illustrations complement the narrative perfectly" and reinforce the story's "universal theme."

Anna and Natalie, a tale by Barbara H. Cole, centers on a disabled third grader who often finds herself overlooked by her classmates. Encouraged by her teacher, Anna enters a letter-writing contest, with the winner chosen to lay a wreath at the Tomb of the Unknown Solider. After her entry—which ends "From Natalie (with help from Anna)"—is selected, the youngster arrives at the ceremony with Natalie, her seeing-eye dog. Blair Christolon noted in *School Library Journal* that Himler's artwork "dramatically fills the spreads."

Himler teams up with David A. Adler and son Michael S. Adler to produce the visual history A Picture Book of John and Abigail Adams. (Illustration copyright © 2010 by Ronald Himler. Reproduced by permission of Holiday House, Inc.)

Based on an incident from the Vietnam War, Ruth Vander Zee's *Always with You* concerns Kim, a young Vietnamese girl who, during the bombing of her village, witnesses her mother's death. Kim is later rescued by U.S. soldiers who take her to an orphanage, which offers safety and security. Here Himler's muted watercolors illustrations "do more to deglorify warfare than any amount of adult preaching," Marian Drabkin wrote in *School Library Journal* review of *Always with You*.

Biographical and Critical Sources

BOOKS

Children's Book Illustration and Design, edited by Julie Cummins, PBC/Library of Applied Design (New York, NY), 1992, pp. 70-72.

Kingman, Lee, and others, *Illustrators of Children's Books 1967-1976,* Horn Book (Boston, MA), 1978, p. 126.

Ward, Martha E., and Dorothy A. Marquardt, *Illustrators of Books for Young People,* Scarecrow Press (Metuchen, NJ), 1975, p. 75.

PERIODICALS

Booklist, October 1, 1976, Denise M. Wilms, review of *The Girl on the Yellow Giraffe,* p. 252; April 1, 1990, Denise M. Wilms, review of *The Wall,* p. 1544; March 1, 1993, Hazel Rochman, review of *Someday a Tree,* p. 1234; April 1, 1993, Ilene Cooper, review of *A Brand Is Forever,* p. 1434; February 15, 1995, Kay Weisman, review of *Bess's Log Cabin,* p. 1085; June 1, 1995, Carolyn Phelan, review of *Sand in My Shoes,* p. 1786; October 1, 1995, Stephanie Zvirin, review of *Sara's City,* p. 325; November 15, 1995, Carolyn Phelan, review of *Dakota Spring,* pp. 559-560; February 1, 1996, Hazel Rochman, review of *Train to Some-where*, p. 930; April 15, 1996, Hazel Rochman, review of *Desert Trip*, p. 1444; December 15, 1996, Carolyn Phelan, review of *The Log Cabin Quilt*, p. 731; April 1, 1997, Hazel Rochman, review of *The Apaches*, p. 1332; September 1, 1997, Hazel Rochman, review of *A Christmas Star*, p. 139; November 15, 1998, Linda Perkins, review of *The Roses in My Carpet*, p. 596; March 1, 1999, Susan Dove Lempke, review of *Mark Twain and Huckleberry Finn*, p. 1210; April 1, 2001, Gillian Engberg, review of *The Caged Birds of Phnom Penh*, p. 1479; May 1, 2001, GraceAnne A. DeCandido, review of *By the Light of the Captured Moon*, p. 1692; September 1, 2001, Hazel Rochman, review of *A Thanksgiving Turkey*, p. 122; October 1, 2002, Kay Weisman, review of *The Log Cabin Church*, p. 345; November 1, 2002, Linda Perkins, review of *The Legend of Blue Jacket*, p. 489; July, 2003, Ilene Cooper, review of *The Blizzard*, p. 1887; April 15, 2004, Julie Cummins, review of *The School at Crooked Creek*, p. 1443; September 1, 2004, Hazel Rochman, review of *Wash Day*, p. 130; November 15, 2004, Hazel Rochman, review of *The Girl on the Yellow Giraffe*, p. 590; January 1, 2005, Carolyn Phelan, review of *My Big Brother*, p. 852; June 1, 2005, Carolyn Phelan, review of *A Picture Book of Samuel Adams*, p. 1815; September 15, 2006, Kay Weisman, review of *Prairie Christmas*, p. 64, and Hazel Rochman, review of *The Log Cabin Wedding*, p. 71; November 1, 2006, Kay Weisman, review of *The Buffalo Soldier*, p. 60; November 15, 2006, Stephanie Zvirin, review of *First Grade Takes a Test*, p. 52; May 1, 2007, Carolyn Phelan, review of *A Picture Book of John Hancock*, p. 94; February 15, 2008, Hazel Rochman, review of *Always with You*, p. 78; February 1, 2010, Carolyn Phelan, review of *A Picture Book of John and Abigail Adams*, p. 52.

Bulletin of the Center for Children's Books, May, 1991, Zena Sutherland, review of *Fly Away Home*, p. 212; October, 1994, review of *A Day's Work*, pp. 38-39; June, 1995, review of *Bess's Log Cabin Quilt*, p. 352; October, 1996, review of *The Log Cabin Quilt*, p. 64; October, 2001, review of *A Thanksgiving Turkey*, p. 75; April, 2003, review of *A Picture Book of Lewis and Clark*, p. 302; November, 2003, Elizabeth Bush, review of *The Blizzard*, p. 130; April, 2004, Elizabeth Bush, review of *The School at Crooked Creek*, p. 334.

Childhood Education, winter, 2000, Smita Guha, review of *William Penn: Founder of Pennsylvania*, p. 107; winter, 2008, Chris Grissom, review of *Anna and Natalie*, p. 126.

Horn Book, July-August, 1991, Ann A. Flowers, review of *Fly Away Home*, p. 445; May-June, 1993, Elizabeth S. Watson, review of *A Brand Is Forever*, pp. 330-331; May-June, 1996, Elizabeth S. Watson, review of *The Cherokees*, p. 353; November-December, 1999, Margaret A. Bush, review of *Why Not, Lafayette?*, p. 756; July, 2002, review of *Sadako and the Thousand Paper Cranes*, p. 425.

Kirkus Reviews, February 1, 1991, review of *Fly Away Home*, p. 172; July 15, 2002, review of *Six Is So Much Less than Seven*, p. 1033; August 1, 2002, review of *The Log Cabin Church*, p. 1133; March 15, 2003, re-

view of *A Picture Book of Lewis and Clark*, p. 458; July 15, 2003, review of *The Blizzard*, p. 969; January 1, 2004, review of *The Best Cat in the World*, p. 40; March 15, 2004, review of *The School at Crooked Creek*, p. 272; October 1, 2004, review of *The Girl on the Yellow Giraffe*, p. 961; January 15, 2005, review of *My Big Brother*, p. 118; October 1, 2006, review of *The Long Cabin Wedding*, p. 1016; November 1, 2006, review of *Prairie Christmas*, p. 1134; January 1, 2009, review of *A Picture Book of Dolley and James Madison*.

New York Times Book Review, October 28, 1979, George A. Woods, review of *Wake up, Jeremiah*, p. 18; May 30, 1993, Marianne Partridge, review of *A Brand Is Forever*, p. 19.

Publishers Weekly, May 21, 1982, review of *Moon Song*, p. 76; March 15, 1993, review of *Someday a Tree*, pp. 86-87; March 29, 1993, review of *A Brand Is Forever*, p. 56; November 8, 1993, review of *The Sioux* and *The Navajos*, p. 80; August 8, 1994, review of *A Day's Work*, pp. 434-435; February 5, 1996, review of *Train to Somewhere*, p. 89; October 6, 1997, review of *A Christmas Star*, p. 55; October 5, 1998, review of *The Roses in My Carpet*, p. 90; September 20, 1999, review of *Why Not, Lafayette?*, p. 89; March 27, 2000, review of *Train to Somewhere*, p. 83; February 26, 2001, review of *By the Light of the Captured Moon*, p. 85; March 5, 2001, review of *The Caged Birds of Phnom Penh*, p. 79; March 26, 2001, review of *Why Not, Lafayette?*, p. 95; September 24, 2001, review of *A Thanksgiving Turkey*, p. 46; September 8, 2003, review of *The Blizzard*, p. 76; September 22, 2003, review of *I Wonder as I Wander*, p. 68; February 2, 2004, review of *The Best Cat in the World*, p. 75; February 2, 2009, review of *A Picture Book of Dolley and James Madison*, p. 49.

School Library Journal, May, 1993, Jacqueline Elsner, review of *Someday a Tree*, p. 81, and Charlene Strickland, review of *A Brand Is Forever*, p. 91; April, 1994, M. Colleen McDougall, reviews of *The Nez Perce*, *The Sioux*, and *The Seminoles*, p. 146; April, 1996, Jacqueline Elsner, review of *The Cherokees*, p. 130; October, 1996, Jane Class, review of *The Log Cabin Quilt*, p. 122; October, 1997, Jane Marino, review of *A Christmas Star*, p. 42; November, 1998, Diane S. Marton, review of *The Roses in My Carpets*, pp. 87-88; April, 1999, Beth Tegart, review of *Redcoats and Petticoats*, p. 100; May, 1999, Shawn Brommer, review of *Mark Twain and Huckleberry Finn*, p. 142; December, 1999, Marlene Gawron, review of *Why Not, Lafayette?*, pp. 149-150; April, 2000, Jackie Hechtkopf, review of *William Penn*, p. 122; June, 2000, Ruth Semrau, review of *Voices of the Alamo*, p. 164; October, 2000, review of *The Log Cabin Christmas*, p. 59; March, 2001, Gay Lynn van Vleck, review of *By the Light of the Captured Moon*, p. 220; May, 2001, Anne Parker, review of *The Caged Birds of Phnom Penh*, p. 128; September, 2001, Pamela K. Bomboy, review of *A Thanksgiving Turkey*, p. 205; October, 2002, Margaret Bush, review of *The Log Cabin Church*, p. 112; November, 2002, Dona Ratterree, review of *The Legend of Blue Jacket*, p. 150; October, 2003, Lisa Dennis, review of *The Blizzard*, p. 143;

February, 2004, Susan Hepler, review of *The Best Cat in the World,* p. 120; June, 2005, Suzanne Myers Harold, review of *A Picture Book of Samuel Adams,* p. 132; July, 2005, Jane Marino, review of *My Big Brother,* p. 71; September, 2005, Rachel G. Payne, review of *Dancing Boy,* p. 173; December, 2006, Pat Leach, review of *The Log Cabin Wedding,* p. 101; July, 2007, Jody Kopple, review of *A Picture Book of John Hancock,* p. 88; December, 2007, Blair Christolon, review of *Anna and Natalie,* p. 87; September, 2008, Marian Drabkin, review of *Always with You,* p. 160; March, 2009, Sarah O'Holla, review of *A Picture Book of Dolley and James Madison,* p. 130; June, 2010, Lucinda Snyder Whitehurst, review of, *A Picture Book of John and Abigail Adams,* p. 86.

ONLINE

Ronald Himler Home Page, http://www.ronhimler.com (September 21, 2011).

* * *

HIMLER, Ronald Norbert
See HIMLER, Ronald

* * *

HOLDER, Jimmy 1962-

Personal

Born 1962; married; children: two. *Education:* College degree.

Addresses

Home—Pasadena, CA. *Agent*—Shannon Associates, 333 W. 57th St., Ste. 809, New York, NY 10019. *E-mail*—jimmy615@att.net.

Career

Illustrator and storyboard artist. Freelance illustrator, beginning 1990; worked in advertising in Atlanta, GA.

Illustrator

Rick Walton, *Pig, Pigger, Piggest,* Gibbs-Smith (Salt Lake City, UT), 1997.

Rick Walton, *Why the Banana Split,* Gibbs Smith (Salt Lake City, UT), 1998.

Rick Walton, *That's What You Get!,* Gibbs Smith (Salt Lake City, UT), 2000.

David Sacks and Brian Ross, *Vigfus the Viking,* Idea & Design, 2008.

Rick Walton, *Pig, Pigger, Piggest: An Adventure in Comparing,* Gibbs Smith (Salt Lake City, UT), 2011.

Todd and Jedd Hafer, *Mischief from the Back Pew,* Bethany House (Bloomington, MN), 2011.

Contributor to periodicals, including *Archaeology, Christian Science Monitor, Delta Sky Magazine, Entrepreneur, Forbes, Inside Sports, Los Angeles Magazine, Saturday Evening Post, Staywell, Sunset, T.V. Guide,* the *Wall Street Journal,* and *Wireless Review.*

"CASTAWAYS" READER SERIES BY SANDY BEECH

Worst Class Trip Ever, Aladdin (New York, NY), 2005.

Weather's Here, Wish You Were Here, Aladdin (New York, NY), 2005.

Isle Be Seeing You, Aladdin (New York, NY), 2005.

"BARNACLE BARB AND HER PIRATE CREW" READER SERIES BY NADIA HIGGINS

Avast, Ye Dog Thief!, Magic Wagon (Edina, MN), 2008.

Aye, My Eye!, Magic Wagon (Edina, MN), 2008.

Blimey, That's Slimy!, Magic Wagon (Edina, MN), 2008.

Break a Sea Leg, Shrimp-breath!, Magic Wagon (Edina, MN), 2008.

Pegleg Gets Stumped, Magic Wagon (Edina, MN), 2008.

Jimmy Holder creates the art capturing the sports action in Rich Wallace's **Game-Day Jitters,** *part of the "Kickers" chapter-book series.* (Illustration copyright © 2011 by Jimmy Holder. Reproduced by permission of Alfred A. Knopf, an imprint of Random house Children's Books, a division of Random House, Inc.)

Walk the Plank, Plankton, Magic Wagon (Edina, MN), 2008.

"KICKERS" BEGINNING CHAPTER BOOK SERIES BY RICH WALLACE

Fake Out, Alfred A. Knopf (New York, NY), 2010.
The Ball Hogs, Alfred A. Knopf (New York, NY), 2010.
Benched, Alfred A. Knopf (New York, NY), 2010.
Game-day Jitters, Alfred A. Knopf (New York, NY), 2011.

Sidelights

Now based in California, artist Jimmy Holder started his career in Atlanta, Georgia, where he created story-boards for advertising campaigns. As the years went by, Holder became interested in other creative options, and in 1990 he relocated to southern California and embarked on a career as an illustrator. In addition to magazine ads, games, and packaging art, he has crafted illustrations for numerous books for young readers, among them stories by authors Sandy Beech, Rich Wallace, and Rick Walton, as well as by Nadia Higgins, whose amusing "Barnacle Barb and Her Pirate Crew" stories gain an extra helping of humor from Holder's cartoon art.

In Wallace's "Kickers" beginning chapter-book series, the author follows a fourth grader named Ben and his experiences as part of the Bobcats, a soccer team. Reviewing series installment *Benched* in *Booklist*, Carolyn Phelan cited Holder for his ability to "underscore the characters' emotions" in his illustrations for Wallace's text. *Game Day Jitters* finds Ben nervous about an upcoming playoff game, while in *Ball Hogs* an aggressive teammate causes tensions on and off the field. In reviewing the latter story, Phelan remarked on Holder's "lively black-and-white drawings," while Blair Christolon remarked in a *School Library Journal* review that the "pen-and-ink" artwork in *Ball Hogs* "augment[s] the enjoyment of the [book's] short chapters." Appraising the entire "Kickers" series, a *Kirkus Reviews* writer concluded that "Holder's simple sketches complement the straightforward narration, which will guide, if not inspire, maturing soccer players."

Walton and Holder "dish out a kid-tickling serving of humor" in *Why the Banana Split,* according to a *Publishers Weekly* critic, and here the illustrator's "fittingly exaggerated cartoons will wring chuckles" from young readers. The fun continues in *Pig, Pigger Piggest* as Walton gives a fresh twist to the traditional story about three little pigs by allowing three greedy witches to enter the mix. "Holder plays along with a jaunty, caricatured style," observed a second *Publishers Weekly* contributor, and "his slightly shiny, rotund pigs . . . give the impression of having been inflated to the point of bursting."

Biographical and Critical Sources

PERIODICALS

Booklist, May 15, 2010, Carolyn Phelan, review of *The Ball Hogs* p. 38; January 1, 2011, Carolyn Phelan, re-

Holder's illustration projects include creating the cartoon art for **Pig Pigger Piggest,** *a humorous story by Rick Walton.* (Illustration copyright © 1997 by Jimmy Holder. Reproduced by permission of Gibbs Smith.)

view of *Benched,* p. 106; April 1, 2011, Carolyn Phelan, review of *Game-Day Jitters,* p. 70.
Kirkus Reviews, May 15, 2010, review of *The Ball Hogs.*
Publishers Weekly, July 14, 1997, review of *Pig Pigger Piggest,* p. 83; October 26, 1998, review of *Why the Banana Split,* p. 65.
School Library Journal, September, 2010, Blair Christolon, review of *The Ball Hogs,* p. 135.

ONLINE

Jimmy Holder Home Page, http://www.jimmyholder.com (September 21, 2011).*

*   *   *

HOPCUS, Anastasia

Personal

Daughter of Peter Hopcus and Candace Camp (an author). *Hobbies and other interests:* Music, horror movies.

Addresses

Home—Manchaca, TX. *Agent*—Meredith Kaffel, Charlotte Sheedy Literary Agency, 928 Broadway, Ste. 901, New York, NY 10010.

Career

Author. Worked variously as an actor, bartender, and receptionist.

Writings

Shadow Hills, Egmont USA (New York, NY), 2010.

Sidelights

As the daughter of prolific romance writer Candace Camp, Anastasia Hopcus grew up around stories, and as a child she dreamed of being an actress and writing film scripts. As she gained more experience of the real world during her late teens, Hopcus's career plans grew more realistic, however, and she decided to channel her creative energy into writing young-adult fiction. Her first novel, *Shadow Hills,* spins a tale of romance and the supernatural into which "epidemics, genetics, and witchcraft intertwine," according to a *Publishers Weekly* contributor.

Cover of Anastasia Hopcus's well-received paranormal suspense novel **Shadow Hills.** (Photograph copyright © 2010 by Veer. Reproduced by permission of Egmont USA.)

California teen Persephone "Phe" Archer is the heroine of *Shadow Hills,* and when readers meet her Phe is attempting to discover the reason for her sister's tragic death. Inspired by entries in the girl's diary, she enrolls at Devenish, a private boarding school in Shadow Hills, Massachusetts, and a place that has haunted both her dreams and those of her late sister. Arriving in town, the West Coast teen immediately senses that something is wrong, and it is not just the town's quaint New England aura. Her dreams of the town had included a graveyard, and when she locates this resting place Phe realizes that everyone buried there has died of a strange illness. Meanwhile, those among the still-living seem to possess strange powers, among them Zach, a handsome but mysterious town resident who she feels drawn to. As the town's strange history gradually reveals itself, Phe realizes that she may play an important role in its future.

While noting that *Shadow Hills* is one of many stories in the growing paranormal romance genre, the *Publishers Weekly* contributor asserted that Hopcus's tale "carries a strong narrative momentum that should appeal to" teens. The novel is enriched by a "dark and believable setting," noted Shari Fesko, the *School Library Journal* contributor adding of *Shadow Hills* that the author's "rich use of language" combines with a cast of interesting characters to mark it as an entry into the supernatural romance genre "with more sweetness and fewer sexual themes."

"If you want to be a writer, be a writer," Hopcus posted on her Web log, encouraging those who share her dream of becoming a writer. "Don't listen to anyone who tells you it can't happen, and don't listen to yourself when you're thinking it can't happen, and most of all, don't give up. I thought about giving up several times, and now I'm just so grateful for my stubborn personality. I'm living my dream, and it was worth every rejection letter, every sleepless night, and every tear shed along the way."

Biographical and Critical Sources

PERIODICALS

Publishers Weekly, July 12, 2010, review of *Shadow Hills,* p. 48.
School Library Journal, August, 2010, Shari Fesko, review of *Shadow Hills,* p. 103.

ONLINE

Anastasia Hopcus Home Page, http://www.anastasiahopcus .com (October 29, 2011).
Anastasia Hopcus Web log, http://hopcusblog.com/ (October 29, 2011).*

J

JACK, Colin

Personal
Born in Vancouver, British Columbia, Canada; married; children: a son. *Education:* Attended Langara Fine Arts Program, 1998-2000; Capilano University, B.A. (commercial animation), 2002.

Addresses
Home—Toronto, Ontario, Canada. *Agent*—Kids Shannon, 333 W. 57th St., Ste. 809, New York, NY 10019. *E-mail*—colinjack8@gmail.com.

Career
Illustrator and character designer. Freelance animator and storyboard artist, with clients including Studio B. Productions, Nerd Corps Entertainment, Elliot Animation, 9story Entertainment, Atomic Cartoons, and Sony Pictures Animation. Capilano University, Vancouver, British Columbia, Canada, adjunct instructor, 2007.

Member
Association Internationale du Film d'Animation (ASIFA), Canadian Animation Resources.

Illustrator
Lori Degman, *One Zany Zoo,* Simon & Schuster Books for Young Readers (New York, NY), 2010.
Russell Punter, *Bad Jack Fox,* Usborne (London, England), 2011.

Biographical and Critical Sources

PERIODICALS

School Library Journal, July, 2010, Richelle Roth, review of *One Zany Zoo,* p. 58.

ONLINE

Colin Jack Interview Web log, http://colin-jack-interview.blogspot.com/ (October 14, 2011).
Colin Jack Web Log, http://jackomtablet.blogspot.com (October 14, 2011).*

* * *

JACOBUS, Tim 1959-

Personal
Born April 21, 1959, in NJ; married, 1980; wife's name Lisa (an artist); children: Jack. *Education:* Spectrum Institute for Advertising Arts, degree, 1981. *Hobbies and other interests:* Skiing.

Addresses
Home—Budd Lake, NJ. *E-mail*—tjacobus@optonline.net.

Career
Illustrator and animator. Worked variously as a machine operator, meter reader, and construction laborer; freelance illustrator, beginning c. 1981; illustrator of book covers for "Goosebumps" series, beginning 1991; D-Scape Interactive, director, beginning 2002. Kubert Art School, instructor, 1995-98. Presenter at schools.

Writings

ILLUSTRATOR

Ellen Conford, *My Sister the Witch,* Little Rainbow/Troll Associates (Mahwah, NJ), 1995.
Ellen Conford, *Norman Newman and the Werewolf of Walnut Street,* Little Rainbow/Troll Associates (Mahwah, NJ), 1995.

Kaza Kingsley, *The Search for Truth* ("Erec Rex" novel series), Simon & Schuster Books for Young Readers (New York, NY), 2009.

ILLUSTRATOR; "TELETUBBIES" SERIES BY ANDREW DAVENPORT; BASED ON THE TELEVISION PROGRAM

Merry Christmas, Teletubbies!, Scholastic (New York, NY), 1999.
The Happy Day, Scholastic (New York, NY), 1999.
The Snow Tubby, Scholastic (New York, NY), 2000.
Happy Time, Publications International (Lincolnwood, IL), 2001.
Teletubbies Love to Sing, Publications International (Lincolnwood, IL), 2001.

SELF-ILLUSTRATED

It Came from New Jersey!: My Life as an Artist, Scholastic (New York, NY), 1998.

Biographical and Critical Sources

BOOKS

Jacobus, Tim, *It Came from New Jersey!: My Life as an Artist,* Scholastic (New York, NY), 1998.

Tim Jacobus creates the scary artwork for the "Goosebumps" books by R.L. Stine, among them The Curse of the Mummy's Tomb. (Jacket cover copyright © 1993 by Scholastic Inc. Reproduced by permission of Scholastic Inc.)

PERIODICALS

School Library Journal, June, 1996, Gale W. Sherman, review of *My Sister the Witch,* p. 120; October, 2009, Eric Norton, review of *The Search for Truth,* p. 129.
Voice of Youth Advocates, June, 2009, Cindy Faughnan, review of *The Search for Truth,* p. 152.

ONLINE

Tim Jacobus Home Page, http://www.timjacobus.com (July 29, 2011).
Scholastic Web site, http://www.scholastic.com/ (October 1, 2011), "Tim Jacobus."*

*   *   *

JALALI, Reza

Personal

Born in Kurdistan, Iran; immigrated to United States as political refugee, c. 1985; married; children: two. *Education:* Earned bachelor's degree in India; Antioch University, M.A.; University of Southern Maine, M.F.A. *Religion:* Muslim. *Hobbies and other interests:* Soccer.

Addresses

Home—Falmouth, ME.

Career

Author and educator. Amnesty International, human-rights worker, beginning 1980s; University of Southern Maine, Portland, adjunct professor; Lewiston-Auburn College, Lewiston, ME, program coordinator of multicultural student affairs. Advocate of immigrant community in southern ME.

Awards, Honors

Maine Literary Award finalist for children's books, and *Skipping Stones* Honor Book selection, both 2011, both for *Moon Watchers.*

Writings

(Coauthor and author of foreword) *New Mainers,* Tilbury House (Gardiner, ME), 2009.
Moon Watchers: Shirin's Ramadan Miracle, illustrated by Anne Sibley O'Brien, Tilbury House (Gardiner, ME), 2010.
God Speaks in Many Accents, Tilbury House (Gardiner, ME), 2011.

Contributor to periodicals, including *Casco Bay Weekly, Deccan Herald, Dissident, Exiled Ink!, Free Press, Maine Progressive, Maine Sunday Telegram, Paivand,*

Portland Press Herald, and *Say.* Contributor to anthologies, including *Child Labor: A Global View,* Greenwood Press, 2004; *Middle East Suitcase Project* (multimedia), 2005; and *The World of Child Labor: An Historical and Regional Survey,* M.E. Sharpe, 2009.

Sidelights

Reza Jalali grew up in Kurdistan, Iran, where, as an ethnic Kurd he encountered discrimination. By the time he was a teen, Jalai and his family had gone into exile, and he attended college in India. Returning to Iran, Jalali attempted to publically promote his ethnic heritage, with the result that he became a political prisoner. With the help of Amnesty International, he became a U.S. citizen, and his appreciation for these efforts prompted him to work on the behalf of the London-based human-rights advocacy organization beginning in the 1980s. Although he has traveled to other parts of the globe that have been torn by cultural and racial antagonisms, Jalali has also continued his education in Maine, which he now considers his home. In his picture book *Moon Watchers: Shirin's Ramadan Miracle* Jalali introduces American children to a holiday tradition of his Muslim culture, drawing on a memorable experience from his Iranian childhood.

In *Moon Watchers* readers meet Shirin, a nine year old who lives in Maine and follows the Muslim faith of her family. As the calendar signals the approach of Ramadan, she and her father watch the night sky for the new moon, the official start of the month-long holy observance. In honor of Ramadan, Muslims fast during daylight hours, pray, and take extra time to do good works. Shirin's parents believe that she is too young to join in the family fast, unlike her twelve-year-old brother Ali. Fortunately, Grandmother is there with a story that suggests a way that the preteen can be included in the Ramadan fasting traditions. *Moon Watchers* also illustrates the true meaning of the holiday, inspiring Shirin to embrace the tradition of doing good deeds in a surprising way.

A "moving picture book," *Moon Watchers* introduces Muslim tradition in a story that also features "a lively drama of sibling rivalry," according to *Booklist* critic Hazel Rochman. A *Kirkus Reviews* critic recognized Jalali's "quiet story" as valuable for depicting a loving Muslim family in a manner contradicting "the often harmful messages seen in the media," and Fawzia Gilani-Williams asserted in *School Library Journal* that *Moon Watchers* is a "thought-provoking tale" in which the colorful watercolor illustrations by Anne Sibley O'Brien "evoke a culturally authentic Persian-American aesthetic."

Biographical and Critical Sources

PERIODICALS

Booklist, June 1, 2010, Hazel Rochman, review of *Moon Watchers: Shirin's Ramadan Miracle,* p. 76.

Kirkus Reviews, May 15, 2010, review of *Moon Watchers.*
School Library Journal, September, 2010, Fawzia Gilani-Williams, review of *Moon Watchers,* p. 126.

ONLINE

Tilbury House Web site, http://www.tilburyhouse.com/ (October 29, 2011), "Reza Jalali."
University of Southern Maine Web site, http://usm.maine.edu/ (March 10, 2008), Jenna Howard, "Iranian in Exile Makes USM Home."

*   *   *

JOHNSON, Mo 1966-

Personal

Born 1966, in Glasgow, Scotland; immigrated to Australia, c. 1991; married, 1991; children: one son. *Education:* University of Stirling, B.A., Dip.Ed.

Addresses

Home—Sydney, New South Wales, Australia. *E-mail*—mojohnson@bigpond.com.

Career

Educator and author. Teacher of English, drama/HSIE/RE in Sydney, New South Wales, Australia, until 2008; freelance writer; co-owner of a mortgage company in Sydney, beginning 2009.

Awards, Honors

Notable Book designation, Children's Book Council of Australia, 2008, for *Boofheads;* New South Wales Premiere's Reading Challenge listee, 2010, for *Noah's Garden.*

Writings

Boofheads, Walker Books (Newton, New South Wales, Australia), 2008.
Something More, Allen & Unwin (Crows Nest, New South Wales, Australia), 2009.
Noah's Garden: When Someone You Love Is in the Hospital, illustrated by Annabelle Josse, Candlewick Press (Sommerville, MA), 2010.

Also author of readers published in Australia, including *CU L8er, Let's Get Physical!,* and *Go for It!* Work anthologized in *Families in Focus, Nutting out Nutrition, Waterwise, Our Energy Choices, Australia, My Country!, Forever Friends, Are You Being Served?,* and *There's More to Me,* all Pearson Rigby; and *Chicken Soup for the Soul for Busy Moms* and *Chicken Soup for the Mother of Preschooler's Soul,* both Health Communications. Contributor of articles to periodicals.

Sidelights

Mo Johnson grew up in Scotland but moved to Australia after marrying a native of Down Uncer whom she met while traveling overseas. Johnson worked as a high-school English and drama teacher for twenty years and channeled her interest in writing into work creating educational texts and publishing articles in magazines. Then, in 2005, she began writing the manuscript that would become her second published novel, *Something More*. Geared for young-adult readers and focusing on a high schooler's difficulties adjusting to a long-distance move, *Something More* was preceded by the humorously titled and critically acclaimed *Boofheads*, another novel for teens. Johnson focuses on younger readers in *Noah's Garden: When Someone You Love Is in the Hospital*, a book illustrated by Annabelle Josse and her first work to be released in the United States. She has also contributed to two books in the inspirational "Chicken Soup for the Soul" series.

Noah's Garden was inspired by Johnson's visits with a good friend while the woman's infant daughter was hospitalized with a heart defect. The whole family spent many weeks living at the hospital which was treating the infant, and this experience was especially taxing on the patient's older brother, who missed playing with his new baby sister. In Johnson's story, Noah and his parents are staying at the hospital where his little sister, Jessica, is undergoing treatment for a life-threatening illness. The hospital garden soon becomes Noah's favorite place, and his imagination allows him to share the area with exotic animals and have adventures involving everything from pirates to penguins to seaplanes. However, for Noah, his favorite daydream is imagining the time when Jessica will be able to play in the garden with him. In her "gentle text," Johnson highlights the boy's "vivid imagination" as well as "the healing powers of nature, and the resilience of family members caring for each other," asserted Kay Weisman in her *Booklist* review of *Noah's Garden*. "Sensitively told and skillfully illustrated" by Josse, according to a *Publishers Weekly* contributor, Johnson's evocative story features a reassuring theme that will appeal to "the very young."

"*Something More* was the first book I ever wrote," Johnson noted on her home page. "It was pulled from a slush pile in 2005 and [took] . . . four years to come into being. If you are reading this and really want to be a writer, don't listen to people who say unknown writers have no chance of publication. Be patient, work hard, listen to all the advice you can get and refuse to give up. There could be something more waiting just around the corner for you."

Biographical and Critical Sources

PERIODICALS

Booklist, June 1, 2010, Kay Weisman, review of *Noah's Garden: When Someone You Love Is in the Hospital*, p, 93.
Publishers Weekly, May 24, 2010, review of *Noah's Garden*, p. 51.

ONLINE

Mo Johnson Home Page, http://www.mojohnson.com.au (September 29, 2011).

*   *   *

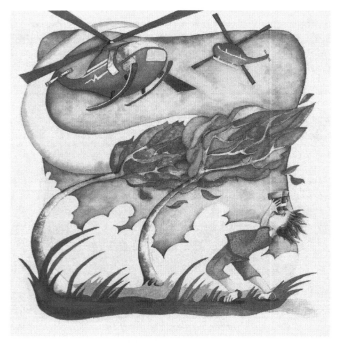

Mo Johnson tells a story that will inspire the curiosity of children in Noah's Garden, *a picture book featuring artwork by Annabelle Josse.* (Illustration copyright © 2010 by Annabelle Josse. Reproduced by permission of Candlewick Press, Somerville, MA on behalf of Walker Books Australia.)

JONES, Diana Wynne 1934-2011

Personal

Born August 16, 1934, in London, England; died of lung cancer, March 26, 2011, in Bristol, England; daughter of Richard Aneurin (an educator) and Marjorie (an educator) Jones; married John A. Burrow (a university professor), December 23, 1956; children: Richard, Michael, Colin. *Education:* St. Anne's College, Oxford, B.A., 1956.

Career

Writer, beginning 1965.

Member

Society of Authors, British Science Fiction Association.

Awards, Honors

Carnegie Medal commendation, 1975, for *Dogsbody;* London *Guardian* commendation, 1977, for *Power of Three;* Carnegie Medal commendation, 1977, and *Guardian* Award, 1978, both for *Charmed Life; Boston Globe/Horn Book* Honor Book selection, 1984, for *Archer's Goon;* Methuen Children's Award, and Carnegie Medal commendation, both 1988, both for *The Lives of Christopher Chant;* Mythopoeic Fantasy Award in children's category, 1996, for *The Crown of Dalemark,* 1999, for *Dark Lord of Derkholm;* Karl Edward Wagner Fantasy Award, British Fantasy Society, 1999; D.Litt., University of Bristol, 2006; Phoenix Award, 2006, for *Howl's Moving Castle;* Life Achievement Award, World Fantasy Awards, 2007.

Writings

FOR CHILDREN

Wilkins' Tooth, illustrated by Julia Rodber, Macmillan (London, England), 1973, published as *Witch's Business,* Dutton (New York, NY), 1974, reprinted, Greenwillow (New York, NY), 2002.

The Ogre Downstairs, Macmillan (London, England), 1974, Dutton (New York, NY), 1975.

Eight Days of Luke, Macmillan (London, England), 1975, Greenwillow (New York, NY), 1988.

Dogsbody, Macmillan (London, England), 1975, Greenwillow (New York, NY), 1977.

Power of Three, Macmillan (London, England), 1976, Greenwillow (New York, NY), 1977.

Who Got Rid of Angus Flint? (also see below), illustrated by John Sewell, Evans Brothers, 1978.

The Four Grannies (also see below), illustrated by Thelma Lambert, Hamish Hamilton (London, England), 1980.

The Homeward Bounders, Greenwillow (New York, NY), 1981, reprinted, Harper Trophy (New York, NY), 2002.

The Time of the Ghost, Macmillan (London, England), 1981, Greenwillow (New York, NY), 1996.

Warlock at the Wheel and Other Stories, Greenwillow (New York, NY), 1984.

Archer's Goon, Greenwillow (New York, NY), 1984, reprinted, 2003.

Fire and Hemlock, Greenwillow (New York, NY), 1985.

Howl's Moving Castle, Greenwillow (New York, NY), 1986, HarperCollins (London, England), 2009.

A Tale of Time City, Greenwillow (New York, NY), 1987.

Chair Person (also see below), illustrated by Glenys Ambrus, Hamish Hamilton (London, England), 1989, Puffin (New York, NY), 1991.

Wild Robert, illustrated by Emma Chichester-Clark, Methuen (London, England), 1989, Greenwillow (New York, NY) 2003.

Castle in the Air (sequel to *Howl's Moving Castle*), Greenwillow (New York, NY), 1991.

Aunt Maria, Greenwillow (New York, NY), 1991.

Black Maria, Methuen (London, England), 1991.

Yes, Dear (picture book), illustrated by Graham Philpot, Greenwillow (New York, NY), 1992.

Stopping for a Spell: Three Fantasies (includes *Chair Person, Who Got Rid of Angus Flint?,* and *The Four Grannies*), illustrated by Jos. A. Smith, Greenwillow (New York, NY), 1993.

Hexwood, Greenwillow (New York, NY), 1994.

Everard's Ride, NESFA (Framingham, MA), 1995.

The Tough Guide to Fantasyland, Vista (London, England), 1996, revised and updated edition, Firebird (New York, NY), 2006.

Minor Arcana, Gollancz (London, England), 1996.

Deep Secret, Gollancz (London, England), 1997, Tor (New York, NY), 1999.

Dark Lord of Derkholm, Greenwillow (New York, NY), 1998.

Seeing Is Believing: Seven Stories, Greenwillow (New York, NY), 1999.

Year of the Griffin (sequel to *Dark Lord of Derkholm*), Greenwillow (New York, NY), 2000.

Wild Robert, Greenwillow (New York, NY), 2003.

The Merlin Conspiracy, Greenwillow (New York, NY), 2003.

Unexpected Magic: Collected Stories, Greenwillow (New York, NY), 2004.

Enna Hittims, illustrated by Peter Utton, Barrington Stoke (Edinburgh, Scotland), 2006.

The Game (novella), Firebird (New York, NY), 2007.

House of Many Ways, Greenwillow Books (New York, NY), 2008.

Enchanted Glass, Greenwillow Books (New York, NY), 2010.

Earwig and the Witch, illustrated by Paul O. Zelinsky, Greenwillow Books (New York, NY), 2012.

FOR CHILDREN; "DALEMARK" CYCLE

Cart and Cwidder, Macmillan (London, England), 1975, Atheneum (New York, NY), 1977, reprinted, Harper-Trophy (New York, NY), 2001.

Drowned Ammet, Macmillan (London, England), 1977, Atheneum (New York, NY), 1978.

The Spellcoats, Atheneum (New York, NY), 1979.

The Crown of Dalemark, Methuen (London, England), 1993, Greenwillow (New York, NY), 1995.

The Dalemark Quartet (omnibus), two volumes, Eos (New York, NY), 2005.

FOR CHILDREN; "CHRESTOMANCI" CYCLE

Charmed Life, Greenwillow (New York, NY), 1977, HarperCollins Children's Books (London, England), 2007.

The Magicians of Caprona, Greenwillow (New York, NY), 1980, HarperCollins Children's Books (London, England), 2008.

Witch Week, Greenwillow (New York, NY), 1982, HarperCollins Children's Books (London, England), 2008.

The Lives of Christopher Chant, Greenwillow (New York, NY), 1988, HarperCollins Children's Books (London, England), 2008.

The Chronicles of Chrestomanci, Volume One (contains *Charmed Life* and *The Lives of Christopher Chant*), HarperCollins (New York, NY), 2001.

The Chronicles of Chrestomanci, Volume Two (contains *The Magicians of Caprona* and *Witch Week*), Harper-Collins (New York, NY), 2001.

Mixed Magics: Four Tales of Chrestomanci, Greenwillow (New York, NY), 2001.

Conrad's Fate, Greenwillow (New York, NY), 2005.

The Pinhoe Egg, Greenwillow Books (New York, NY), 2006.

FOR CHILDREN; PLAYS

The Batterpool Business, first produced in London, England, 1968.

The King's Things, first produced in London, England, 1970.

The Terrible Fisk Machine, first produced in London, England, 1971.

OTHER

Changeover (adult novel), Macmillan (London, England), 1970.

The Skiver's Guide, illustrated by Chris Winn, Knight Books, 1984, Barn Owl Books (London, England), 2006.

(Editor) *Hidden Turnings: A Collection of Stories through Time and Space,* Greenwillow (New York, NY), 1990.

A Sudden Wild Magic, Morrow (New York, NY), 1992.

(Editor) *Fantasy Stories,* illustrated by Robin Lawrie, Kingfisher (New York, NY), 1994, published as *Spellbound: Fantasy Stories,* Kingfisher (Boston, MA), 2007.

(Author of introduction) Louise Cooper, *Spiral Garden,* British Fantasy Society, 2000.

Contributor to books, including *The Cat-Flap and the Apple Pie,* W.H. Allen, 1979; *Hecate's Cauldron,* DAW Books, 1981; *Hundreds and Hundreds,* Puffin, 1984; *Dragons and Dreams,* Harper, 1986; and *Guardian Angels,* Viking Kestrel, 1987.

Adaptations

Archer's Goon was adapted as a television series by Marilyn Fox, 1992; *Howl's Moving Castle* was adapted as the animated film *Hauro no ugoku shiro* by Japanese filmmaker Hayao Miyazaki, 2004.

Sidelights

When Diana Wynne Jones died in 2011, she left behind a rich literary legacy. Her prolific talents and wry humor, as well as her ability to blend Norse, Greek, and Celtic mythologies with fantastic elements such as magic, ghosts, enchanted animals, and witches, resulted in an impressive body of work. In a career spanning four decades," according to a London *Independent* contributor, Jones "influenced generations of readers, in-cluding many who went on to become authors themselves, and she displayed a range and originality in her approach to fantasy writing that made her unique among British novelists." She found the fantasy genre—her particular interpretation of it, at any rate—to be an effective way to tell coming-of-age tales with a twist; she not only peopled her mythical worlds with wizards, witches, fire demons, ghosts, djinns, genies, and the like, but also introduced seemingly "normal" characters whose lives become complicated through the introduction of a magical element, such as the strange chemical sets in *The Ogre Downstairs.* According to Bruce Weber in the *New York Times,* Jones "created generally recognizable worlds except for the ubiquity of spells, trances and hocus-pocus." A London *Times* writer noted that "the imaginary worlds [she] invented running parallel with the ordinary and everyday lent her writing a wild unpredictability, turning each story into an individual process of discovery. This rich mix, while not to the taste of every reader, proved just the thing for children able and willing to make the effort of imagination required to follow stories unlike anything they had come across before."

Mixing a potent brew of magic, myth, and fantasy, Jones typically related the story of a youngster between the ages of ten and thirteen—one often operating in a difficult relationship with the adults in his or her life—who undergoes some crisis as a result of the realization of magical powers. "Though avoiding criminally dysfunctional families or unwanted pregnancies," as Christopher Priest observed in the London *Guardian,* "her cleverly plotted and amusing adventures deal frankly with emotional clumsiness, parental neglect, jealousy between siblings and a general sense of being an outcast. Rather than a deliberately cruel stepmother, a Jones protagonist might have a real mother far more wrapped up in her own career than in the discoveries and feelings of her child. The child protagonist would realise this, but get on with the adventure anyway."

Born in London in 1934, Jones had a childhood ideal for one intending to become a writer—or even a recluse. Much of her youth was informed by the horrors and vicissitudes of World War II. Evacuated at the age of five from London to the relative safety of Wales, Jones and her younger sister stayed with their grandmother. Soon joined by their mother and a new baby sister, the family's reunion was anything but warm: Jones' mother, Marjorie, did not care for the Welsh-isms she now detected in her daughters' speech. In 1940 the family moved to Westmorland in northern England, where Jones and her siblings lived with other children evacuated from southern, urban areas. Here Jones had her first encounters with authors: both Arthur Ransome and Beatrix Potter lived nearby, and neither seemed to like children very much. Relocation continued during the war years, landing the family next in a Yorkshire nunnery, and then back in a London suburb in 1942 after the worst of the Blitz was over.

It was at about this time that Jones determined she would be an author, a notion her parents scoffed at despite the fact that her mother was Oxford educated and was herself searching for a suitable career. An opportunity seemed to present itself to Jones' parents when, in 1943, they took jobs running a cultural center for young adults in the rural Essex village of Thaxted. Jones' experience at Thaxted was anything but a country idyll, however. With the main house on the grounds used for the center, the three young girls were housed in a hastily prepared two-room shack with inadequate heating and no water. Left to their own devices by their busy and distant parents, the three girls bonded with each other for support and community. Irony and a strong sense of humor proved to be survival skills in such a situation.

Of all the privations of village life, the worst for Jones was the absence of reading material. By then a voracious reader, she quickly made her way through the small local library, as well as the bookshelves at the school her parents ran. Such reading included the Greek myths as well as *The Arabian Nights* and works by Homer. Each Christmas the girls' father would go to the cupboard where he kept a complete set of Arthur Ransome's "Swallows and Amazons" novels and pick one out for the three daughters as their communal present. To fill the literary void, Jones took to composing her own works and filled the pages of several exercise books with cliché-filled epics.

Jones eventually attended Oxford's St. Anne's College, accepted in part because of her near-photographic memory. There she studied under both C.S. Lewis and J.R.R. Tolkien, both of whom greatly influenced not only her writing style but also her choice of genres. Graduating in 1956, Jones was married in that same year to a young man whom she had met in Thaxted several years before. For the next decade, she kept busy with motherhood, raising three boys born in 1958, 1961, and 1963, respectively. Although she had never thought of writing children's books, this tour of duty as a mom encouraged her in that direction. Determined that her children should never feel as deprived of good books as she had been during her childhood, Jones went in search of stories to read to them. When she could not find well-crafted contemporary fantasy tales, she decided to create some herself.

Although she did publish one adult novel in 1970, Jones' first children's work, *Wilkins' Tooth,* did not appear until 1973. A story of two children who set up in the revenge business and eventually tangle with a local witch, this first novel—published in the United States as *Witch's Business*—is important in that it "shows the unflagging inventiveness and sense of humor characteristic of Jones' style," according to Donna R. White in the *Dictionary of Literary Biography.* Also, as Christopher Davis pointed out in the *New York Times Book Review,* no "authority but the child's own is ever recognized and adults are never appealed to." Thus, *Wilkins'*

Tooth established Jones' twin pillars: a sense of humor and an adolescent protagonist largely bereft of parental supervision who must fend for him-or herself.

Jones' *The Ogre Downstairs* relates the story of five stepchildren who deal with the trials of a blended family by creating magical spells with a chemistry set. Compared to the fantasy works of Edwardian writer E. Nesbit, Jones' second novel won favorable reviews and also introduced themes such as displacement and alienation, which she would develop in subsequent novels. Much of Jones' more-recent work hearkens back to the difficulties of her own childhood, when she was continually displaced during the war years and left to fend for herself emotionally.

Jones went on to write several dozen books for young readers, each dealing in some way with magic and fantasy. Some of these works, such as *The Homeward Bounders* and *A Tale of Time City,* with their alternate worlds, could be classified as science fiction. Her first book to win recognition, in the form of a Carnegie Medal commendation, was *Dogsbody,* in which the Dog Star Sirius is banished to earth in the form of a newborn puppy, there to become the object of the adoration of Kathleen, a neglected young girl whose father is in prison for terrorist activities. Indeed, this year, 1975, was something of a watershed year for Jones, as she published two other novels, one of them, *Cart and Cwidder,* initiating the "Dalemark" quartet of books that concluded with *The Crown of Dalemark.*

The "Dalemark" series, which also includes *Drowned Ammet* and *The Spellcoats,* was described by White as "a more conventional kind of fantasy than Jones usually writes—almost High Fantasy." Here the author creates a mythical medieval land, Dalemark, and tells the story of the North and South kingdoms and of characters young and old who go in search of the kingdom's lost crown. Reviewing *The Spellcoats, Booklist* reviewer Chris Sherman noted that "treachery, mystery, humor, and magic abound in this intriguing, well-crafted fantasy," and that Jones' "quirky characters" are so well drawn that "readers will feel they know them."

Jones also wrote another fantasy series, the "Chrestomanci" books, which includes *Charmed Life, The Lives of Christopher Chant,* and *The Pinhoe Egg.* As Margaret Meek observed in *School Librarian,* the "Chrestomanci Cycle" takes place "in a universe where magic is normal and the unexpected commonplace." The books in this cycle are loosely linked together by the enchanter Chrestomanci, who appears in all six volumes. He even appears as a young man in *Conrad's Fate,* which displays Jones' "characteristic blend of magic, mystery and snortingly funny slapstick," according to a *Publishers Weekly* critic. In *The Pinhoe Egg,* the concluding entry in the series, Chrestomanci tries to ease tensions between warring clans of witches. "Witty, wise and wonderfully imaginative—this novel ranks among the author's best," according to a *Publishers Weekly* critic.

Cover of Jones' fantasy-focused chapter book Enchanted Glass, *featuring artwork by Brandon Dorman.* (Illustration copyright © 2010 by Brandon Dorman. Reproduced by permission of HarperCollins Children's Books, a division of HarperCollins Publishers.)

Jones' standalone novels include the award-winning *Howl's Moving Castle* and its sequel, *Castle in the Air.* Inspired by *The Arabian Nights* as well as by fairy tales from Europe, *Howl's Moving Castle* and *Castle in the Air* tell the story of Sophie Hatter, who must work as an apprentice hat-maker while her sisters go out into the world to seek their fortunes. Sophie is transformed into an old crone and the Wizard Howl follows his moving castle around the countryside in the award-winning novel, in which "wit and humor glint from the pages," according to *Horn Book* reviewer Ethel R. Twichell. The castle of the sequel is again Howl's, and this time he has become a genie in a bottle, while a young rug merchant purchases a magic carpet straight out of *The Arabian Nights.* Ann A. Flowers, writing in *Horn Book,* commented that *Castle in the Air* "contains enough material for any number of books" and that it is "cleverly written, with flowing Middle-Eastern expressions and amusing, sardonic remarks."

After an absence of almost two decades, Jones revisited the world of *Howl's Moving Castle* and *Castle in the Air* in *House of Many Ways,* "an equally rollicking, enchantment-filled tale," in the words of *Booklist* reviewer Sally Estes. This story focuses on Charmain Baker, a bookish young woman who, while serving as the caretaker of her uncle's magical home, discovers some surprising hidden powers of her own and ultimately saves the land of High Norland from a diabolical lubbock. S.E.G. Hopkin, writing in the *Spectator,* described *House of Many Ways* as "one of Jones' lighter works, but it is characteristically stylish and witty, and *Horn Book* contributor Deirdre F. Baker stated that Jones' "comic pacing and wit are amply evident" in *House of Many Ways.*

Ranked among Jones' "most powerful novels" by White in the *Dictionary of Literary Biography, The Homeward Bounders* and *The Time of the Ghost* both feature themes of alienation and displacement. In *The Homeward Bounders* Jamie discovers that his world is simply a giant game-board for the masters he calls "Them." Having discovered the secret, he is discarded from the game and destined to walk the borders between the worlds forever in a novel *Times Literary Supplement* critic Judith Elkin described as "strangely compelling—rather like a monster jigsaw-puzzle in which the reader can become totally and intensely absorbed."

Published in England the same year as *The Homeward Bounders, The Time of the Ghost* was eventually released in the United States fifteen years later. Dealing in a fictional manner with Jones' years in Thaxted, the novel introduces four neglected sisters who live in a converted shack next to a boys' boarding school. In this tale, a ghost returns to the past and attempts to prevent her own death in order to change history in effect. *Horn Book* reviewer Flowers concluded of *The Time of the Ghost* that the "complex plot . . . is absorbing, but equally interesting and frequently amusing are the family dynamics and the character sketches of the four fascinatingly eccentric sisters." *A Tale of Time City* also deals with Jones' childhood experiences during World War II.

An eclectic author, Jones often pushed the boundary of the fantasy genre. *Aunt Maria,* for example, is a horror story involving werewolves and zombies while *Fire and Hemlock*—Jones' "most challenging book for adolescents," in White's opinion—is a book with a convoluted structure and shifting time perspectives which examines deep emotional states. *Hexwood* walks the line between science fiction and fantasy and deals with virtual reality. When young Ann, the teenaged daughter of a British couple, notices strangers arriving at Hexwood Farm but never reemerging, she investigates, only to find that the boundaries of time and space are not what she thought. Sally Estes, writing in *Booklist,* called *Hexwood* "fast-paced" and the mystery "compelling." Estes also commented on the Jones trademark: "There's even a nice bit of humor." Joan Zahnleiter concluded in *Magpies* that "this challenging book is a satisfying read and one that is likely to be re-read in order to extract full flavor from its many layers of meaning."

A commentator for *Publishers Weekly* noted of *Dark Lord of Derkholm* that "this expansive novel" is on a par with the author's best, managing to be at once "an affectionate send-up of the sword-and-sorcery genre and a thrilling fantasy adventure in its own right." Each year, package tours come looking for excitement in Derkholm, but this year, teenager Blade and his magical siblings must do something to set things right and free the land from the tyranny of evil bureaucrat Mr. Chesney. "Thought-provoking and utterly engaging, this tour-de-force succeeds on numerous levels," the reviewer concluded. Flowers noted in *Horn Book* that one of the charms of the book "is the staggering magnitude of the invention," and concluded that the novel is "the author's best fantasy in some time."

Year of the Griffin, set eight years after *Dark Lord of Derkholm,* "retains the goofiness of its predecessor," according to *Booklist* contributor Sally Estes, by "continuing Jones' spoof of traditional fantasy conventions." The book centers on six students who have recently begun to study at Wizard's University, despite their parents' objections and the declining quality of the education provided there. At least four of the six are hiding their whereabouts from someone: Elda's father (Derk the wizard from *Dark Lord of Derkholm*) does not know that his daughter has enrolled at the university and would not approve if he did; Lukin's father, the king of Luteria, forbade him to study magic at all; and Felim and Claudia are under death threats from the Emir and the Senate, respectively. As for the other two members of this study group, one is a dwarf who hopes to use the magical powers he is acquiring to lead a dwarf revolution and the other refuses to talk about her past. As Beth Wright noted in *School Library Journal,* "the misdeeds ensuing from various attempts to retrieve or retaliate against the young wizards provide most of the dramatic thrust for this hilarious ensemble piece." The novelist "skillfully pulls together an enormous cast, a dozen convergent plots, an entertaining and well developed setting, and her trademark humor for the rousing finale," Anita L. Burkam commented in *Horn Book,* the critic adding that Jones demonstrates a solid "command of her material."

The Merlin Conspiracy is another complex fantasy that "shows the author's signature style and imagination," as Beth L. Meister declared in *School Library Journal.* The novel's action is spread out across several different parallel worlds, primarily the Islands of Blest, an alternate, magical England. One of the book's two narrators, Arianrhod "Roddy" Hyde, lives on the Islands of Blest with her parents, who are mages in the king's traveling court. The other narrator, Nick Mallory, begins in the normal, modern-day Earth but goes on a journey that takes him to several different worlds. Reaching Blest, he teams up with Roddy and her friend Grundo to discover who murdered the old Merlin (the name/title for the court official who is responsible for keeping magic under control) and who is apparently trying to destroy the magical balance of the multiverse. Featuring a large cast of characters and spanning multiple worlds, *The Merlin Conspiracy* might be daunting to those unfamiliar with Jones' other writings, commented a *Kirkus Reviews* contributor. "Those accustomed to Jones' labyrinthine narrative pyrotechnics will settle back to enjoy everything crashing together in a universe-tilting climax," the critic added. "Infused with humor as well as exciting adventure," *The Merlin Conspiracy* "makes compelling reading," Sally Estes concluded in *Booklist,* and a *Publishers Weekly* critic predicted that readers will find themselves "ensorcelled by this exuberant tale and Jones' unmistakable wit."

Wild Robert is aimed at a slightly younger audience than some of Jones' tales. The title character of this novella is a naughty young magician who was executed at Castlemaine 350 years ago. He has remained safely trapped underground until Heather, the daughter of Castlemaine's curators, now accidentally summons him. At first Heather is happy to have someone to keep her company while her parents lead tours through the castle grounds, but she soon comes to realize that an impulsive magician with a grudge against those who purportedly stole his inheritance can be quite a handful. "Light and fun, this fantasy is fine for children who aren't old enough for Jones' more complex fare," Eva Mitnick suggested in *School Library Journal.* However, Mitnick and other critics also saw a deeper side to Wild Robert's story; by the end of the tale "both Heather and the reader will see the pathos behind Wild Robert's frenetic chaos," noted a *Kirkus Reviews* critic.

Unexpected Magic: Collected Stories pulls together sixteen of Jones' tales, including "The Girl Jones," an autobiographical story about Jones as a nine-year-old, and the novella "Everard's Ride." Speaking of the latter story, Carolyn Phelan wrote in *Booklist* that "this excellent romantic adventure is worth the price of the book." Other tales contained in *Unexpected Magic* are "Enna Hittims," in which a sick child left at home amuses herself by conjuring up tiny magical characters who proceed to destroy her house; "The Girl Who Loved the Sun," a romance; and "Little Dot," a story narrated by a wizard's helpful pet cat. "Each story smoothly draws readers in and brings its own mood and adventure," Beth L. Meister noted in *School Library Journal,* and the characters in all these tales "are both appealing and realistically flawed." "Great work from one of the best modern fantasy authors," concluded a *Kirkus Reviews* critic.

Jones received a lifetime achievement award at the World Fantasy Convention in 2007, the same year she released *The Game,* a novella in which she draws on classical mythology for her tale of a young girl who learns that her parents are held hostage in the "mythosphere," an alternate reality populated by characters from story and legend. Matt Warman, writing in the London *Daily Telegraph,* commented that the work "will grip young readers for every page, and encourage further encounters with the ancient myths found in its subplots." *Enchanted Glass,* one of the author's final works, centers on the relationship between Andrew Hope, a magician's grandson, and Aidan Cain, an orphan who is on the run from magical beings. According to Lynn Rutan in *Booklist,* "Jones hits all the bases, combining fluid storytelling, sly humor, and exquisitely drawn characters." *Enchanted Glass,* observed Marcus Sedgwick in the London *Guardian,* "is no exception to . . . Jones' general rule of using, and possibly abusing, folklore and fantasy for her own splendid ends, mixing the spectacularly ordinary life of a university town satellite village with everyday magic, and a potent dash of *A Midsummer Night's Dream.*"

Biographical and Critical Sources

BOOKS

Butler, Charles, *Four British Fantasists: Place and Culture in the Children's Fantasies of Penelope Lively, Alan Garner, Diana Wynne Jones, and Susan Cooper,* Scarecrow Press (Lanham, MD), 2006.

Children's Literature Review, Volume 23, Gale (Detroit, MI), 1991.

Contemporary Literary Criticism, Volume 26, Gale (Detroit, MI), 1983.

Dictionary of Literary Biography, Volume 161: *British Children's Writers since 1960,* Gale (Detroit, MI), 1996.

Marcus, Leonard S., *The Wand in the Word: Conversations with Writers of Fantasy,* Candlewick Press (Cambridge, MA), 2006.

Mendleson, Farah, *Diana Wynne Jones: Children's Literature and the Fantastic Tradition,* Routledge (New York, NY), 2005.

Rosenberg, Teya, and others, editors, *Diana Wynne Jones: An Exciting and Exacting Wisdom,* Peter Lang (New York, NY), 2002.

St. James Guide to Fantasy Writers, St. James Press (Detroit, MI), 1996.

Twentieth-Century Young-Adult Writers, St. James Press (Detroit, MI), 1994.

PERIODICALS

Booklist, June 1, 1994, Sally Estes, review of *Hexwood,* pp. 1803-1804; December 15, 1995, Chris Sherman, review of *The Crown of Dalemark,* p. 698; November, 2000, Sally Estes, review of *Year of the Griffin,* p. 535; April 15, 2001, Carolyn Phelan, review of *Mixed Magics: Four Tales of Chrestomanci,* p. 1558, Sally Estes, review of *Year of the Griffin,* p. 1561; April 15, 2002, Sally Estes, review of *Year of the Griffin,* p. 1416; April 15, 2003, Sally Estes, review of *The Merlin Conspiracy,* p. 1464; September 15, 2003, Kay Weisman, review of *Wild Robert,* p. 237; April 15, 2004, Carolyn Phelan, review of *Unexpected Magic: Collected Stories,* p. 1450; May 15, 2008, Sally Estes, review of *House of Many Ways,* p. 55; February 15, 2010, Lynn Rutan, review of *Enchanted Glass,* p. 76.

Bulletin of the Center for Children's Books, July-August, 1993, review of *Stopping for a Spell,* p. 348; May, 1994, review of *Hexwood,* p. 290; October, 1996, review of *The Time of the Ghost,* p. 65.

Daily Telegraph (London, England), March 15, 2008, Matt Warman, review of *The Game,* p. O29.

Guardian (London, England), February 20, 2010, Marcus Sedgwick, review of *Enchanted Glass,* p. 18.

Horn Book, May-June, 1986, Ethel R. Twichell, review of *Howl's Moving Castle,* pp. 331-1332; March-April, 1991, Ann A. Flowers, review of *Castle in the Air,* p. 206; May, 1994, review of *Witch Week,* p. 345; March, 1996, Ann A. flowers, review of *The Crown of Dalemark,* p. 209; November-December, 1996, Ann A. Flowers, review of *The Time of the Ghost,* pp. 736-737; November, 1998, Ann A. Flowers, review of *Dark Lord of Derkholm,* p. 732; November, 2000, Anita L. Burkam, review of *Year of the Griffin,* p. 755; May, 2001, review of *Mixed Magics,* p. 327; May-June, 2003, Susan Dove Lempke, review of *The Merlin Conspiracy,* p. 359; July-August, 2004, Diana Wynne Jones, "Birthing a Book," p. 379, and Kristi Elle Jemtegaard, review of *Charmed Life,* p. 474; May-June, 2005, Deirdre F. Baker, review of *Conrad's Fate,* p. 327; November-December, 2005, Jeannine M. Chapman, review of *Witch Week,* p. 743; September-October, 2006, Jeannine M. Chapman, review of *The Pinhoe Egg,* p. 587; May-June, 2008, Deirdre F. Baker, review of *House of Many Ways,* p. 315; May-June, 2010, Deirdre F. Baker, review of *Enchanted Glass,* p. 83.

Independent (London, England), January 29, 2010, Nicholas Tucker, review of *Village Magic from the Gentle Fairy Queen,* p. 26.

Journal of the Fantastic in the Arts, Volume 21, number 2, special Diana Wynne Jones issue.

Kirkus Reviews, May 15, 1993, review of *Stopping for a Spell,* p. 663; March 15, 2003, review of *The Merlin Conspiracy,* p. 469; August 15, 2003, review of *Wild Robert,* p. 1074; April 15, 2004, review of *Unexpected Magic,* p. 395.

Kliatt, May, 2003, Stacey Conrad, review of *Deep Secret,* p. 26; September, 2004, Sherri Ginsberg, review of *Charmed Life,* p. 54; November, 2004, Sherri Ginsberg, review of *The Lives of Christopher Chant,* p. 48.

Magpies, July, 1994, Joan Zahnleiter, review of *Hexwood,* p. 34.

New York Times Book Review, May 5, 1974, Christopher Davis, review of *Witch's Business,* pp. 22, 24, 26; July 10, 2010, Polly Shulman, review of *Conrad's Fate,* p. 20.

Publishers Weekly, February 22, 1991, Kit Alderdice, "Diana Wynne Jones," pp. 201-202; May 24, 1993, review of *Stopping for a Spell,* p. 88; October 19, 1998, review of *Dark Lord of Derkholm,* p. 82; October 16, 2000, review of *Year of the Griffin,* p. 77; April 23, 2001, review of *Mixed Magics,* p. 79; March 10, 2003, review of *The Merlin Conspiracy,* p. 73; March 21,

2005, review of *Conrad's Fate,* p. 52; September 11, 2006, review of *The Pinhoe Egg,* p. 55; March 5, 2007, review of *The Game,* p. 62; May 19, 2008, review of *House of Many Ways,* p. 54; February 22, 2010, review of *Enchanted Glass,* p. 68.

School Librarian, December, 1977, Margaret Meek, review of *Charmed Life,* pp. 363-364.

School Library Journal, October, 1992, Linda Greengrass, review of *Yes, Dear,* p. 89; March, 1994, Vanessa Elder, review of *Hexwood,* p. 236; October, 1998, Steven Engelfried, review of *Dark Lord of Derkholm,* p. 136; October, 2000, Beth Wright, review of *Year of the Griffin,* p. 161; July, 2001, Patricia A. Dollisch, review of *Mixed Magics,* p. 110; May, 2003, Beth L. Meister, review of *The Merlin Conspiracy,* p. 154; October, 2003, Eva Mitnick, review of *Wild Robert,* p. 128; September, 2004, Louise L. Sherman, review of *The Lives of Christopher Chant,* p. 78, Beth L. Meister, review of *Unexpected Magic,* p. 209; October, 2004, Sarah Flowers, review of *Charmed Life,* p. 84; December, 2010, Necia Blundy, review of *Enchanted Glass,* p. 66.

Spectator, July 12, 2008, S.E.G. Hopkin, review of *Magic and Laundry,* p. 44.

Times Literary Supplement, March 27, 1981, Judith Elkin, "Walking the Bounds," p. 339; November 20, 1981, Elaine Moss, "Ghostly Forms," p. 1354.

U.S. News & World Report, November 29, 1999, Holly J. Morris, "Mad about Harry? Try Diana," p. 80.

Voice of Youth Advocates, February, 1994, review of *Witch Week,* p. 382; October, 1994, review of *Hexwood,* p. 223; August, 1995, review of *The Spellcoats,* p. 172; April, 1997, review of *The Time of the Ghost,* p. 42.

ONLINE

Diana Wynne Jones Home Page, http://www.dianawynnejones.com (September 15, 2011).

HarperCollins Web site, http://www.harpercollins.com/ (September 15, 2011), "Diana Wynne Jones."

Publishers Weekly Online, http://www.publishersweekly.com/ (June 19, 2008), Kit Alderdice, interview with Jones.

Obituaries

PERIODICALS

Booklist, May 15, 2011, Michael Cart, "The Possibilities of the Impossible."

Daily Telegraph (London, England), March 30, 2011, Rowan Pelling, "Wizard Writer Whose Young Life Was Far from Magical," p. 20, and "Author of Children's Fantasies Who Was Inspired to Write after Learning at the Feet of Tolkien and C.S. Lewis," p. 29; April 2, 2011, Tim Martin, "More Charm and Wit than Harry Potter," p. 3.

Guardian (London, England), March 28, 2011, Christopher Priest, "Diana Wynne Jones: Renowned Children's Fantasy and Science-fiction Author with a Dedicated Following," p. 35.

Independent (London, England), March 31, 2011, p. 8.
New York Times, March 29, 2011, p. B19.
Times (London, England), March 28, 2011, p. 45.*

* * *

JUDGE, Lita

Personal

Born in Ketchikan, AK; father a soil scientist; married; husband's name Dave. *Education:* Oregon State University, degree. *Hobbies and other interests:* Travel, reading, gardening, yoga.

Addresses

Home—Peterborough, NH. *Office*—Wilder Farm Studio, 77 Wilder Farm Rd., Peterborough, NH 03458. *E-mail*—Lita@litajudge.com.

Career

Author and illustrator. Has worked as an environmental geologist and a paleobotanist.

Member

Society of Children's Book Writers and Illustrators.

Awards, Honors

One Hundred Books for Reading and Sharing selection, New York Public Library, and Gold Award, National Parenting Publications Awards, both 2007, Children's Book Award and Notable Book for a Global Society designation, both International Reading Association, Notable Children's Book selection, American Library Association, Jane Addams Children's Book Award Honor designation, Notable Children's Books in the Language Arts designation, National Council of Teachers of English, and *Storytelling World* Resource Award, all 2008, all for *One Thousand Tracings;* New Hampshire Outstanding Work of Children's Literature selection, 2009, for *Pennies for Elephants; Smithsonian* Notable Book selection, 2009, for *Yellowstone Moran;* Oppenheim Toy Portfolio Gold Medal, and One Hundred Books for Reading and Sharing selection, both 2010, and Cooperative Children's Books Center Choice selection, 2011, all for *Born to Be Giants.*

Writings

SELF-ILLUSTRATED

One Thousand Tracings: Healing the Wounds of World War II, Hyperion Books (New York, NY), 2007.

(With Todd Chapman) *D Is for Dinosaur: A Prehistoric Alphabet,* Sleeping Bear Press (Chelsea, MI), 2007.

Lita Judge (Reproduced by permission.)

Pennies for Elephants, Disney-Hyperion Books (New York, NY), 2009.

Yellowstone Moran: Painting the American West, Viking (New York, NY), 2009.

Born to Be Giants: How Baby Dinosaurs Grew to Rule the World, Flash Point (New York, NY), 2010.

Bird Talk: What Birds Are Saying and Why, Roaring Brook Press (New York, NY), 2011.

Strange Creatures: The Story of Walter Rothschild and His Museum, Hyperion (New York, NY), 2011.

Red Sled, Atheneum Books for Young Readers (New York, NY), 2011.

ILLUSTRATOR

Donna Jo Napoli, *Ugly,* Hyperion Books (New York, NY), 2006.

Helen Foster James, *S Is for S'mores: A Camping Alphabet,* Sleeping Bear Press (Chelsea, MI), 2007.

Donna Jo Napoli, *Mogo, the Third Warthog,* Hyperion Books (New York, NY), 2008.

Sidelights

A former environmental geologist and paleobotanist, Lita Judge now writes and illustrates children's books. While Judge has created the original, self-illustrated stories *Pennies for Elephants* and *Red Sled,* most of her work has been in the area of nonfiction and includes *One Thousand Tracings: Healing the Wounds of World War II, Yellowstone Moran: Painting the American West,*

Born to Be Giants: How Baby Dinosaurs Grew to Rule the World, and *Strange Creatures: The Story of Walter Rothschild and His Museum.* As an illustrator, she has also provided artwork to several stories by Donna Jo Napoli, among them *Ugly,* Napoli's adaptation of Hans Christian Andersen's "The Ugly Duckling."

Born in Ketchikan, Alaska, Judge developed an early interest in her surroundings due to her father's career as a soil scientist. The job required him to travel and Judge's mother packed up her twins and accompanied her husband on several trips to islands off the Alaskan coast. The family also moved several times. Fortunately, visiting her grandparents' rustic farm in Wisconsin became a summer tradition, and the couple inspired the soon-to-be author/illustrator with their enthusiasm as biologists and bird watchers with a special interest in raptors. "I've loved drawing from as early as I can remember," Judge recalled on her home page. "I especially loved drawing birds from life and dinosaurs from my imagination. Writing came later for me. I think my love of reading finally led me to want to write my own stories."

In *One Thousand Tracings* Judge mines her family history by describing her grandparents' effort to assist European survivors following World War II. "When I was cleaning out my grandmother's attic after her death, I found a dusty box stuffed with aged yellowed envelopes," the author noted on the *One Thousand Tracings* Web site. "I was intrigued when I lifted out the first envelope; it had a German stamp postmarked 1947 and inside were two paper foot tracings." As Judge discovered, her grandparents had founded The Action, a relief organization that provided food and clothing to more than 3,000 refugees in thirteen countries; the tracings helped volunteers determine refugees' shoe sizes. "I wish my grandmother could have shared these memories with me, but I feel closer to her now for having discovered the truth," Judge observed. "I wish I had known about it when she was alive so I could tell her how proud I am. Instead, I wrote my book as a tribute to her."

In *One Thousand Tracings* a six-year-old Midwestern girl and her mother take action after receiving a letter from a friend describing the horrific conditions in postwar Germany. The "narration offers a child's perspective on the tragedies and hope of the era, making the story especially accessible to young audiences," noted a critic in *Publishers Weekly.* Marianne Saccardi commented in *School Library Journal* that Judge's "soft-edged paintings" in *One Thousand Tracings* "are colorful and fluid and create a strong sense of time and place."

Judge taps her longtime interest in dinosaurs in *Born to Be Giants* which focuses on the growing insight of paleontologists into the way several dinosaur species raised their young. In researching the book, Judge followed the studies by scientists of fossilized nests, eggs, and hatchlings of eight species of dinosaurs. In her text she introduces young readers to the scientific method, showing the framing and testing of different hypotheses based on these findings. In *Booklist* John Peters praised the author for injecting her story with "a full measure of visual appeal" via her colorful and realistic paintings, while Patricia Manning praised *Born to Be Giants* as "an interesting and attractive introduction" to the subject in her *School Library Journal* review. Judge's "text is a model of logical reasoning," asserted *Horn Book* contributor Danielle J. Ford, the critic adding that the book's "detailed, richly colored" artwork exhibits "the same care in balancing accuracy and imagination."

Another large creature stars in Judge's picture-book story for *Pennies for Elephants,* which was inspired by an actual event. Set in Boston, Massachusetts, in 1914, *Pennies for Elephants* is narrated by Dorothy, who joins her brother Henry and numerous other children in earning the funds needed to purchase three trained elephants for Boston's Franklin Park Zoo. The siblings host a benefit costume party and, with the addition of their own life savings, raise almost two dollars for the cause; their funds combine with similar contributions from thousands of other children throughout New England who have learned of the zoo's need by reading newspaper coverage. Judge's "uplifting tale will surely capti-

Judge tells a story that focuses on the strength of a close-knit rural family during wartime in her self-illustrated **One Thousand Tracings.**
(Illustration copyright © 2007 by Lita Judge. Reprinted by permission of Disney-Hyperion, an imprint of Disney Book Group LLC. All rights reserved.)

vate—and hopefully inspire—contemporary children," wrote Kathleen Finn in her *School Library Journal* review of *Pennies for Elephants,* and in *Booklist* Ilene Cooper praised the book's illustrations as "varied and appealing." The author/illustrator "weaves a compelling tale based on a true, heartwarming incident," concluded a *Publishers Weekly* critic, calling *Pennies for Elephants* "an inspired celebration of kid power."

Judge's interest in biology has led her to discover the work of others who share her passion. In *Yellowstone Moran* she profiles painter Thomas Moran, who in 1871 joined Dr. Ferdinand Hayden and his fellow scientists in exploring the wild region that is now part of Yellowstone National Park. The trip was an arduous one, and required the city dweller to learn to travel by horseback over the rough and rocky terrain and also sleep under the stars. In his paintings and his journals, Moran captured the beauty of the region's canyons, geysers, and other natural wonders, helping to spark the movement to preserve Yellowstone by establishing a national park. In a text that *School Library Journal* contributor Donna Cardon described as "interesting and engaging," Judge inserts Moran's own journal entries, and her illustrations reflect the style of the nineteenth-century painter. Her art incorporates "energetic lines and the rich, earthy colors of the American West," noted Cardon, while in *Kirkus Reviews* a contributor wrote that her "watercolors effectively capture the monumental landscapes" of the region. "Rare is the book that makes painting seem adventurous, but this true-life account of Thomas Moran's journey to the land called 'Yellowstone' does just that," asserted Daniel Kraus in his *Booklist* review of *Yellowstone Moran.*

Another picture-book biography, Judge's *Strange Creatures,* focuses on Walter Rothschild and the museum he created in Tring, England. The oldest son of Lord Nathan Rothschild, patriarch of the wealthy British banking family, Walter Rothschild began his collection of bugs, butterflies, and animals when he was seven years old. As an adult he left the running of the family business to others, preferring instead to collect and house all manner of living animals in a building on his family's estate. In 1892, the twenty-four-year-old naturalist opened his collection to the public, and it grew to become the largest private zoological collection ever amassed, with Rothschild discovering and naming thousands of new species. At the time, biologists were limited in their studies to live animals, so Rothschild's collection was a great contribution to biologists because it brought so many creatures to one location. In reviewing *Strange Creatures* for *Booklist,* Kara Dean cited the "dramatic watercolor spreads" that capture the man's lifelong "obsession with nature," and a *Publishers Weekly* reviewer wrote that "Judge's expressive watercolors convey Rothschild's inquisitiveness." While noting that the Rothschild family's wealth enabled Walter to pursue his interest unrestrained, Kathy Piehl added in *School Library Journal* that "Judge's picture-book biography of the shy genius may encourage readers to follow their own creative ideas."

Biographical and Critical Sources

PERIODICALS

Booklist, May 15, 2007, Hazel Rochman, review of *One Thousand Tracings: Healing the Wounds of World War II,* p. 47; June 1, 2008, Carolyn Phelan, review of *Mogo, the Third Warthog,* p. 76; September 1, 2009, Ilene Cooper, review of *Pennies for Elephants,* p. 102; November 1, 2009, Daniel Kraus, review of *Yellowstone Moran: Painting the American West,* p. 60; March 1, 2010, John Peters, review of *Born to Be Giants: How Baby Dinosaurs Grew to Rule the World,* p. 64; February 15, 2011, Kara Dean, review of *Strange Creatures: The Story of Walter Rothschild and His Museum,* p. 67.

Horn Book, May-June, 2010, Danielle J. Ford, review of *Born to Be Giants,* p. 108.

Kirkus Reviews, December 15, 2005, review of *Ugly,* p. 1326; June 15, 2007, review of *One Thousand Tracings*; June 1, 2008, review of *Mogo, the Third Warthog*; August 1, 2009, review of *Yellowstone Moran.*

Publishers Weekly, February 6, 2006, review of *Ugly,* p. 70; June 11, 2007, review of *One Thousand Tracings,* p. 59; June 22, 2009, review of *Pennies for Elephants,* p. 43; March 29, 2010, review of *Born to Be Giants,* p. 57; December 20, 2010, review of *Strange Creatures,* p. 52.

School Library Journal, March, 2006, Susan Hepler, review of *Ugly,* p. 199; July, 2007, Marianne Saccardi, review of *One Thousand Tracings,* p. 92; August, 2008, Ellen G. Fader, review of *Mogo, the Third Warthog,* p. 99; September, 2009, Donna Cardon, review of *Yellowstone Moran,* p. 143; November, 2009, Kathleen Finn, review of *Pennies for Elephants,* p. 82; May, 2010, Patricia Manning, review of *Born to Be Giants,* p. 132; February, 2011, Kathy Piehl, review of *Strange Creatures,* p. 97.

ONLINE

Lita Judge Home Page, http://www.litajudge.com (September 21, 2011).

Lita Judge Web log, http://wpblog.litajudge.com (September 21, 2011).

One Thousand Tracings Web site, http://tracings.litajudge.com/ (August 15, 2008).

K

KADE, Stacey
(Stacey Klemstein)

Personal

Father a Lutheran minister, mother a teacher; married Greg Klemstein (a realtor). *Education:* Valparaiso University, B.A. (English), 1997.

Addresses

Home—Metro Chicago, IL. *E-mail*—stacey@staceykade .com.

Career

Copywriter and author. Caterpillar, Inc., communications representative, 1997-98; Watson Wyatt Worldwide, communications specialist, 1998-99; Allstate Insurance Company, copywriter and project manager, 1999-2006; freelance writer.

Member

Romance Writers of America.

Writings

"GHOST AND THE GOTH" YOUNG-ADULT NOVEL SERIES

The Ghost and the Goth, Hyperion (New York, NY), 2010.
Queen of the Dead, Hyperion (New York, NY), 2011.
Body and Soul, Hyperion (New York, NY), 2012.

ADULT NOVELS; UNDER NAME STACEY KLEMSTEIN

The Silver Spoon, Echelon Press, 2007.
Bitter Pill, Echelon Press, 2008.
Eye of the Beholder, Echelon Press, 2008.

Sidelights

Apart from her work as a corporate copywriter, Stacey Kade is a novelist who wears two hats. Teen readers

Cover of Stacey Kade's entertaining paranormal romance **The Ghost and the Goth,** *featuring artwork by Tom Corbett.* (Photograph copyright © 2010 by Tom Corbett. Reproduced by permission of Disney-Hyperion, an imprint of Disney Book Group LLC. All rights reserved.)

know her as the author of the "Ghost and the Goth" series, while adult fans of romance-laced science fiction know her as Stacey Klemstein, author of the novels *The Silver Spoon, Bitter Pill,* and *Eye of the Beholder.*

Kade's fictional focus was inspired by a childhood love of *Star Trek* and the "Star Wars" films as well as by the fascination with otherworldly intersections that science fiction inspires. Because she enjoyed writing her own stories, she majored in English at Valparaiso University and embarked on a copywriting career. She published her first adult novel, *The Silver Spoon,* in 2007, then produced two other sci-fi romances before turning to an adolescent readership.

Kade gives supernatural teen romance a fanciful twist in her "Ghost and the Goth" novel series, which includes *The Ghost and the Goth* and *Queen of the Dead.* Alona Dare was the queen of Groundsboro High until she met her demise under the tires of a school bus transporting the high-school band. Now a ghost, Alona haunts her high school, where few of her so-called friends seem to be grieving over her death. Although she is surprised, geeky fellow senior Will Killian can actually see and talk to her and it turns out that he has the ability to interact with the dead. Tapping her well-developed skill at persuading guys to do her bidding, Alona convinces Will to aid her in moving on toward her ultimate resting place, but their communication alerts the other ghosts haunting the school as to Will's spirit-world sensitivity. *Queen of the Dead* continues the adventures of Alona and Will as Alona resigns herself to being the reigning ghost at Groundsboro High. She also discovers a compassionate side to her self-absorbed personality, one likely inspired by her growing affection for Will. Her efforts to help other ghosts on their way to the hereafter are interrupted by worries, however, including concerns about family members who are still among the living. Another problem rears its head in the form of Mina, a pretty and very-much-alive ghost seer who seems bent on capturing Will's attention.

Predicting that *The Ghost and the Goth* will be a hit among teen fans of supernatural romance, Laura Amos added in *School Library Journal* that Kade's "absorbing" YA novel "shows how two people can grow tremendously over time." "With plenty of humor, this quirky debut will appeal to both genders," asserted *Booklist* contributor Melissa Moore, and a *Publishers Weekly* reviewer praised the way Kade's story "becomes steadily more engrossing as . . . her characters' voices and identities develop."

Biographical and Critical Sources

PERIODICALS

Booklist, August 1, 2010, Melissa Moore, review of *The Ghost and the Goth,* p. 45.

Publishers Weekly, July 5, 2010, review of *The Ghost and the Goth,* p. 44.
Reviewer's Bookwatch, January, 2005, Alisa McCune, review of *The Silver Spoon.*
School Library Journal, August, 2010, Laura Amos, review of *The Ghost and the Goth,* p. 104.

ONLINE

Stacy Kade Home Page, http://www.staceykade.com (October 1, 2011).
Stacey Klemstein Home Page, http://www. staceyklemstein. com (October 1, 2011).*

*　　*　　*

KINCY, Karen 1986-

Personal

Born 1986, in Snohomish, WA. *Education:* Evergreen State College, B.A. (linguistics and literature), 2010; graduate study (computational linguistics). *Hobbies and other interests:* Digital photography, gardening.

Addresses

Home—Redmond, WA. *Agent*—Sara Crowe, Harvey Klinger, Inc., 300 W. 55th St., Ste. 11V, New York, NY 10019. *E-mail*—karenkincy@hotmail.com.

Career

Writer.

Member

Society of Children's Book Writers and Illustrators.

Writings

Other, Flux (Woodbury, MN), 2010.
Bloodborn, Flux (Woodbury, MN), 2011.
Foxfire, Flux (Woodbury, MN), 2012.

Sidelights

As a teen growing up in western Washington State, Karen Kincy dreamed of becoming a novelist. Kincy read published novels written by other teens, then decided to write her own. This first effort satirized the fantasy genre, but Kincy thought better of such an approach after struggling through a few drafts. Although she discarded that particular plot, the characters she had created continued to haunt her. She researched unusual paranormal creatures in stories and legends from around the world, cast them in a new tale, and this time the story rang true. Although it took several years to find a

Karen Kincy (Reproduced by permission.)

publisher, Kincy remained undaunted, and her young-adult paranormal debut, *Other,* hit bookstore shelves the same year its author graduated from college.

Set in Klikamuks, Washington, a fictionalized version of its author's home town, *Other* introduces Gwen, a seventeen year old who struggles with how to tell her conservative boyfriend, Zack, a secret: Gwen's mother is human, but her father was a pooka, a shapeshifting spirit from Wales. In Gwen's alternate America, people recognize that supernatural creatures such as centaurs, pookas, water sprites, werewolves, and the like do live among them, although these "Others" keep to the shadows due to often deadly prejudice and hatred.

Gwen's secret becomes even more dangerous when a pack of werewolves begins roaming the forest near Klikamuks and a mysterious killer also starts hunting Others. The teen is determined to find the murderer, aided by a dryad (tree-spirit) named Chloe. Meanwhile, a handsome kitsune (Japanese fox-spirit) named Tavian urges her to explore her pooka side. In *School Library Journal* Genevieve Gallagher praised *Other* for presenting readers with a "fresh take on a modern fantasy," adding that "the emotional turmoil of the characters is evident and will appeal to readers who have felt misunderstood." *Other* "is a standout blend of paranormal thriller and sweet teen romance," wrote Krista Huntley in *Booklist,* and its "extremely likeable" heroine helps make Kincy's novel a "suspenseful mystery."

Kincy continues to explore a world where Others and humans openly coexist in *Bloodborn,* but here her protagonist is Brock Koeman. Having grown up despising supernatural creatures, Brock becomes the very thing he hates after he and his brother Chris are bitten by a werewolf. While Chris fights for his life in the local

hospital, Brock fights the slow transformation. Despite medication, he begins to evolve physically, at the same time recognizing that his new powers will allow him a life without restraints. Throughout Brock's story, Kincy touches on themes such as racism and adolescent angst, and a *Kirkus Reviews* writer noted similarities to the work of Neal Schusterman. *Bloodborn* presents a rare paranormal adventure that will appeal to male readers through its "realism about thugs and delinquents," the critic added.

Biographical and Critical Sources

PERIODICALS

Booklist, June 1, 2010, Krista Hutley, review of *Other,* p. 56.
Cicada, January-February, 2011, interview with Kincy, p. 27.

Cover of Kincy's haunting young-adult novel Other, *the first novel in her series about a teenaged shapeshifter.* (Photography copyright © 2010 by Ebby May/Digital Vision/PunchStock. Reproduced by permission of Flux, an imprint of Llewellyn Publication.)

Kirkus Reviews, July 1, 2011, review of *Bloodborn.*
School Library Journal, July, 2010, Genevieve Gallagher, review of *Other,* p. 92.

ONLINE

Karen Kincy Home Page, http://www.karenkincy.com (September 29, 2011).

* * *

KLEMSTEIN, Stacey
See KADE, Stacey

* * *

KNIGHT, Steven 1959-

Personal

Born 1959, in Marlborough, England. *Education:* University College London, B.A. (English literature).

Addresses

Home—London, England.

Career

Writer for film and television. Copywriter and producer for advertising agency in Birmingham, England; Capital Radio, former copywriter/producer; freelance screenwriter beginning 1988. Director of episodes for television series *The Detectives,* 1995-97. Owner of brewery.

Awards, Honors

W.H. Smith Fresh Talent Award, 1993, for *The Movie House;* BIFA Award for Best Screenplay, Edgar Award for Best Motion-Picture Screenplay, Best British Screenwriter honor, London Film Critics' Circle Awards, and British Academy of Film and Television Arts (BAFTA) Award nomination for Best Original Screenplay, and Alexander Korda Award for Outstanding British Film, all 2003, and Writers Guild of America Best Original Screenplay Award nomination, Best Screenplay Award runner up, Los Angeles Film Critics Awards, and Academy Award nomination for Best Screenplay Written Directly for the Screen, all 2004, all for *Dirty Pretty Things.*

Writings

ADULT FICTION

The Movie House, Penguin (London, England), 1994.
Alphabet City, Penguin (London, England), 1995.
Out of the Blue, Viking (London, England), 1996.

FOR CHILDREN

The Last Words of Will Wolfkin, Walden Pond Press (New York, NY), 2010.

OTHER

Gypsy Woman (screenplay), 2001.
Dirty Pretty Things (screenplay), 2002.
The President of an Empty Room: A Story of Voodoo, Heroin, and Tobacco (stage play; produced in London, England, 2005), Nick Hern Books (London, England), 2005.
Amazing Grace (screenplay), 2006.
Eastern Promises (screenplay), Focus Features, 2007.
Wrath of the Titans (screenplay), 2012.

Writer, with Mike Whitehill, for television, including *Commercial Breakdown,* 1989; *Canned Carrott,* 1990; *Aunties Big Bloomers,* 1990; *Frankie Howerd on Campus,* 1990; *Frankie's On . . . ,* 1992; *The Detectives File,* 1993-97; *Comedy Playhouse,* 1994; *Carrott U Like,* 1994; and *Who Wants to Be a Millionaire,* 1998.

Sidelights

Steven Knight worked as an advertising copywriter in his native England before moving into radio and beginning a writing partnership with his friend, Mike Whitehill. Since the mid-1980s, Knight and Whitehill have written for television series and even helped develop the popular game show *Who Wants to Be a Millionaire?,* which first aired in the United Kingdom. Knight has expanded his list of credits with several adult novels as well as with screenplays for such award-winning films as *Dirty Pretty Things, Amazing Grace,* and the David Cronenberg-directed *Eastern Promises.* He has also earned a legion of younger fans with his middle-grade adventure novel *The Last Words of Will Wolfkin.*

In *The Last Words of Will Wolfkin* readers meet fourteen-year-old Toby, who is in an unhappy situation. Paralyzed, Toby lives in a quiet English convent where he is taken care of and shielded by a group of Carmelite nuns. A fan of Icelandic mythology, Toby's vivid imagination crafts a fantasy world, Langjoskull, and there he is sent through the power of his magical pet cat, Egil. In Langjoskull, Toby meets another young teen, Emma, and learns that they both bear the birthright of the ancient Icelandic adventurer Will Wolfkin. Armed with the power of shapeshifting as part of this birthright, Toby and Emma now face an heroic quest: to save the entire world by squelching the spreading evil wrought by Helva Gullkin. Toby's story is compelling and so real that it leaves readers pondering: did he really transcend his illness, or "was it all a dream?," according to Wendy Smith-D'Arezzo in *School Library Journal. The Last Words of Will Wolfkin* treats readers to "an imaginative, truly fascinating entrance to another world," according to Smith-D'Arezzo, the critic expressing the hope that Knight has plans to produce a sequel.

Biographical and Critical Sources

PERIODICALS

Bulletin of the Center for Children's Books, September, 2010, Kate Quealy-Gainer, review of *The Last Words of Will Wolfkin,* p. 26.

Kirkus Reviews, May 15, 2010, review of *The Last Words of Will Wolfkin.*

School Library Journal, September, 2010, Wendy Smith-D'Arezzo, review of *The Last Words of Will Wolfkin,* p. 156.

Voice of Youth Advocates, June, 2010, Jan Chapman, review of *The Last Words of Will Wolfkin,* p. 166.*

L

LaFEVERS, R.L.
(Robin LaFevers)

Personal
Born in Los Angeles, CA; married; children: two sons. *Hobbies and other interests:* Reading, writing, research.

Addresses
E-mail—robin@rllafevers.com.

Career
Children's author. Formerly did design and marketing for a wedding accessories company.

Member
Society of Children's Book Writers and Illustrators.

Awards, Honors
Texas Bluebonnet list inclusion, 2006-07, for *The Forging of the Blade;* Agatha Award nomination, Malice Domestic, and Mitten Award Honor Book designation, Michigan Library Association, both 2007, both for *Theodosia and the Serpents of Chaos;* Agatha Award nomination, 2010, for *Theodosia and the Eyes of Horus.*

Writings

The Falconmaster, Dutton (New York, NY), 2003.
Werewolf Rising, Dutton (New York, NY), 2006.

"LOWTHAR'S BLADE" NOVEL TRILOGY

The Forging of the Blade, Dutton (New York, NY), 2004.
The Secrets of Grim Wood, Dutton (New York, NY), 2005.
The True Blade of Power, Dutton (New York, NY), 2005.

R.L. LaFevers (Photograph by Rick Carter. Courtesy of R.L. LaFevers.)

"THEODOSIA THROCKMORTON" NOVEL SERIES; ILLUSTRATED BY YOKO TANAKA

Theodosia and the Serpents of Chaos, Houghton Mifflin (Boston, MA), 2007.
Theodosia and the Staff of Osiris, Houghton Mifflin (Boston, MA), 2008.
Theodosia and the Eyes of Horus, Houghton Mifflin (Boston, MA), 2010.
Theodosia and the Last Pharaoh, Houghton Mifflin Harcourt (New York, NY), 2011.

"NATHANIEL FLUDD, BEASTOLOGIST" NOVEL SERIES; ILLUSTRATED BY KELLY MURPHY

The Flight of the Phoenix, Houghton Mifflin (Boston, MA), 2009.
The Basilisk's Lair, Houghton Mifflin (Boston, MA), 2010.

The Wyverns' Treasure, Houghton Mifflin (Boston, MA), 2010.

The Unicorn's Tale, Houghton Mifflin Harcourt (New York, NY), 2011.

"HIS FAIR ASSASSIN" NOVEL TRILOGY

(Under name Robin LaFevers) *Grave Mercy,* Houghton Mifflin Harcourt (Boston, MA), 2012.

Sidelights

Combining her love of research and history—particularly the middle ages—with a talent for writing and storytelling, R.L. LaFevers is the author of historical fiction and fantasy for upper-elementary and middle-grade readers. In addition to her "Lowthar's Blade," "Theodosia Throckmorton," and "Nathanial Fludd, Beastologist" novel series, LaFevers is also the author of several stand-alone fantasy novels. "I am like a magpie, collecting ideas and snippets and personality traits from everyone around me: my kids, myself, my brothers, family, friends," the author admitted in an interview with Hayley Schroeder for *Creative Kids.* "But it all gets tossed into this big cauldron in my head and stirred around and mixed with other ingredients so that what comes out is never wholly one person or another. It's an entirely new creation based on what I've learned from all of the people in my life."

LaFevers knew from an early age that she wanted to be a writer. "I began writing long boring poetry at age seven," she recalled on her home page, "then graduated to short stories that were (thankfully!) a little more interesting. At age fourteen I knew that what I wanted more than anything else was to be a fantasy writer." Raised in Los Angeles, California, as one sister in a group of brothers, she was surrounded by animals as a child: family pets ranged from cats and dogs to goats, chipmunks, and even a baby anteater. As a writer, LaFevers has drawn on that childhood love of wild creatures as well as on the trouble she got into growing up with her brothers, and many of her novels feature young male protagonists. "I learned a lot about how boys think and the kinds of trouble they can get into," the author once explained.

LaFevers' first novel, *The Falconmaster,* introduces a young boy named Wat, who is called "Devil's Spawn" by other villagers due to his lame leg and blind eye. Set in Norman England, the story follows Wat as he steals two of his lord's peregrine falcon nestlings and raises them in the forest. While hiding there he learns that he is more than just a boy; in fact, Wat is heir to a magic that will allow him to protect the surrounding woodlands. LaFevers "successfully blends rich descriptions of the medieval world and flights of fantasy into an exciting adventure," according to Todd Morning in a *Booklist* review of *The Falconmaster.* As Jane G. Connor wrote in *School Library Journal,* LaFevers "has done a fine job of integrating elements of fantasy into a historical setting" her fiction debut.

LaFevers crafts an original fantasy world in her "Lowthar's Blade" trilogy. Beginning with *The Forging of the Blade* and continuing with *The Secrets of Grim Wood* and *The True Blade of Power,* the series tells the story of Prince Kenric, whose father has been overthrown by an evil lord, Mordig. Now in power, Mordig starts kidnaping skilled blacksmiths in an effort to forge a new sword of power. Kenric sides with the goblin Hnagi to both save his father and redeem his beloved kingdom. LeFevers' story "moves smoothly from start to finish; the action is continuous without being overly violent," according to Beth L. Meister in *School Library Journal* in her review of *The Forging of the Blade.*

In *Theodosia and the Serpents of Chaos* and its sequels LaFevers returns to historical fantasy, this time setting her story in Edwardian England as British interests extended to the mysterious lands of India and Egypt. Theodosia Throckmorton is not fond of surprises, as the shocks she has experienced at her parents' Museum of Legends & Antiquities have tended to be rather wicked. It is Theo—and only Theo—who can see all the curses and black magic still clinging to the ancient artifacts. Then her mother returns from Egypt with the "Heart of Egypt," an artifact with a curse so vile that it threatens to topple the British Empire. Theo will have to call

Cover of LaFevers' fantasy novel The Secrets of Grim Wood, *featuring artwork by Hunter Brown.* (Jacket art © 2005 by Hunter Brown. All rights reserved. Reproduced by permission of Puffin Books, a division of Penguin Young Readers Group, a member of Penguin Group (USA) Inc., 345 Hudson Street, New York, NY 10014. All rights reserved.)

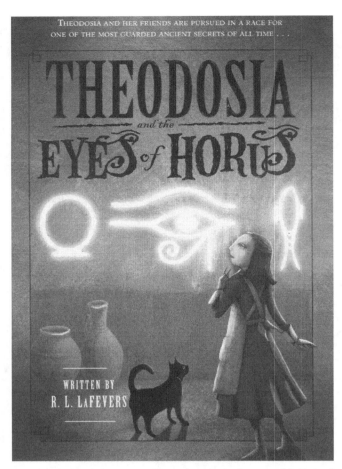

A girl with the ability to travel into the past is the star of LaFevers' middle-grade novel Theodosia and the Eyes of Horus, *featuring artwork by Yoko Tanaka.* (Illustration copyright © 2010 by Yoko Tanaka. Reproduced by permission of Houghton Mifflin Harcourt Publishing Company. All rights reserved.)

upon everything she has ever learned in order to prevent the resulting chaos from destroying her country—and herself. Using "delicious, precise, and atmospheric details," according to *Booklist* critic Gillian Engberg, *Theodosia and the Serpents of Chaos* is "a sure bet for Harry Potter fans," while a *Publishers Weekly* critic recommended LaFevers' novel as "the perfect blend of mystery and humor."

Theo returns in *Theodosia and the Staff of Osiris, Theodosia and the Eyes of Horus,* and *Theodosia and the Last Pharaoh.* In *Theodosia and the Staff of Osiris* the eleven year old is busy shutting down the curses and other malevolence lurking in the objects in her family's Museum of Legends & Antiquities. Her attention is diverted, however, by the appearance of Mr. Tetley and his latest effort to marshal the power of the Serpents of Chaos. When she takes time to watch a performance of the Great Awi Bubu in *Theodosia and the Eyes of Horus,* Theo is drawn into yet another hidden threat to life as we know it, while more adventures involving the occult can be enjoyed by Theo's fans in *Theodosia and the Last Pharaoh.*

Suggesting that the "Theodosia Throckmorton" novels are "best read in order," *School Library Journal* critic

Clare A. Dombrowski recommended *Theodosia and the Eyes of Horus* "enthusiastically to any reader who likes Egyptian history, a good mystery, or fast-paced action." "Theodosia's first-person narration is often very funny," asserted Samantha Larsen Hastings in a review of *Theodosia and the Staff of Osiris* for the same periodical, the critic adding that LaFevers' "plot is quick and multilayered like a well-wrapped mummy." In *Booklist* Ilene Cooper praised the same novel for treating readers to "nonstop action in a delightful English package."

Illustrated by Kelly Murphy, LaFevers' "Nathaniel Fludd, Beastologist" novel series begins with *The Flight of the Phoenix,* in which readers meet the intrepid ten-year-old hero. Now that his parents are presumed lost somewhere in the North Pole, Nathaniel Fludd is put in the care of his Aunt Phil and helps in her business of making maps and caring for mythical creatures such as griffins, dodo birds, gremlins, and the like. A trip to Arabia to administer to a newly hatched phoenix results in Phil's abduction, leaving Nate to mother the mythical bird when others would do it harm.

The Basilisk's Lair finds Nate and his aunt on the trail of a deadly desert serpent whose venom threatens several Sudanese villages. As snippets of information regarding his parents' whereabouts begin to surface and inspire his curiosity, Nate's worries over the efforts of someone to steal the irreplaceable *Fludd Book of Beasts* also vie for his attention. His return to England with Phil is disheartening in *The Wyverns' Treasure;* First they find that the Fludd home has been ransacked and then they must leave for Wales to calm a group of fire-breathing wyverns (dragons) before the household can be set to rights and the *Fludd Book of Beasts* fully protected. Worries over his still-missing parents surface again in *The Unicorn's Tale,* although his growing confidence over his skill as a beastologist makes Nate able to juggle all his responsibilities.

Citing the first "Nathaniel Fludd, Beastologist" novel for its "promising premise," a *Kirkus Reviews* writer added that LaFevers' "exciting tale" will pull even reluctant readers in with its "straightforward sentences, chronological narrative, short chapters," and engaging artwork. In *School Library Journal* Jan Cronkhite also praised *The Flight of the Phoenix,* describing it as "a quick and enriching read that will appeal to a wide variety of children," and Kara Dean wrote in *Booklist* that Nate is "a resourceful and brave protagonist [for] whom readers will root." "The action is non-stop," wrote Cronkhite in appraising Nate's second outing: "The elements of fantasy, mystery, and humor will appeal to a wide audience," she asserted. Also reviewing *The Basilisk's Lair,* a *Kirkus Reviews* writer noted the effective combination of "a hesitant, unskilled hero, a miniature sidekick straight from [Maurice Sendak's] *Where the Wild Things Are* and an exotic setting in colonial British West Africa."

LaFevers' first young-adult novel, *Grave Mercy,* begins her "His Fair Assassin" trilogy and tells the story of seventeen-year-old Ismae. After escaping from the brutality of an arranged marriage, Ismae finds sanctuary at the convent of St. Mortain, where the dedicated sisters still serve the gods of old. Here she learns that the god of Death himself has blessed her with dangerous gifts . . . and a violent destiny. If she chooses to stay at the convent, the teen will be trained as an assassin and serve as a handmaiden to Death.

"My husband jokes that I am a writer so I have an excuse to do research, and he's only half kidding," LaFevers once told *SATA.* "The truth is, I am mad about research. I've always loved it. Even when I was little I adored walking into libraries or museums because I knew I was in the presence of Knowledge. Answers to the Ancient Mysteries lay all around me and I only had to know which books to read in order to find those answers. It's always struck me that the myths from ancient civilizations weren't just a story, but were something the people of the time truly believed were true. What if they were real? What would that be like and how would that affect our world?"

On her home page, LaFevers encourages beginning writers to learn the basics of plotting and style. However, she is quick to add that each person brings an unique viewpoint to their writing, and that uniqueness should be cultivated rather than hidden in order to fit with current trends. A writer's secret weapon "is you," she assured budding wordsmiths. "Your secret, crazy self. Maybe it's even the part of yourself that gets you in trouble sometimes. Are you angry? Sassy? Goofy? Do you get scared easily? Tell wild tales? Make sure and put parts of your secret crazy self into your writing."

Biographical and Critical Sources

PERIODICALS

Booklist, November 1, 2003, Todd Morning, review of *The Falconmaster,* p. 490; May 1, 2007, Gillian Engberg, review of *Theodosia and the Serpents of Chaos,* p. 48; November 15, 2008, Ilene Cooper, review of *Theodosia and the Staff of Osiris,* p. 40; October 1, 2009, Kara Dean, review of *Flight of the Phoenix,* p. 44; May 15, 2010, Kara Dean, review of *The Basilisk's Lair,* p. 51; April 1, 2011, Kara Dean, review of *The Unicorn's Tale,* p. 70.
Bulletin of the Center for Children's Books, December, 2003, Krista Hutley, review of *The Falconmaster,* p. 156; May, 2007, Cindy Welch, review of *Theodosia and the Serpents of Chaos,* p. 373.
Creative Kids, spring, 2010, Hayley Schroeder, interview with LaFevers, p. 8.
Kirkus Reviews, November 1, 2003, review of *The Falconmaster,* p. 1312; April 1, 2007, review of *Theodosia and the Serpents of Chaos;* July 15, 2009, review of *The Flight of the Phoenix;* May 15, 2010, review of *The Basilisk's Lair.*
Publishers Weekly, November 24, 2003, review of *The Falconmaster,* p. 64; April 9, 2007, review of *Theodosia and the Serpents of Chaos,* p. 54.
School Library Journal, January, 2004, Jane G. Gonnor, review of *The Falconmaster,* p. 132; December, 2004, Beth L. Meister, review of *The Forging of the Blade,* p. 112; April, 2007, Margaret A. Chang, review of *Theodosia and the Serpents of Chaos,* p. 140; December, 2008, Samantha Larsen Hastings, review of *Theodosia and the Staff of Osiris,* p. 130; July, 2010, Clare A. Dombrowski, review of *Theodosia and the Eyes of Horus,* p. 92; September, 2009, Jane Cronkhite, review of *The Flight of the Phoenix,* p. 127; July, 2010, Jane Cronkhite, review of *The Basilisk's Lair,* p. 63, and Clare A. Dombrowski, review of *Theodosia and the Eyes of Horus,* p. 92.
Voice of Youth Advocates, April, 2011, review of *Theodosia and the Eyes of Horus,* p. 10.

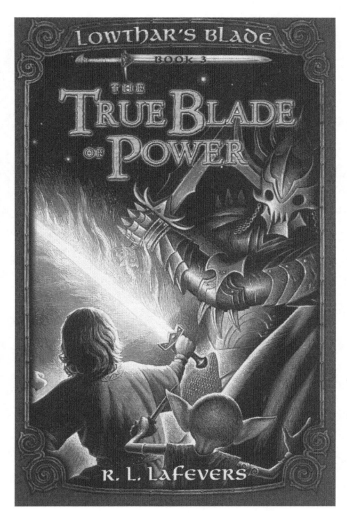

Cover of LaFevers' novel **The True Blade of Power,** *featuring artwork by Hunter Brown.* (Jacket art © 2005 by Hunter Brown. All rights reserved. Reproduced by permission of Puffin Books, a division of Penguin Young Readers Group, a member of Penguin Group (USA) Inc., 345 Hudson Street, New York, NY 10014. All rights reserved.)

ONLINE

Enchanted Inkpot Web log, http://enchantedinkpot.
livejournal.com/ (June 9, 2010), interview with
LaFevers.
R.L. LaFevers Home Page, http://www.rllafevers.com (October 21, 2011).
R.L. LaFevers Web log, http://rllafevers.blogspot.com (October 21, 2011).

*   *   *

LaFEVERS, Robin
See LaFEVERS, R.L.

*   *   *

LANG, Diane
(Lang Buchanan, a joint pseudonym)

Personal

Married. *Education:* University of Cincinnati, degree;
attended University of Iowa writer's workshop, 2000.

Addresses

Home—Richmond, GA.

Career

Educator and author. Former high-school drama and
language-arts teacher in Atlanta, GA. Tin Roof Films,
Atlanta, GA, creative development executive. Speaker
at conferences; presenter at schools.

Awards, Honors

Named Teacher of the Year; Disney Teacher Award
nomination.

Writings

(With Michael Buchanan, under joint pseudonym Lang
Buchanan) *Micah's Child,* Dragonon, Inc., 2006.
(With Michael Buchanan) *The Fat Boy Chronicles* (also
see below), Sleeping Bear Press (Ann Arbor, MI),
2010.
(With Michael Buchanan) *The Fat Boy Chronicles* (screenplay; adapted from the novel), Tin Roof Films, 2010.

Also coauthor, under joint pseudonym Lang Buchanan,
of the novel *Cry of the Quetzal* as well as screenplays
including *Treasure of the Four Lions, Ryan's Heart,
Bait and Tackle.* Former food critic for *Cincinnati Inquirer;* columnist for *50Plus* magazine; contributor to
other periodicals, including *Lakewood Ranch News.*

Sidelights

Diane Lang and writing partner Michael Buchanan have
produced novels as well as screenplays since they began their creative collaboration in 2000. In writing their
middle-grade novel *The Fat Boy Chronicles* Lang and
Buchanan were inspired by a true story as well as by
their own backgrounds as award-winning educators.

Lang and Buchanan met while working as teachers in
Atlanta, Georgia, where Buchanan taught math and science and Lang taught language arts. Their interest in
combining literature with their classroom subjects in
unique ways forged their friendship, and eventually
Lang convinced Buchanan to join her at a writer's
workshop. By 2006, they had published their first novel,
Micah's Child, under the joint pseudonym Lang
Buchanan. An historical romance, the novel has been
followed by several other works, including several
screenplays.

The genesis of *The Fat Boy Chronicles* occurred during
a book signing for *Micah's Child,* when the two authors
met Mr. Hennig and his son, Doug, and learned how
Doug had endured merciless bullying during middle
school due to his weight. Then, by sticking to an exercise regimen and learning about proper nutrition, during
ninth grade the determined teen managed to lose sixty
pounds. Clearly Doug had a story to tell about overcoming obstacles, and Lang and Buchanan fictionalized
his story in journal form as *The Fat Boy Chronicles.*

Jimmy Winterpock is the overweight hero of *The Fat
Boy Chronicles,* and by the time he turns fifteen the
five-foot-five-inch teen weighs almost 200 pounds.
Through Jimmy's eyes readers see the classmates who
taunt him, as well as the way he is discounted by his
schoolmates to the point where he feels he does not
exist. Readers also watch as Jimmy decides to opt
against self-pity and depression. Instead, the teen decides to make positive changes in his life by researching obesity and combating it. While Jimmy is battling
his weight, he also comes to the aid of Paul, a classmate whose foolish attempt to jump from a moving
train resulted in the loss of both his legs. Another outsider at school, Paul now immerses himself in following a local unsolved murder, and Jimmy helps him compensate for his lack of mobility and eventually solve the
crime. In *The Fat Boy Chronicles* Lang and Buchanan
give their teen narrator "a refreshingly down-to-earth
point of view," asserted *Booklist* contributor Miriam
Aronin, and "many readers will both relate to and learn
from Jimmy."

Biographical and Critical Sources

PERIODICALS

Booklist, July 1, 2010, Miriam Aronin, review of *The Fat
Boy Chronicles,* p. 50.

Chesterfield Observer (Chesterfield County, VA), September 2, 2009, Gwen Sadler, "*The Fat Boy Chronicles* Goes to Hollywood."

School Library Journal, December, 2010, Joanna K. Fabicon, review of *The Fat Boy Chronicles,* p. 118.

ONLINE

Fat Boy Chronicles Web site, http://www.thefatboy chronicles.com/ (October 21, 2011).

Lang Buchanan Home Page, http://www.langbuchanan. com (October 21, 2011).

Lang Buchanan Web log, http://langbuchanan.blogs.com (October 21, 2011).*

* * *

LATYK, Olivier 1976-

Personal

Born 1976, in Strasbourg, France; married; children: Rose. *Education:* Studied in Paris and Strasbourg, France. *Hobbies and other interests:* Aikido, sea fishing.

Addresses

Home—La Rochelle, France. *Agent*—Good Illustration, Ltd., 11-15 Betterton St., Covent Garden, London WC2H 9BP, England. *E-mail*—olivier.latyk@wanadoo. fr.

Career

Illustrator for children's books and advertising, beginning c. 2002. Designer of puzzles and mobiles.

Writings

SELF-ILLUSTRATED

A comme, Éditions l'Édue (Andernos-les-Bains, France), 2007.

ILLUSTRATOR

Bruno Hourst, *Au bon plaisir d'apprendre,* InterÉditions (Paris, France), 1997, third edition, 2008.

Jean-Pierre Kerloc'h, *Les deux moitiés de rêve,* Albin Michel Jeunesse (Paris, France), 1997.

Juliette Mellon, *Change de voix, Lapinou!,* Éditions Nathan (Paris, France), 1999.

(With others) Ann Rocard, *Contes d'Europe,* Éditions Lito (Campigny-sur-Marne, France), 1999.

(With others) Valérie Guidoux, *Au fil des saisons,* Éditions Nathan (Paris, France), 1999.

Christian Lamblin, *Le pouvoir du froid,* Éditions Nathan (Paris, France), 1999.

Frédéric Lenormand, *Je m'envole!,* Éditions Milan (Toulouse, France), 2000.

Jean-Baptiste de Panafieu, *Les bords de mer,* Éditions Nathan (Paris, France), 2000.

(With Étienne Butterlin) James Gourier, *La montagne,* Éditions Nathan (Paris, France), 2000.

Michel Boucher, *Manger comme un ogre,* Actes Sud Junior (Arles, France), 2000.

Jo Hoestlandt, *Mes petites étoiles,* Éditions Milan (Toulouse, France), 2000.

Anouk Bloch-Henry, *Le roi superbe,* Milan (Toulouse, France), 2001.

Dominique Dupriez, *Quel tintamarre!,* Éditions Milan (Toulouse, France), 2001.

Jo Hoestlandt, *Réponds-moi quant je t'écris!,* Casterman (Paris, France), 2001.

Rachel Hausfater-Douïeb, *Le petit garçon étoile,* Casterman (Paris, France), 2001.

Nathalie Tordjman, *Des jardins à croquer,* Actes Sud Junior (Arles, France), 2001.

Syllvie Dugeay, reteller, *Étonnantes mesures,* Albin Michel Jeunesse (Paris, France), 2001.

Ghislaine Roman and Bruno Pilorget, *Bientôt Noël!: une histoire par jour et des jeux pour attendre Noël,* Milan (Toulouse, France), 2001.

(With others) Isabelle Bézard, *101 poèmes pour les petits,* Bayard Jeunesse (Paris, France), 2002.

Ester Rota Gasperoni, *La porte d'en face,* Actes Sud Junior (Arles, France), 2002.

Béatrice Tanaka, *Le songe de la princesse Adetola,* Albin Michel Jeunesse (Paris, France), 2002.

Falzar, *Vacances joyeuses,* Casterman (Paris, France), 2002.

Rachel Hausfater-Douïeb, *Je ne joue plus!,* Casterman (Paris, France), 2002.

Kochka, *Le liseron de Jules,* Belin Jeunesse (Paris, France), 2002.

Olivier Mau, *Armand dur à cuire et moi!,* Syros Jeunesse (Paris, France), 2002.

Jean-Pierre Guéno, *Les enfants du silence,* Milan (Toulouse, France), 2003.

Michel Boucher, *Faire la pluie et le beau temps,* Actes Sud Junior (Arles, France), 2003.

Sophie Loubière, *Éléphanfare,* Albin Michel Jeunesse (Paris, France), 2003.

Anouk Bloch-Henry, *Un bateau pour demain,* Milan Juenesse (Toulouse, France), 2003.

André Maurois, *Le pays de 36000 volontés,* Hachette Jeunesse (Paris, France), 2003.

Ghislaine Roman, *Le 4 saisons: deux histoires par mois et des jeux pour toutes les saisons,* Milan Jeunesse (Toulouse, France), 2003.

Jacob and Wilhelm Grimm, *Tom Pouce,* Tourbillon (Paris, France), 2003.

(With Anne Eydoux) Valérie Videau, *Les animaux du froid,* Éditions Nathan (Paris, France), 2003, translated by Al Daigen as *Animals of the Cold,* Firefly Books (Richmond Hill, Ontario, Canada), 2005.

Corinne Albaut and Sylvie Pierre, *La merveilleuse légende de sainte Nicholas,* Actes Sud Junior (Arles, France), 2003.

Henriette Bichonnier, *Lutin et Lutinette: un histoire écrite*, Bayard Jeunesse (Paris, France), 2004.

Virginie Aladjidi and Caroline Pellissier, adapters, *L'arche d Noé* (from the book of Genesis), Éditions Nathan (Paris, France), 2004.

Virginie Aladjidi and Caroline Pellissier, adapters, *La création du monde* (from the book of Genesis), Éditions Nathan (Paris, France), 2004.

(With Philippe Mignon) Marie Kolaczek, *L'espace*, Éditions France Loisirs (Paris, France), 2004, translated by Al Daigen as *Exploring Space*, Firefly Books (Richmond Hill, Ontario, Canada), 2005.

Marie Houblon, *Si j'étais . . .*, Casterman (Paris, France), 2004.

(With others) Jean-Hugues Malineau, *Premier poèmes pour tous les jours*, Milan Jeunesse (Toulouse, France), 2004.

Charles Perrault, *Cendrillon*, Larousse (Paris, France), 2004.

Sylvie Poillevé, *Le rêve de Mehdi*, Père Castor-Flammarion (Paris, France), 2005.

Anouk Bloch-Henry, *Le bon côté des choses*, Actes Sud Junior (Arles, France), 2005.

Stéphane Daniel, *Un cadeau pour le Père Noël*, Casterman (Paris, France), 2005.

Anne Jonas, *Là-bas tout au fond du dessin*, Éditions Sarabacane (Paris, France), 2005, new edition, 2007.

Jo Hoestlandt, *Le moulin à paroles*, Bayard Jeunesse (Paris, France), 2006.

Béatrice Vincent, *Le festind de Coco*, Albin Michel Jeunesse (Paris, France), 2006.

Hélène Juvigny and Brigitte Labbé, *Maman a une maladie grave*, Milan Jeunesse (Toulouse, France), 2007.

(With others) Julien Hirsinger and Séverine Charon, *Le monde où je vis*, Éditions Nathan (Paris, France), 2007.

Charles Perrault, *Le chat botté*, Hachette Jeunesse (Paris, France), 2007.

Anouk Bloch-Henry, *Qu'est-ce-que tu préfères?*, Milan Jeunesse (Toulouse, France), 2007.

Ghislaine Roman, *Bientôt Noël!: 24 histoires pour attendre Noël*, Milan Jeunesse (Toulouse, France), 2007.

Hubert Ben Kemoun, *Monsieur Boniface*, Tourbillon (Paris, France), 2008.

Rudyard Kipling, *La baleine et son gosier*, translation by Robert d'Humières and Louis Fabulet, Père Castor-Flammarion (Paris, France), 2008.

Éric Sanvoisin, *La petite buveuse de couleurs*, Éditions Nathan (Paris, France), 2008.

Claire Clément, *En avant, petit train!*, Bayard Jeunesse (Montrouge, France), 2008.

Éric Sanvoisin, *Le buveur de fautes d'orthographe*, Éditions Nathan (Paris, France), 2009.

(With Yann Le Béchec and Sébastien Telleschi) Jean-Michel Billioud, *L'Europe*, Éditions Nathan (Paris, France), 2009.

Éric Sanvoisin, *La cité des buveurs d'encre*, Éditions Nathan (Paris, France), 2009.

Olivier Ka, *La vie merveilleuse de la princesse Olga*, Éditions l'Édune (Andernous-les-Bains, France), 2009.

Agnès de Lestrade, *Arto et la fée des livres*, Milan Jeunesse (Toulouse, France), 2010.

Éric Sanvoisin, *Le livre des petits buveurs d'encre*, Éditions Nathan (Paris, France), 2010.

Alain Doressoundiram, *C'est comment la station spatiale?*, Belin (Paris, France), 2010.

Jo Hoestlandt, *Mathématic et tac: 30 casse-tête pas casse-pieds!*, Éditions Nathan (Paris, France), 2010.

Douglas Rees, *Jeannette Claus Saves Christmas*, Margaret K. McElderry Books (New York, NY), 2010.

Ruth Martin, *Where on Earth Is the Moon?*, Templar (London, England), 2010, published as *Moon Dreams*, Templar Books (Somerville, MA), 2010.

(With others) Julien Hirsinger and Séverine Charon, *Le monde où je vis*, Éditions Nathan (Paris, France), 2010.

Èric Sanvoisin, *Le mystère des buveurs d'encre*, Éditions Nathan (Paris, France), 2011.

Contributor to periodicals, including *Boston Globe, New York Times,* and *Wall Street Journal.*

Biographical and Critical Sources

PERIODICALS

Booklist, July 1, 2010, Abby Nolan, review of *Moon Dreams*, p. 67; November 15, 2010, Daniel Kraus, review of *Jeannette Claus Saves Christmas*, p. 50.

Horn Book, November-December, 2010, Kitty Flynn, review of *Jeannette Claus Saves Christmas*, p. 67.

Publishers Weekly, July 5, 2010, review of *Moon Dreams*, p. 40.

School Librarian, spring, 2011, Angela Lepper, review of *Where on Earth Is the Moon?*, p. 27.

School Library Journal, October, 2010, Mara Alpert, review of *Jeannette Claus Saves Christmas*, p. 76; April, 2011, Barbara Elleman, review of *Moon Dreams*, p. 149.

ONLINE

Children's Illustrators Web site, http://www.childrens illustrators.com/ (September 29, 2011), "Olivier Latyk."

Olivier Latyk Home Page, http://www.olivierlatyk.com (September 29, 2011).*

*   *   *

LEONHARDT, Alice 1950-
(Alison Hart)

Personal

Born April 16, 1950, in Baltimore, MD; daughter of Karl and Dorothy Leonhardt; married Bruce Thompson; children: Brian, Beth Anne Thompson. *Education:* University of Maryland, B.S.; John Hopkins University, M.S. *Hobbies and other interests:* Horses.

Alice Leonhardt (Photograph by Woods Pierce, Jr. Reproduced by permission.)

Addresses

Home—Mt. Sidney, VA. *E-mail*—alison@alisonhart books.com.

Career

Writer and educator. Special education teacher, Howard County, MD, 1976-94; writer, 1988—; Blue Ridge Community College, Weyers Cave, VA, adjunct instructor, 1995—; court-appointed special advocate for abused children, beginning 1996.

Member

Society of Children's Book Writers and Illustrators, Mystery Writers Association, Children's Book Guild.

Awards, Honors

Edgar Allan Poe Award nomination, Mystery Writers of America, 2000, for *Shadow Horse;* Honor Book Award, Society of School Librarians International, 2004, for *Return of the Gypsy Witch;* Teacher's Choice selection, International Reading Association, 2006, for *Anna's Blizzard;* honors from numerous state reading associations.

Writings

Wild Cats, Steck-Vaughn (Austin, TX), 1999.
Mystery of the Vanishing Leopard, Steck-Vaughn (Austin, TX), 1999.

Why the Ocean Is Salty, Steck-Vaughn (Austin, TX), 1999.
Ocean Life: Tide Pool Creatures, Steck-Vaughn (Austin, TX), 2000.
Turtle's Big Race, Steck-Vaughn (Austin, TX), 2000.
Save the Sea Turtles, Steck-Vaughn (Austin, TX), 2000.
The Princess and the Castle, Steck-Vaughn (Austin, TX), 2000.
Castles, Steck-Vaughn (Austin, TX), 2000.
Trash Is Dash, Steck-Vaughn (Austin, TX), 2002.
Animals You Will Never Forget, Steck-Vaughn (Austin, TX), 2002.
One Special Dog, Steck-Vaughn (Austin, TX), 2002.
Mystery at the White House, Steck-Vaughn (Austin, TX), 2002.
Presidents, Steck-Vaughn (Austin, TX), 2002.

Also author of books in the "Nancy Drew Casefiles" series. Contributor to *Highlights for Children, Ladybug,* and other periodicals.

"LINDA CRAIG" NOVEL SERIES

Kathy in Charge, Simon & Schuster (New York, NY), 1990.
The Riding Club, Simon & Schuster (New York, NY), 1990.
A Horse for Jackie, Simon & Schuster (New York, NY), 1990.
The Glimmering Ghost, Simon & Schuster (New York, NY), 1990.
The Silver Stallion, Simon & Schuster (New York, NY), 1990.

"THOROUGHBRED" NOVEL SERIES

Melanie's Last Ride, HarperCollins (New York, NY), 1998.
A Home for Melanie, HarperCollins (New York, NY), 1998.
Living Legend, HarperCollins (New York, NY), 2000.
The Bad Luck Filly, HarperCollins (New York, NY), 2000.
Perfect Image, HarperCollins (New York, NY), 2000.
Team Player, HarperCollins (New York, NY), 2001.
Racing Image, HarperCollins (New York, NY), 2001.
Perfect Challenge, HarperCollins (New York, NY), 2002.
Faith in a Long Shot, HarperCollins (New York, NY), 2003.

Also author of *Christina's Courage, Dead Heat,* and *Star in Danger.*

"NEW ADVENTURES OF MARY-KATE AND ASHLEY" NOVEL SERIES

The Case of the High Seas Secret, HarperEntertainment (New York, NY), 2001.
The Case of the Jingle Bell Jinx, HarperEntertainment (New York, NY), 2001.

The Case of the Mall Mystery, HarperEntertainment (New York, NY), 2002.

UNDER PSEUDONYM ALISON HART

Shadow Horse, Random House (New York, NY), 1999, new edition, 2010.

Chase: A Police Story, Random House (New York, NY), 2002.

Rescue: A Police Story, Random House (New York, NY), 2002.

Fires of Jubilee, Aladdin (New York, NY), 2003.

Return of the Gypsy Witch, Aladdin (New York, NY), 2003.

Anna's Blizzard, Peachtree (Atlanta, GA), 2005.

A Spy on the Home Front: A Molly Mystery, illustrated by Jean-Paul Tibbles, American Girl (Middleton, WI), 2005.

Bell's Star ("Horse Diaries" series), illustrated by Ruth Sanderson, Random House (New York, NY), 2009.

Emma's River, illustrated by Paul Bachem, Peachtree (Atlanta, GA), 2010.

Taking the Reins ("American Girl Innerstar University" series), illustrated by Arcana Studios, American Girl (Middleton, WI), 2010.

Whirlwind (sequel to *Shadow Horse*), Random House (New York, NY), 2010.

Dive Right In ("American Girl Innerstar University" series), illustrated by Arcana Studios, American Girl (Middleton, WI), 2011.

Risky Chance ("Horse Diaries" series), illustrated by Ruth Sanderson, Random House (New York, NY), 2011.

"RIDING ACADEMY" SERIES; UNDER PSEUDONYM ALISON HART

A Horse for Mary Beth, Random House (New York, NY), 1994.

Andie out of Control, Random House (New York, NY), 1994.

Jina Rides to Win, Random House (New York, NY), 1994.

Mary Beth's Haunted Ride, Random House (New York, NY), 1994.

Andie Shows Off, Random House (New York, NY), 1994.

Jina's Pain-in-the-Neck Pony, Random House (New York, NY), 1995.

The Craziest Horse Show Ever, Random House (New York, NY), 1995.

Andie's Risky Business, Random House (New York, NY), 1995.

Trouble at Foxhall, Random House (New York, NY), 1995.

Foxhunt!, Random House (New York, NY), 1995.

Lauren Rides to the Rescue, Random House (New York, NY), 1995.

Haunted Horseback Holiday, Random House (New York, NY), 1996.

"RACING TO FREEDOM" NOVEL TRILOGY; UNDER PSEUDONYM ALISON HART

Gabriel's Horses, Peachtree (Atlanta, GA), 2007.

Gabriel's Triumph, Peachtree (Atlanta, GA), 2007.

Gabriel's Journey, Peachtree (Atlanta, GA), 2007.

Sidelights

Alice Leonhardt, a prolific author who writes under the pen name Alison Hart, recognizes literacy as a serious issue in contemporary society. In addition to penning stories that include *Return of the Gypsy Witch, Gabriel's Horses,* and *Anna's Blizzard,* Leonhardt works as an educator at a community college near her home in Virginia. With each book she writes, her goal is to capture readers with intriguing plot twists, drawing them into books they cannot put down. As she stated on her home page, "I love writing books that keep young readers glued to the pages."

Under her pen name Alison Hart, Leonhardt has published horse stories and nonfiction as well as works of historical fiction. On the *Cynsations* Web log, the author explained that "each novel I write must be filled with vivid scenes that not only convey our history, but bring it to life for readers." As Hart she is the author of books such as *Shadow Horse, Fires of Jubilee,* and *Return of the Gypsy Witch,* as well as the books in the "Racing to Freedom" trilogy. *Return of the Gypsy Witch* showcases Leonhardt's ability to keep readers intrigued by spinning a suspense-filled plot that follows detective sisters Allie and Kat as they try to catch a thief. While Kat follows all the rules, Allie is more rebellious and mischievous. However, despite her careful nature, Kat ultimately winds up in danger when her plan to lure the thief into a trap takes an unwanted turn. It is now up to Allie to save her sister and solve the mystery. While the dialogue in *Return of the Gypsy Witch* was described by some reviewers as occasionally excessive, John Green wrote in *Booklist* that Hart's plot features "exciting, but never terrifying, twists and turns."

Set at the end of the U.S. Civil War, *Fires of Jubilee* concerns thirteen-year-old Abby Joyner. A former slave, Abby now leaves the plantation that was her home to embark on a search for her mother, who disappeared under mysterious circumstances years earlier. According to *School Library Journal* critic Nancy P. Reeder, Leonhardt's novel offers "an interesting look at a sad time in this nation's history."

Gabriel's Horses, the first work in the author's "Racing to Freedom" trilogy, also explores the issue of slavery. A young slave who dreams of becoming a jockey, Gabriel trains under his father, a freed man who works as a horse trainer on a Kentucky plantation belonging to Master Giles. Hoping to earn money to purchase his wife and son's freedom, Gabriel's father joins the Union Army, leaving Gabriel at the hands of a merciless new trainer. Alone one night, Gabriel proves his worth to Master Giles by courageously protecting a group of horses from a band of Confederate raiders. "Readers will find this wonderful blend of history and horses appealing," Ann Robinson observed in her *School Library Journal* review of *Gabriel's Horses.* In *Gabriel's Triumph,* the second installment in the series, the talented young horseman has earned his freedom and now ventures to New York, where he plans to ride Giles' prized thoroughbred in a prestigious race at Saratoga. Leonhardt's trilogy concludes in *Gabriel's Journey*, as Gabriel reunites with his father, now a sergeant in the cavalry. As Reeder stated, "The narrative is well written and the major characters have depth and realism."

Also published under Leonhardt's Alison Hart pseudonym, *Anna's Blizzard* is based on a tragic event from U.S. history: the "Schoolchildren's Blizzard" of 1888 during which more than 200 people perished on the high plains, many of them children. When an unexpected snowstorm traps her classmates in their one-room schoolhouse, Nebraska farm girl Anna Vail braves the elements to lead the children to safety with help from her pony, Top Hat. "Anna is a strong, appealing heroine," Kathleen E. Gruver maintained in *School Library Journal,* and a contributor in *Kirkus Reviews* predicted that "readers should identify with Anna and admire her spunk."

Set in 1852, *Emma's River* centers on Emma Wright, a spoiled ten year old who travels with her mother by steamboat along the Mississippi and Missouri rivers. While sneaking down to the main deck to visit her prized pony in its stall, Emma meets Patrick O'Brien,

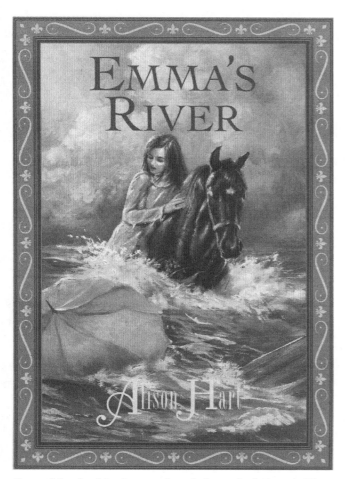

Cover of Leonhardt's adventure-themed chapter book **Emma's River,** *featuring artwork by Paul Bachem.* (Illustration copyright © 2010 by Paul Bachem. Reproduced by permission of Peachtree Publishers.)

an Irish stowaway. The two form an unlikely friendship and later assist other passengers when the steamboat's boiler explodes. "Hart well conveys . . . Emma's gradual move away from willfulness and muddled thinking," Abby Nolan stated in her *Booklist* review of *Emma's River,* while Necia Blundy observed in *School Library Journal* that "readers will enjoy following her as she learns and grows."

"I knew that children, *all* children, desperately wanted to read," Leonhardt once told *SATA,* recalling her experiences as a special education teacher. "Most children pick it up naturally. However, the students I taught, although just as desperate to read, struggled mightily with every word. I tried many different techniques to unlock the mysteries of reading. One method that worked was having them read stories that I wrote using their names and personal information. So you can say I started my career as an author writing stories for reading disabled students. The stories weren't works of literary genius, but my students loved them—and slowly, they learned.

"Not only is reading literacy a huge issue, so is reading *aliteracy.* Aliteracy is defined as the lack of interest in reading. Today I teach college-level students. Like my beginning readers, some continue to struggle with reading. But what really scares me is their lack of interest in reading. One eighteen year old told me he had never read an entire book!"

Leonhardt further noted, "I constantly question how I, how *we,* can help get children excited about reading. I haven't found any magic answers, but when I write a book, literacy and aliteracy are very much on my mind. Is my story filled with suspense? Does it hook readers from the first chapter? Can readers relate to my characters? Will the story fill them with a sense of wonder? *Will they love reading my book?* When young readers tell me they couldn't put my book down, I know I'm on the right track. Obviously, my books will not solve reading literacy problems, but I hope they, and I, can do a small part."

Biographical and Critical Sources

PERIODICALS

Booklist, June, 1994, Carolyn Phelan, review of *Andie out of Control,* p. 1948; July, 1999, Shelle Rosenfeld, review of *Shadow Horse,* p. 1946; April 15, 2000, Roger Leslie, review of *Rescue: A Police Story,* p. 1542; May 1, 2003, John Green, review of *Return of the Gypsy Witch,* p. 1529; November 1, 2003, Hazel Rochman, review of *Fires of Jubilee,* p. 496; May 15, 2007, Hazel Rochman, review of *Gabriel's Horses,* p. 41; December 1, 2007, Hazel Rochman, review of *Gabriel's Triumph,* p. 42; June 1, 2010, Abby Nolan, review of *Emma's River,* p. 66.

Kirkus Reviews, September 15, 2005, review of *Anna's Blizzard,* p. 1027; March 1, 2010, review of *Emma's River.*

School Library Journal, September, 1996, Carol Schene, review of *Haunted Horseback Holiday,* p. 202; October, 2000, Timothy Capehart, review of *Rescue,* p. 161; March, 2004, Nancy P. Reeder, review of *Fires of Jubilee,* p. 212; October, 2005, Kathleen E. Gruver, review of *Anna's Blizzard,* p. 115; June, 2007, Ann Robinson, review of *Gabriel's Horses,* p. 146; January, 2008, Nancy P. Reeder, review of *Gabriel's Triumph,* p. 120; July, 2010, Necia Blundy, review of *Emma's River,* p. 90.

ONLINE

Alison Hart Home Page, http://www.alisonhartbooks.com (September 1, 2011).

Cynsations Web log, http://cynthialeitichsmith.blogspot.com/ (February 18, 2010), "Guest Post: Author Alison Hart on Writing about Horses."

*   *   *

LLEWELLYN, Tom 1964-

Personal

Born 1964, in WA; married; wife's name Deb; children: Ben, Abel, Bizayehu, Genet. *Education:* University of Washington, Seattle, B.A. (creative writing). *Hobbies and other interests:* Camping, skiing, playing bass.

Addresses

Home—Tacoma, WA. *Agent*—Abigail Samoun, Red Fox Literary, 129 Morro Ave., Shell Beach, CA 93449. *E-mail*—tommyllew@yahoo.com.

Career

Copywriter, journalist, and author. Russell (investment company), Tacoma, WA, creative director. Editorial curator of *Rotator* magazine, beginning 2011. Volunteer coach for soccer and lacrosse.

Writings

The Tilting House, illustrated by Sarah Watts, Tricycle Press (Berkeley, CA), 2010.

Letter Off Dead (originally serialized in a Web log), illustrated by James Stowe, Tricycle Press (Berkeley, CA), 2011.

Sidelights

A native of the Pacific Northwest, Tom Llewellyn now lives in a late-nineteenth-century house located in western Washington. With its canted floors and strange history, this home has evoked Llewellyn's memories of growing up in an old house where chilly drafts and frozen water lines and loose, squeaky boards were the norm. These images from past and present melded into an eerie setting that, peopled with characters also based in real life, ultimately inspired Llewellyn's darkly humorous fiction debut, *The Tilting House.*

Featuring appropriately macabre black-and-white art by Sarah Watts, *The Tilting House* introduces narrator Josh Peshik as he and his family move into an old house in Tacoma. The house was purchased at a bargain price and Josh's parents initially view it as a definite step up from apartment living. However, Josh quickly recognizes that many things in the Peshik's new home seem a bit "off": handwriting and mathematical equations are scrawled on the dingy plaster walls, the floorboards bowl down to the center of each room, and things that family members unpack keep going missing. As Josh and his brother Aaron begin to investigate, they discover that they are sharing the house with talking rats. Soon rumors surface regarding a mad scientist and a body that is supposedly buried somewhere beneath the squeaky floorboards of the front porch. Then there are the things that suddenly expand to enormous size, supposedly the result of a strange blue powder. Clearly the Peshiks now share their living space with a growing malevolence, and it is up to the two brothers to keep their family safe.

Llewellyn's "decidedly nonlinear" plot in *The Tilting House* "ranges from exaggerated humor to Gothic horror to downright grotesque," noted *School Library Journal* contributor Elaine E. Knight, and a *Kirkus Reviews* writer commented that the book's colorful narration "nails the sibling cadences and camaraderie" to produce a "genre-blending page-turner." A *Publishers Weekly* reviewer cited the "quick pace" and unusual storyline of *The Tilting House,* noting that "Watts' shadowy woodblock-style illustrations . . . will keep readers attentive." In *Booklist* Ian Chipman also recommended the novel, writing that Llewellyn "takes the classic family-in-a-new-house motif and mixes in just the right creaky touches of the macabre."

Since writing *The Tilting House,* Llewellyn has continued to pursue other innovative ways to tell a story. Using the blog format, he decided to craft a second novel, *Letter Off Dead,* in "real time," writing one segment every day. Asked how the unusual format affected the structure of his story, Llewellyn told *Seattle Post-Intelligencer* online interviewer Mark Baumgarten: "It was figuring out, if you were writing a book as a blog, what would be a good format? What could fit into that page-a-day, max? I didn't want to take a novel and cut it up into increments, because that seems kind of phony and a bad reading experience. So, I thought that the letter format . . . seemed like just a great way to do it."

By creating the same anticipation among readers that nineteenth-century novelists Charles Dickens and Anthony Trollope nourished with their serialized novels,

Tom Llewellyn teams up with artist Sarah Watts to craft an eerie adventure in **The Tilting House.** (Illustration copyright © 2010 by Sarah Watts. Reproduced by permission of Tricycle Press, an imprint of Random House Children's Books, a division of Random House, Inc.)

Llewellyn was committed to finishing *Letter Off Dead,* which focuses on the feelings of a boy whose father is now dead. That meant creating a new post each day, whether he was in the writing mood or not. Soon he had thousands of readers following *LetterOffDead.com,* which played out, live, from September of 2009 to June of 2010. *Letter Off Dead* has since been picked up for publication by Tricycle Press, retaining the original illustrations by Llewellyn's friend, artist James Stowe.

Biographical and Critical Sources

PERIODICALS

Booklist, August 1, 2010, Ian Chipman, review of *The Tilting House,* p. 56.

Kirkus Reviews, May 15, 2010, review of *The Tilting House.*

News Tribune (Tacoma, WA), February 7, 2010, Rosemary Ponnekanti, "Book as Blog: Writer Finds Format Works, Forces Discipline"; June 4, 2010, Rosemary Ponnekanti, review of *The Tilting House.*

Publishers Weekly, June 21, 2010, review of *The Tilting House,* p. 46.

School Library Journal, June, 2010, Elaine E. Knight, review of *The Tilting House,* p. 110.

ONLINE

Tom Llewelyn Web log, http://tomllewellyn.blogspot.com (October 15, 2011).

Seattle Post-Intelligencer Web log, http://blog.seattlepi.com/city-arts/ (November 15, 2010), Mark Baumgarten, interview with Llewellyn.*

M

MacHALE, D.J. 1956-

Personal

Born Donald James MacHale, March 11, 1956, in Port Chester, NY; married; wife's name Evangeline; children: Keaton (daughter). *Education:* New York University, B.F.A. *Hobbies and other interests:* Running, playing guitar, skiing, backpacking.

Addresses

Home—Southern CA. *Agent*—Richard Curtis, Richard Curtis Associates, 171 E. 74th St., Fl. 2, New York, NY 10021. *E-mail*—djmac@djmachalebooks.com.

Career

Writer, film director, and executive producer of television programming. Worked variously as a filmmaker, freelance writer/director, and teacher of photography and film production. Cocreator and producer of television series, including *Are You Afraid of the Dark?*, Nickelodeon, and *Flight 29 Down*, Discovery Kids/NBC.

Awards, Honors

CableAce Award nomination for Best Writer, for "The Tale of Cutter's Treasure" (episode of *Are You Afraid of the Dark?*); Gemini Award nomination for Best Director, for "The Tale of the Dangerous Soup" (episode of *Are You Afraid of the Dark?*); CableAce Award for Best Youth Television Series, for *Chris Cross;* CableAce Award nomination for Best Writing, for *Encyclopedia Brown, Boy Detective* (television program); Gemini Award for Best Youth Television Series, for *Are You Afraid of the Dark?;* Director's Guild of America Award for Children's Program nomination, and Writers Guild of America Award, 2008, both for *Flight 29 Down.*

Writings

"PENDRAGON" YOUNG-ADULT NOVEL SERIES

The Merchant of Death, Aladdin (New York, NY), 2002.
The Lost City of Faar, Aladdin (New York, NY), 2003.
The Never War, Aladdin (New York, NY), 2003.
The Reality Bug, Aladdin (New York, NY), 2003.
Black Water, Aladdin (New York, NY), 2004.
(With Victor Lee and Peter Ferguson) *Pendragon: The Guide to the Territories of Halla* (atlas of places from the series), Aladdin (New York, NY), 2005.
The Rivers of Zadaa, Simon & Schuster (New York, NY), 2005.
The Quillan Games, Simon & Schuster (New York, NY), 2006.
The Pilgrims of Rayne, Simon & Schuster (New York, NY), 2007.
Raven Rise, Simon & Schuster (New York, NY), 2008.
The Soldiers of Halla, Simon & Schuster (New York, NY), 2009.

"THE TRAVELERS" YOUNG-ADULT NOVEL SERIES

(With Carla Jablonski) *Pendragon before the War: Book One,* Simon & Schuster (New York, NY), 2009.
(With Walter Sorrells) *Pendragon before the War: Book Two,* Simon & Schuster (New York, NY), 2009.
(With Walter Sorrells) *Pendragon before the War: Book Three,* Simon & Schuster (New York, NY), 2009.

"MORPHEUS ROAD" YOUNG-ADULT NOVEL TRILOGY

The Light, Aladdin (New York, NY), 2010.
The Black, Aladdin (New York, NY), 2011.

OTHER

(Reteller), *East of the Sun, West of the Moon,* Rabbit Ears (Westport, CT), 1991, illustrated by Vivienne Flesher, Abdo (Edina, MN), 2006.
The Monster Princess (picture book), illustrated by Alexandra Boiger, Aladdin Paperbacks (New York, NY), 2010.

Scriptwriter for television programs, including *ABC Afterschool Specials; Ghostwriter,* PBS; and *Encyclopedia Brown, Boy Detective,* HBO. Executive producer, writer, and director of *Are You Afraid of the Dark?* (television series), and Disney television movie *Tower of Terror.* Cocreator and writer of television series, including *Chris Cross*, Showtime, and *Flight 29 Down*, Discovery Kids/ NBC. Coauthor of *The Tale of the Nightly Neighbors.*

Adaptations

The "Pendragon" series was adapted for audiobook by Brilliance Audio; *The Merchant of Death* was adapted for a graphic novel by Carla Speed McNeil.

Sidelights

An award-winning screenwriter, D.J. MacHale is best known as the author of the hugely popular "Pendragon" fantasy novels, a series centering on a fourteen year old whose life takes a dramatic turn when he learns of his wondrous heritage. MacHale has also garnered praise for his "Morpheus Road" trilogy of supernatural thrillers, as well as for *The Monster Princess,* his debut picture book. Having found success in a number of mediums, MacHale stated in a Simon & Schuster online interview that there is one constant in his writing efforts: "Storytelling is storytelling. Good stories need compelling characters and interesting conflicts. That's the bottom line no matter what medium you're writing for."

A collection of ten young-adult novels, MacHale's "Pendragon" series spins a tale of adventure as Bobby Pendragon joins other Travelers—beings who can travel through space and time—to secure the territories of Halla from the evil doings of the shape-shifting Saint Dane. With over five million copies in print, the "Pendragon" books are more adventure than science fiction: Bobby must rely not on magic or superhuman powers but rather on his skills and acumen to foil the machinations of the cleve Saint Dane. MacHale focused on this realistic aspect of the fantasy series in his Simon & Schuster online interview. "I believe Bobby's appeal comes from the fact that he never loses sight of the person he was before the adventure began," he explained. "When he's faced with a challenge, he reacts the way a regular person would. I believe readers put themselves into Bobby's shoes, imagining how they would deal with the same challenges." Another aspect of the "Pendragon" series that keeps readers hooked is the fact that Bobby would much rather be at home with his family in Connecticut, shooting hoops and hanging out with friends. The problem is that once he became a Traveler, his family disappeared. Part of the mystery that unfolds during "Pendragon" concerns why Bobby was chosen to become a Traveler, as well as what happened to his family.

MacHale grew up in Greenwich, Connecticut, and enjoyed reading. "I had an odd history in that I went from Dr. Seuss, straight to Ian Fleming," he told *Writers Write* online interviewer Claire E. White. "I'm sad to say that I missed out on the wealth of terrific 'middle

reader' literature . . . out there. But I believe that reading the adventure thrillers written by Fleming and Alistair McLean developed my love for the genre." By high school MacHale's focus had turned to filmmaking, and he graduated from New York University with a degree in fine arts and film.

After college, MacHale worked filming advertisements and public-service announcements. "But the whole time I was writing screenplays and teleplays and trying to break into entertainment," he recalled to White. "It wasn't until I started writing for kids that my stories started to sell. So . . . I guess you could say that, through trial and error, I eventually found my true calling." MacHale forged a successful career in television, directing, producing, writing, and creating children's content for channels from Nickelodeon to Discovery Kids. He was the cocreator and writer behind such television shows as *Are You Afraid of the Dark? Flight 29 Down,* and *Chris Cross.*

Through his work in television, MacHale gained experience writing for children. When asked about his turn from screen to printed page, he explained to White:

Cover of D.J. MacHale's novel **Raven Rise,** *part of his "Pendragon" series and featuring artwork by Dawn Austin.* (Illustration copyright © 2008 by Dawn Austin. Reproduced by permission of Simon & Schuster Books for Young Readers and Dawn Austin.)

"Any screenwriter will tell you that as satisfying and wonderful a career as that is, outside of the people you work with, nobody actually reads what you write. Your writing goes through a process, touched by multiple dozens of people, until it becomes a finished piece of film. . . . Writing a book is much more pure than that, and I wanted to experience it."

MacHale had long planned to write the story at the heart of the "Pendragon" books, but he realized that the depth of detail involved was not appropriate for television. Instead, in 2001, he began to write the story in book form. The result was *The Merchant of Death.* Content with his basketball career, his girlfriend, and his suburban Connecticut life, fourteen-year-old Bobby receives the shock of his life when his uncle Press explains to the teen that they are both actually Travelers: beings able to make the leap between parallel realities and on whom many worlds depend. Uncle Press now asks Bobby to travel with him to the territory of Denduron, a medieval civilization that is about to experience civil war. In Denduron the two learn of the vicious Saint Dane, a shape changer who hopes to take over all the worlds the Travelers have sworn to protect. Reviewing *The Merchant of Death* for *School Library Journal,* Celeste Steward recommended the series as "perfect for reluctant readers."

Bobby's adventures continue in further "Pendragon" novels, among them *The Lost City of Faar, The Never War,* and *The Reality Bug.* In each book he travels to a new world via an interplanetary wormhole, visiting underwater cities, parallel Earths, and unusual societies. Along the way the teen meets fellow Travelers, including Spader and Loor, and sends his journal chronicles to his best friends back home in Connecticut. MacHale tells each of the stories by combining a third-person narrative with Bobby's viewpoint as noted in the letters he sends home. "With Pendragon," he told White, "I've tried very hard to have the stories feel as if they are being told by Bobby, directly to the reader. I wanted to make Bobby as accessible as possible, so that readers will feel as if he could actually be somebody they know in real life, which then adds to the whole wonder of the experience because the reader can then imagine what it would be like to have someone they know off on an impossible adventure."

In *The Lost City of Faar* Bobby and Uncle Press travel to the watery world of Cloral, hoping there to locate a legendary city beneath the waves before Saint Dane can gain control of it and wreak havoc on the territories of Halla. Reviewing the second book of the series, a *Kirkus Reviews* critic noted that MacHale "displays a flair for action-packed pacing." A *Publishers Weekly* critic recommended *The Lost City of Faar* to fans of Jules Verne's adventures, adding that the author "embellishes his science fiction with just enough silly touches to leaven the mood."

The Never War, one of MacHale's favorite installments in the "Pendragon" series, finds Bobby, along with buddy Spader, sent to a variant of Earth circa 1937. Gangsters rule New York City here, and the duo must dodge bullets to stop Saint Dane's latest evil plot. Writing about *The Never War,* Sharon Rawlins noted in *School Library Journal* that while the book "may not be great literature," readers will enjoy its "fast pace, suspenseful plotting, and cliff-hanger chapter endings."

With book four, *The Reality Bug,* Bobby travels to Veelox, a world that appears to be deserted because all of the inhabitants are living a sort of virtual reality, escaping into their own dream worlds. It seems like a peaceful place, but Bobby knows that Saint Dane has evil plans for Veelox. Book five, *Black Water,* takes Bobby and friends to the territory of Eelong, a jungle world populated by huge and ferocious cats. White deemed this "Pendragon" installment "a fast-paced, exciting adventure that has an underlying theme of choice."

In *The Rivers of Zadaa* the Travelers arrive on the home planet of Loor, a young warrior woman who has become Bobby's fellow soldier in the fight against Saint Dane as well as his romantic interest. Here they discover that the once-peaceful relationship between the two civilizations—one the subterranean Rokadors, who supply water above ground, and the other the Batu, who protect the Rokador from invasion by uncivilized tribes—has now turned hostile because of a drought. Saint Dane, meanwhile, is thwarting every peace initiative between the two, hoping to turn the altercation into death-dealing war. "The Travelers are faced with a seemingly impossible task, especially with Saint Dane countering their every move," wrote James Blasingame in a *Journal of Adolescent & Adult Literacy* review of book number six. Blasingame went on to comment that *The Rivers of Zadaa* "is as good if not better than its predecessors," comparing Bobby to "Harry Potter, Frodo Baggins, and a host of other characters." Writing in *School Library Journal,* Walter Minkel remarked of the same book that "the action never stops for long, and Zadaa is sure to hold the interest of fans of the series."

According to *Kliatt* reviewer Deirdre Root, the seventh "Pendragon" book, *The Quillan Games,* shows that, with each new adventure, the series "gets better and better." Here Bobby and his friends discover a world on the brink of destruction. Causing the society's decay are the Quillan Games, a combination of sport and combat, are masterminded by a strange pair: Veego and LeBerge. The games are played to the death for the amusement of the game masters. Bobby knows that the only way to save Quillan is by competing in the games and defeating Veego and LeBerge.

The eighth "Pendragon" book, *The Pilgrims of Rayne,* marked a change of pace for the series; the first book of a trilogy within the series, it takes MacHale's saga to its conclusion. Here, and in *Raven Rise* and *Soldiers of Halla,* Bobby and the Travelers must battle Saint Dane as he attempts to take over all of the territories. *The*

Pilgrims of Rayne is set on the seemingly blissful world of Ibara, but, as Bobby soon discovers, it is blissful only because its leader is hiding a dreadful secret. After battling Saint Dane through eight worlds, it appears in *Raven Rise* that Bobby and the Travelers have lost the war for control of the territories. Now Bobby, Uncle Press, and the others must liberate Halla. MacHale's "Travelers" series, a group of three novels, serves as a prequel to the "Pendragon" epic.

MacHale's "Morpheus Road" trilogy begins with *The Light,* a "creepy, tension-filled adventure," in the words of a *Publishers Weekly* critic. After his mother's death, sixteen-year-old Marshall Seaver finds himself tormented by strange sights and sounds, the most terrifying of these being an encounter with the Gravedigger, a skeletal creature that Marshall created in his sketchbook. When Marshall discovers that his best friend, Cooper Foley, has suddenly disappeared, he senses danger and asks Cooper's aloof sister, Sydney, to help locate her brother. "This lengthy fantasy, full of twists and turns, keeps the reader working to unravel the illusive plot line while Marshall flirts with death," Laura Woodruff noted in *Voice of Youth Advocates,* and *School Library Journal* critic Sharon Rawlins praised Marshall's first-person narrative, stating that readers will "experience what he is feeling as the suspense builds and events spiral out of his control to the twisty ending."

The Black, the second installment in MacHale's "Morpheus Road" series, continues its focus on the travails of Cooper Foley. After he is killed in a mysterious boating accident, Cooper finds himself transported to the Black, a spiritual limbo where he meets Damon. A vengeful figure from ancient Macedonia, Damon threatens Marshall's life unless Cooper agrees to help him retrieve a magical poleax. "The reader learns about various realms along the Morpheus Road, connecting the living and the dead," Woodruff commented, and *School Library Journal* reviewer Kathy Kirchoefer applauded *The Black* for featuring a "narrative . . . intriguing enough to hook even reluctant readers."

Switching his focus away from young adults, MacHale's *The Monster Princess* is geared for younger readers and features illustrations by Alexandra Boiger. Tired of living underground, Lala, a sweet but scaly monster, travels to a mountaintop castle to pursue her dream of becoming a princess. Befriended by three scheming human princesses, the monster is invited to a grand ball, where she becomes the target of a cruel and humiliating prank. When the unkind princesses later find themselves in danger from a foul-smelling beast, Lala comes to their rescue, prompting the trio to view the monster in a new light. Lala's "irrepressible spirit makes her a creature kids will root for," Diane Foote stated in *Booklist,* and a *Publishers Weekly* contributor concluded of *The Monster Princess* that MacHale "delivers his message about handling mean girls with sincerity."

Sharing his pointers for budding authors, MacHale told White that it is "classic advice: Write about what you know. That way your writing will be real and people will respond to it. It's as simple as that. And never give up."

Biographical and Critical Sources

PERIODICALS

Booklist, September 1, 2010, Diane Foote, review of *The Monster Princess,* p. 114; April 15, 2011, Debbie Carton, review of *The Black,* p. 56.
Journal of Adolescent & Adult Literacy, October, 2006, James Blasingame, review of *The Rivers of Zadaa,* p. 161.
Kirkus Reviews, January 1, 2003, review of *The Lost City of Faar,* p. 63; July 1, 2010, review of *The Monster Princess;* March 1, 2011, review of *The Black.*
Kliatt, July, 2003, Deirdre B. Root, review of *The Never War,* p. 33; May, 2006, Deirdre Root, review of *The Quillan Games,* p. 11.
Publishers Weekly, December 2, 2002, review of *The Lost City of Faar,* p. 53; May 30, 2005, review of *Pendragon: The Guide to the Territories of Halla,* p. 62; July 5, 2010, review of *The Monster Princess,* p. 42; March 8, 2010, review of *The Light,* p. 57.
School Librarian, summer, 2003, review of *The Merchant of Death,* p. 100.
School Library Journal, November, 2002, John Peters, review of *The Merchant of Death,* p. 173; May, 2003, Susan L. Rogers, review of *The Lost City of Faar,* p. 156; July, 2003, Sharon Rawlins, review of *The Never War,* p. 133; July, 2005, Walter Minkel, review of *The Rivers of Zadaa,* p. 106; May, 2010, Sharon Rawlins, review of *The Light,* p. 120; July, 2011, Kathy Kirchoefer, review of *The Black,* p. 102.
Voice of Youth Advocates, December, 2002, review of *The Merchant of Death,* p. 400; April, 2003, review of *The Lost City of Faar,* p. 66; October, 2003, review of *The Never War,* p. 325; April, 2010, Laura Woodruff, review of *The Light,* p. 72; June, 2011, Laura Woodruff, review of *The Black,* p. 188.

ONLINE

D.J. MacHale Home Page, http://djmachalebooks.com (September 1, 2011).
Scholastic Web site, http://www2.scholastic.com/ (May 5, 2007), Aaron Broder, interview with MacHale.
Simon & Schuster Web site, http://authors.simonand schuster.com/ (April 20, 2009), interview with MacHale.
Writers Write Web site, http://www.writerswrite.com/ (October 1, 2004), Claire E. White, interview with MacHale.

*   *   *

MACK, W.C.
See FRENCH, Wendy

MACK, Winnie
    See FRENCH, Wendy

*   *   *

MALAWER, Ted
    See MICHAEL, Ted

*   *   *

MARTIN, Ann M. 1955-

Personal

Born August 12, 1955, in Princeton, NJ; daughter of Henry Read (a cartoonist) and Edith Aiken (a teacher) Martin. *Education:* Smith College, A.B. (cum laude), 1977. *Politics:* Democrat. *Hobbies and other interests:* "Reading and needlework, especially smocking and knitting."

Addresses

Home—Woodstock, NY. *Agent*—Amy Berkower, Writers House, Inc., 21 W. 26th St., New York, NY 10010.

Career

Author and educator. Elementary school teacher in Noroton, CT, 1977-78; Pocket Books, Inc., New York, NY, editorial assistant for Archway Paperbacks, 1978-80; Scholastic Book Services, New York, NY, copywriter for Teen Age Book Club, 1980-81, associate editor, 1981-83, editor, 1983; Bantam Books, Inc., New York, NY, senior editor of Books for Young Readers, 1983-85; writer and freelance editor, 1985—. Founder of Lisa Libraries (charitable organization); founder of Ann M. Martin Foundation, 1990.

Member

PEN, Authors Guild, Society of Children's Book Writers and Illustrators.

Awards, Honors

New Jersey Author awards, New Jersey Institute of Technology, 1983, for *Bummer Summer,* 1987, for *Missing since Monday;* Children's Choice, 1985, for *Bummer Summer;* Child Study Association of America Children's Books of the Year selection, 1986, for *Inside Out,* 1987, for *Stage Fright, With You and without You,* and *Missing since Monday;* Keystone State Reading Award, 1998, for *Leo the Magnificat;* (with Paula Danziger) California Young Reader Medal nomination, 2000, and Washington Sasquatch Reading Award nomination, 2001, both for *P.S. Longer Letter Later;* Newbery Medal Honor Book designation, 2003, for *A Corner of the Universe.*

Ann M. Martin (Reproduced by permission.)

Writings

Bummer Summer, Holiday House (New York, NY), 1983.
Just You and Me, Scholastic (New York, NY), 1983.
(With Betsy Ryan) *My Puppy Scrapbook,* illustrated by father, Henry Martin, Scholastic (New York, NY), 1983.
Inside Out, Holiday House (New York, NY), 1984.
Stage Fright, illustrated by Blanche Sims, Holiday House (New York, NY), 1984.
Me and Katie (the Pest), illustrated by Blanche Sims, Holiday House (New York, NY), 1985.
With You and without You, Holiday House (New York, NY), 1986.
Missing since Monday, Holiday House (New York, NY), 1986.
Just a Summer Romance, Holiday House (New York, NY), 1987.
Slam Book, Holiday House (New York, NY), 1987.
Yours Turly, Shirley, Holiday House (New York, NY), 1988.
Ten Kids, No Pets, Holiday House (New York, NY), 1988.
Fancy Dance in Feather Town, illustrated by Henry Martin, Western Publishing, 1988.
Ma and Pa Dracula, illustrated by Dirk Zimmer, Holiday House (New York, NY), 1989.
Moving Day in Feather Town, illustrated by Henry Martin, Western Publishing, 1989.
Eleven Kids, One Summer, Holiday House (New York, NY), 1991.

Enchanted Attic, Bantam (New York, NY), 1992.

Rachel Parker, Kindergarten Show-off, illustrated by Nancy Poydar, Holiday House (New York, NY), 1992.

Chain Letter, Scholastic (New York, NY), 1993.

(With Margot Becker) *Ann M. Martin: The Story of the Author of the Baby-Sitters Club,* Scholastic (New York, NY) 1993.

Leo the Magnificat, illustrated by Emily A. McCully, Scholastic (New York, NY), 1996.

(With Paula Danziger) *P.S. Longer Letter Later,* Scholastic (New York, NY), 1998.

(With Paula Danziger) *Snail Mail No More,* Scholastic (New York, NY), 2000.

Belle Teal, Scholastic (New York, NY), 2001.

A Corner of the Universe, Scholastic (New York, NY), 2002.

Here Today, Scholastic (New York, NY), 2004.

(Editor, with David Levithan) *Friends: Stories about New Friends, Old Friends, and Unexpectedly True Friends,* Scholastic (New York, NY), 2005.

A Dog's Life: The Autobiography of a Stray, Scholastic (New York, NY), 2005.

On Christmas Eve, illustrated by Jon J. Muth, Scholastic (New York, NY), 2006.

Everything for a Dog (sequel to *A Dog's Life*), Feiwel & Friends (New York, NY), 2009.

Ten Rules for Living with My Sister, Feiwel & Friends (New York, NY), 2011.

Author's books have been translated into numerous languages.

"BABY-SITTERS CLUB" SERIES

Kristy's Great Idea, Scholastic (New York, NY), 1986.

Claudia and the Phantom Phone Calls, Scholastic (New York, NY), 1986.

The Truth about Stacey, Scholastic (New York, NY), 1986.

Mary Anne Saves the Day, Scholastic (New York, NY), 1987.

Dawn and the Impossible Three, Scholastic (New York, NY), 1987.

Kristy's Big Day, Scholastic (New York, NY), 1987.

Claudia and Mean Janine, Scholastic (New York, NY), 1987.

Boy-Crazy Stacey, Scholastic (New York, NY), 1987.

The Ghost at Dawn's House, Scholastic (New York, NY), 1988.

Logan Likes Mary Anne!, Scholastic (New York, NY), 1988.

Kristy and the Snobs, Scholastic (New York, NY), 1988.

Claudia and the New Girl, Scholastic (New York, NY), 1988.

Good-bye Stacey, Good-bye, Scholastic (New York, NY), 1988.

Hello, Mallory, Scholastic (New York, NY), 1988.

Little Miss Stoneybrook . . . and Dawn, Scholastic (New York, NY), 1988.

Jessi's Secret Language, Scholastic (New York, NY), 1988.

Mary Anne's Bad-Luck Mystery, Scholastic (New York, NY), 1988.

Stacey's Mistake, Scholastic (New York, NY), 1988.

Claudia and the Bad Joke, Scholastic (New York, NY), 1988.

Kristy and the Walking Disaster, Scholastic (New York, NY), 1989.

Mallory and the Trouble with the Twins, Scholastic (New York, NY), 1989.

Jessi Ramsey, Pet-Sitter, Scholastic (New York, NY), 1989.

Dawn on the Coast, Scholastic (New York, NY), 1989.

Kristy and the Mother's Day Surprise, Scholastic (New York, NY), 1989.

Mary Anne and the Search for Tigger, Scholastic (New York, NY), 1989.

Claudia and the Sad Good-bye, Scholastic (New York, NY), 1989.

Jessi and the Superbrat, Scholastic (New York, NY), 1989.

Welcome Back, Stacey!, Scholastic (New York, NY), 1989.

Mallory and the Mystery Diary, Scholastic (New York, NY), 1989.

Mary Anne and the Great Romance, Scholastic (New York, NY), 1990.

Dawn's Wicked Stepsister, Scholastic (New York, NY), 1990.

Kristy and the Secret of Susan, Scholastic (New York, NY), 1990.

Claudia and the Great Search, Scholastic (New York, NY), 1990.

Mary Anne and Too Many Boys, Scholastic (New York, NY), 1990.

Stacey and the Mystery of Stoneybrook, Scholastic (New York, NY), 1990.

Jessi's Baby-Sitter, Scholastic (New York, NY), 1990.

Dawn and the Older Boy, Scholastic (New York, NY), 1990.

Kristy's Mystery Admirer, Scholastic (New York, NY), 1990.

Poor Mallory, Scholastic (New York, NY), 1990.

Claudia and the Middle School Mystery, Scholastic (New York, NY), 1991.

Mary Anne vs. Logan, Scholastic (New York, NY), 1991.

Jessi and the Dance School Phantom, Scholastic (New York, NY), 1991.

Stacey's Emergency, Scholastic (New York, NY), 1991.

Dawn and the Big Sleepover, Scholastic (New York, NY), 1991.

Kristy and the Baby Parade, Scholastic (New York, NY), 1991.

Mary Anne Misses Logan, Scholastic (New York, NY), 1991.

Mallory on Strike, Scholastic (New York, NY), 1991.

Jessi's Wish, Scholastic (New York, NY), 1991.

Claudia and the Genius of Elm Street, Scholastic (New York, NY), 1991.

Dawn's Big Date, Scholastic (New York, NY), 1992.

Stacey's Ex-Best Friend, Scholastic (New York, NY), 1992.

Mary Anne and Too Many Babies, Scholastic (New York, NY), 1992.

Kristy for President, Scholastic (New York, NY), 1992.

Mallory and the Dream Horse, Scholastic (New York, NY), 1992.

Jessi's Gold Medal, Scholastic (New York, NY), 1992.

Keep out, Claudia!, Scholastic (New York, NY), 1992.

Dawn Saves the Planet, Scholastic (New York, NY), 1992.

Stacey's Choice, Scholastic (New York, NY), 1992.

Mallory Hates Boys (and Gym), Scholastic (New York, NY), 1992.

Mary Anne's Makeover, Scholastic (New York, NY), 1993.

Jessi and the Awful Secret, Scholastic (New York, NY), 1993.

Kristy and the Worst Kid Ever, Scholastic (New York, NY), 1993.

Claudia's Friend, Scholastic (New York, NY), 1993.

Dawn's Family Feud, Scholastic (New York, NY), 1993.

Stacey's Big Crush, Scholastic (New York, NY), 1993.

Maid Mary Anne, Scholastic (New York, NY), 1993.

Dawn's Big Move, Scholastic (New York, NY), 1993.

Jessi and the Bad Baby-Sitter, Scholastic (New York, NY), 1993.

Get Well Soon, Mallory, Scholastic (New York, NY), 1993.

Stacey and the Cheerleaders, Scholastic (New York, NY), 1993.

Claudia and the Perfect Boy, Scholastic (New York, NY), 1994.

Dawn and the We Love Kids Club, Scholastic (New York, NY), 1994.

Mary Anne and Miss Priss, Scholastic (New York, NY), 1994.

Kristy and the Copycat, Scholastic (New York, NY), 1994.

Jessi's Horrible Prank, Scholastic (New York, NY), 1994.

Stacey's Lie, Scholastic (New York, NY), 1994.

Dawn and Whitney, Friends Forever, Scholastic (New York, NY), 1994.

Claudia and Crazy Peaches, Scholastic (New York, NY), 1994.

Mary Anne Breaks the Rules, Scholastic (New York, NY), 1994.

Mallory Pike, Number One Fan, Scholastic (New York, NY), 1994.

Kristy and Mr. Mom, Scholastic (New York, NY), 1995.

Jessi and the Troublemaker, Scholastic (New York, NY), 1995.

Stacey vs. the BSC, Scholastic (New York, NY), 1995.

Dawn and the School Spirit War, Scholastic (New York, NY), 1995.

Claudia Kishi, Live from WSTO, Scholastic (New York, NY), 1995.

Mary Anne and Camp BSC, Scholastic (New York, NY), 1995.

Stacey and the Bad Girls, Scholastic (New York, NY), 1995.

Farewell, Dawn, Scholastic (New York, NY), 1995.

Kristy and the Dirty Diapers, Scholastic (New York, NY), 1995.

Welcome to the BSC, Abby, Scholastic (New York, NY), 1995.

Claudia and the First Thanksgiving, Scholastic (New York, NY), 1995.

Mallory's Christmas Wish, Scholastic (New York, NY), 1995.

Mary Anne and the Memory Garden, Scholastic (New York, NY), 1996.

Stacey McGill, Super Sitter, Scholastic (New York, NY), 1996.

Kristy + Bart =?, Scholastic (New York, NY), 1996.

Abby's Lucky Thirteen, Scholastic (New York, NY), 1996.

Claudia and the World's Cutest Baby, Scholastic (New York, NY), 1996.

Dawn and Too Many Sitters, Scholastic (New York, NY), 1996.

Stacey's Broken Heart, Scholastic (New York, NY), 1996.

Kristy's Worst Idea, Scholastic (New York, NY), 1996.

Claudia Kishi, Middle School Drop Out, Scholastic (New York, NY), 1996.

Mary Anne and the Little Princess, Scholastic (New York, NY), 1996.

Happy Holidays, Jessi, Scholastic (New York, NY), 1996.

Abby's Twin, Scholastic (New York, NY), 1997.

Stacey the Match Whiz, Scholastic (New York, NY), 1997.

Claudia, Queen of the Seventh Grade, Scholastic (New York, NY), 1997.

Mind Your Own Business, Kristy!, Scholastic (New York, NY), 1997.

Don't Give up, Mallory, Scholastic (New York, NY), 1997.

Mary Anne to the Rescue, Scholastic (New York, NY), 1997.

Abby the Bad Sport, Scholastic (New York, NY), 1997.

Stacey's Secret Friend, Scholastic (New York, NY), 1997.

Kristy and the Sister War, Scholastic (New York, NY), 1997.

Claudia Makes up Her Mind, Scholastic (New York, NY), 1997.

The Secret Life of Mary Anne Spier, Scholastic (New York, NY), 1997.

Jessi's Big Break, Scholastic (New York, NY), 1997.

Abby and the Best Kid Ever, Scholastic (New York, NY), 1997.

Claudia and the Terrible Truth, Scholastic (New York, NY), 1997.

Kristy Thomas, Dog Trainer, Scholastic (New York, NY), 1997.

Stacey's Ex-Boyfriend, Scholastic (New York, NY), 1997.

Mary Anne and the Playground Fight, Scholastic (New York, NY), 1997.

Abby in Wonderland, Scholastic (New York, NY), 1997.

Kristy in Charge, Scholastic (New York, NY), 1997.

Claudia's Big Party, Scholastic (New York, NY), 1998.

Stacey McGill . . . Matchmaker?, Scholastic (New York, NY), 1998.

Mary Anne in the Middle, Scholastic (New York, NY), 1998.

The All-New Mallory Pike, Scholastic (New York, NY), 1998.

Abby's Un-Valentine, Scholastic (New York, NY), 1998.

Claudia and the Little Liar, Scholastic (New York, NY), 1999.

Kristy at Bat, Scholastic (New York, NY), 1999.

Stacey's Movie, Scholastic (New York, NY), 1999.

The Fire at Mary Anne's House, Scholastic (New York, NY), 1999.

Graduation Day, Scholastic (New York, NY), 2000.

The Summer Before (prequel), Scholastic (New York, NY), 2010.

"BABY-SITTERS CLUB MYSTERY" SERIES

Stacey and the Missing Ring, Scholastic (New York, NY), 1991.

Beware, Dawn!, Scholastic (New York, NY), 1991.

Mallory and the Ghost Cat, Scholastic (New York, NY), 1992.

Kristy and the Missing Child, Scholastic (New York, NY), 1992.

Mary Anne and the Secret in the Attic, Scholastic (New York, NY), 1992.

The Mystery at Claudia's House, Scholastic (New York, NY), 1992.

Dawn and the Disappearing Dogs, Scholastic (New York, NY), 1993.

Jessi and the Jewel Thieves, Scholastic (New York, NY), 1993.

Kristy and the Haunted Mansion, Scholastic (New York, NY), 1993.

Stacey and the Mystery Money, Scholastic (New York, NY), 1993.

Claudia and the Mystery at the Museum, Scholastic (New York, NY), 1993.

Dawn and the Surfer Ghost, Scholastic (New York, NY), 1993.

Mary Anne and the Library Mystery, Scholastic (New York, NY), 1994.

Stacey and the Mystery at the Mall, Scholastic (New York, NY), 1994.

Kristy and the Vampires, Scholastic (New York, NY), 1994.

Claudia and the Clue in the Photograph, Scholastic (New York, NY), 1994.

Dawn and the Halloween Mystery, Scholastic (New York, NY), 1994.

Stacey and the Mystery at the Empty House, Scholastic (New York, NY), 1994.

Kristy and the Missing Fortune, Scholastic (New York, NY), 1995.

Mary Anne and the Zoo Mystery, Scholastic (New York, NY), 1995.

Claudia and the Recipe for Danger, Scholastic (New York, NY), 1995.

Stacey and the Haunted Masquerade, Scholastic (New York, NY), 1995.

Abby and the Secret Society, Scholastic (New York, NY), 1996.

Mary Anne and the Silent Witness, Scholastic (New York, NY), 1996.

Kristy and the Middle-School Vandal, Scholastic (New York, NY), 1996.

Dawn Schafer, Undercover Baby-Sitter, Scholastic (New York, NY), 1996.

Claudia and the Lighthouse Ghost, Scholastic (New York, NY), 1996.

Abby and the Mystery Baby, Scholastic (New York, NY), 1997.

Stacey and the Fashion Victim, Scholastic (New York, NY), 1997.

Kristy and the Mystery Train, Scholastic (New York, NY), 1997.

Mary Anne and the Music Box Secret, Scholastic (New York, NY), 1997.

Claudia and the Mystery in the Painting, Scholastic (New York, NY), 1997.

Stacey and the Stolen Hearts, Scholastic (New York, NY), 1997.

Mary Anne and the Haunted Bookstore, Scholastic (New York, NY), 1997.

Abby and the Notorious Neighbor, Scholastic (New York, NY), 1997.

Kristy and the Cat Burglar, Scholastic (New York, NY), 1997.

"BABY-SITTERS CLUB SUPER SPECIALS" SERIES

Baby-Sitters on Board!, Scholastic (New York, NY), 1988.

Baby-Sitters' Summer Vacation, Scholastic (New York, NY), 1989.

Baby-Sitters' Winter Vacation, Scholastic (New York, NY), 1989.

Baby-Sitters' Island Adventure, Scholastic (New York, NY), 1990.

California Girls!, Scholastic (New York, NY), 1990.

New York, New York!, Scholastic (New York, NY), 1991.

Snowbound, Scholastic (New York, NY), 1991.

Baby-Sitters at Shadow Lake, Scholastic (New York, NY), 1992.

Starring the Baby-Sitters Club, Scholastic (New York, NY), 1992.

Sea City, Here We Come!, Scholastic (New York, NY), 1993.

The Baby-Sitters Remember, Scholastic (New York, NY), 1994.

Here Come the Bridesmaids!, Scholastic (New York, NY), 1994.

Aloha, Baby-Sitters!, Scholastic (New York, NY), 1996.

"BABY-SITTERS LITTLE SISTERS" SERIES

Karen's Witch, Scholastic (New York, NY), 1988.

Karen's Roller Skates, Scholastic (New York, NY), 1988.

Karen's Worst Day, Scholastic (New York, NY), 1989.

Karen's Kittycat Club, Scholastic (New York, NY), 1989.

Karen's School Picture, Scholastic (New York, NY), 1989.

Karen's Little Sister, Scholastic (New York, NY), 1989.

Karen's Birthday, Scholastic (New York, NY), 1990.

Karen's Haircut, Scholastic (New York, NY), 1990.

Karen's Sleepover, Scholastic (New York, NY), 1990.

Karen's Grandmothers, Scholastic (New York, NY), 1990.

Karen's Prize, Scholastic (New York, NY), 1990.

Karen's Ghost, Scholastic (New York, NY), 1990.

Karen's Surprise, Scholastic (New York, NY), 1990.

Karen's New Year, Scholastic (New York, NY), 1991.

Karen's in Love, Scholastic (New York, NY), 1991.

Karen's Goldfish, Scholastic (New York, NY), 1991.

Karen's Brothers, Scholastic (New York, NY), 1991.

Karen's Home Run, Scholastic (New York, NY), 1991.

Karen's Good-Bye, Scholastic (New York, NY), 1991.

Karen's Carnival, Scholastic (New York, NY), 1991.

Karen's New Teacher, Scholastic (New York, NY), 1991.

Karen's Little Witch, Scholastic (New York, NY), 1992.

Karen's Doll, Scholastic (New York, NY), 1992.
Karen's School Trip, Scholastic (New York, NY), 1992.
Karen's Pen Pal, Scholastic (New York, NY), 1992.
Karen's Ducklings, Scholastic (New York, NY), 1992.
Karen's Big Joke, Scholastic (New York, NY), 1992.
Karen's Tea Party, Scholastic (New York, NY), 1992.
Karen's Cartwheel, Scholastic (New York, NY), 1992.
Karen's Kittens, Scholastic (New York, NY), 1992.
Karen's Bully, Scholastic (New York, NY), 1992.
Karen's Pumpkin Patch, Scholastic (New York, NY), 1992.
Karen's Secret, Scholastic (New York, NY), 1992.
Karen's Snow Day, Scholastic (New York, NY), 1993.
Karen's Doll Hospital, Scholastic (New York, NY), 1993.
Karen's New Friend, Scholastic (New York, NY), 1993.
Karen's Tuba, Scholastic (New York, NY), 1993.
Karen's Big Lie, Scholastic (New York, NY), 1993.
Karen's Wedding, Scholastic (New York, NY), 1993.
Karen's Newspaper, Scholastic (New York, NY), 1993.
Karen's School, Scholastic (New York, NY), 1993.
Karen's Pizza Party, Scholastic (New York, NY), 1993.
Karen's Toothache, Scholastic (New York, NY), 1993.
Karen's Big Weekend, Scholastic (New York, NY), 1993.
Karen's Twin, Scholastic (New York, NY), 1994.
Karen's Baby-Sitter, Scholastic (New York, NY), 1994.
Karen's Kite, Scholastic (New York, NY), 1994.
Karen's Two Families, Scholastic (New York, NY), 1994.
Karen's Stepmother, Scholastic (New York, NY), 1994.
Karen's Lucky Penny, Scholastic (New York, NY), 1994.
Karen's Big Top, Scholastic (New York, NY), 1994.
Karen's Mermaid, Scholastic (New York, NY), 1994.
Karen's School Bus, Scholastic (New York, NY), 1994.
Karen's Candy, Scholastic (New York, NY), 1994.
Karen's Magician, Scholastic (New York, NY), 1994.
Karen's Ice Skates, Scholastic (New York, NY), 1994.
Karen's School Mystery, Scholastic (New York, NY), 1995.
Karen's Ski Trip, Scholastic (New York, NY), 1995.
Karen's Leprechaun, Scholastic (New York, NY), 1995.
Karen's Pony, Scholastic (New York, NY), 1995.
Karen's Tattletale, Scholastic (New York, NY), 1995.
Karen's New Bike, Scholastic (New York, NY), 1995.
Karen's Movie, Scholastic (New York, NY), 1995.
Karen's Lemonade Stand, Scholastic (New York, NY), 1995.
Karen's Toys, Scholastic (New York, NY), 1995.
Karen's Monsters, Scholastic (New York, NY), 1995.
Karen's Turkey Day, Scholastic (New York, NY), 1995.
Karen's Angel, Scholastic (New York, NY), 1995.
Karen's Big Sister, Scholastic (New York, NY), 1996.
Karen's Grandad, Scholastic (New York, NY), 1996.
Karen's Island Adventure, Scholastic (New York, NY), 1996.
Karen's New Puppy, Scholastic (New York, NY), 1996.
Karen's Dinosaur, Scholastic (New York, NY), 1996.
Karen's Softball Mystery, Scholastic (New York, NY), 1996.
Karen's County Fair, Scholastic (New York, NY), 1996.
Karen's Magic Garden, Scholastic (New York, NY), 1996.
Karen's School Surprise, Scholastic (New York, NY), 1996.
Karen's Half Birthday, Scholastic (New York, NY), 1996.
Karen's Big Fight, Scholastic (New York, NY), 1996.
Karen's Christmas Tree, Scholastic (New York, NY), 1996.

Karen's Accident, Scholastic (New York, NY), 1997.
Karen's Secret Valentine, Scholastic (New York, NY), 1997.
Karen's Bunny, Scholastic (New York, NY), 1997.
Karen's Big Job, Scholastic (New York, NY), 1997.
Karen's Treasure, Scholastic (New York, NY), 1997.
Karen's Telephone Trouble, Scholastic (New York, NY), 1997.
Karen's Pony Camp, Scholastic (New York, NY), 1997.
Karen's Puppet Show, Scholastic (New York, NY), 1997.
Karen's Unicorn, Scholastic (New York, NY), 1997.
Karen's Haunted House, Scholastic (New York, NY), 1997.
Karen's Pilgrim, Scholastic (New York, NY), 1997.
Karen's Sleigh Ride, Scholastic (New York, NY), 1997.
Karen's Cooking Contest, Scholastic (New York, NY), 1997.
Karen's Snow Princess, Scholastic (New York, NY), 1997.
Karen's Promise, Scholastic (New York, NY), 1997.
Karen's Big Move, Scholastic (New York, NY), 1997.
Karen's Paper Route, Scholastic (New York, NY), 1997.
Karen's Fishing Trip, Scholastic (New York, NY), 1997.
Karen's Big City Mystery, Scholastic (New York, NY), 1997.
Karen's Book, Scholastic (New York, NY), 1997.
Karen's Chain Letter, Scholastic (New York, NY), 1997.
Karen's Black Cat, Scholastic (New York, NY), 1998.
Karen's Movie Star, Scholastic (New York, NY), 1998.
Karen's Christmas Carol, Scholastic (New York, NY), 1998.
Karen's Nanny, Scholastic (New York, NY), 1998.
Karen's President, Scholastic (New York, NY), 1998.
Karen's Copycat, Scholastic (New York, NY), 1998.
Karen's Field Day, Scholastic (New York, NY), 1998.
Karen's Show and Share, Scholastic (New York, NY), 1998.
Karen's Swim Meet, Scholastic (New York, NY), 1998.
Karen's Spy Mystery, Scholastic (New York, NY), 1998.
Karen's New Holiday, Scholastic (New York, NY), 1998.
Karen's Hurricane, Scholastic (New York, NY), 1998.
Karen's Chicken Pox, Scholastic (New York, NY), 1999.
Karen's Runaway Turkey, Scholastic (New York, NY), 1999.
Karen's Reindeer, Scholastic (New York, NY), 1999.
Karen's Mistake, Scholastic (New York, NY), 2000.
Karen's Figure Eight, Scholastic (New York, NY), 2000.
Karen's Yo-Yo, Scholastic (New York, NY), 2000.
Karen's Easter Parade, Scholastic (New York, NY), 2000.
Karen's Gift, Scholastic (New York, NY), 2000.
Karen's Cowboy, Scholastic (New York, NY), 2000.

"BABY-SITTERS LITTLE SISTERS SUPER SPECIAL" SERIES

Karen's Wish, Scholastic (New York, NY), 1990.
Karen's Plane Trip, Scholastic (New York, NY), 1991.
Karen's Mystery, Scholastic (New York, NY), c. 1991.
Karen, Hannie, and Nancy: The Three Musketeers, Scholastic (New York, NY), 1992.
Karen's Baby, Scholastic (New York, NY), 1992.
Karen's Campout, Scholastic (New York, NY), 1993.

"BABY-SITTERS CLUB PORTRAIT COLLECTION" SERIES

Dawn's Book, Scholastic (New York, NY), 1993.
Stacey's Book, Scholastic (New York, NY), 1994.
Claudia's Book, Scholastic (New York, NY), 1995.
Mary Anne's Book, Scholastic (New York, NY), 1996.
Kristy's Book, Scholastic (New York, NY), 1996.
Abby's Book, Scholastic (New York, NY), 1997.

"BABY-SITTERS CLUB SUPER MYSTERIES" SERIES

Baby-Sitters' Haunted House, Scholastic (New York, NY), 1995.
Baby-Sitters Beware, Scholastic (New York, NY), 1995.
Baby-Sitters' Fright Night, Scholastic (New York, NY), 1996.

OTHER "BABY-SITTERS CLUB" SPECIAL EDITIONS

Logan Bruno, Boy Baby-Sitter, Scholastic (New York, NY), 1993.
Baby-Sitters Little Sister School Scrapbook, Scholastic (New York, NY), 1993.
Baby-Sitters Club Guide to Baby-Sitting, Scholastic (New York, NY), 1993.
Shannon's Story, Scholastic (New York, NY), 1994.
Secret Santa, Scholastic (New York, NY), 1994.
Baby-Sitters Little Sister Summer Fill-in Book, Scholastic (New York, NY), 1995.
Baby-Sitters Little Sister Jump Rope Rhymes, Scholastic (New York, NY), 1995.
Baby-Sitters Little Sister Playground Games, Scholastic (New York, NY), 1996.
Complete Guide to the Baby-Sitters Club, Scholastic (New York, NY), 1996.
The BSC Notebook, Scholastic (New York, NY), 1996.
BSC Chain Letter, Scholastic (New York, NY), 1996.
The Baby-Sitters Club Trivia and Puzzle Fun Book, Scholastic (New York, NY), 1996.
The Baby-Sitters Club Postcard Book, Scholastic (New York, NY), 1996.
Little Sister Photo Scrapbook, Scholastic (New York, NY), 1997.
Baby-Sitters Little Sister Secret Diary, Scholastic (New York, NY), 1997.
Baby-Sitters Little Sister Laugh Pack, Scholastic (New York, NY), 1997.

"THE KIDS IN MS. COLMAN'S CLASS" SERIES

Teacher's Pet, illustrated by Charles Tang, Scholastic (New York, NY), 1996.
Author Day, illustrated by Charles Tang, Scholastic (New York, NY), 1996.
Class Play, illustrated by Charles Tang, Scholastic (New York, NY), 1996.
The Second Grade Baby, illustrated by Charles Tang, Scholastic (New York, NY), 1996.
Snow War, illustrated by Charles Tang, Scholastic (New York, NY), 1997.

Twin Trouble, illustrated by Charles Tang, Scholastic (New York, NY), 1997.
Science Fair, illustrated by Charles Tang, Scholastic (New York, NY), 1997.
Summer Kids, illustrated by Charles Tang, Scholastic (New York, NY), 1997.
Halloween Parade, illustrated by Charles Tang, Scholastic (New York, NY), 1998.
Holiday Time, illustrated by Charles Tang, Scholastic (New York, NY), 1998.
Spelling Bee, illustrated by Charles Tang, Scholastic (New York, NY), 1998.
Baby Animal Zoo, illustrated by Charles Tang, Scholastic (New York, NY), 1998.

"CALIFORNIA DIARIES" SERIES

Dawn, Scholastic (New York, NY), 1997.
Sunny, Scholastic (New York, NY), 1997.
Maggie, Scholastic (New York, NY), 1997.
Amalia, Scholastic (New York, NY), 1997.
Ducky, Scholastic (New York, NY), 1997.
Dawn Diary Two, Scholastic (New York, NY), 1998.
Sunny Diary Two, Scholastic (New York, NY), 1998.
Maggie Diary Two, Scholastic (New York, NY), 1998.
Amalia Diary Two, Scholastic (New York, NY), 1998.
Ducky Diary Two, Scholastic (New York, NY), 1998.
Dawn Diary Three, Scholastic (New York, NY), 1999.
Sunny Diary Three, Scholastic (New York, NY), 1999.
Maggie Diary Three, Scholastic (New York, NY), 2000.
Amalia Diary Three, Scholastic (New York, NY), 2000.
Ducky Diary Three, Scholastic (New York, NY), 2001.

"FRIENDS FOREVER" SERIES

Kristy's Big News, Scholastic (New York, NY), 1999.
Stacey vs. Claudia, Scholastic (New York, NY), 1999.
Mary Anne's Big Break Up, Scholastic (New York, NY), 1999.
Claudia and the Friendship Feud, Scholastic (New York, NY), 1999.
Kristy Power, Scholastic (New York, NY), 1999.
Stacey and the Boyfriend Trap, Scholastic (New York, NY), 1999.
Claudia Gets Her Guy, Scholastic (New York, NY), 2000.
Mary Anne's Revenge, Scholastic (New York, NY), 2000.
Kristy and the Kidnapper, Scholastic (New York, NY), 2000.
Stacey's Problem, Scholastic (New York, NY), 2000.
Welcome Home, Mary Anne, Scholastic (New York, NY), 2000.
Claudia and the Disaster Date, Scholastic (New York, NY), 2000.

"FRIENDS FOREVER SPECIAL" SERIES

Everything Changes, Scholastic (New York, NY), 1999.
Graduation Day, Scholastic (New York, NY), 2000.

"DOLL PEOPLE" CHAPTER-BOOK SERIES

(With Laura Godwin) *The Doll People,* illustrated by Brian Selznick, Hyperion (New York, NY), 1999.
(With Laura Godwin) *The Meanest Doll in the World,* illustrated by Brian Selznick, Hyperion (New York, NY), 2003.
(With Laura Godwin) *The Runaway Dolls,* illustrated by Brian Selznick, Hyperion (New York, NY), 2008.

"MAIN STREET" SERIES

Welcome to Camden Falls, Scholastic (New York, NY), 2007.
Needle and Thread, Scholastic (New York, NY), 2007.
'Tis the Season, Scholastic (New York, NY), 2007.
Best Friends, Scholastic (New York, NY), 2008.
The Secret Book Club, Scholastic (New York, NY), 2008.
September Surprises, Scholastic (New York, NY), 2008.
Keeping Secrets, Scholastic (New York, NY), 2009.
Special Delivery, Scholastic (New York, NY), 2009.
Coming Apart, Scholastic (New York, NY), 2010.
Staying Together, Scholastic (New York, NY), 2011.

Adaptations

The *Baby-Sitters Club* television series was produced by Scholastic Productions and broadcast on Home Box Office (HBO) and the Disney Channel. *The Baby-Sitters Club Movie,* co-produced by Scholastic Productions and Beacon Communications, was distributed by Columbia, 1995, and several "Baby-Sitters Club" stories appeared on video and audio cassette. A "Baby-Sitters Club" board game was released by Milton-Bradley. Illustrator/author Raina Telgemeier adapted several "Baby-Sitters Club" books into graphic novels, among them *Kristy's Great Idea, The Truth about Stacey, Mary Anne Saves the Day,* and *Claude and Mean Janine,* published by Graphix (New York, NY), 2006-08.

Sidelights

When the curtain came down on the final act of the "Baby-Sitters Club" series in 2000, author and co-originator Ann M. Martin was one of the best-known names in juvenile publishing. What started in 1986 as an idea for a four-book series to be published over the course of one year had ballooned fourteen years later into a mini-publishing industry with several spin-off titles, a television series, a movie, games, and enough "Baby-Sitters Club" (BSC) merchandise to satisfy the needs of legions of faithful readers. With over 180 million books in print in nineteen languages, the "Baby-Sitters Club" had obviously, as Sally Lodge noted in *Publishers Weekly,* "struck a resounding chord with pre-teen girls all over the world."

Martin's success with the BSC is nothing short of a publishing phenomenon. Millions of teens and pre-teens grew up with the antics and adventures of Kristy, Mary Anne, Stacey, and Claudia, and they found new friends with whom to identify with the addition of Dawn, Jessi, Mallory, and Abby to the club. The spin-off titles include over 130 of the original "Baby-Sitters Club" editions as well as 120 more titles in the "Little Sisters" series, twenty-five books in the "Mystery" series, a baker's dozen in the "BSC Friends Forever" series, another fifteen in the "California Diaries" series, and dozens of titles in super editions, not to mention the twelve books in the "Kids in Ms. Colman's Class" series—a spin-off of a spin-off.

After fourteen years, both Martin and her publisher, Scholastic, were ready to move on to new projects. Although she bid adieu to her BSC readers with the final volume in the series, *Graduation Day,* she did not say good-bye to publishing. Martin has continued to write for middle-school readers, producing several other multi-volume series as well as highly regarded standalone novels, among them *A Dog's Life: The Autobiography of a Stray,* the Newbery Honor Book *A Corner of the Universe,* and *Ten Rules for Living with My Sister,* the last which prompted a *Kirkus Review* writer to note her "gift for creating appealing characters in an atmosphere of caring and forgiveness." In her "Main Street" series, Martin follows the adventures of two orphaned sisters as they adjust to life in small-town Massachusetts, while she joins coauthor Laura Godwin and artist Brian Selznick to create the popular "Doll People" novels.

Born in 1955, Martin grew up in Princeton, New Jersey, in a tight-knit family that included her parents and younger sister, Jane. "I grew up in a very imaginative family," Martin once noted. "My mother was a preschool teacher and my father, an artist. Both liked fantasy and children's literature, so my world was one of circuses, animals, Beatrix Potter, *Winnie-the-Pooh, The Wizard of Oz,* elves and gnomes and fairies. It was a lot of fun, and it stayed with me. I'm often off in some other world, and all my daydreaming goes into my books." Martin was an enterprising child, running a library at one point and charging her friends overdue fines. She also was a babysitter; her oddest "client" was a snake which she had to tend one weekend. The author subsequently modeled many of the events and characters of her popular series from those of her youth, including best friend Beth Perkins who inspired the character of Kristy, leader of the Baby-Sitters Club.

Reading and writing were among her favorite childhood activities. "I had always enjoyed writing, even as a child," Martin once commented. "Before I could write, I dictated stories to my mother. I took creative writing classes and that sort of thing as a kid, but I wanted desperately to be a teacher, so that was what I prepared for." At Smith College, she double-majored in psychology and early childhood education. Out of college, Martin taught elementary school for a year, working with students challenged by learning disabilities such as dyslexia. Soon, however, Martin realized that she wanted to work in children's books rather than in education. She cut her literary teeth first on the "other" side of the desk, working as an editorial assistant, then assistant editor, and finally editor and senior editor at a succession of publishers that included Pocket Books, Scholastic, and Bantam between 1978 and 1985.

Martin published her first book, *Bummer Summer,* in 1983. A popular story for young readers that focuses on a first overnight camp experience, this debut paved the way for further teen and preteen books such as *Inside Out, Stage Fright,* and *Me and Katie (the Pest).* "Some of my books are based on actual experiences," Martin once said; "others are based more on imagination, and memories of feelings. *Me and Katie (the Pest)* is loosely based on riding lessons I took in the third grade. . . . *With You and without You* is about the death of a parent. *Inside Out* was based on my work as a therapist for autistic children; it wasn't really something that happened in my childhood. *Stage Fright* is probably the most autobiographical of my books. I had terrible stage fright when I was a kid, . . . and that was the inspiration for that book."

Increasingly Martin began to see herself as a writer rather than an editor. In 1985, Jean Feiwel, editor-in-

Martin's "Babysitter's Club" series includes girl-friendly stories such as **Stacey's Problem.** *(Jacket cover copyright © 2000 by Scholastic, Inc. Reproduced by permission of Scholastic, Inc.)*

chief of the book group at Scholastic, came up with the idea of a miniseries about a babysitting cooperative, and she asked Martin to write the first four stories. When the inaugural title, *Kristy's Great Idea,* quickly sold out its 30,000-copy first printing, Feiwel and Martin thought they might just be on to something. The subsequent books were popular enough that Martin was tapped to write two more stories for the series. "Scholastic decided the books were doing exceptionally well when the sixth book of the series hit number one on the B. Dalton Juvenile Bestseller list, sometime in 1987," Martin once noted. "That was when we decided that we really had something. We stepped up the schedule to one book every other month and eventually one every month."

From the outset the BSC series was a collaborative effort. Martin and Feiwel determined early on that, while sometimes dealing with serious issues such as death, racism, divorce, and peer pressure, the series would not deal with other hot button issues such as child abuse, alcohol or drug abuse, or the death of a parent. Geared for readers aged eight through twelve, the "Baby-Sitters Club" series is intended as entertainment: light, breezy, and conversational. It has often been touted as the perfect introduction to books for reluctant readers. In all of the books, the characters remain the same age. "Two of them are permanently in the sixth grade, and the rest are permanently in the eighth grade," Martin once explained. "I can't let them grow up because the books come out too fast. I try not to allude to birthdays or summer vacations. . . . Otherwise the characters would soon be thirty-five." Martin was also careful to avoid slang and the use of time-fixers such as the names of current rock groups; the "Baby-Sitters Club" books take place in a time capsule, a sort of all-time and any-time.

Books in the series deal with the adventures of a group of girls who band together to operate a child-care business, and individual titles explore a range of topics. *Kristy and the Secret of Susan* deals with an autistic savant, *Claudia and the Sad Good-Bye* is about the death of a grandparent, *Kristy and the Snobs* relates the death of Kristy's pet, and *Jessi's Secret Language* finds Jessi baby-sitting for a deaf boy who communicates only in American Sign Language. Such books demonstrate Martin's own interests and proclivities, and her personal favorite is *Kristy's Big Day.* Martin herself admitted in *Time* magazine that while her books are "not great literature," they "attract kids who are reluctant readers, if not children with definite learning problems such as dyslexia, and turn them into readers. And for kids who are already readers, I don't think there's anything wrong with picking up a series and reading it. I write the books as pure entertainment for myself as well as for the kids, but I am hoping that avid readers who are reading series are reading other things as well, and I also hope that reluctant readers who get hooked on reading through series reading, whether it's the 'Baby-Sitters Club' or another series, will then 'graduate' to other kinds of books."

Cover of Martin's young-adult novel Sunny, *part of her "California Diaries" series.* (Jacket cover copyright © 1998 by Scholastic, Inc. Reproduced by permission of Scholastic, Inc.)

Over the years, Martin and her editors added new series to explore different age levels and also update and enliven the BSC series with a contemporary veneer. The final such addition, the "Baby-Sitters Club Friends Forever" series, ended with a title in a letters-and-journal-entries format in which the original four members of the club are left to carry on the traditions of their enterprise. The "California Diaries" series, inaugurated in 1997, features Dawn, one of the original baby-sitters, who moves to the West Coast to be with one of her divorced parents full-time. That series is, as the name implies, told in diary format. The eighth-grade girls in this series are involved in somewhat edgier and more sophisticated activities than those found in the original "Baby-Sitters Club" books.

Contrary to the way most multi-volume children's book series are produced, Martin penned much of the BSC series herself, rising at 5:30 each morning to start her writing day and completing nearly two books each month. As the number of series grew, however, it was impossible for her to keep up with the flow of books, and other writers were brought on to help produce some of the installments until the final BSC volume, *Graduation Day,* reached series fans.

Martin continued publishing hardcover novels during the years she was churning out the BSC. One of her personal favorites of these is *Ten Kids, No Pets,* about the boisterous Rosso family. In a sequel to that book, *Eleven Kids, One Summer,* the Rossos spend the summer on New York's Fire Island. Each chapter focuses the lens on the activities of one of the "amiable Rosso offspring," according to a *Publishers Weekly* reviewer, and these young characters range in age from six months to fifteen years. There is a movie being filmed on the island with a handsome star for the eldest Rosso, Abbie, to form a friendship with; there is a house that the sensitive Candy believes is haunted; and there are plenty of seashells for enterprising Woody to paint and then sell. "Martin . . . knows well what pleases young readers," the same reviewer concluded, "and [*Eleven Kids, One Summer*] . . . is filled with characters, escapades and dialogue that will do just that."

Humor takes center stage in Martin's picture book *Leo the Magnificat,* a story based on an actual cat who adopted an entire church congregation. The cat in question sauntered into the yard of a Louisville, Kentucky, church one Sunday morning and remained there for the next twelve years. Martin shows how this cat wormed its way into the hearts of the entire congregation and surrounding neighborhood, insinuating itself into events ranging from potluck dinners to church services. When Leo the cat finally passes on, he is buried in the church garden. A reviewer for *Publishers Weekly* dubbed *Leo the Magnificat* a "charmer like its feline hero," and further noted that its author is a "pro at age-appropriate writing." In *Booklist,* Stephanie Zvirin commented that "Martin's picture book reads just like what it is—a story drawn from life," and concluded that her "gently humorous, poignant (never sentimental)" tale "won't disappoint."

In 1998 Martin teamed up with long-time friend and fellow children's book author Paula Danziger to write *P.S. Longer Letter Later.* In this book the two authors (both who specialize in writing for young girls) blend their disparate writing styles to create an epistolary novel told from two points of view. When seventh graders Elizabeth and Tara*Starr are separated by a family move, they promise to maintain their friendship through letters. The two girls are a study in contrasts: Tara*Starr is the type to put purple streaks in her hair, to joke incessantly, and to write scathingly funny columns for the school paper while staid Elizabeth is into cross-stitching and poetry and would never think of piercing her ears, let alone her nose. Suddenly Tara*Starr's free-spirited parents become responsible, begin holding regular jobs, think about having another baby, and move to Ohio. Outrageous, flamboyant, creative Tara*Starr—whose letters are written by Danziger—struggles against the overnight change and has a hard time adjusting to her new school and making new friends. Meanwhile the more reserved, introspective, and affluent Elizabeth—her letters written by Martin—undergoes her own transformations. Her father loses his job, turns to alcohol, and then abandons the family amid the throes of downsizing to life in a small apartment. In letters that are at once humorous and painful, the two girls maintain their long-distance friendship. They survive tiffs and personal crises and even silence when one or the other fails to write for a time.

"If Danziger and Martin had been childhood pen pals," commented a reviewer for *Publishers Weekly,* "their correspondence might have read much like this strikingly insightful epistolary novel." The same writer further observed of *P.S. Longer Letter Later* that the "venerable authors here do a splendid job of creating a story based on . . . letters." *Booklist* contributor Hazel Rochman predicted that "the immediacy of the letters format will draw kids in, especially as the tension mounts in Elizabeth's home and her friend replies with humor and heartfelt sympathy." Lynda Drill Comerford, writing in *Publishers Weekly,* commented that the collaboration, "a celebration of friendship, ends on a happy note, with characters overcoming personal conflicts and forgiving each other's shortcomings." Comerford concluded, "For characters and authors alike, [*P.S. Longer Letter Later*] . . . represents the unique meshing of two creative,

Cover of Martin's middle-grade novel **P.S. Longer Letter Letter,** *featuring cover art by Paul Colin.* (Illustration copyright © 1998 by Paul Colin. Reprinted by permission of Scholastic, Inc.)

witty and very different personalities." Renee Steinberg, reviewing the same novel in *School Library Journal,* observed that the "authenticity of the well-drawn characters gives life and vitality to the story" and concluded that readers "will thoroughly enjoy this fast-paced story."

In *Snail Mail No More* the coauthors continue Elizabeth and Tara*Starr's correspondence, this time by e-mail. With her mother pregnant, Tara*Starr is not so sure she wants to be a sister. Meanwhile, Elizabeth's wayward father has shown up again with less-than-positive results. The girls now turn thirteen and make new friends, including boys. The green-eyed monster pops up between the two for a time, but even jealousy is vanquished by their strong friendship. "Seasoned pros Danziger and Martin couldn't write a dull book if they tried," noted *Booklist* critic Michael Cart, "and this one . . . is a funny, thought-provoking page-turner that will delight readers and leave them ready for more messages." While *School Library Journal* reviewer Linda Bindner found that *Snail Mail No More* "lacks the energy and freshness" of *P.S. Longer Letter Later,* she also commented that "fans will find it to be an enjoyable sequel." A contributor for *Publishers Weekly* dubbed *Snail Mail No More* a "funny and poignant sequel" and concluded that the "two characters approach life differently enough that there will likely be a response or suggestion that resonates with every reader, and both heroines share one important trait: they are all heart."

Another collaborative effort, Godwin and Martin's "Doll People" series, chronicles the culture clash between members of a Victorian doll household and their new, plastic neighbors, the Funcrafts. In series opener *The Doll People* the Funcrafts are the birthday present of the younger sister of Kate Palmer, current owner of the Victorian dollhouse and its occupants. Tiffany, a Funcraft doll, is the same age as Annabelle, of the Victorian dollhouse, and the two opposites oddly enough hit it off as they join forces to hunt for missing Auntie Sarah, a longtime doll resident of the Victorian dollhouse. Kathie Meizner, writing in *School Library Journal,* commented of *The Doll People* that a "lighthearted touch and a dash of drama make this a satisfying read," while a writer for *Publishers Weekly* concluded that doll lovers "may well approach their imaginative play with renewed enthusiasm and a sense of wonder after reading this fun-filled adventure."

The "Doll People" saga continues in *The Meanest Doll in the World* and *The Runaway Dolls,* both featuring artwork by award-winning illustrator Selznick. In *The Meanest Doll in the World* Annabelle and Tiffany inadvertently wind up at the home of Kate's classmate, where they encounter the diabolical Princess Mimi doll. After the two doll friends help the household dolls stand up to Mimi, the princess doll makes her way to the Palmers' home and threatens the sanctity of the Victorian doll world. A mysterious package that has been

Cover of **The Doll People**, *a fanciful story coauthored by Martin and Laura Godwin and featuring illustrations by Brian Selznick.* (Illustration copyright © 2000 by Brian Selznick. Reprinted by permission of Hyperion Books for Children, an imprint of Disney Book Group. All rights reserved.)

mislaid by the post office for over a century arrives at the Palmers' while the human household is on vacation in *The Runaway Dolls.* When Annabelle and Tiffany realize that Tiffany's toddler doll sister is trapped inside they risk losing their ability to be moveable dolls by opening the package. The "truly evil nemesis will keep the pages turning," noted *School Library Journal* contributor Eva Mitnick of *The Meanest Doll in the World,* and in *Horn Book* Martha V. Parravano stated that the book's "broad humor and action balance with smaller, more personal dramas." Noting that Selznick's pencil drawings "lure readers into the story," a *Publishers Weekly* contributor asserted of *The Runaway Dolls* that the coauthors' "fast-paced, satisfyingly developed" tale "is doubly enjoyable for its foundation in a solidly imagined doll culture," and *School Library Journal* critic Debra Banna dubbed the same book a "fun, magical entry in the series." "Young children like to believe that their toys come alive," asserted a *New York Times Book Review* writer. "And in the pantheon of living toys, . . . Ann M. Martin and Laura Godwin's admired Doll People series reign[s] supreme."

Eleven-year-old Flora Northrup and her younger sister, Ruby, are the featured characters in Martin's "Main Street" novels, which are set in the quiet New England town of Camden Falls and follow the sisters through

several years in installments such as *Welcome to Camden Falls, Needle and Thread, 'Tis the Season, Keeping Secrets,* and *Special Delivery.* After their parents are killed in a car accident, the Northrup girls come to live with their grandmother, Min, who owns a fabric store in town. As the sisters settle into their new environment, they meet a host of intriguing neighbors, including an elderly man caring for his wife, a rebellious teen, and a boy with Down syndrome.

In *Needle and Thread* and *'Tis the Season* the coming holidays find the sisters reminded of their parents' death, while in *Keeping Secrets* they join new friends Olivia and Nikki in welcoming several new neighbors to their row-house community. Little Nikki is the focus of *Coming Apart,* as her father returns to live with the family after spending time apart due to anger issues, and in *Staying Together* she and Olivia join Min in helping Flora and Ruby work through the disagreements that come with growing up together.

Reviewing *Welcome to Camden Falls* in *Booklist,* critic Ilene Cooper predicted that "Martin's easy style, appealing characters, and obvious love of place will keep readers going," while *School Library Journal* critic Kathryn Kosiorek remarked that the "Main Street" books will "appeal to readers more interested in characters and values than true action and adventure." Although Martin addresses the difficulties of typical families in her series, Eva Mitnick observed in her *School Library Journal* review of *'Tis the Season* that her "gentle, clear-eyed narration keeps readers focused on the positive."

Martin's positive focus can also be found in her standalone novels for young readers. Set in the rural South during the 1960s, *Belle Teal* centers on a spunky fifth-grade girl and her experiences in an integrated classroom. When the other white children taunt Darryl, their new African-American schoolmate, Belle reacts with sensitivity, offering her friendship to the boy. Martin's "portrayal of integration in a small school is low key yet quite effective," noted Denise Wilms in *Booklist.* "The writing is graceful and easy, with Belle Teal's narration distinctly and convincingly evoked," Roger Sutton wrote in *Horn Book,* while a contributor in *Publishers Weekly* concluded that the fifth-grade narrator's "observations and realizations provide an eye-opening introduction to social and personal injustice."

Martin's award-winning *A Corner of the Universe* was inspired by the tragic story of her uncle Stephen, her mother's younger brother. As the author told Lynda Brill Comerford in *Publishers Weekly,* Stephen "was diagnosed with schizophrenia at a young age, and he killed himself when he was 23, before my parents met. I remember that what surprised me more than the existence of this uncle and the story behind him was the fact that he had been kept a secret." In the novel, twelve-year-old Hattie Owen meets her uncle Adam, who suffers from a mental illness, for the first time after he returns to the family's boarding house. Adam's exuberant personality helps shy Hattie come out of her shell, until his problems prove to be more than she can handle. According to *Kliatt* reviewer Paula Rohrlick, Martin "offers a sympathetic portrait of the mentally ill in this sensitive, tender coming-of-age tale."

Martin shifts her focus from people to animal protagonists in *A Dog's Life*. In the story a dog named Squirrel becomes lost as a puppy but manages to make her way through life as a stray dog. Told by the elderly Squirrel as she looks back on her younger years, the story features a "convincing animal perspective," acccording to *Booklist* critic Jennifer Mattson, "though some sad events may shock . . . softer hearted" readers. Three more personal perspectives are added to the chorus in the companion volume, *Everything for a Dog,* and here Squirrel's brother Bone tells his life story alongside the present-tense comments of dog-owning Charlie as he sadly recalls his late brother's high-school graduation day. The wish of eleven-year-old Henry for a dog of his own is captured in yet another intertwining narrative, and ultimately all three stories come together in a surprising way. "Touching and ultimately happy," *Everything for a Dog* "also touches upon growing up, facing hardship, and the importance of companionship, no matter its form," according to *School Library Journal* critic Nicole Waskie. Praising Martin's story in *Horn Book,* Susan Dove Lempke described the work as "a serious and very fine book about life, death, and the need to keep going in order to find joy again," while a *Publishers Weekly* contributor predicted that "animal lovers of all ages will cherish this moving tale."

In addition to writing, Martin is very active in supporting various community activities. She is co-founder of the Lisa Novak Community Libraries and has established the Ann M. Martin Foundation, which benefits children, education and literacy programs, and homeless people and animals. Even without the 'Baby-Sitters Club' on the back burner, it is clear that Martin will not be changing her early rising habits. "I love to feel that every week is full of a lot of different kinds of things," she told Lodge. "I've always worked better when I'm working on many things at one time."

Biographical and Critical Sources

PERIODICALS

Booklist, September 1, 1996, Stephanie Zvirin, review of *Leo the Magnificat,* p. 143; June 1, 1998, Hazel Rochman, review of *P.S. Longer Letter Later,* p. 1765; March 15, 2000, Michael Cart, review of *Snail Mail No More,* p. 1376; August, 2000, Ilene Cooper, review of *The Doll People,* p. 2140; October 1, 2001, Denise Wilms, review of *Belle Teal,* p. 319; December 1, 2002, Ilene Cooper, review of *A Corner of the Universe,* p. 659; November 15, 2005, Hazel Rochman,

review of *Friends: Stories about New Friends, Old Friends, and Unexpectedly True Friends,* p. 45; December 1, 2005, Jennifer Mattson, review of *A Dog's Life: The Autobiography of a Stray,* p. 49; August, 2007, Ilene Cooper, reviews of *Welcome to Camden Falls* and *Needle and Thread,* both p. 76; October 1, 2008, Kathleen Isaacs, review of *The Runaway Dolls,* p. 46; June 1, 2009, Daniel Kraus, review of *Everything for a Dog,* p. 55; April 1, 2010, Shelle Rosenfeld, review of *The Summer Before,* p. 42; August 1, 2011, Karen Cruze, review of *Ten Rules for Living with My Sister,* p. 50.

Horn Book, January-February, 2002, Roger Sutton, review of *Belle Teal,* p. 81; November-December, 2003, Martha V. Parravano, review of *The Meanest Doll in the World,* p. 751; November-December, 2004, Susan Dove Lempke, review of *Here Today,* p. 712; November-December, 2009, Susan Dove Lempke, review of *Everything for a Dog,* p. 679.

Journal of Adolescent and Literacy, October, 2010, Donna L. Miller, review *Everything for a Dog,* p. 157.

Kirkus Reviews, May 1, 2007, review of *Welcome to Camden Falls*; September 1, 2008, review of *The Runaway Dolls*; July 15, 2009, review of *Everything for a Dog;* April 15, 2011, review of *Ten Rules for Living with My Sister.*

Kliatt, November, 2002, Paula Rohrlick, review of *A Corner of the Universe,* p. 12; January, 2007, Jennifer Feigelman, review of *The Truth about Stacey,* p. 32; August 15, 2011, review of *Ten Rules for Living with My Sister.*

People, August 21, 1989, Kristin McMurran, "Ann Martin Stirs up a Tiny Tempest in Preteen Land with Her Bestselling 'Baby-Sitters Club,'" pp. 55-56.

Publishers Weekly, August 23, 1991, review of *Eleven Kids, One Summer,* p. 62; September 2, 1996, review of *Leo the Magnificat,* p. 131; September 1, 1997, Sally Lodge, "Another Busy Season for Ann M. Martin," pp. 31-32; February 16, 1998, review of *P.S. Longer Letter Later,* p. 212; March 9, 1998, Lynda Drill Comerford, "A True Test of Friendship," p. 26; January 10, 2000, review of *Snail Mail No More,* p. 68; July 3, 2000, review of *The Doll People,* p. 71; September 32, 2001, review of *Belle Teal,* p. 88; July 22, 2002, Lynda Brill Comerford, interview with Martin, p. 181; January 15, 2006, review of *A Dog's Life,* p. 68; April 16, 2007, review of *Welcome to Camden Falls,* p. 51; August 25, 2008, review of *The Runaway Dolls,* p. 74; August 10, 2009, review of *Everything for a Dog,* p. 55; March 15, 2010, review of *The Summer Before,* p. 53; June 20, 2011, review of *Ten Rules for Living with My Sister,* p. 54.

St. Louis Post-Dispatch (St. Louis, MO), May 6, 2007, Sarah Bryan Miller, "'Baby-Sitters Club' Creator Moves to 'Main Street,'" p. F11.

School Library Journal, May, 1998, Renee Steinberg, review of *P.S. Longer Letter Later,* p. 141; March, 2000, Linda Bindner, review of *Snail Mail No More,* p. 234; November, 2000, Kathie Meizner, review of *The Doll People,* p. 128; October, 2003, Eva Mitnick, review of *The Meanest Doll in the World,* p. 130; November, 2005, Laura Scott, review of *A Dog's Life,* p. 142;

January, 2006, Nancy P. Reeder, review of *Friends,* p. 138; July, 2006, Ronnie Gordon, review of *Kristy's Great Idea,* p. 128; March, 2007, Sadie Mattox, review of *The Truth about Stacey,* p. 238; August, 2007, Kathryn Kosiorek, reviews of *Welcome to Camden Falls* and *Needle and Thread,* both p. 120; October, 2007, Eva Mitnick, review of *'Tis the Season,* p. 102; October, 2008, Debra Banna, review of *The Runaway Dolls,* p. 116; September, 2009, Nicole Waskie, review of *Everything for a Dog,* p. 166.

Time, June 11, 1990, "Wake-up Call," p. 75.

ONLINE

Chronogram Web site, http://www.chronogram.com/ (June 26, 2008), Nina Shergold, "Paperback Writer: Ann M. Martin Lifts the Corners."
Scholastic Web site, http://www.scholastic.com/annmartin/ (October 21, 2011), "Ann M. Martin."

OTHER

Good Conversation!: A Talk with Ann M. Martin (video), Tim Podell Productions, 2005.*

* * *

MASS, Wendy 1967-

Personal

Born April 22, 1967, in Livingston, NJ; daughter of Norman (a lawyer) and Linda (a psychotherapist); married; husband's name Michael; children: twins. *Education:* Tufts University, B.A. (English); California State University at Long Beach, M.A. (English); Drew University, D.Litt. *Hobbies and other interests:* Photography, hiking, reading, music, genealogy, archaeology.

Addresses

Home—NJ. *Agent*—Ginger Knowlton, Curtis Brown, Ltd., Ten Astor Place, New York, NY 10003. *E-mail*—wendy@wendymass.com.

Career

Author of novels and nonfiction for children and young adults. Worked variously for a literary agent, a television casting company, as a script reader for a film producer, and as a book editor at publishing houses in New York, NY, and CT. Cofounder, with Laura Hoffman, of *Writes of Passage* (literary journal for teenagers).

Member

Authors Guild, Writers Guild of America East, Society of Children's Book Writers and Illustrators.

Awards, Honors

Schneider Family Book Award, American Library Association, 2004, and New York Public Library Best Books for the Teen Age designation, and Great Lakes Great Book Award, Michigan State Reading Council, both 2005, and *Booksense* Choice designation, and several state reader awards, all for *A Mango-shaped Space;* International Reading Association Young-Adult Choice designation, 2006, for *Leap Year;* New York Public Library Books for the Teen Age designation, and *Booksense* Choice designation, both 2007, and nominations for several state reader awards, all for *Jeremy Fink and the Meaning of Life;* National Parenting Publication Awards Gold Medal, 2008, for *Every Soul a Star;* Colorado Children's Book Award nomination, 2012, for *Finally;* several state awards, c. 2008, for *11 Birthdays.*

Writings

YOUNG-ADULT FICTION

Getting a Clue: Tammy, Silhouette Books (New York, NY), 1996.
A Mango-shaped Space, Little, Brown (New York, NY), 2003.
Leap Day, Little, Brown (New York, NY), 2004.
Jeremy Fink and the Meaning of Life, Little, Brown (New York, NY), 2006.
Heaven Looks a Lot like the Mall, Little, Brown (New York, NY), 2007.
Every Soul a Star, Little, Brown (New York, NY), 2008.
The Candymakers, Little, Brown (New York, NY), 2010.

Author's work has been translated into thirteen languages.

"TWICE UPON A TIME" NOVEL SERIES

Rapunzel: The One with All the Hair, Scholastic (New York, NY), 2005.
Sleeping Beauty: The One Who Took the Really Long Nap, Scholastic (New York, NY), 2006.
Beauty and the Beast: The Only One Who Didn't Run Away, Scholastic (New York, NY), 2012.

"WILLOW FALLS" NOVEL SERIES

11 Birthdays, Scholastic (New York, NY), 2009.
Finally, Scholastic Press (New York, NY), 2010.
13 Gifts, Scholastic (New York, NY), 2011.

NONFICTION

Stonehenge, Lucent Books (San Diego, CA), 1998.
Teen Drug Abuse, Lucent Books (San Diego, CA), 1998.
Women's Rights, Lucent Books (San Diego, CA), 1998.
(Editor) *Readings on Night,* Greenhaven Press (San Diego, CA), 2000.
Great Authors of Children's Literature, Lucent Books (San Diego, CA), 2001.

(Editor) *A Guide to Children's Literature,* Greenhaven Press (San Diego, CA), 2001.

(Editor, with Stuart P. Levine) *A Guide to Fantasy Literature,* Greenhaven Press (San Diego, CA), 2002.

Gods and Goddesses, Lucent Books (San Diego, CA), 2002.

John Cabot: Early Explorer, Enslow (Berkeley Heights, NJ), 2004.

Ray Bradbury: Master of Science Fiction and Fantasy, Enslow (Berkeley Heights, NJ), 2004.

Celebrate Halloween, Enslow (Berkeley Heights, NJ), 2005.

OTHER

The Bad Hair Day (picture book), Longmeadow Press (Stamford, CT), 1996.

Contributor to periodicals, including *Storyworks* and *Girls' Life.* Short fiction included in anthology *Geektastic,* Little, Brown (New York, NY), 2009.

Adaptations

All Mass's novels were adapted as audiobooks by Recorded Books and Scholastic Audio.

Sidelights

Wendy Mass is an award-winning author of young-adult fiction and nonfiction whose books have been translated into over a dozen languages. Mass, a former book editor who co-created the teen literary journal *Writes of Passage,* began her writing career in nonfiction. However, since earning the Schneider Family Book Award from the American Library Association for her debut novel *A Mango-shaped Space,* she has focused on fiction for teen and preteen readers, producing the critically praised books *Leap Day, Jeremy Fink and the Meaning of Life, Heaven Looks a Lot like the Mall,* and *The Candymakers* as well as the lighthearted stories in her "Willow Falls" and "Twice upon a Time" series.

After graduating from Tufts University with a degree in English, Mass moved to Los Angeles, California, to work in the entertainment industry. She later attended graduate school where she made the decision to write for children and young adults. Moving back east to begin her career in publishing, Mass was soon afforded the opportunity to write nonfiction. Her first works, *Stonehenge, Teen Drug Abuse,* and *Women's Rights,* appeared in 1998. She has also written and edited a number of books about authors, including *Great Authors of Children's Literature* and *Ray Bradbury: Master of Science Fiction and Fantasy.* In *Ray Bradbury,* Mass "presents a well-organized biography of the writer," according to *Booklist* critic Carolyn Phelan.

In *A Mango-shaped Space* Mass introduces an unusual protagonist who sees the world in an unusual way. Thirteen-year-old Mia Winchell discovers that she has a rare neurological condition called synesthesia. As Mass told Beverly Rowe for *MyShelf.com,* "synesthesia is a condition that some people have where the different senses—touch, taste, hearing, vision, and smell—get mixed up instead of remaining separate. The most common variety is called lexical synesthesia, which is where letters and numbers each have individual colors. For instance, someone with this condition might say that the letter 'A' has a sunflower yellow tint with a crumbly feel to it. The number 'two' might be the color of wet cement." In Mia's case, synesthesia allows her to see sounds, letters, and numbers in color, but she keeps her abilities a secret, fearing that her family and classmates will view her as a freak. Mia's struggles with math and Spanish, a consequence of her condition, eventually prove too much for her, and she ultimately seeks help from her parents and a sympathetic doctor.

A Mango-shaped Space was well received by critics. A *Publishers Weekly* contributor remarked that the book's "well-defined characterizations, natural-sounding dialogue, and concrete imagery allow readers to feel Mia's emotions and see through her eyes a kaleidoscopic world." Reviewing Mass's book for *School Library*

Cover of Wendy Mass's debut young-adult novel A Mango-shaped Space, *which introduces readers to an unique way of mapping out one's world.* (Jacket cover copyright © 2003 by Billy Kelly. Reproduced by permission of Little, Brown & Company, a division of Hachette Book Group.)

Cover of Mass's coming-of-age novel **Leap Day,** *featuring artwork by* **Billy Kelly.** (Jacket cover copyright © 2004 by Billy Kelly. Reproduced by permission of Little, Brown & Company, a division of Hachette Book Group.)

Journal, Eva Mitnick stated that "Mia's voice is believable and her description of the vivid world she experiences, filled with slashes, blurs, and streaks of color, is fascinating."

Leap Day concerns Josie, a sixteen year old who, having been born on February 29th, is celebrating only her fourth "official" birthday. During this busy day, Josie plans to take her driver's test, audition for the school play, and join her friends on a scavenger hunt. *Leap Day* employs a dual narrative: Josie's version of events is interspersed with third-person accounts that describe the same incidents from a different perspective. According to Michele Winship in *Kliatt,* "Readers get to see beyond Josie's point of view and find out the motivations and inner thoughts of the people she interacts with throughout her birthday." *Horn Book* contributor Jennifer M. Brabander called *Leap Day* a work "that highlights the potentially life-altering results of our most fleeting daily interactions."

An important birthday is also central to the plot of *Jeremy Fink and the Meaning of Life.* Here cautious Manhattan preteen Jeremy is weeks away from turning thirteen when he received an interesting box in the mail.

Made of wood and with four locks but no keys, the box was made by Jeremy's dad five years before, just before the man's untimely death. Along with instructions to open the box on his upcoming birthday, Jeremy is also informed that the box contains the meaning of life. Determined to honor his late father's wishes—and satisfy his own growing curiosity—Jeremy and adventurous friend Lizzy go on a quest to find the four missing keys before the sun sets on his thirteenth birthday. Featuring what a *Publishers Weekly* critic described as a "exquisitely executed plot twist, combined with an ending that requires a few tissues," *Jeremy Fink and the Meaning of Life* is a "soulful novel one ought not miss." For Faith Brautigam, reviewing Mass's novel for *School Library Journal,* the story is enriched by a "warm picture of parental love and wisdom and of a boy growing into his own understanding and acceptance of life."

The junior year of unhappy high-schooler Tessa Reynolds yields both ups and downs in Mass's verse novel *Heaven Looks a Lot like the Mall.* Hit in the head by a ball during gym class, Tessa suffers a coma and re-experiences important times in her own short life. While wandering through a heaven that looks a lot like the lo-

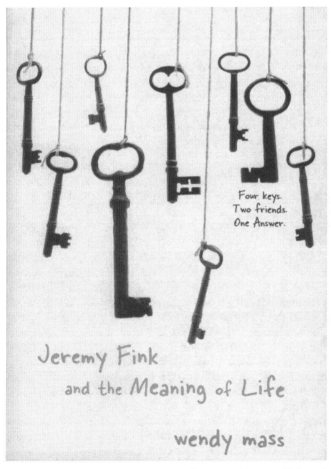

Cover of Mass's middle-grade coming-of-age novel **Jeremy Fink and the Meaning of Life.** (Little, Brown, 2008. Photograph © by Gary S. Chapman/Getty Images. Reproduced by permission of Little, Brown & Company, a division of Hachette Book Group.)

cal shopping mall, Tessa finds that each storefront reveals another of the mean-spirited acts and poor choices that comprise her past. Her unconscious experiences prompt the comatose teen to evaluate her life from a fresh perspective and realize the potential that still exists for a more positive future. "Tessa's journey and authentic voice is one that readers will appreciate," Lynn Rashid predicted in *School Library Journal*, the critic adding that *Heaven Looks a Lot like the Mall* "will entertain and inspire" middle-grade readers. Writing that Mass "takes a chance by offering readers an unlikable protagonist" in the angry and dishonest Tessa, *Booklist* critic Ilene Cooper asserted that *Heaven Looks a Lot like the Mall* is an "emotionally realistic novel [that] will resonate with many" teens.

Mass introduces readers to three unusual tweens in *Every Soul a Star,* a novel for middle-grade readers that alternates first-person narratives with interesting facts about astronomy. The youngest of the three main characters, twelve-year-old Ally, enjoys puzzles and anything to do with astronomy. She also loves living at the Moon Shadow Campground, which her family owns. Popular and pretty, Bree is thirteen and needs access to a shopping mall nearby to survive. To her horror, Bree's academic parents have decided to purchase Moon Shadow. Jack is also thirteen, but unlike Bree, he is gawky and overweight and in the process of failing his favorite science class. When the three children meet up at the campground amidst a gathering of hundreds of people hoping to witness a once-in-a-lifetime solar eclipse, the friendships they form change each of their lives for the better. Commenting on *Every Soul a Star,* Hazel Rochman wrote in *Booklist* that "Bree's hilarious account of her experience as a glamour queen in the wilderness is right-on." "Confirming her mastery of the middle-grade novel, Mass . . . [presents] a well-balanced look at friendships and the role they play in shaping identity," maintained a *Publishers Weekly* critic in reviewing *Every Soul a Star.*

In *The Candymakers* Logan, Miles, Philip, and Daisy are the contestants selected for an annual contest sponsored by the Confectionery Association, their challenge to craft a delicious new candy. All four twelve year olds arrive at the Life Is Sweet Candy Factory, and their interspersed narratives reveal that winning the grand prize will help each child achieve a personal goal as well. For Logan, his candymaker father's respect is the true goal, while Miles uses the challenge of candymaking as a way to avoid dealing with a family tragedy. However, when a theft occurs at the factory, all four children band together to save the business, and the story's "subtle message of teamwork over greed and growth through friendship will resonate with readers," according to *School Library Journal* critic Caitlin Augusta. Noting that the author reveals "clues about misunderstandings, spies, and sabotage . . . along the way," Abby Nolan concluded in her *Booklist* review of *The Candymakers* that "attentive, candy-loving readers will be richly rewarded." In *Horn Book* Susan Dove Lempke

Cover of Mass's young-adult novel **Finally,** *which finds a preteen impatient to make the decisions that frame her life.* (Jacket cover photograph copyright © by Michael Frost. Reproduced by permission of Scholastic, Inc.)

predicted that Mass's novel will find fans among "mystery lovers" who will find that its story "satisfies without being sticky-sweet."

In her middle-grade novels *11 Birthdays, Finally,* and *13 Gifts* Mass takes readers to the small town of Willow Falls, where several young residents have life-changing experiences with the help of a wise elderly woman named Angelina D'Angelo. In *11 Birthdays* Leo and Amanda used to be best friends until Amanda overheard Leo joking about her with his friends. After the preteens become somehow stuck in time (with the help of Angelina), their friendship is pulled back onto rock-solid ground. *Finally* finds almost-twelve-year-old Rory Swenson counting down the minutes until she reaches the age where many things forbidden by her parents will finally be allowed, like drinking coffee, piercing her ears, staying home alone, wearing makeup, and being allowed to babysit. Through Rory's narration, readers learn that growing up comes with a cost, although her life lesson is cushioned by Angelina's compassionate guidance. After her misguided antics cause trouble for her parents, Tara Brennan arrives in Willow Falls to spend the summer with her aunt and uncle and her eleven-year-old cousin Emily. In *13 Gifts* readers follow her efforts to work out her problems through a set of thirteen tasks, one for every year of her upcoming birthday, while befriended by Leo, Amanda, and Rory and once again aided by Angelina.

Praising the "winning story" in *11 Birthdays,* a *Publishers Weekly* contributor added that Mass's "expertise with pacing keeps the story moving at a lively clip, and her understanding of this age group is . . . finely honed." In *Booklist,* Carolyn Phelan wrote that the same novel "offers a fresh twist on the familiar themes of middle-grade family and school dynamics," while *13 Gifts* continues the quasi-magical adventures of Mass's "wonderfully supportive" characters. Reviewing *Finally,* Phelan praised "Rory's lively first-person narrative," and *School Library Journal* critic Madigan McGillicuddy predicted that middle-graders "will relate to this warm, funny story of a heroine who can't wait to grow up." Typical of the series' upbeat protagonists, Rory's "chatty, friendly [narration] . . . and relentless optimism in the face of her many mishaps are heartwarming," concluded a *Publishers Weekly* reviewer in appraising *Finally,* and each novel's story "skillfully resolves mysteries while perpetuating Willow Falls' mystique," according to a *Kirkus Reviews* writer.

Asked by Rowe why she chooses to write for teenagers, Mass explained: "When I was that age, reading was such a huge part of my life. I wouldn't be the same person today if I didn't have those wonderful stories living inside my head. It seems to me that those years, be-

tween ten and fourteen, are when kids figure out what kind of person they want to be—both inside and outside—and how they want to live their life." "We can experience things in books that we can never experience in life," she added, "but these experiences show us what is possible in our own life."

Biographical and Critical Sources

PERIODICALS

Booklist, April 1, 2003, Debbie Carton, review of *A Mango-shaped Space,* p. 1390; February 15, 2004, Cindy Welch, review of *Leap Day,* pp. 1051-1052; November 1, 2004, Carolyn Phelan, review of *Ray Bradbury: Master of Science Fiction and Fantasy,* p. 474; December 15, 2006, Hazel Rochman, review of *Jeremy Fink and the Meaning of Life,* p. 49; October 15, 2007, Ilene Cooper, review of *Heaven Looks a Lot like the Mall,* p. 44; December 1, 2006, Hazel Rochman, review of *Every Soul a Star,* p. 51; December 15, 2008, Carolyn Phelan, review of *11 Birthdays;* February 1, 2010, Carolyn Phelan, review of *Finally,* p. 42; November 15, 2010, Abby Nolan, review of *The Candymakers,* p. 46; August 1, 2011, Carolyn Phelan, review of *13 Gifts,* p. 47.

Bulletin of the Center for Children's Books, March, 2007, Karen Coats, review of *Jeremy Fink and the Meaning of Life,* p. 302; October, 2007, Deborah Stevenson, review of *Heaven Looks a Lot like the Mall,* p. 98; December, 2010, Kate Quealy-Gainer, review of *The Candymakers,* p. 196.

Horn Book, July-August, 2003, Jennifer M. Brabander, review of *A Mango-shaped Space,* p. 463; May-June, 2004, Jennifer M. Brabander, review of *Leap Day,* p. 333; January-February, 2007, Jennifer M. Brabander, review of *Jeremy Fink and the Meaning of Life,* p. 70; November-December, 2008, Jennifer M. Brabander, review of *Every Soul a Star,* p. 709; November-December, 2010, Susan Dove Lempke, review of *The Candymakers,* p. 95.

Kirkus Reviews, March 1, 2003, *A Mango-shaped Space,* p. 392; January 15, 2004, review of *Leap Day,* p. 85; October 15, 2006, review of *Jeremy Fink and the Meaning of Life,* p. 1074; August 1, 2007, review of *Heaven Looks a Lot like the Mall;* September 1, 2008, review of *Every Soul a Star;* December 15, 2008, review of *11 Birthdays;* February 15, 2010, review of *Finally;* July 15, 2011, review of *13 Gifts.*

Kliatt, March, 2003, Paula Rohrlick, review of *A Mango-shaped Space,* p. 14; January, 2004, Michele Winship, review of *Leap Day,* p. 10; September, 2006, Joanna Solomon, review of *Jeremy Fink and the Meaning of Life,* p. 15; September, 2007, Janis Flint-Ferguson, review of *Heaven Looks a Lot like the Mall,* p. 15; November, 2008, Janis Flint-Ferguson, review of *Every Soul a Star,* p. 130.

Publishers Weekly, April 14, 2003, *A Mango-shaped Space,* p. 71; December 11, 2006, review of *Jeremy Fink and the Meaning of Life,* p. 70; October 13, 2008, review

Cover of Mass's "Twice upon a Time" retelling of **Rapunzel,** *featuring artwork by James Dignan.* (Copyright © 2005 by Scholastic, Inc. Reproduced by permission of Scholastic, Inc.)

of *Every Soul a Star,* p. 54; December 22, 2008, review of *11 Birthdays,* p. 52; February 1, 2010, review of *Finally,* p. 47.

School Library Journal, June, 2000, Timothy Capehart, review of *Great Authors of Children's Literature,* p. 169; January, 2001, Marilyn Heath, review of *Readings on Night,* p. 151; March, 2003, Eva Mitnick, review of *A Mango-shaped Space,* p. 237; March, 2004, Paula J. LaRue, review of *Leap Day,* pp. 216-217; December, 2004, Kathleen Simonetta, review of *Ray Bradbury,* p. 164; December, 2006, Faith Brautigam, review of *Jeremy Fink and the Meaning of Life,* p. 151; September, 2007, Lynn Rashid, review of *Heaven Looks a Lot like the Mall,* p. 203; November, 2008, Kristin Anderson, review of *Every Soul a Star,* p. 130; July, 2010, Madigan McGillicuddy, review of *Finally,* p. 93; November, 2010, Caitlin Augusta, review of *The Candymakers,* p. 122.

Voice of Youth Advocates, October, 2007, Stephanie L. Petruso, review of *Heaven Looks a Lot like the Mall,* p. 333.

ONLINE

MyShelf.com, http://www.myshelf.com/ (May 26, 2005), Beverly Rowe, interview with Mass.

Teenreads.com, http://www.teenreads.com/ (January 5, 2009), "Wendy Mass."

Wendy Mass Home Page, http://www.wendymass.com (October 10, 2011).

*   *   *

McCAHAN, Erin

Personal

Born in East Grand Rapids, MI; married April 17, 1999; husband's name Tim. *Education:* Attended Hope College; Capital University, bachelor's degree, 1991; attended Methodist Theological School, 1993.

Addresses

Home—Upper Arlington, OH. *Agent*—Faye Bender Literary Agency, 19 Cheever Pl., Brooklyn, NY 11231.

Career

Writer. Freelance writer, c. mid-1990s; youth minister at St. John's Episcopal Church in Worthington, OH, and St. Mark's Episcopal Church, Upper Arlington, OH, for ten years; full-time writer, 2007—. Certified peer mentor for Tragedy Assistance Program for Survivors (TAPS).

Member

Mensa, Society of Children's Book Writers and Illustrators, Sons and Daughters in Touch, Athletic Club of Columbus.

Awards, Honors

Rita Award nominations for Best First Book and Best Young-Adult Romance, both Romance Writers of America, both 2010, both for *I Now Pronounce You Someone Else.*

Writings

I Now Pronounce You Someone Else, Arthur A. Levine Books (New York, NY), 2010.

Sidelights

A high-school senior contemplates her disdain for ketchup, an alternate identity, and marriage in *I Now Pronounce You Someone Else,* Erin McCahan's debut novel. Described as "a coming-of-age story with surprising twists and turns" by *Booklist* critic Hazel Rochman, the work centers on Bronwen Oliver, a sensitive and imaginative young woman who, feeling alienated from her family, enters a whirlwind romance with a charming college student. Writing about a seventeen-year-old protagonist seemed an obvious choice for McCahan, an experienced freelance writer who also spent ten years working as a youth minister. During that time, she discovered her talent for connecting with teens, and tapped her talent for writing as well.

Bronwen's troubled relationship with her family members is at the heart of *I Now Pronounce You Someone Else.* Since the death of her father years earlier, Bronwen has grown distant from her mother and older brother, and she now struggles to maintain a close bond with her stepdad. To assuage her feelings of loneliness, Bronwen concocts a fictional personality, Phoebe Lilywhite, and imagines herself part of a secure, loving home. When she begins dating an old acquaintance, Jared Sondervan, she quickly falls in love, and on her eighteenth birthday she accepts Jared's proposal of marriage. As the wedding approaches, though, Bronwen realizes that she has rushed into the situation and begins having second thoughts about her decision.

In *I Now Pronounce You Someone Else* McCahan examines "that time period of high school and college when young adults try on and discard personalities in search of their true selves," explained *School Library Journal* contributor Suanne Roush. A *Publishers Weekly* reviewer praised the work, stating that "this intelligent romance teaches a hard but relevant lesson about living dreams and letting them go."

Biographical and Critical Sources

PERIODICALS

Booklist, July 1, 2010, Hazel Rochman, review of *I Now Pronounce You Someone Else,* p. 51.

Bulletin of the Center for Children's Books, September, 2010, Deborah Stevenson, review of *I Now Pronounce You Someone Else,* p. 29.

Columbus Dispatch, June 10, 2010, Kristine Gill, "Youth Work Provided Insight for Author's Inaugural Book."

Grand Rapids Press, July 11, 2010, Erin Albanese, "West Michigan Roots Inspire Erin McCahan's First Novel."

Kirkus Reviews, May 15, 2010, review of *I Now Pronounce You Someone Else.*

Publishers Weekly, May 31, 2010, review of *I Now Pronounce You Someone Else,* p. 48.

School Library Journal, June, 2010, Suanne Roush, review of *I Now Pronounce You Someone Else,* p. 110.

ONLINE

Erin McCahan Home Page, http://www.erinmccahan.com (September 15, 2011).*

* * *

MENCHIN, Scott

Personal

Married Yvetta Fedorova (an artist); children: Karina. *Education:* Attended Art Students' League; Pratt Institute, degree, 1980.

Addresses

Office—640 Broadway, Ste. 3E, New York, NY 10012. *Agent*—Pippin Properties, 155 E. 38th St., Ste. 2H, New York, NY 10016. *E-mail*—s.menchin@verizon.net.

Career

Illustrator. Former art director for *How* magazine and *Seven Days.* Pratt Institute, Brooklyn, NY, adjunct associate professor in graduate-design program, beginning 1996. *Exhibitions:* Work included in exhibition at Eric Carle Museum of Picture-Book Art, 2007.

Awards, Honors

Choices selection, Cooperative Children's Book Council, and Please Touch Museum Book Award, both 2006, both for *Wiggle* by Doreen Cronin; Christopher Award, 2008, and Best Children's Books of the Year designation, Bank Street College of Education, both for *Taking a Bath with the Dog and Other Things That Make Me Happy.*

Writings

SELF-ILLUSTRATED

Taking a Bath with the Dog and Other Things That Make Me Happy, Candlewick Press (Cambridge, MA), 2007.

What If Everything Had Legs?, Candlewick Press (Somerville, MA), 2010.

ILLUSTRATOR

Eve Bunting, *The Day the Whale Came,* Harcourt (San Diego, CA), 1998.

Bob Dylan, *Man Gave Names to All the Animals,* Harcourt (San Diego, CA), 1999.

Ann Braybrooks, *Plenty of Pockets,* Harcourt (San Diego, CA), 2000.

Mat Connolley, compiler, *Butter Comes from Butterflies: When I Was a Kid I Used to Believe—,* Chronicle Books (San Francisco, CA), 2004.

Doreen Cronin, *Wiggle,* Atheneum (New York, NY), 2005.

Doreen Cronin, *Bounce,* Atheneum (New York, NY), 2007.

Doreen Cronin, *Stretch,* Atheneum Books for Young Readers (New York, NY), 2009.

Alison McGhee, *Song of Middle C,* Candlewick Press (Somerville, MA), 2009.

Doreen Cronin, *Rescue Bunnies,* Balzer and Bray (New York, NY), 2010.

George Shannon and Lynn Brunelle, *Chicken Scratches: Poultry Poetry and Rooster Rhymes,* Chronicle Books (San Francisco, CA), 2010.

Contributor of illustrations to periodicals, including *Newsweek, Rolling Stone, Time,* and the *New York Times.*

Sidelights

An instructor at the prestigious Pratt Institute, Scott Menchin created advertising art for companies such as Toyota, Intel, and Dr. Pepper before he began writing and illustrating children's books. Menchin's first picture-book project, Eve Bunting's text for *The Day the Whale Came,* involves a dead whale that was transported through the streets of a town in Illinois during the early 1900s. The illustrator's "quirky pen-and-ink pictures effectively contrast the ordinary Midwestern town with the surrealism of the event," Linda Perkins wrote in *Booklist.* As a *Publishers Weekly* contributor noted of the same book, "Menchin's unconventional pictures . . . subtly incorporate photographs with stylized drawings."

The art in Menchin's second picture-book project, an adaptation of Bob Dylan's song "Man Gave Name to All the Animals," was highly praised in *Publishers Weekly.* Menchin turns the song into a "guessing game," the magazine's reviewer explained, noting that the artist reveals only part of each animal being sung about in his mixed-media collage art. Despite the lack of musical accompaniment, the illustrator "makes visual the rollicking, reggae-inflected sounds" of Dylan's music, according to *Booklist* critic GraceAnne A. DeCandido. *Man Gave Names to All the Animals* is not the only book in which Menchin incorporates clues into his artwork. Describing *Plenty of Pockets,* a picture book with a story by Ann Braybrooks, *Booklist* contributor Connie Fletcher concluded that "Menchin's collage illustrations . . . pack in surprises."

Menchin collaborates with writer Doreen Cronin on several books which follow an energetic spotted dog through its day, among them *Wiggle* and *Bounce.* "The delightful cartoon-style, ink-and-watercolor art is highlighted by tidbits of collage," wrote Ilene Cooper in her *Booklist* review of *Wiggle.* Noting Menchin's use of collage, Kathy Krasniewicz commented in *School Library Journal* that photographs and other materials "are well integrated into broad, bright cartoon illustrations," while a *Publishers Weekly* critic dubbed the artist's use of "whimsical photographic images" a form of "comic punctuation." In *Bounce,* which finds the effervescent canine frolicking with a host of animal friends, Menchin's "cartoon art is eye-catching and as playful as the text," according to *School Library Journal* critic Marge Loch-Wouters, and a contributor in *Publishers Weekly* noted that the artist "works in bold ink outlines and bright, even digital colors, and uses whimsical photographic images here and there for comic punctuation." The limber pooch practices his yoga skills in *Stretch,* a third collaboration between Menchin and Cronin. The artist's collage creations here drew praise from *Booklist* reviewer Daniel Kraus, who described the illustrations in *Stretch* as "playful and wildly colorful"

Menchin and Cronin also joined forces on *Rescue Bunnies,* which follows the adventures of Newbie, a trainee on a team of courageous emergency workers. When the rabbits receive a distress signal notifying them that a giraffe has gotten stuck in a pool of mud, Newbie gets the opportunity to pass her field test by standing guard over the creature as a band of hyenas approaches and

devising a bunny-centric solution to the giraffe's predicament. "Menchin's cartoon art is as sharply lined and colorful as they come," a critic in *Kirkus Reviews* noted, and Marge Loch-Wouters observed in *School Library Journal* that the artist "uses minimalist backgrounds and simple shapes to focus readers' eyes on the action."

A young musician turns tragedy into triumph in Alison McGhee's *Song of Middle C,* another work illustrated by Menchin. To prepare for her first recital, a talented pianist practices virtually around the clock, memorizing every note of her song, "Dance of the Wood Elves." When it comes time to play on stage, however, the youngster comp letely freezes, remembering how to play only one note, the middle C, which she manages to turn into a command performance. "Menchin's digitally colored pen-and-ink cartoons are remarkably detailed while appearing deceptively simple and childlike," remarked a contributor in *Kirkus Reviews,* and *School Library Journal* critic Joy Fleischhacker maintained that the book's "cartoon artwork merrily depicts the action while illustrating the young maestro's funny flights of fancy."

Menchin's first self-illustrated title, *Taking a Bath with the Dog and Other Things That Make Me Happy,* begins when a mother asks her sobbing young daughter what would make her happy. Unsure, the unhappy girl asks the dog, then the rabbit, then other people and animals what makes them happy, thereby learning how many things there are to smile about. The tale "will likely inspire youngsters who are in a funk to seek joy in the unexpected as well as in the perfectly ordinary," observed a *Publishers Weekly* critic. In *Kirkus Reviews,* a contributor wrote that, with "striking effect," Menchin's "illustrations contrast the characters painted in textured watercolors against a backdrop of one vivid color."

An exhausted but inventive child is the focus of *What If Everything Had Legs?,* another self-illustrated story by Menchin. While reluctantly trudging home with her mother, an exasperated youngster wonders why their house couldn't sprout legs and come to meet them. Before long, the pair are engaged in a spirited discussion about the possibilities for attaching legs to a variety of inanimate objects, including cupcakes, rakes, and snails. A number of critics complimented the colorful, mixed-media illustrations in *What If Everything Had Legs?* "Menchin's figures have the wide eyes and stiff limbs of people in Egyptian friezes," a reviewer stated in *Publishers Weekly,* According to Kathleen Finn in *School Library Journal,* the book's "simple text and wacky, hybrid illustrations . . . combine for an entertaining read-aloud," and a *Kirkus Reviews* critic described *What If Everything Had Legs?* as an "amusing tale that may spark readers to embark on their own imaginative journeys."

Cover of Scott Menchin's lighthearted self-illustrated picture book **Taking a Bath with the Dog, and Other Things That Make Me Happy.**

Biographical and Critical Sources

PERIODICALS

Booklist, April 15, 1998, Linda Perkins, review of *The Day the Whale Came,* p. 1449; December 15, 1999, GraceAnne A. DeCandido, review of *Man Gave Names to All the Animals,* p. 785; July, 2000, Connie Fletcher, review of *Plenty of Pockets,* p. 2037; May 1, 2005, Ilene Cooper, review of *Wiggle,* p. 1586; May 15, 2009, Daniel Kraus, review of *Stretch,* p. 47; July 1, 2010, Daniel Kraus, review of *Rescue Bunnies,* p. 68.

Children's Bookwatch, September, 2007, review of *Taking a Bath with the Dog.*

Horn Book, September-October, 2005, review of *Wiggle,* p. 560; July-August, 2009, Kitty Flynn, review of *Song of Middle C,* p. 412; September-October, 2010, Kitty Flynn, review of *Rescue Bunnies,* p. 58.

Kirkus Reviews, June 1, 2005, review of *Wiggle,* p. 635; April 15, 2007, review of *Bounce;* May 15, 2007, review of *Taking a Bath with the Dog and Other Things That Make Me Happy;* April 1, 2009, review of *Song of Middle C;* July 15, 2011, review of *What If Everything Had Legs?*

Publishers Weekly, February 23, 1998, review of *The Day the Whale Came,* p. 76; November 15, 1999, review of *Man Gave Names to All the Animals,* p. 1999; May 23, 2005, review of *Wiggle,* p. 77; March 5, 2007, review of *Bounce,* p. 59; July 9, 2007, review of *Taking a Bath with the Dog and Other Things That Make Me Happy,* p. 52; August 5, 2010, review of *Rescue Bunnies,* p. 43; June 6, 2011, review of *What If Everything Had Legs?,* p. 41.

School Library Journal, May, 2000, Tina Hudak, review of *Plenty of Pockets,* p. 130; June, 2005, Kathy Krasniewicz, review of *Wiggle,* p. 107; June, 2007, Shelley B. Sutherland, review of *Taking a Bath with the Dog and Other Things That Make Me Happy,* p. 81, and Marge Loch-Wouters, review of *Bounce.* p. 96; August, 2009, Lisa Glasscock, review of *Stretch,* p. 73, and Joy Fleischhacker, review of *Song of Middle C,* p. 80; September, 2010, Marge Loch-Wouters, review of *Rescue Bunnies,* p. 120; July, 2011, Kathleen Finn, review of *What If Everything Had Legs?,* p. 72.

ONLINE

Pippin Properties Web site, http://www.pippinproperties.com/ (September 28, 2011), "Scott Menchin."

Pratt Institute Web site, http://www.pratt.edu/ (September 21, 2011), "Scott Menchin."

Scott Menchin Home Page, http://www.scottmenchin.com (September 21, 2011).

MICHAEL, Ted 1984-
[A pseudonym]
(Ted Malawer)

Personal

Born January, 1984, on Long Island, NY. *Education:* Columbia College, B.A. (English and comparative literature), 2006; Juilliard School of Music, degree (opera).

Addresses

Home—NY. *Office*—Upstart Crow Literary, P.O. Box 25404, Brooklyn, NY 11202.

Career

Literary agent and author. Opera singer; former theatrical performer.

Writings

The Diamonds, illustrated by Kate Berthold, Delacorte Press (New York, NY), 2009.
Crash Test Love, Delacorte Press (New York, NY), 2010.

Sidelights

Publishing under the pen name Ted Michael, Ted Malawer began writing novels after establishing his reputation as a literary agent specializing in middle-grade and young-adult fiction. A graduate of Columbia College, where he studied comparative literature, Malawer also studied at New York City's prestigious Juilliard School of Music, where he trained as an opera singer. His novels *The Diamonds* and *Crash Test Love* are based on his memories of growing up on Long Island and focus on the romance, intrigue, jealousies, and competition that characterize contemporary teen culture.

Malawer wrote his first novel, *The Diamonds,* shortly after graduating from Columbia College. It is set at Bennington School, a prestigious private high school where a clique of popular senior girls are known as the Diamonds and rule over their classmates. The group of four is led by popular and beautiful Clarissa, and Marni enjoys her role as Clarissa's best friend. However, when Marni begins a friendship with Anderson, the ex-boyfriend of the Diamond's queen bee, she quickly becomes the focus of the Diamonds' wrath. The teen is not willing to accept her new role as social outcast, however, and Marni fights back with ammunition that may threaten Clarissa's own status. Reviewing *The Diamonds* in *School Library Journal,* Jill Heritage Maza noted that Marni "spearheads a group of students from across the social spectrum" to break her former friend's dictatorial hold on Bennington, perhaps bringing about her own form of social justice.

Malawer also taps into contemporary high-school culture in *Crash Test Love,* the second novel written under his Ted Michael pseudonym. Here readers meet Henry Arlington, a self-described "player" whose talent lies in amassing a string of one-night relationships. Henry's hobby is crashing the Sweet Sixteen parties that are held within striking distance of his Long Island home, but at one party he finally meets his match. Garrett Lennox has just moved to town from Chicago, and she is desperate to be accepted by East Shore High's ruling clique, the J. Squad. The battle is on when Garrett is challenged by the squad to woo Henry, get him to commit as her steady, and then give him a dose of his own medicine by dumping him publicly. Not surprisingly, the scheme backfires when feelings get in the way, resulting in a story that weaves "interspersed movie-script format for dialogue and song references throughout," according to *School Library Journal* critic Lynn Rashid. In *Publishers Weekly* a critic noted the "emotional intensity" Malawer kindles between his two main characters, and Rashid recommended *Crash Test Love* to "romance fans [who] will enjoy the familiar theme of reluctant, ill-fated love."

Biographical and Critical Sources

PERIODICALS

Bulletin of the Center for Children's Books, July-August, 2009, Karen Coats, review of *The Diamonds,* p. 452; July-August, 2010, Karen Coats, review of *Crash Test Love,* p. 495.
Kirkus Reviews, May 15, 2010, review of *Crash Test Love.*
Publishers Weekly, May 31, 2010, review of *Crash Test Love,* p. 50.
School Library Journal, June, 2009, Jill Heritage Maza, review of *The Diamonds,* p. 132; July, 2010, Lynn Rashid, review of *Crash Test Love,* p. 94.

ONLINE

Upstart Crow Literary Web site, http://www.upstartcrow literary.com/ (October 21, 2011), "Tom Malawer."
Pacific Coast Children's Writers Workshop, http://www.childrenswritersworkshop.com/ (October 21, 2011), Nancy Sondel, interview with Malawer.*

N

NEWMAN, Lesléa 1955-

Personal

Born November 5, 1955, in Brooklyn, NY. *Education:* University of Vermont, B.S. (education), 1977; Naropa Institute, certificate in poetics, 1980. *Religion:* Jewish

Addresses

Office—Write from the Heart, P.O. Box 815, Northampton, MA 01061. *Agent*—Elizabth Harding, Curtis Brown, Ltd., 10 Astor Pl., New York, NY 10003. *E-mail*—leslea@lesleakids.com.

Career

Educator and author. Reader for *Mademoiselle* and *Redbook* magazines, New York, NY, 1982; *Valley Advocate*, Hatfield, MA, journalist and book reviewer, 1983-87; Mount Holyoke College, South Hadley, MA, director and teacher of writing at summer program, 1986-90; Write from the Heart: Writing Workshops for Women, Northampton, MA, founder and director, 1986—. University of Southern Maine, member of M.F.A. faculty, 2005-09; instructor at Clark University; M.F.A. faculty mentor at Spalding University. Lecturer and presenter at workshops at colleges and universities, including Amherst College, Smith College, Swarthmore College, Trinity College, and Yale University. Presenter at schools and libraries.

Member

Society of Children's Book Writers and Illustrators, Poets and Writers, Cat Writers Association, Dog Writers Association.

Awards, Honors

Massachusetts Artists Foundation poetry fellowship, 1989; James Baldwin Award for Cultural Achievement, Greater Boston Area Lesbian/Gay Political Alliance, 1993; Silver Award, Parents' Choice Foundation, 1994,

Lesléa Newman (Photograph copyright by Mary Vazquez. Reproduced by permission.)

for *Fat Chance;* Gemini Award for Best Short Drama, Canadian Academy of Film and Television, 1995, for *Spoken Word: A Letter to Harvey Milk;* Books for the Teen Age selection, New York Public Library, 1996, for *A Loving Testimony: Remembering Loved Ones Lost to AIDS;* National Endowment for the Arts poetry fellowship, 1997; first place winner in humor category, Vice Versa Awards for Excellence in Gay and Lesbian Press, 1999, for "Cher Heaven"; *Americus Review* Poetry Contest winner, 2000, for "The Politics of Buddy"; Gold Seal Award, Oppenheim Toy Portfolio, 2005, and Amelia Bloomer List inclusion, American Library Association (ALA), 2006, both for *A Fire Engine for Ruthie;* Children's Choice selection, Children's Book Council/International Reading Association, 2004, for *The Best Cat in the World;* ASPCA Henry Bergh Honor Book designation, Kiriyama Prize honor, and Best Children's Book selection, Bank Street College of Education, all

2005, all for *Hachiko Waits;* Continuing the Legacy of Stonewall Award, University of Massachusetts Stonewall Center, 2006; named poet laureate of Northampton, MA, 2008-10; Gold Seal Award, Oppenheim Toy Portfolio, 2009, and Cooperative Children's Book Center Choice selection, 2010, both for both *Mommy, Mama, and Me* and *Daddy, Papa, and Me;* ALA Notable Book designation, 2010, for *Mommy, Mama, and Me;* Hachamat Lev Award, Keshet Foundation, 2010; Certificate of Excellence, Dog Writers Association of America and Cat Writers of America; numerous awards for poetry.

Writings

PICTURE BOOKS

Heather Has Two Mommies, illustrated by Diana Souza, In Other Words/Inland, 1989, 10th anniversary, Alyson Books (Los Angeles, CA), 2000, 20th anniversary edition, with new illustrations, 2009.

Gloria Goes to Gay Pride, Alyson Books (Los Angeles, CA), 1991.

Belinda's Bouquet, Alyson Books (Los Angeles, CA), 1991.

Saturday Is Pattyday, illustrated by Annette Hegel, New Victoria Publishers (Norwich, VT), 1993.

Too Far Away to Touch, illustrated by Catherine Stock, Clarion Books (New York, NY), 1996.

Remember That, illustrated by Karen Ritz, Clarion Books (New York, NY), 1996.

Matzo Ball Moon, illustrated by Elaine Greenstein, Clarion Books (New York, NY), 1998.

Cats, Cats, Cats!, illustrated by Erika Oller, Simon & Schuster (New York, NY), 2001.

Dogs, Dogs, Dogs!, illustrated by Erika Oller, Simon & Schuster (New York, NY), 2002.

Runaway Dreidel!, illustrated by Kyrsten Brooker, Henry Holt (New York, NY), 2002.

Felicia's Favorite Story, illustrated by Alaiyo Bradshaw, Two Lives Publishing (Ridley Park, PA), 2003.

Pigs, Pigs, Pigs!, illustrated by Erika Oller, Simon & Schuster (New York, NY), 2003.

Daddy's Song, illustrated by Karen Ritz, Henry Holt (New York, NY), 2004.

A Fire Engine for Ruthie, illustrated by Cyd Moore, Clarion Books (New York, NY), 2004.

The Best Cat in the World, illustrated by Ronald Himler, Eerdmans Books for Young Readers (Grand Rapids, MI), 2004.

The Boy Who Cried Fabulous, illustrated by Peter Ferguson, Tricycle Press (Berkeley, CA), 2004.

Where Is Bear?, illustrated by Valeri Gorbachev, Gulliver Books/Harcourt (Orlando, FL), 2004.

The Eight Nights of Chanukah, illustrated by Elivia Savadier, Harry N. Abrams (New York, NY), 2005.

Skunk's Spring Surprise, illustrated by Valeri Gorbachev, Harcourt (San Diego, CA), 2007.

Daddy, Papa, and Me, illustrated by Carol Thomas, Tricycle Press (Berkeley, CA), 2009.

Mommy, Mama, and Me, illustrated by Carol Thomas, Tricycle Press (Berkeley, CA), 2009.

Just like Mama, illustrated by Julia Gorton, Abrams Books for Young Readers (New York, NY), 2010.

Miss Tutu's Star, illustrated by Carey Armstrong-Ellis, Abrams Books for Young Readers (New York, NY), 2010.

Donovan's Big Day, illustrated by Mike Dutton, Tricycle Press (Berkeley, CA), 2011.

MIDDLE-GRADE NOVELS

Fat Chance, Putnam (New York, NY), 1994.

Hachiko Waits, illustrated by Machiyo Kodaira, Henry Holt (New York, NY), 2004.

FOR YOUNG ADULTS

Still Life with Buddy, Pride Publications (Radwor, OH), 1998.

Jailbait, Delacorte Press (New York, NY), 2005.

FOR ADULTS

Just Looking for My Shoes (poetry), Back Door Press, 1980.

Good Enough to Eat (novel), Firebrand Books, 1986.

Love Me like You Mean It (poetry), HerBooks (Santa Cruz, CA), 1987.

A Letter to Harvey Milk: Short Stories (also see below), Firebrand Books, 1988, reprinted, University of Wisconsin Press/Terrace Books (Madison, WI), 2004.

(Editor) *Bubba Meisehs by Shayneh Maidelehs: An Anthology of Poetry by Jewish Granddaughters about Our Grandmothers,* HerBooks (Santa Cruz, CA), 1989.

Secrets (short stories), New Victoria Publishers (Norwich, VT), 1990.

Sweet Dark Places (poetry), HerBooks (Santa Cruz, CA), 1991.

Somebody to Love: A Guide to Loving the Body You Have, Third Side Press, 1991.

In Every Laugh a Tear (novel), New Victoria Publishers (Norwich, VT), 1992.

(Editor) *Eating Our Hearts Out: Women and Food,* Crossing Press (Freedom, CA), 1993.

Writing from the Heart: Inspiration and Exercises for Women Who Want to Write, Crossing Press (Freedom, CA), 1993.

Every Woman's Dream (essays and short fiction), New Victoria Publishers (Norwich, VT), 1994.

(Editor) *A Loving Testimony: Remembering Loved Ones Lost to AIDS,* Crossing Press (Freedom, CA), 1995.

Spoken Word: A Letter to Harvey Milk (television program; adapted from *A Letter to Harvey Milk*), Sleeping Giants Productions, 1995.

(Editor) *The Femme Mystique,* Alyson Publications (Boston, MA), 1995.

(Editor) *My Lover Is a Woman: Contemporary Lesbian Love Poems,* Ballantine Books (New York, NY), 1996.

Out of the Closet and Nothing to Wear, Alyson Books (Los Angeles, CA), 1997.

(Editor) *Pillow Talk: Lesbian Stories between the Covers,* Alyson Books (Los Angeles, CA), 1998.

The Little Butch Book, illustrated by Yohah Ralph, New Victoria Publishers (Norwich, VT), 1998.

Girls Will Be Girls (short fiction), Alyson Books (Los Angeles, CA), 1999.

Pillow Talk II: More Lesbian Stories between the Covers, Alyson Books (Los Angeles, CA), 2000.

Signs of Love (poetry), Windstorm Creative, 2000.

Just like a Woman (short stories), Fluid Words (Los Angeles, CA) 2001.

She Loves Me, She Loves Me Not (short stories), Alyson Books (Los Angeles, CA), 2002.

Nobody's Mother (poetry), Orchard House Press, 2008.

The Reluctant Daughter (novel), Bold Strokes Books, 2009.

Contributor to anthology *Am I Blue?,* edited by Marion Dane Bauer, HarperCollins (New York, NY), 1994; and to magazines, including *Backbone, Common Lives, Conditions, Cricket, Heresies, Highlights for Children, Horn Book, Seventeen, Sinister Wisdom, Sojourner,* and *Spider.*

Adaptations

A Letter to Harvey Milk was adapted for film and stage.

Sidelights

Lesléa Newman is an author, poet, and teacher of creative writing who is strongly motivated by her Jewish heritage and strong feminist beliefs. Newman's list of writings is diverse, both in genre and theme, ranging from fiction to nonfiction and focusing on AIDS, lesbian identity, sexual abuse, eating disorders, Jewish identity, and dealing with the death of a loved one. Among her works for young readers are picture books such as *Remember That, Cats, Cats, Cats!,* and *Miss Tutu's Star.* Her groundbreaking *Heather Has Two Mommies,* a controversial work first published in 1989 and still in print, was the first picture book to respond to the growing need for literature about young children raised by same-sex couples. In addition to books for young children, Newman has authored a novel for young teens about the "thinner is better" philosophy promoted by modern culture, and has addressed women-focused issues in her many essays, poems, short stories, and works of adult nonfiction. As Newman once commented: "Writing continues to teach me, surprise me, and inform me in new and exciting ways."

Deciding to become a writer after earning her bachelor's degree in education at the University of Vermont, Newman spent several years working in New York City before moving north to the college town of Northampton, Massachusetts. Active in that area's vibrant gay community, she soon realized that there was a need for books to help lesbian couples who chose to become parents deal with questions common to all children, especially the universal question: "Where did I come from?" Responding to this need, Newman wrote several books for both lesbian parents and the offspring of such non-traditional families that portray their unique circumstances in a sensitive and informed manner.

Heather Has Two Mommies answers a little girl's questions about where she came from and why she has no "Daddy." While the adult characters attempt to do so in a loving and sympathetic manner, Robert Burke took issue with Newman's approach, noting in the *Bloomsbury Review* that "on the one hand, they hope to console her with an explanation of her uniqueness. On the other hand, they also seem to be trying to convince Heather that she is just the same as everyone else." A reviewer for *Bulletin of the Center for Children's Books* was more positive, describing the book as "a positive, if idealized, portrait of a loving lesbian family," and commending it for "preach[ing] . . . a respect for all kinds of families." As Heather's teacher informs the kindergarten class in *Heather Has Two Mommies,* "The most important thing about a family is that all the people in it love each other."

Like *Heather Has Two Mommies, Donovan's Big Day* and *Felicia's Favorite Story* also deal with two-mommy households. A very special wedding is the focus of *Donovan's Big Day,* and young Donovan will play an important part as ring-bearer when Mommy and Mama finally get married. Adirana Romo creates the pastel-tinted watercolor art for *Felicia's Favorite Story,* in which a little girl delights in every retelling of her adoption by loving parents Mama Linda and Mama Nessa. "Plain and poetic," according to *Booklist* contributor Hazel Rochman, "the swiftly flowing free verse" in *Donovan's Big Day* "perfectly captures the day's excitement," and Donna Cardon recommended the story as "appealingly nonthreatening" in her *School Library Journal* review. Also in *School Library Journal,* Marge Loch-Wouters praised *Felicia's Favorite Story* as "a comforting book for children in alternative families as well as a pleasant tale" for general story hours.

Same-sex-parent households are also Newman's focus in several other picture books. With its strong board covers and engaging artwork by Carol Thompson, *Mommy, Mama, and Me* taps the same audience as *Heather Has Two Mommies* by following the events of a single day in a close-knit family formed by a lesbian couple. In *Daddy, Papa, and Me* Newman shifts her focus genderwise, as another toddler has its attention divided between Papa's efforts to bake a pie and Daddy's enjoyment in painting pictures. Both books "present warm, matter-of-fact depictions of same-sex parents doting on their child," asserted Claire E. Gross in *Horn Book,* while Linda Staskus concluded in *School Library Journal* that Thompson's "soft, realistic illustrations expand the simple texts." Another portrayal of a loving parent-child relationship is captured in Newman's rhythmic text for *Daddy's Song,* which features a bedtime

Newman's engaging family-centered story in **Just like Mama** *is brought to life in Julia Gorton's unique, graphic-style illustrations.* (Illustration copyright © 2010 by Julia Gorton. Reproduced by permission of Harry Abrams.)

song "filled with silly, fantastic, and humorous images," according to *School Library Journal* critic Catherine Callegari. Also reviewing this story, a *Kirkus Reviews* writer predicted that *Daddy's Song* will allow readers to share "cherished times between father and daughter."

Unfortunately, children of lesbian or gay parents are not immune to the pain of separation or divorce, as Newman shows in *Saturday Is Pattyday*. Called "reassuring" by *Booklist* contributor Rochman, *Saturday Is Pattyday* depicts the changing relationship between young Frankie and his mom Patty after Patty leaves him and his other mom and moves away from home. A more

permanent loss is dealt with by Newman in *Too Far Away to Touch*, as Uncle Leonard attempts to let his young niece know that he is dying of AIDS in a text that *Horn Book* contributor Maeve Visser Knoth called "effective" and "understated." Reviewing *Too Far Away to Touch* for *Booklist*, Carolyn Phelan asserted that Newman's tale "has a universality that will touch readers of any age" who have experienced the death of someone close to them.

While several of Newman's picture books focus on homosexuality and alternative families, she has also written stories geared to a mainstream readership. The celebration of the Jewish holiday of Passover is the focus of *Matzo Ball Moon*, as Eleanor's grandmother Bubbe makes her yearly holiday visit to help fix the holiday feast. Calling the book "a warm story of intergenerational sharing of holiday preparations within a loving family," *Booklist* contributor Ellen Mandel cited Newman's inclusion of explanations referencing Passover rituals and traditional foods. A *Publishers Weekly* reviewer had special praise for the character of Bubbe; she "says the unexpected, she is also credible and has some chutzpah," the critic noted. The relationship between Bubbe and her granddaughter is also the focus of *Remember That*, another story grounded in Jewish culture. After several years, the ageing Bubbe is moved to a nursing home and the weekly Friday-night Sabbath ritual the two share is altered. Including a introduction to Shabbos and the translations of some of Bubbe's Yiddish expressions, Newman's book "leaves readers with a warm, happy feeling," according to Susan Scheps in *School Library Journal*. Hazel Rochman also had praise for the sentimental story in *Remember That*, noting in her *Booklist* review that "Bubbe's story will help children cope with the changes age brings to those they love."

In *Cats, Cats, Cats!*, which features artwork by Erika Oller, Newman presents the first in a trio of picture books featuring energetic rhymes about familiar and sometimes unfamiliar household pets. Mrs. Brown loves cats, and although there are cats and kittens in every corner, cupboard, and cranny of her home she continues to bring home more strays in *Cats, Cats, Cats! Dogs,*

A houseful of playful felines sleep all day but get wild at night in Cats, Cats, Cats!, *written by Newman and illustrated by Erika Oller.* (Illustration copyright © 2001 by Erika Oller. Reproduced in the U.S. by permission of Simon & Schuster, Inc.)

Dogs, Dogs! continues the rhyming fun, as Newman conceals a lesson in counting within a rhyming story about an ever-growing pack of dogs roaming the city streets and playing in the city park. Hogs by the dozens are featured in *Pigs, Pigs, Pigs!*, as the promise of a free meal draws carloads of pigs from far and wide to the streets of one small town, where singing and dancing are also on the menu. In a *Publishers Weekly* review, a critic praised *Cats, Cats, Cats!* as "a real find for cat fanciers and their furry companions" and added that Oller's illustrations, "with their indistinct edges and softly blurred colors, capture all the fuzzy charm of the capering kitties." "Newman's rollicking, action-filled text" in *Dogs, Dogs, Dogs!* "is playful and cheerful," asserted a *Kirkus Reviews* writer, noting that the book's "wonderfully subtle watercolors are full of motion and humorous details." Reviewing the same book, Jody McCoy wrote in *School Library Journal* that *Dogs, Dogs, Dogs!* serves up a "splendid celebration" of canines in its "joyful readaloud text," while Andrea Tarr concluded in the same periodical that *Pigs, Pigs, Pigs!* "will be a storytime delight" that is "sure to bounce right of the shelves."

Newman continues to highlight animals in In *The Best Cat in the World*, which finds Victor coming to terms with the death of his beloved cat Charlie. When the boy is finally ready to accept a new cat into the household, a frisky kitten named Shelley joins the family. However, Shelley will not sleep on Victor's bed like Charlie did, and she is not interested in his offer of secret treats from the dinner table. Although the boy is first sad that the new kitten does not fill Charlie's place, he eventually learns that Shelley's frisky personality also adds its own new element to family life. Noting the "warm pencil-and-watercolor illustrations" by Ronald Himler, Susan Hepler concluded in *School Library Journal* that, "for comfort and catharsis, Newman's fine story is the cat's pajamas," and a *Kirkus Reviews* writer concluded that *The Best Cat in the World* "skillfully manages to convey sympathy without being cloying."

A little girl with a dream is the star of *Miss Tutu's Star*, as young Selena joins the ballet class that will start her on her way to ballet-dancer stardom. The recital is just days away when Selena begins to have doubts about her abilities, but an encouraging teacher rebuilds the confidence that makes the girl's performance a hit. Newman's "text flows smoothly in rhymed couplets, documenting Selena's . . . emotional ups and downs," wrote *Booklist* critic Carolyn Phelan, while *School Library Journal* contributor Martha Simpson noted that the "gouache and colored-pencil illustrations" by Carey Armstrong-Ellis "add comic touches" to Newman's tale. Roger shares a similar enthusiasm in *The Boy Who Cried Fabulous*, as he finds magic and wonderment everywhere he goes. "This silly but entertaining story is told in lilting rhyme and . . . expressive paintings" by Peter Ferguson, according to *School Library Journal* critic Linda L. Walkins, and a *Publishers Weekly* critic maintained that the book's brightly colored and retro-styled illustrations "firmly plant the story in a whimsical realm."

In conjunction with several books she has authored for adults that focus on body image, Newman published the YA novel *Fat Chance* in 1994. Written in the form of a diary, *Fat Chance* is a realistic look at the effect of an eating disorder on a young girl. It follows thirteen-year-old, five-foot-four Judi, whose obsession about weight prompts her to idolize fellow student Nancy, the thinnest and most popular girl in the entire eighth grade. Discovering Nancy's trick, Judi begins the binge-purge cycle characteristic of the bulimic, and she goes out of her way to keep it a secret from friends and family. A desire to fit in and be popular fuels Judi's resolve, and the compliments that come her way as her weight begins to drop and she sheds her baggy clothes provides more encouragement. Praising Newman for her ability to create a teen voice that rings true, *Booklist* contributor Stephanie Zvirin added that *Fat Chance* "will sound achingly familiar to girls struggling with self-image." Noting that the story goes "further than the average 'problem' novel" in examining the motivations of the bulimic protagonist, a *Publishers Weekly* contributor commented praised Newman for focusing on "the importance of professional help" in her "compelling, thought-provoking narrative."

Newman's first historical novel, *Hachiko Waits*, recounts a true story that took place in Tokyo, Japan, during the first decades of the twentieth century and is now commemorated by a statue. A loyal Akita named Hachiko walked its master to the train each morning and waited at the station to walk the man back home each night. One day the man died, leaving the loyal dog waiting at the station where he was fed and cared for by compassionate citizens until its own death a decade later. Brought to life in woodcut-style art by Machiyo Kodaira, Newman's retelling benefits from "her many details about Tokyo and passages of dialogue," according to a *Publishers Weekly* critic.

Newman turns to an older readership in *Jailbait*, which is set on Long Island during the early 1970s. Andi Kaplan is beginning tenth grade and dreading it now that the school bully has singled her out. With her parents involved in their own personal dysfunctions and her pot-smoking older brother idling away his time in college, Andi feels alone until she meets Frank, who is almost old enough to be her dad. Feeling secure in Frank's love, the teen agrees to keep their sexual relationship a secret, but gradually the dynamic shifts and the man becomes increasingly volatile and controlling. Praising *Jailbait* as "a cautionary tale," *Kliatt* critic Myrna Marler added that Newman's "evocative" prose causes readers to care about Andi "and her painful rise from the ashes . . . is to be cheered." *Jailbait* "will keep teen girls listening as the tale unfolds," according to *School Library Journal* critic Karen Hoth, "whether they've loved and lost or not."

"Writing is hard work," Newman noted on her home page. "It is also lots of fun and very rewarding. If you want to be a writer, you must practice your art. Try to do it every day. Do other things that support the writing life: read as much as you can, visit the library, go to readings at bookstores, join or start a writer's group. Everyone has interesting and important stories to tell. Allow your writing to take you on a journey. Don't try to control it—let your writing lead you to new and exciting places. The wonderful thing about writing is, you don't need much: just a pen, a piece of paper, and your own imagination."

Biographical and Critical Sources

PERIODICALS

Bloomsbury Review, June, 1992, Robert Burke, review of *Heather Has Two Mommies*, p. 19.
Booklist, November 1, 1993, Hazel Rochman, review of *Saturday Is Pattyday*, p. 531; September 1, 1994, Stephanie Zvirin, review of *Fat Chance*, p. 35; March 15, 1995, Carolyn Phelan, review of *Too Far Away to Touch*, p. 1336; February 1, 1996, Hazel Rochman, review of *Remember That*, p. 939; April, 1998, Ellen Mandel, review of *Matzo Ball Moon*, p. 1332; February 15, 2001, Helen Rosenberg, review of *Cats, Cats, Cats!*, p. 1141; September 1, 2002, Ilene Cooper, review of *Runaway Dreidel!*, p. 139; February 15, 2003, Kathleen Odean, review of *Pigs, Pigs, Pigs!*, p. 1075; October 15, 2005, Stephanie Zvirin, review of *The Eight Nights of Chanukah*, p. 58; February 15, 2007, Shelle Rosenfeld, review of *Skunk's Spring Surprise*, p. 84; September 1, 2010, Carolyn Phelan, review of *Miss Tutu's Star*, p. 1; April 1, 2011, Hazel Rochman, review of *Donovan's Big Day*, p. 73.
Bulletin of the Center for Children's Books, February, 1990, review of *Heather Has Two Mommies*, p. 144.
Entertainment Weekly, January 29, 1993, Rebecca Ascher-Walsh, "Writer on the Storm," and Michele Landsberg, reviews of *Heather Has Two Mommies* and *Gloria Goes to Gay Pride*, all p. 66.
Horn Book, May-June, 1995, Maeve Visser Knoth, review of *Too Far Away to Touch*, p. 328; May-June, 2009, Claire E. Gross, review of *Daddy, Papa, and Me*, p. 285.
Kirkus Reviews, May 15, 2002, review of *Dogs, Dogs, Dogs!*, p. 738; November 1, 2002, review of *Runaway Dreidel!*, p. 1623; January 1, 2004, review of *The Best Cat in the World*, p. 40; November 1, 2005, review of *The Eight Nights of Chanukah*, p. 1195; December 1, 2006, review of *Skunk's Spring Surprise*, p. 1224; April 15, 2007, review of *Daddy's Song*; May 15, 2009, review of *Daddy, Papa, and Me*.
Kliatt, May, 2005, Myrna Marler, review of *Jailbait*, p. 17.
Lambda Book Report, August-September, 2003, Marissa Pareles, review with Newman, p. 6.
New York Times Book Review, August 27, 1995, Roger Sutton, review of *Too Far Away to Touch*, p. 27; July 28, 1996, Judith Viorst, review of *Remember That*, p. 21.

Publishers Weekly, September 19, 1994, review of *Fat Chance,* p. 72; February 6, 1995, review of *Too Far Away to Touch,* p. 85; February 23, 1998, review of *Matzo Ball Moon,* p. 76; January 15, 2001, review of *Cats, Cats, Cats!,* p. 75; April 12, 2004, review of *The Boy Who Cried Fabulous,* p. 65; December 13, 2004, review of *Hachiko Waits,* p. 68; October 19, 2009, Leslea Newman, "The More Things Change . . . *Heather Has Two Mommies* Turns Twenty," p. 58; August 2, 2010, review of *Miss Tutu's Star,* p. 44; February 21, 2011, review of *Donovan's Big Day,* p. 130.

School Library Journal, January, 1995, Melissa Yurechko, review of *Fat Chance,* p. 138; September, 1995, Mary Rinato Berman, review of *Too Far Away to Touch,* p. 183; March, 1996, Susan Scheps, review of *Remember That,* p. 179; June, 1998, Susan Pine, review of *Matzo Ball Moon,* p. 116; March, 2001, Lauralyn Persson, review of *Cats, Cats, Cats!,* p. 215; August, 2002, Jody McCoy, review of *Dogs, Dogs, Dogs!,* p. 162; February. 2003, Andrea Tarr, review of *Pigs, Pigs, Pigs!,* p. 118; October, 2003, Marge Loch-Wouters, review of *Felicia's Favorite Story,* p. 132; February, 2004, Susan Hepler, review of *The Best Cat in the World,* p. 120; October, 2004, Linda L. Walkins, review of *The Boy Who Cried Fabulous,* p. 125; November, 2004, John Peters, review of *Hachiko Waits,* and Rosalyn Pierini, review of *Where Is Bear?,* both p. 113; June, 2005, Karen Hoth, review of *Jailbait,* p. 167; June, 2007, Catherine Callegari, review of *Daddy's Song,* p. 118; November, 2009, Linda Staskus, reviews of *Daddy, Papa, and Me* and *Mommy, Mama, and Me,* both p. 85; August, 2010, Martha Simpson, review of *Miss Tutu's Star,* p. 82; April, 2011, Donna Cardon, review of *Donovan's Big Day,* p. 150.

ONLINE

Lesléa Newman Home Page, http://www.lesleanewman. com (October 21, 2011).*

*   *   *

NIELSON, Sheila A.

Personal

Born in San Jose, CA. *Education:* Brigham Young University, B.F.A. (children's illustration). *Hobbies and other interests:* Doll and miniatures collecting, jewelry making.

Addresses

Home—Lehi, UT. *Agent*—Amy Boggs, Donald Maass Literary Agency, Ste. 801, 121 W. 27th St., New York, NY 10001. *E-mail*—sheilanielsonauthor@gmail.com.

Career

Author/illustrator and librarian. Children's librarian, beginning c. 1996.

Sheila A. Nielson (Reproduced by permission.)

Writings

Forbidden Sea, Scholastic Press (New York, NY), 2010.

Sidelights

"I used to be afraid of the dark when I was little," Sheila A. Nielson told *SATA.* "I'd make up stories to keep myself from thinking about the monsters I was sure were hiding under my bed at night. All that creative energy eventually led me to become an author.

"Before I learned to write my stories down, I drew pictures of them. Any scrap of paper (even the blank margins of math tests) would quickly become my canvas—a doorway into the fantastical worlds that constantly swirled about inside my head. I wrote down my first (fully illustrated) story in sixth grade. My journals were always filled up with fictional accounts of made-up characters and their adventures. Talking animals, magical creatures, and mysterious ghosts—all, the things I loved to read about most were written into those early stories of my youth.

"I haunted the library as a teenager, checking out towering stacks of books almost too heavy for me to carry. I spent my summers engrossed in the works of such authors as L.M. Montgomery, Lois Duncan, and Robin McKinley. It wasn't long before I decided I wanted to be a story teller just like them.

"I never did properly settle on what I wanted to be when I grew up. I graduated from college with a B.F.A.

in children's illustration. I have worked as a children's librarian for fifteen years but would still like to be a full-time author someday.

"I got the idea for my first novel, *Forbidden Sea,* when lots of girls kept coming into the library asking for mermaid books. In those days, there were very few available. These girls were always so disappointed when we didn't have more stories for them to read. I could see that someone needed to write a new mermaid novel. Why not me? That is how the idea for *Forbidden Sea* was born."

Biographical and Critical Sources

PERIODICALS

Bulletin of the Center for Children's Books, September, 2010, April Spisak, review of *Forbidden Sea,* p. 35.
School Library Journal, September, 2010, Samantha Larsen Hastings, review of *Forbidden Sea,* p. 160.
Voice of Youth Advocates, August, 2010, Cynthia Grady, review of *Forbidden Sea,* p. 269.

ONLINE

Sheila A. Nielson Web Log, http://sheilanielson.blogspot.com (September 29, 2011).

*   *   *

NORCLIFFE, James 1946-

Personal
Born March 3, 1946, in Greymouth, New Zealand; married Joan Melvyn.

Addresses
Home—Church Bay, Lyttelton Harbour, New Zealand.

Career
Author, editor, poet, and educator. English teacher throughout the world, including in Brunei, Darussalam, China, and Christchurch, New Zealand; Lincoln University, Christchurch, teacher of English. Artist-in-residence, Arts Centre, Palmerston North and Massey University; children's-writer-in-residence at University of Otago College of Education, 2012. Christchurch Press, poetry editor; *Takahe* magazine, poetry and fiction editor. Presenter at festivals.

Awards, Honors
PEN Jessie Mackay Award shortlist, 1987, for *The Sportsman, and Other Poems;* PEN Lilian Ida Smith Award, 1990; New Zealand Poetry Society International Competition winner, 1992; New Zealand Book Awards shortlist, 1994, for *Letters to Dr Dee and Other Poems;* Aim Children's Book Award Honour designation, 1995, for *The Emerald Encyclopaedia;* Christchurch Press Literary Liaisons Honour Award, 2003; Sir Julius Vogel Award for Best New Zealand Fantasy Novel, 2006, for *The Assassin of Gleam; New Zealand Post* Children's Book Award in junior fiction category, Sir Julius Vogel Award shortlist, and Esther Glen Award shortlist, all 2010, all for *The Loblolly Boy;* New Zealand Children's Writers' bursary; various fellowships.

Writings

POETRY

The Sportsman, and Other Poems: Rites of Admission, Hard Echo Press (Auckland, New Zealand), 1987.
Letters to Dr Dee and Other Poems, Hazard Press (Christchurch, New Zealand), 1993.
A Kind of Kingdom, Victoria University Press (Wellington, New Zealand), 1998.
(With John Allison and David Howard) *Passport Stamps,* Firebrand (Christchurch, New Zealand), 2001.
Rat Tickling, Sudden Valley Press (Christchurch, New Zealand), 2003.
Along Blueskin Road, Canterbury University Press (Christchurch, New Zealand), 2005.
Villon in Millerton, Auckland University Press (Auckland, New Zealand), 2007.

Contributor of poetry to periodicals, including *Sport.*

FOR CHILDREN

Under the Rotunda, Hazard Press (Christchurch, New Zealand), 1992.
Penguin Bay, Hazard Press (Christchurch, New Zealand), 1993.
The Emerald Encyclopedia, Hazard Press (Christchurch, New Zealand), 1994.
The Carousel Experiment, Hazard Press (Christchurch, New Zealand), 1995.
The Strange and Diverting Story of the Loblolly Boy: A Fantasy Novel Involving Enchantment, Mystery, One Garden Gnome, and a Wombat's Bottom, Longacre Press (Dunedin, New Zealand), 2009, published as *The Loblolly Boy,* Allen & Unwin (New South Wales, Australia), 2009, published as *The Boy Who Could Fly,* Egmont USA (New York, NY), 2010.
The Loblolly Boy and the Sorcerer, Longacre (Auckland, New Zealand), 2011.

"GLEAM" NOVEL TRILOGY; FOR CHILDREN

The Assassin of Gleam, Hazard Press (Christchurch, New Zealand), 2006.

The Mistress of Yewfire, Hazard Press (Christchurch, New Zealand), 2006.

The Witch of Aboraxus, Hazard Press (Christchurch, New Zealand), 2006.

OTHER

The Chinese Interpreter (short stories), Hazard Press (Christchurch, New Zealand), 1994.

(Editor with Bernadette Hall) *Big Sky: A Collection of Canterbury Poems,* Shoal Bay Press (Christchurch, New Zealand), 2002.

(Editor with Marissa Johnpillai and Alan Bunn) *The Fun-House Mirror: Ten Years of Write On,* Clerestory Press/School for Young Writers (Christchurch, New Zealand), 2003.

(Editor with Alan Bunn) *Re-draft 3: A Collection of Teenage Writing,* Clerestory Press/School for Young Writers (Christchurch, New Zealand), 2003.

(Editor with Alan Bunn) *Cupid on a Friday Night,* Clerestory Press/School for Young Writers), 2005.

(Editor with Alan Bunn) *Re-draft 4: A Collection of Teenage Writing,* Clerestory Press/School for Young Writers (Christchurch, New Zealand), 2005.

Cover of James Norcliffe's magical young-adult novel **The Boy Who Could Fly,** *which echoes a message about being careful what you wish* **for.** (Photograph copyright © 2010 by Grafissimo/iStockphoto.com. Reproduced by permission of Egmont USA.)

(Editor with Alan Bunn) *Tennis with Raw Eggs,* Clerestory Press/School for Young Writers), 2007.

(Editor with Tessa Duder) *DIY Graffiti: The Eighth in the Re-draft Series,* Clerestory Press/School for Young Writers (Christchurch, New Zealand), 2009.

(Editor with Tessa Duder) *Fishing for Birds,* Clerestory Press/School for Young Writers (Christchurch, New Zealand), 2010.

(Editor with Tessa Duder) *The World's Steepest Street,* Clerestory Press/School for Young Writers (Christchurch, New Zealand), 2010.

Contributor of short fiction and poetry to periodicals, including *Antigonish Review, Ariel, Baltimore Review, Confrontations, Dalhousie Review, Fiddlehead, Greensboro Review, Harvard Review, Independent, Landfall, London Magazine, Malahat Review, Manhattan Review, Nimrod, Overland, Poetry Australia, Prism International, Queen's Quarterly, Southerly, Sport, Stand,* and *Sycamore Review.* Contributor to anthologies, including *Essential New Zealand Poems, New Zealand Love Poems: An Oxford Anthology, Oxford Book of New Zealand Poetry in English, Spinning a Line, Tabla Book of New Verse; The Fun-house Mirror: Ten Years of Write On,* Clerestory Press, 2003; and *Contemporary New England Poets in Performance,* Auckland University Press, 2007.

Sidelights

James Norcliffe is well known in his native New Zealand, where his poetry, short fiction, and edited anthologies have made him one of his country's honored literary exports. In addition, Norcliffe's work as a teacher has enriched generations of writers. His first book, *The Sportsman, and Other Poems: Rites of Admission,* has been followed by several other published collections, and his work coediting the annual "Re-draft" series for the Clerestory Press/School for Young Writers has contributed greatly to showcasing the work of talented young New Zealanders.

Norcliffe began writing for young people early in his career; his second book, *Under the Rotunda,* features a magical story geared for preteens. *Under the Rotunda* has been followed by several other children's novels as well as Norcliffe's popular "Gleam" fantasy trilogy. In *Penguin Bay* a group of siblings stirs up some slumbering ghosts when they vacation at a secluded seaside town, while *The Emerald Encyclopedia* finds a book seducing a boy named Fraser into a web of malevolent magic. The award-winning *The Assassin of Gleam,* Norcliffe's first "Gleam" novel, has been followed by *The Mistress of Yewfire* and *The Witch of Aboraxus.* Set in the distant past, in a fiefdom ruled by the tyrannical Markgrave Twyll, the "Gleam" trilogy explores the machinations ongoing within this powerful world of secrets as Tobias and his sister Johanna discover themselves to be an integral part of an age-old prophecy to restore freedom to Twyll.

Norcliffe has earned many of his young fans through *The Strange and Diverting Story of the Loblolly Boy: A Fantasy Novel Involving Enchantment, Mystery, One Garden Gnome, and a Wombat's Bottom,* a story published in the United States as *The Boy Who Could Fly* and released in Australia as *The Loblolly Boy.* Growing up the behind tall brick walls of a miserable orphanage, unhappy Michael has always dreamed of being able to fly, to sail the skies with the birds. However, when he gets what he wished for Michael realizes that it comes with a cost: he has unknowingly traded places with the legendary Loblolly Boy and is now invisible to all but a few Sensitives. As loneliness sets in, Michael longs to regain his human form, and when he meets twin sisters who can sense his presence he asks for their help. Unfortunately, there is one person who hopes to keep Michael in his current form and even capture the boy: the Collector, who has been relentless in pursuing the Loblolly Boy. Michael's quest continues in a sequel, *The Loblolly Boy and the Sorcerer,* which finds the boy pursued by still more sinister forces.

Noting that Norcliffe begins his fantasy about the Loblolly Boy by presenting "a sort of existential crisis—Are we human if we lose the capacity to connect with other people?," Emma Burkhart added in her *School Library Journal* review of *The Boy Who Could Fly* that the novel resolves itself into "a concrete adventure story" that mends a "quick pace and intriguing themes." Michael's story mixes "suspense" with "whimsical moments," in the opinion of a *Publishers Weekly* contributor, but his story also touches on deeper issues: "the tenuous nature of identity-issues young readers face even if they don't have wings." In *Booklist* Michael Cart hailed the novel as "an imaginative and richly atmospheric fantasy with sympathetic characters," predicting that *The Boy Who Could Fly* "will capture most

readers' imaginations," while Jonathan Hunt concluded in *Horn Book* that Norcliffe exhibits "storytelling [that] is accomplished and leisurely."

Biographical and Critical Sources

BOOKS

Robinson, Roger, and Nelson Wattie, editors, *Oxford Companion to New Zealand Literature,* Oxford University Press (Oxford, England), 1998.

PERIODICALS

Booklist, July 1, 2010, Michael Cart, review of *The Boy Who Could Fly,* p. 58.
Bulletin of the Center for Children's Books, September, 2010, Kate Quealy-Gainer, review of *The Boy Who Could Fly,* p. 35.
Horn Book, September-October, 2010, Jonathan Hunt, review of *The Boy Who Could Fly,* p. 87.
Publishers Weekly, June 28, 2010, review of *The Boy Who Could Fly,* p. 129.
School Library Journal, April, 2011, Emma Burkhart, review of *The Boy Who Could Fly,* p. 181.

ONLINE

Christchurch City Libraries Web site, http://christchurch citylibraries.com/ (July, 2007), interview with Norcliffe.
James Norcliffe Home Page, http://jamesnorcliffe.com (October 21, 2011).
New Zealand Book Council Web site, http://www. bookcouncil.org.nz/ (October 21, 2011), "James Norcliffe."*

P-S

PATTERSON, James 1947-
(James B. Patterson)

Personal

Born March 22, 1947, in Newburgh, NY; son of Charles (an insurance broker) and Isabelle (a teacher and homemaker) Patterson; married; wife's name Susan; children: Jack. *Education:* Manhattan College, B.A. (English; summa cum laude), 1969; Vanderbilt University, M.A. (English; summa cum laude), 1970. *Hobbies and other interests:* Golf.

Addresses

Home—Palm Beach County, FL.

Career

Writer. J. Walter Thompson Co., New York, NY, junior copywriter, beginning 1971, vice president and associate creative supervisor of JWT/U.S.A., 1976, senior vice president and creative director of JWT/New York, 1980, executive creative director and member of board of directors, 1984, chair and creative director, 1987, and chief executive officer, 1988, chair of JWT/North America, 1990-96. Full-time novelist, beginning 1996.

Awards, Honors

Edgar Allan Poe Award, Mystery Writers of America, 1977, for *The Thomas Berryman Number.*

Writings

MYSTERY NOVELS; FOR ADULTS

The Thomas Berryman Number, Little, Brown (Boston, MA), 1976, reprinted, Compass Press (Boston, MA), 1997.
The Season of the Machete, Ballantine (New York, NY), 1977, reprinted, 1997.

The Jericho Commandment, Crown (New York, NY), 1979, published as *See How They Run,* Warner Books (New York, NY), 1997.
Virgin, McGraw Hill (New York, NY), 1980, revised as *Cradle and All,* Little, Brown (Boston, MA), 2000.
Black Market, Simon & Schuster (New York, NY), 1986, published as *Black Friday,* Warner Books (New York, NY), 2002.
The Midnight Club, Little, Brown (Boston, MA), 1989.
(With Peter de Jonge) *Miracle on the 17th Green,* Little, Brown (Boston, MA), 1996.
Hide and Seek, Little, Brown (Boston, MA), 1996.
When the Wind Blows, Little, Brown (Boston, MA), 1998.
(With Peter de Jonge) *The Beach House,* Little, Brown (Boston, MA), 2002.
The Lake House (sequel to *When the Wind Blows*), Little, Brown (Boston, MA), 2003.
(With Andrew Gross) *The Jester,* Little, Brown (Boston, MA), 2003.
(With Howard Roughan) *Honeymoon,* Little, Brown (New York, NY), 2005.
(With Andrew Gross) *Lifeguard,* Little, Brown (New York, NY), 2005.
(With Andrew Gross) *Judge and Jury,* Little, Brown (New York, NY), 2006.
(With Peter de Jonge) *Beach Road,* Little, Brown (New York, NY), 2006.
(With Michael Ledwidge) *The Quickie,* Little, Brown (New York, NY), 2007.
(With Howard Roughan) *You've Been Warned,* Little, Brown (New York, NY), 2007.
(With Howard Roughan) *Sail,* Little, Brown (New York, NY), 2008.
(With Gabrielle Charbonnet) *Sundays at Tiffany's,* Little, Brown (New York, NY), 2008.
(With Maxine Paetro) *Swimsuit,* Little, Brown (New York, NY), 2009.
(With Howard Roughan) *Don't Blink,* Little, Brown (New York, NY), 2010.
(With Maxine Paetro) *Private,* Little, Brown (New York, NY), 2010.
(With Ned Rust) *Game Over,* Little, Brown (New York, NY), 2011.

(With Marshall Karp) *Kill Me If You Can,* Little, Brown (New York, NY), 2011.

(With Michael Ledwidge) *Now You See Her,* Little, Brown (New York, NY), 2011.

(With Richard DiLallo) *The Christmas Wedding,* Little, Brown (New York, NY), 2011.

(With Neil McMahon) *Toys,* Little, Brown (New York, NY), 2011.

(With Maxine Paetro) *Number One Suspect* (sequel to *Private*), Little, Brown (New York, NY), 2012.

(With David Ellis) *Guilty Wives,* Little, Brown (New York, NY), 2012.

"WOMEN'S MURDER CLUB" SERIES; FOR ADULTS

First to Die, Little, Brown (Boston, MA), 2001.

(With Andrew Gross) *Second Chance,* Little, Brown (Boston, MA), 2002.

(With Andrew Gross) *Third Degree,* Little, Brown (New York, NY), 2004.

(With Maxine Paetro) *Fourth of July,* Little, Brown (New York, NY), 2005.

(With Maxine Paetro) *The Fifth Horseman,* Little, Brown (New York, NY), 2006.

(With Maxine Paetro) *The Sixth Target,* Little, Brown (New York, NY), 2007.

(With Maxine Paetro) *Seventh Heaven,* Little, Brown (New York, NY), 2008.

(With Maxine Paetro) *The Eighth Confession,* Little, Brown (New York, NY), 2009.

(With Maxine Paetro) *The Ninth Judgment,* Little, Brown (New York, NY), 2010.

(With Maxine Paetro) *Tenth Anniversary,* Little, Brown (New York, NY), 2011.

"ALEX CROSS" MYSTERY SERIES; FOR ADULTS

Along Came a Spider, Little, Brown (Boston, MA), 1993.
Kiss the Girls, Little, Brown (Boston, MA), 1995.
Jack and Jill, Little, Brown (Boston, MA), 1996.
Cat and Mouse, Little, Brown (Boston, MA), 1997.
Pop Goes the Weasel, Little, Brown (Boston, MA), 1999.
Roses Are Red, Little, Brown (Boston, MA), 2000.
Violets Are Blue, Little, Brown (Boston, MA), 2001.
Four Blind Mice, Little, Brown (Boston, MA), 2002.
The Big Bad Wolf, Little, Brown (Boston, MA), 2003.
London Bridges, Little, Brown (New York, NY), 2004.
Mary, Mary, Little, Brown (New York, NY), 2005.
Cross, Little, Brown (New York, NY), 2007.
Double Cross, Little, Brown (New York, NY), 2007.
Cross Country, Little, Brown (New York, NY), 2008.
I, Alex Cross, Little, Brown (New York, NY), 2009.

(With Richard DiLallo) *Alex Cross's Trial,* Little, Brown (New York, NY), 2009.

Cross Fire, Little, Brown (New York, NY), 2010.

"MICHAEL BENNETT" ADULT NOVEL SERIES

(With Michael Ledwidge) *Step on a Crack,* Little, Brown (New York, NY), 2007.

(With Michael Ledwidge) *Run for Your Life,* Little, Brown (New York, NY), 2009.

(With Michael Ledwidge) *Worst Case,* Grand Central Pub. (New York, NY), 2010.

(With Michael Ledwidge) *Tick Tock,* Little, Brown (New York, NY), 2011.

FOR YOUNGER READERS

SantaKid (picture book), illustrated by Michael Garland, Little, Brown (Boston, MA), 2004.

(With Chris Tebbetts) *Middle School, the Worst Years of My Life,* illustrated by Laura Park, Little, Brown (New York, NY), 2011.

"MAXIMUM RIDE" NOVEL SERIES; FOR YOUNG ADULTS

The Angel Experiment, Little Brown (New York, NY), 2005.
School's Out—Forever, Little, Brown (New York, NY), 2006.
Saving the World, and Other Extreme Sports, Little, Brown (New York, NY), 2007.
The Final Warning, Little, Brown (New York, NY), 2008.
Max, Little, Brown (New York, NY), 2009.
Fang, Little, Brown (New York, NY), 2010.
Angel, Little, Brown (New York, NY), 2011.

"DANIEL X" YOUNG-ADULT NOVEL SERIES

(With Michael Ledwidge) *The Dangerous Days of Daniel X* (also see below), Little, Brown (New York, NY), 2008.

(With Leopoldo Gout) *Daniel X: Alien Hunter* (graphic-novel adaptation of *The Dangerous Days of Daniel X*), illustrated by Klaus Lyngeled and Jonathan Girin, Little, Brown (New York, NY), 2008.

(With Ned Rust) *Watch the Skies,* Little, Brown (New York, NY), 2009.

(With Adam Sadler) *Demons and Druids,* Little, Brown (New York, NY), 2010.

"WITCH AND WIZARD" YOUNG-ADULT NOVEL SERIES

(With Gabrielle Charbonnet) *Witch and Wizard,* Little, Brown (New York, NY), 2009.

(With Ned Rust) *The Gift,* Little, Brown (New York, NY), 2010.

(With Jill Dembowski) *The Fire,* Little, Brown (New York, NY), 2012.

OTHER

(With Peter Kim) *The Day America Told the Truth: What People Really Believe about Everything That Matters* (nonfiction), Prentice Hall (Englewood Cliffs, NJ), 1991.

(With Peter Kim) *The Second American Revolution* (nonfiction), Morrow (New York, NY), 1994.

Suzanne's Diary for Nicholas (adult fiction), Little, Brown (Boston, MA), 2001.

Sam's Letters to Jennifer (adult fiction), Little, Brown (New York, NY), 2004.

(Editor) *Thriller* (short stories), Mira (Toronto, Ontario, Canada), 2006.

Against Medical Advice: A True Story, Little, Brown (New York, NY), 2008.

(With Martin Dugard) *The Murder of King Tut: The Plot to Kill the Child King: A Nonfiction Thriller,* Little, Brown (New York, NY), 2009.

(Coauthor) Hal Friedman, *Med Head: My Knock-down, Drag-out, Drugged-up Battle with My Brain,* Little, Brown (New York, NY), 2010.

Adaptations

Kiss the Girls was adapted for film and produced by Paramount, 1997. *Along Came a Spider* was produced by Paramount, 2001, starring Morgan Freeman and directed by Lee Tamahori. *Roses Are Red* was adapted for film by Ben Ramsey. *First to Die* was adapted for an NBC television mini-series. *Virgin* was adapted as a television film titled *Child of Darkness, Child of Light.* Film rights to *When the Wind Blows* and *Maximum Ride* were sold to Warner Bros, for production by Avi Arad. The "Women's Murder Club" books were adapted as a television series by ABC. Film rights to *SantaKid* and *Honeymoon* were sold to New Line Cinema. All Patterson's mystery novels and "Maximum Ride" books were adapted as audiobooks. *Maximum Ride* was adapted as a graphic novel written and illustrated by NaRae Lee, Yen, 2009. The "Witch and Wizard" series was adapted for manga and published by IDW Publishing, 2011.

Sidelights

A best-selling novelist whose "Alex Cross" mystery thrillers have won him a loyal following since they first appeared in the mid-1970s, James Patterson moved to fiction writing after a stellar career in advertising where, as former chair of the J. Walter Thompson advertising agency, he created advertising campaigns for Kodak, Toys 'R' Us, Burger King, and other companies. His first novel to crack the bestseller list was *Along Came a Spider,* the story of a crazed math teacher who kidnaps two of his students. In addition to introducing Cross, a black police psychologist, the 1993 novel was the second of Patterson's books to be adapted as a feature film. Known for his addictive, fast-moving plots, the prolific Patterson responds to what readers want: he dedicated his eighth "Alex Cross" mystery, *Pop Goes the Weasel,* to "the millions of Alex Cross readers who so frequently ask 'Can't you write faster?'"

Shortly after leaving the advertising business to write full time in 1996, Patterson showed his willingness to listen to fans as well as his publisher, producing series fiction in his "Women's Murder Club" and "Michael Bennett" novel sequences as well as dozens of standalone novels in a variety of genres. He now collaborates

with other writers, sketching the plot of many of his novels and then approving his collaborator's completed manuscript. Even so, Patterson continues to work on his writing every day, seven days a week, and he can spend up to two months structuring a plot. His co-writers receive 70 to 90 chapter summaries, each about four lines long, and they use those to produce their first drafts. Patterson takes these drafts and works on them, sometimes producing three or four more revisions before the final manuscript is prepared. His productivity has been such that by 2010 Patterson had set several publishing records, including the *Guiness World Record* for most hardcover novel bestsellers produced by a single author.

While Patterson was strengthening his reputation by writing adult mystery/thrillers (and revolutionized mass-market publishing along the way), a sidestep into science-fiction territory earned him an unintended new audience: teens. His adult thriller *When the Wind Blows* focuses on a Colorado veterinarian and his experiences with a strange preteen named Max. Max is being pursued by a group of thugs that is attempting to return her to a secret genetic research laboratory located nearby. As the novel continues, five other children—nicknamed Fang, Iggy, Nudge, the Gasman, and Angel and known

James Patterson's "Maximum Ride" series profiles a teen's singular adventure in Fang, *featuring artwork by Larry Rostant.* (Illustration copyright © 2010 by Larry Rostant. Reproduced by permission of Hachette Book Group Inc.)

as "The Flock"—are introduced and all are half-human clones who possess extraordinary abilities. A sequel, *The Lake House,* continues their story, as the teen members of The Flock confront a new threat in the form of a maniacal physician who wants to subject them to unpleasant forms of medical experimentation.

Learning that *When the Wind Blows* and *The Lake House* gained him many teen readers, Patterson decided to rework Max's story in a novel specifically geared for a young-adult audience. In *Maximum Ride: The Angel Experiment* Max is now fourteen, and her five friends are discovering how to use the retractable wings and other super-abilities resulting from the bird DNA that has been grafted onto their human genes. Orphans, the children were held in cages at a place known only as the "School"; since their escape, The Flock has lived in hiding, migrating to New York City in search of answers and hoping to escape the half-wolf Erasers who are hunting them down.

Dubbing *Maximum Ride* "an action-packed cross between Gertrude Chandler Warner's "Boxcar Children" and Marvel Comics' X-Men," *Booklist* contributor Stephanie Zvirin predicted that Patterson's novel would attract both teen and adult readers. Noting that the book's "fast-moving plot" is conveyed primarily through Max's first-person narration, Sharon Rawlins praised *Maximum Ride* as a "compelling read," while a *Kirkus Reviews* contributor noted that "nonstop action" propels Patterson's "page-turner breathlessly from start to finish." While several reviewers commented that *Maximum Ride* leaves several questions unanswered, the *Kirkus Reviews* contributor wrote that the novel closes, "leaving layers of mystery" for Patterson's planned sequel.

Patterson continues Max's adventures in several other "Maximum Ride" novels in which the young woman is guided toward her ultimate destiny: to save the world. In *School's Out—Forever* Max and her wingéd friends Fang, Iggy, Nudge, the Gasman, and Angel are flying south when their location is made known to the FBI after Fang becomes injured and must be taken to the hospital. Although FBI agent Anne Walker hides the six teens on her Virginia farm, The Flock's flirtation with real life proves to be short lived. *Saving the World, and Other Extreme Sports* moves the action closer to the final countdown, as Max combats a group of scientists attempting to re-engineer humans into a superior master race. In *The Final Warning* The Flock travels to Antarctica, hoping to combat climate change, but their creator lies in wait, hoping to capture the six teens and sell them to the highest bidder, while the novels *Max, Fang,* and *Angel* detail the unique individual journeys of several of the super-evolved teens.

"Patterson, an accomplished storyteller, . . . demonstrates his ability to write page-turning action scenes," concluded *Booklist* critic Diana Tixier Herald in her review of *School's Out—Forever,* the critic also citing the author's inclusion of "some surprising humor" in his "Maximum Ride" novels. In *Booklist* Jennifer Mattson predicted that in *Saving the World, and Other Extreme Sports* "affection for the dauntless characters and [their] misadventures" "will hold readers" transfixed, while Herald maintained that *Fang* "will excite the legions of fans waiting for this installment" in the popular series.

Patterson began another young-adult novel series in *The Dangerous Days of Daniel X,* a collaboration with Michael Ledwidge. *The Dangerous Days of Daniel X* finds fifteen-year-old Daniel working in the family trade: hunting alien life forms and exterminating the top twenty creatures on the official List of Alien Outlaws on Terra Firma. In addition to appearing in novel form and spawning several sequels, *The Dangerous Days of Daniel X* was also adapted as the graphic novel *Alien Hunter.* In *Watch the Skies* Daniel X must eradicate an evil threatening every television viewer and computer user in the quiet town of Holliswood, while his attention turns to tracking Alien Outlaw number three: Fire, in *Demons and Druids.* The teen's further adventures play out in *Game Over,* as Daniel X discovers a plot whereby gamers will be brainwashed into an army of mindless, thoughtless avengers. Reviewing the graphic-novel adaptation of *The Dangerous Days of Daniel X,* a *Kirkus Reviews* writer observed that Patterson's story plays out "fast and furious, neatly resolving itself by the end."

Patterson moves into fantasy territory in his coauthored "Witch and Wizard" novels, which include *Witch and Wizard, The Gift,* and *The Fire.* In the series opener, brother-and-sister team Whitford and Wisteria Allgood share their amazing story. Living under a totalitarian government known as the New Order, the teens were marked for imprisonment, just as thousands of others had been. Abducted by police and trapped in a teen reformatory, Whit and Wisty were accused of wizardry and witchcraft, respectively, but fortunately they escaped and joined a community of teens living in hiding. While most teens disappeared due to their unconventional views and willingness to challenge the status quo, fifteen-year-old Wisty is of special interest to the One, leader of the New Order and a man who knows of the teen's special talent. As their adventures play out, the siblings encounter dead friends living in the Shadowland, perform in a rock band, fight in the teen army resisting the New Order, and learn to harness their own special powers as well as mastering some nifty magical tools. Citing *Witch and Wizard* for its "enticing prologue," Daniel Kraus added in his *Booklist* review that "Patterson's trademark bite-size chapters . . . keep things zippy," while *School Library Journal* critic Tara Kehoe wrote that *The Gift* exhibits the author's "trademark mastery of gruesome and terrifying imagery." Noting that popular musicians, novels, and visual artists are mentioned throughout the text, Lona Trulove concluded in her *Voice of Youth Advocates* review of *The Gift* that Patterson's "Witch and Wizard" saga communicates "a very powerful message to children to believe in themselves, each other, and their own special talents."

In his books for both teens and adults, Patterson remains known for his high-speed plots and his tendency to avoid in-depth character development in favor of high-octane storytelling. As he explained to Steven Womak in a *Bookpage.com* interview, "I read *Ulysses* and figured I couldn't top that, so I never had any desire to write literary fiction." However, when he read William Peter Blatty's *The Exorcist* and Frederick Forsyth's *The Day of the Jackal,* he had a different reaction. "I went, 'Ooh! This is cool.' . . . And I set out to write that kind of book, the kind of book that would make an airplane ride disappear." As Patterson's teen fiction has become increasingly popular, the author has become increasingly involved in the effort to encourage reading among young people. In addition to providing a book guide for parents on his *ReadKiddoRead.com* Web site, he also established the James Patterson Pageturner Awards to honor those who discover imaginative ways to inspire children to become bookworms.

In an interview posted on his home page, Patterson explained that writing for younger readers is an especially fulfilling experience: "I love the idea of getting people reading." "I'm a fan of character best revealed by action," he noted in a *Bookseller* interview with Katherine Rushton. "What we do is more important than how we cerebrate about a certain moral problem."

Biographical and Critical Sources

PERIODICALS

Booklist, May 15, 2001, Kristine Huntley, review of *Suzanne's Diary for Nicholas,* p. 1708; October 15, 2001, Kristine Huntley, review of *Violets Are Blue,* p. 356; January 1, 2002, Kristine Huntley, review of *Second Chance,* p. 777; July, 2004, Kristine Huntley, review of *Sam's Letters to Jennifer,* p. 1799; February 1, 2005, Stephanie Zvirin, review of *Maximum Ride: The Angel Experiment,* p. 918; May 15, 2006, Diana Tixier Herald, review of *School's Out—Forever,* p. 54; August, 2007, Jennifer Mattson, review of *Saving the World, and Other Extreme Sports,* p. 62; October 1, 2008, Jesse Karp, review of *Daniel X: Alien Hunter,* p. 40; December 15, 2009, Daniel Kraus, review of *Witch and Wizard,* p. 36; April 15, 2010, Diana Tixier Herald, review of *Fang,* p. 43; December, 2010, Cindy Welch, review of *The Gift,* p. 60; March 15, 2011, Kristine Huntley, review of *Tenth Anniversary,* p. 23.

Bookseller, October 5, 2007, Katherine Rushton, interview with Patterson, p. 26.

Bulletin of the Center for Children's Books, April, 2005, Krista Hutley, review of *The Angel Experiment,* p. 353.

Kirkus Reviews, December 15, 2001, review of *Second Chance,* p. 1712; June 1, 2004, review of *Sam's Letters to Jennifer,* p. 513; April 1, 2005, review of *Maxi-*

mum Ride, p. 422; April 1, 2006, review of *School's Out—Forever,* p. 353; May 1, 2007, review of *Saving the World, and Other Extreme Sports;* November 1, 2008, review of *The Dangerous Days of Daniel X.*

Kliatt, March, 2005, Paula Rohrlick, review of *Maximum Ride,* p. 15; March, 2006, Paula Rohrlick, review of *School's Out—Forever,* p. 16; May, 2007, Paula Rohrlick, review of *Saving the World, and Other Extreme Sports,* p. 17.

Library Journal, October 1, 2000, Rebecca House Stankowski, review of *Roses Are Red,* p. 148; July 2001, Margaret Hanes, review of *Suzanne's Diary for Nicholas,* p. 126.

New York Times, July 24, 2001, Janet Maslin, "Love Story, or Is That Death Story?," p. 6; November 29, 2001, Janet Maslin, "Bodies Hang in California, and Bullets Fly in Florida," p. 7; January 20, 2010, Jonathan Mahler, "James Patterson Inc.," p. 32.

Publishers Weekly, August 2, 1999, review of *Pop Goes the Weasel,* p. 69; March 20, 2000, review of *Cradle and All,* p. 68; February 18, 2002, review of *Second Chance,* p. 75; March 18, 2002, Daisy Maryles and Dick Donahue, "Don't Get Mad, Get Even," p. 19; June 7, 2004, review of *Sam's Letters to Jennifer,* p. 33; July 12, 2004, Daisy Maryles, "A Passionate Patterson," p. 12; September 27, 2004, review of *SantaKid,* p. 60; March 21, 2005, review of *Maximum Ride,* p. 52; November 16, 2009, review of *Witch and Wizard,* p. 55; November 1, 2010, review of *Battle for Shadowland,* p. 47.

School Library Journal, May, 2005, Sharon Rawlins, review of *Maximum Ride,* p. 135; August, 2006, Heather M. Campbell, review of *School's Out—Forever,* p. 127; July, 2007, Vicki Reutter, review of *Saving the World, and Other Extreme Sports,* p. 108; November, 2008, Douglas P. Davey, review of *Daniel X: Alien Hunter,* p. 152; March, 2010, Jake Pettit, review of *Witch and Wizard,* p. 165; February, 2011, Tara Kehoe, review of *The Gift,* p. 117.

Voice of Youth Advocates, April, 2005, Jenny Ingram, review of *Maximum Ride,* p. 60; February, 2007, review of *School's Out—Forever;* August, 2007, Jenny Ingram, review of *Saving the World, and Other Extreme Sports;* February, 2011, Lona Trulove, review of *The Gift,* p. 575, and Lisa Martincik, review of *Battle for Shadowland,* p. 576.

ONLINE

Bookpage.com, http://www.bookpage.com/ (April 2, 2002), Steven Womak, interview with Patterson.

James Patterson Home Page, http://www.jamespatterson.com (October 21, 2011).*

* * *

PATTERSON, James B.
See PATTERSON, James

PLACE, François 1957-

Personal

Born April 26, 1957, in Ézanville, Val-d'Oise, France. *Education:* École Estienne (Paris, France), B.T.S. (graphics), 1977.

Addresses

Home—France.

Career

Illustrator and author of books for children. Collaborated in creating Web site for the Louvre, Paris, France, 2008. Presenter at festivals.

Awards, Honors

Grand Prix, Bologne Biennal, for "Atlas des Géographes d'Orbase" series; awards from numerous other exhibitions.

Writings

SELF-ILLUSTRATED

Le livre des navigateurs, Gallimard (Paris, France), 1988.
Le livre des explorateurs, Gallimard (Paris, France), 1989.
Le livre des marchands, Gallimard (Paris, France), 1990.
Les derniers géants, Casterman (Paris, France), 1992, translated by William Rodarmor as *The Last Giants,* David R. Godine (Boston, MA), 1993.
(With Christophe Besse) *Le camion fantôme,* Hachette Jeunesse (Paris, France), 1996.
(Adaptor) *Le vieux fou de dessin,* Gallimard Jeunesse (Paris, France), 1997, translated by William Rodarmor as *The Old Man Mad about Drawing: A Tale of Hokusai,* David R. Godine (Boston, MA), 2004.
Le désert des Pierreux, Casterman (Paris, France), 2002.
Le deux royaumes de Nilandâr, Casterman (Paris, France), 2003.
Le fleuve Wallawa, Casterman (Paris, France), 2003.
Le pays des Frissons, Casterman (Paris, France), 2003.
Les montagnes de la Mandragore, Casterman (Paris, France), 2004.
Grand ours, Casterman (Paris, France), 2005.
Le prince bégayant, Gallimard Jeunesse (Paris, France), 2006.
Le roi des trois orients, Rue du Monde (Voisins-le-Bretonneux, France), 2006.
La fille des batailles, Casterman (Paris, France), 2007.
La douane volante, Gallimard Jeunesse (Paris, France), 2010.

Author's work has been translated into several languages, including German.

SELF-ILLUSTRATED; "ATLAS DES GÉOGRAPHES D'ORBASE" SERIES

Du pays des Amazones au îles Indigo, Casterman (Paris, France), 1996.

Du pays de Jade á l'île Quinookta, Casterman (Paris, France), 1998.
De la rivière Rouge au pays de Zizotls, Casterman (Paris, France), 2000.
Le pays de Korakâr, Casterman (Paris, France), 2005.

FOR CHILDREN

L'ombre du chasseur, illustrated by Philippe Pourier, Albin Michel Jeunesse (Paris, France), 1998.

ILLUSTRATOR

Sophie de Ségur, *Quel amour d'enfant!,* Hachette (Paris, France), 1983.
Bernard Planche, *Le livre de la découverte du monde,* Gallimard (Paris, France), 1986.
Odile Bombarde and Claude Moatti, *Comment vivaient les Romains?,* Gallimard Jeunesse (Paris, France), 1987, translated by Sarah Matthews as *Living in Ancient Rome,* Young Discovery Library (Ossining, NY), 1988, new edition, 2005.
Henriette Bichonnier, *Kiki la casse,* Librairie générale française (Paris, France), 1987.
Bernard Planche, *Le livre des conquérants,* Gallimard (Paris, France), 1987.
Roselyne Morel, *Panique à Plexipolis,* Librarie générale française (Paris, France), 1987.
Henriette Bichonnier, *Micmac à la casse,* Hachette (Paris, France), 1988.
Sophie de Ségur, *Les bons enfants,* Hachette (Paris, France), 1989.
Sophie de Ségur, *Les deux nigauds,* Hachette (Paris, France), 1991.
Sophie de Ségur, *Jean qui grogne et Jean qui rit,* Hachette (Paris, France), 1991.
Sophie de Ségur, *Nouveaux conted de fées: Histoire de Blondine, la petite souris grise, ourson,* Hachette (Paris, France), 1991.
Leigh Sauerwein, *Groumf le grognon,* Gallimard (Paris France), 1991.
Michael Morpurgo, *Le roi de la forêt des brumes* (translation of *King of the Cloud Forest*), Gallimard (Paris, France), 1992.
Alexandre Jardin, *Le petit sauvage,* Gallimard (Paris, France), 1992.
Penelope Lively, *Le vitrail* (translation of *The Stained Glass Window*), Gallimard (Paris, France), 1992.
Michael Morpurgo, *Le naufrage du "Zanzibar",* Gallimard Jeunesse (Paris, France), 1994, published in original English as *The Wreck of the Zanzibar,* Viking (New York, NY), 1995.
Robert Louis Stevenson, *L'île au trésor,* Gallimard Jeunesse (Paris, France), 1994, published in original English as *Treasure Island,* Viking (New York, NY), 1996.
Marie Luise Knott, *Die letzten Riesen,* Bertelsmann (Munich, Germany), 1995.
François Bon, *Voleurs de feu: Le vies singulières de poètes,* Hatier (Paris, France), 1996.

Marie Luise Knott, *Phantastische Reisen,* three volumes, Bertelsmann (Munich, Germany), 1997–2000.

Robert Louis Stevenson, *L'etrange cas du Dr. Jekyll et de M. Hyde,* Gallimard Jeunesse (Paris, France), 1999, published in original English as *The Strange Case of Dr. Jekyll and Mr. Hyde,* Viking (New York, NY), 2000.

Michael Morpurgo, *Jeanne d'Arc* (translated from the English), Gallimard Jeunesse (Paris, France), 2000.

Jean-Pierre Kerloch'h, *Le peintre et le guerrier,* Albin Michel Jeunesse (Paris, France), 2000.

Michael Morpurgo, *Le royaume de Kensuké* (translation of *Kensuke's Kingdom*), Gallimard Jeunesse (Paris, France), 2000.

Iain Lawrence, *Les contrebandiers* (translation of *The Smugglers*), Gallimard Jeunesse (Paris, France), 2000.

Jean-François Chabas, *Trèfle d'or,* Casterman (Paris, France), 2001.

Thierry Aprile, reteller, *Aladdin,* Gallimard Jeunesse (Paris, France), 2001.

Iain Lawrence, *Les flibustiers* (translation of *The Buccaneers*), Gallimard Jeunesse (Paris, France), 2002.

Daniel Conrod, *Siam,* Rue du Monde (Voisins-le-Bretonneux, France), 2002.

Thierry Aprile, reteller, *Pirates,* Gallimard Jeunesse (Paris, France), 2003.

Arnauld Pontier, *La légende du jardin japonais,* Albin Michel Jeunesse (Paris, France), 2003.

Érik L'Homme, *Contes d'un royaume perdu,* Gallimard Jeunesse (Paris, France), 2003, translated by Claudia Zoe Bedrick as *Tales of a Lost Kingdom: A Journey into Northwest Pakistan,* Enchanted Lion Books (New York, NY), 2007.

Alice Leader, *Marcus et les brigantes* (translation of *Power and Stone*), Gallimard Jeunesse (Paris, France), 2004.

Michael Morpurgo, *Cheval de guerre* (translation of *War Horse*), Gallimard Jeunesse (Paris, France), 2004.

(With Erwann Fagès) Sandrine Mirza, reteller, *Prisonnier des pirates: Gabriel, les Antilles, 1720,* Gallimard Jeunesse (Paris, France), 2004.

Alphonse Daudet, *La chèvre de M. Seguin,* Gallimard Jeunesse (Paris, France), 2005.

Alice Leader, *Il faut sauver Athènes!* (translation of *Shield of Fire*), Gallimard Jeunesse (Paris, France), 2005.

Timothée de Fombelle, *Tobie Lolness: La vie suspendue,* Gallimard Jeunesse (Paris, France), 2006, translated by Sarah Ardizzone as *Toby Alone,* Candlewick Press (Somerville, MA), 2009.

Timothée de Fombelle, *Les yeux d'Elisha* (sequel to *Tobie Lolness*), Gallimard Jeunesse (Paris, France), 2007, translated by Sarah Ardizzone as *Toby and the Secrets of the Tree,* Candlewick Press (Somerville, MA), 2010.

Jean-Yves Loude, *Tanuk le maudit,* Belin (Paris, France), 2007.

Jean Giono, *Le petit garçon qui avait envie d'espace,* Gallimard (Paris, France), 2007.

Bernadette Ott, *Der König der vier Winde,* Gerstenberg (Hildesheim, Germany), 2008.

Jennifer Dalrymple, *Manju et les samouraïs,* Bayard Poche (Paris, France), 2008.

Florence Thinard, *Mesdemoiselles de la vengeance,* Gallimard Jeunesse (Paris, France), 2009.

Bernadette Ott, *Gwen: Der Lehrling des Heilers,* Gerstenberg (Hildesheim, Germany), 2011.

Biographical and Critical Sources

BOOKS

François Bon, *François Place illustrateur,* Casterman/ Centre de promotion du livre de jeunesse de Seine-Saint-Denis (Seine Saint-Denis, France), 1994, new edition published as *François Place illustrateur, ou, "Comment s'invente un livre?",* 2000.

PERIODICALS

Booklist, November 15, 1995, Carolyn Phelan, review of *The Wreck of the Zanzibar,* p. 560; May 1, 2000, Carolyn Phelan, review of *The Strange Case of Dr. Jekyll and Mr. Hyde,* p. 1670; March 15, 2004, Linda Perkins, review of *The Old Man Mad about Drawing: A Tale of Hokusai,* p. 1302; January 1, 2008, Carolyn Phelan, review of *Tales of a Lost Kingdom: A Journey into Northwest Pakistan,* p. 72.

Horn Book, March-April, 1994, Elizabeth S. Watson, review of *The Last Giants,* p. 201; March-April, 1996, Elizabeth S. Watson, review of *The Wreck of the Zanzibar,* p. 198l; March-April, 2004, Lolly Robinson, review of *The Old Man Mad about Drawing,* p. 188; May-June, 2009, Sarah Ellis, review of *Toby Alone,* p. 295.

Kirkus Reviews, February 15, 2009, review of *Toby Alone.*

Publishers Weekly, August 9, 1993, review of *The Last Giants,* p. 475; March 23, 2009, review of *Toby Alone,* p. 60.

School Library Journal, May, 2004, Margaret A. Chang, review of *The Old Man Mad about Drawing,* p. 156; December, 2007, Marilyn Taniguchi, review of *Tales of a Lost Kingdom,* p. 154; May, 2009, Jane Henriksen Baird, review of *Toby Alone,* p. 104; November, 2010, Kim Dare, review of *Toby and the Secrets of the Tree,* p. 110.

ONLINE

Internationales Literaturfestival Berlin Web site, http:// www.literaturfestival.com/ (October 21, 2011), "François Place."

Walker Books Web site, http://www.walker.co.uk/ (July 29, 2011), "François Place."*

*   *   *

PRICEMAN, Marjorie 1958-

Personal

Born 1958. *Education:* Rhode Island School of Design, B.F.A.; graduate-level writing classes. *Hobbies and other interests:* Films.

Addresses

Home—Lewisburg, PA.

Career

Author and illustrator.

Awards, Honors

Top Ten Picture Books of the Year citation, *Redbook* magazine, 1989, for *Friend or Frog;* Caldecott Honor Book designation, and Honor Book designation, American Library Association (ALA), both 1995, both for *Zin! Zin! Zin!* by Lloyd Moss; *New York Times* Best Illustrated Children's Book award, 1999, for *Emeline at the Circus;* Caldecott Honor Book designation, ALA Honor Book designation, and Best Book selection, Bank Street College of Education, all 2005, all for *Hot Air;* Notable Children's Book in Social Studies selection, Children's Book Council/National Council for the Social Studies, 2010, for *The Ride* by Kitty Griffin.

Writings

SELF-ILLUSTRATED

Friend or Frog, Houghton Mifflin (Boston, MA), 1989.
How to Make an Apple Pie and See the World, Knopf (New York, NY), 1994.
My Nine Lives: by Clio, Atheneum (New York, NY), 1998.
Emeline at the Circus, Knopf (New York, NY), 1999.
(Reteller) *Froggie Went a-Courting: An Old Tale with a New Twist,* Little, Brown (Boston, MA), 2000.
It's Me, Marva!: A Story about Color and Optical Illusions, Knopf (New York, NY), 2001.
Little Red Riding Hood (pop-up book), Simon & Schuster (New York, NY), 2001.
Princess Picky, Roaring Brook Press (Brookfield, CT), 2002.
Hot Air: The (Mostly) True Story of the First Hot-Air Balloon Ride, Atheneum (New York, NY), 2005.
How to Make a Cherry Pie and See the U.S.A., Alfred A. Knopf (New York, NY), 2008.

ILLUSTRATOR

Amy MacDonald, *Rachel Fister's Blister,* Houghton Mifflin (Boston, MA), 1990.
Nancy Van Laan, *A Mouse in My House,* Random House (New York, NY), 1990.
Jack Prelutsky, selector, *For Laughing out Loud: Poems to Tickle Your Funnybone,* Random House (New York, NY), 1991.
Jack Prelutsky, selector, *A. Nonny Mouse Writes Again! Poems,* Random House (New York, NY), 1993.
Nancy Van Laan, *The Tiny, Tiny Boy and the Big, Big Cow: A Scottish Folk Tale,* Knopf (New York, NY), 1993.

Lloyd Moss, *Zin! Zin! Zin! A Violin,* Simon & Schuster (New York, NY), 1995.
Jack Prelutsky, selector, *For Laughing out Louder: More Poems to Tickle Your Funnybone,* Knopf (New York, NY), 1995.
Susan Garrison, *How Emily Blair Got Her Fabulous Hair,* BridgeWater (New York, NY), 1995.
Amy MacDonald, *Cousin Ruth's Tooth,* Houghton (Boston, MA), 1996.
Elsa Okon Rael, *What Zeesie Saw on Delancey Street,* Simon & Schuster (New York, NY), 1996.
Elsa Okon Rael, *When Zaydeh Danced on Eldridge Street,* Simon & Schuster (New York, NY), 1997.
Mary Ann Hoberman, *One of Each,* Little, Brown (Boston, MA), 1997.
Wendy Gelsanliter and Frank Christian, *Dancin' in the Kitchen,* Putnam (New York, NY), 1998.
Phyllis Theroux, *Serefina under the Circumstances,* Greenwillow (New York, NY), 1999.
Katie Couric, *The Brand New Kid,* Doubleday (New York, NY), 2000.
Avi, *Things That Sometimes Happen: Very Short Stories for Little Listeners,* Atheneum Books for Young Readers (New York, NY), 2002.
Katie Couric, *The Blue Ribbon Day,* Doubleday (New York, NY), 2004.
Jacqueline K. Ogburn, *The Bake Shop Ghost,* Houghton Mifflin (Boston, MA), 2005.
Phillis Gershator, adaptor, *This Is the Day!,* Houghton Mifflin (Boston, MA), 2007.
Amy MacDonald, *Rachel Fister's Blister* (with sound recording), Houghton Mifflin (Boston, MA), 2008.
Joan Yolleck, *Paris in the Spring with Picasso,* Schwartz & Wade Books (New York, NY), 2010.
Kitty Griffin, *The Ride: The Legend of Betsy Dowdy,* Atheneum Books for Young Readers (New York, NY), 2010.
Eileen Spinelli, *Cold Snap,* Alfred A. Knopf (New York, NY), 2012.

Sidelights

Author and artist Marjorie Priceman began her career in the 1980s and quickly found her humorous and energetic illustrations in demand by children's book publishers. Although her artwork has appeared alongside stories by such noted writers as Jack Prelutsky, Amy MacDonald, Phillis Gershator, Eileen Spinelli, and Nancy Van Laan, Priceman has found that illustrating someone else's story is not nearly as fun as illustrating her own. Since taking an advanced writing course, she has created the original picture books *My Nine Lives: by Clio, Emeline at the Circus,* and *Princess Picky,* and *How to Make a Cherry Pie and See the U.S.A.* Priceman's books "are rollicking and riotous," commented a *Publishers Weekly* reviewer; "It often seems as though the borders of the pages are unable to contain the energy of her artwork and creations." Also praising the illustrator in a profile for the *Bulletin of the Center for Children's Books* online, Deborah Stevenson wrote that "there's a delicious artistic gaiety" to Priceman's work that recalls "earlier styles; the result is not retro effect, but a feeling that something that's been missing has been restored."

Priceman's first published picture book, *Friend or Frog,* is based on the frog-related experiences of her family and friends. Her parents were concerned about the welfare of neighborhood frogs; in fact, as Priceman explained to interviewer Diane Roback for *Publishers Weekly,* "I'd be talking to my mother, and she'd say, 'Hold on, I have to go save a frog.'" In *Friend or Frog,* a young girl named Kate meets a green, spotted frog carrying a towel with the word "Hilton" woven onto it. Naming the frog after its towel, Kate takes Hilton home to live with her. The two become best friends and live happily in New York City until Hilton makes an unscheduled appearance in a dinner guest's teacup. When Kate's unreasonable mother insists that the frog must go, Kate advertises for a new owner for her pet. Monsieur Fromage, a chef, wants to cook Hilton; Miss Lavender kisses the frog in hopes that he will turn into a prince; and Donald, a school boy, plans a role for the

amphibian in a particularly unpleasant science project. Weighing the options, Hilton decides to return to his home in Florida and Kate enjoys his subsequent postcards. Writing in *School Library Journal,* Marcia Hupp praised *Friend or Frog* as a "rollicking romp" told with "exuberance and humor," while *Booklist* reviewer Ilene Cooper wrote that Priceman's watercolor illustrations "energetically glide across the pages" and bring to life "every humorous nuance" of her cold-blooded protagonist.

How to Make an Apple Pie and See the World introduces a young girl who wants to make an apple pie but does not have what she needs at home. Although the stores are closed, the young baker refuses to give up. Instead, she travels around the world to gather the necessary ingredients: to Italy to find wheat for the flour, to France to get a chicken's eggs, to Sri Lanka for cinnamon from the bark of a tree, to England for the milk of a cow, to Jamaica for sugar cane, and to Vermont for tart, ripe apples. Priceman also includes a recipe, enabling ambitious readers to make a pie right alongside

Marjorie Priceman adapts her version of a classic fairy tale into an interactive experience for young readers in her self-illustrated **Little Red Riding Hood.** (Copyright © 2001 Marjorie Priceman. Reprinted with the permission of Little Simon, an imprint of Simon & Schuster Children's Publishing Division.)

the story's protagonist. A reviewer for the *Bulletin of the Center for Children's Books* described *How to Make an Apple Pie and See the World* as a "delightful contrast to more sober-sided narratives of food origins."

Priceman treats readers to a second helping of her young heroine's story in *How to Make a Cherry Pie and See the U.S.A.*, which celebrates the Fourth of July and also treats readers to a wonderful fruit pie recipe. Here Priceman's heroine decides to make the perfect cherry pie, and her determination sends her on a round-the-country that leads from New Mexico for a clay mixing bowl to a Pennsylvania coal mine to get the fuel to mold the steel pie pan, to Hawai'i for the sand needed to form the glass for her measuring cup. In the girl's "madcap adventure," readers "will get a sense of the breadth and scope of the country," according to *Booklist* critic Cooper. For *School Library Journal* critic Marilyn Taniguchi, *How to Make a Cherry Pie and See the U.S.A.* is enlivened by Priceman's "spunky" young traveler, and the girl's chronicle comes to life in the author/illustrator's "loose and sketchy, vivid and childlike" gouache paintings. "The visuals take the cake . . . in this folksy jaunt across the country," quipped a *Kirkus Reviews* writer.

Clio the cat is introduced to readers through the faux autobiography *My Nine Lives, by Clio.* Beginning her nine incarnations in Mesopotamia in 3000 B.C., the precocious puss names the constellations, invents the alphabet, catches a ride with explorer Leif Eriksson, and makes Mona Lisa smile while living out her nine lives. While noting that the story has more appeal for adults than younger readers due to its historic references, Michael Cart noted in his *Booklist* appraisal that "Priceman's hand-lettered text and illustrations rendered in various period-appropriate styles are engaging and witty." "This beguiling spoof is the cat's meow," added a *Publishers Weekly* contributor, the critic also praising the feline narrator's inclusion of several interesting and accurate historical facts.

In *Emeline at the Circus* Priceman serves up what a *Horn Book* reviewer called "a rambunctious parody of earnest and over-serious teaching" in the person of second-grade teacher Ms. Splinter. Even a trip to the circus is drained of all fun by Ms. Splinter, who drones on about significant factoids. Young student Emeline is treated to a more-interesting learning experience when she is picked up by a peanut-hungry elephant and made a part of the show under the big top. "Priceman captures the show's frenzied grace in freely painted forms that dance and swirl," noted the *Horn Book* critic, while *Booklist* reviewer Hazel Rochman praised the illustrator's "wildly exuberant style." Calling *Emeline at the Circus* "one of Priceman's most intriguing picture books," a *Publishers Weekly* contributor noted that each scene of "controlled chaos—as animals and performers in all manner of glitzy costume tumble, prance and parade about—attests to why this is called the greatest show on earth."

Priceman capture the high-energy hijinks woven through Jack Prelutsky's verse anthology For Laughing Out Loud: Poems to Tickle Your Funnybone. *(Illustration copyright © 1991 by Marjorie Priceman. Reproduced by permission of Alfred A. Knopf, an imprint of Random House Children's Books, a division of Random House, Inc.)*

Other self-illustrated stories by Priceman include *Froggie Went a-Courting,* a modernized rendition of a Scottish folk tune that finds a love-struck amphibian hopping a cab to visit the object of his affections—Ms. Mouse. The engagement and the wedding go smoothly, but during the reception a feline party crasher spoils the fun by making off with Auntie Rat. Priceman "more than matches [her] story's zip with gouache and cut-paper compositions in kicky color," noted a *Publishers Weekly* contributor of the light-hearted tale, while in *School Library Journal* Faith Brautigam praised the "inventive design and engaging details."

Readers are transported skyward, along with a duck, a sheep, and a rooster in *Hot Air: The (Mostly) True Story of the First Hot-Air Balloon Ride,* which details a little slice of history that makes a perfect subject for the whimsical author/illustrator. Based on the first successful test flight of French inventors Etienne and Joseph Montolfier, which was undertaken in 1783, the book follows the adventures of a sheep, a rooster, and a duck who, with no say in the matter, suddenly find themselves airborne, riding the winds over the king's palace in a wicker basket connected to the first hot-air balloon. Noting the "slapstick" quality of Priceman's story, Roger Sutton wrote in *Horn Book* that *Hot Air* "has a sort of charm-run-amok extravagance that keeps it aloft," while in *Booklist* Julie Cummins praised the "buoyant artwork full of swirls and clever details" that brings to life the book's brief text.

Described as "a playful and painless exploration of optical-illusion concepts," *It's Me, Marva!: A Story about Colors and Optical Illusions* introduces readers to a somewhat confused inventor whose innovations generate surprising and often-unintended consequences. When Marva decides to adjust her Ketcho-matic machine, a sudden eruption of tomato red colors her blonde hair a vibrant orange (red plus yellow). A trip to the beauty parlor and a dose of bleach generates another lesson about the color wheel: when the beautician doses Marva's bleached-white hair with red, it turns pink! The transformations continue as Marva makes her way through a color-filled day full of surprises that ultimately result in a budding romance highlighted by Priceman's spunky collage-and-ink artwork. In *Publishers Weekly* a reviewer praised the author/illustrator's "snappy, humorous" text and added that her "vibrant, kinetic artwork keep readers sailing through an optical wonderland," while *Horn Book* reviewer Lolly Robinson praised *It's Me, Marva!* as "an excellent introduction to color theory and optical illusion."

In addition to writing and illustrating her own stories, Priceman also collaborates with other children's book authors by enhancing picture-book texts with her humorous illustrations. She earned her first Caldecott honor designation for the artwork she created for Lloyd Moss's *Zin! Zin! Zin! A Violin,* which provides a rhyming introduction to the orchestra for young children. In Phyllis Theroux's *Serefina under the Circumstances* Priceman's "bright gouache . . . pictures are packed with witty details that extend the story and show a magical world," noted *Booklist* contributor Hazel Rochman, echoing praise by other critics. In *School Library Journal,* Miriam Lang Budin dubbed the paintings for the same book "clever, colorful, and energetic," while the artist's "breezy watercolor illustrations" add an extra helping of humor to Gershator's "lyrical, joyous, and somewhat silly" song adaptation in *This Is the Day!,* according to *School Library Journal* critic Martha Simpson.

Several stories by author Elsa Okon Rael also benefit from Priceman's entertaining illustrations. *What Zeesie Saw on Delancey Street* finds seven-year-old birthday girl Zeesie gaining a lesson in the spirit of giving when she attends a "package party" where money is raised to help newly arrived immigrant families. In *When Zaydeh Danced on Eldridge Street* Rael explains the Jewish holiday of Simchas Torah by depicting a girl and her grandfather sharing the solemn holiday celebration. The book's illustrations were praised by *Booklist* reviewer Rochman for "captur[ing] the Jewish immigrant neighborhood in New York City in the 1930s." A *Publishers Weekly* contributor commented that Priceman's artwork for *When Zaydeh Danced on Eldridge Street* reflects "the sacredness and beauty of religious symbolism" while also reflecting the illustrator's characteristic "playful, deceptively casual style."

Author Kitty Griffin takes readers back to the era of the American Revolution in *The Ride: The Legend of Betsy Dowdy,* which shares a North Carolina legend about a girl who warned colonists about a planned British attack led by Lord Dunmore on an off-shore island, their aim to capture ponies and other supplies. Along with Griffin's "nicely paced" tale, Priceman contributes artwork featuring what *School Library Journal* contributor Grace Oliff described as her "signature swirling backgrounds and slightly off-kilter perspectives." Another illustration project, creating artwork for Jacqueline K. Ogburn's picture book *The Bake Shop Ghost,* finds the artist depicting a busy kitchen that is shared by one real-life pastry chef and one mischievous ghostly baker. Priceman's illustrations, in ink and water color, "capture [the] . . . ghostly hauntings with all the right swoops and swirls," according to a *Kirkus Reviews* writer. In *School Library Journal* Elaine Lesh Morgan dubbed the art for *The Bake Shop Ghost* a "charming" addition to "a delightful story."

Biographical and Critical Sources

PERIODICALS

Booklist, April 15, 1989, Ilene Cooper, review of *Friend or Frog,* p. 1470; April 15, 1994, review of *How to Make an Apple Pie and See the World,* p. 1532; May 15, 1995, Julie Yates Walton, review of *Zin! Zin! Zin! A Violin,* p. 1650; October 1, 1997, Hazel Rochman, review of *When Zaydeh Danced on Eldridge Street,* p. 324; November 1, 1997, review of *One of Each,* p. 466; October 15, 1998, GraceAnne A. DeCandido, review of *Dancin' in the Kitchen,* p. 416; November 15, 1998, Michael Cart, review of *My Nine Lives: by Clio,* p. 591; April 1, 1999, H. Rochman, review of *Emeline at the Circus,* p. 1408; September 1, 1999, Hazel Rochman, review of *Serefina under the Circumstances,* p. 144; April 1, 2000, Gillian Engberg, review of *Froggie Went a-Courting: An Old Tale with a New Twist,* p. 1463; July, 2001, Ilene Cooper, review of *Red Riding Hood,* p. 2014; October 1, 2002, Gillian Engberg, review of *Things That Sometimes Happen: Very Short Stories for Little Listeners,* p. 332; July, 2005, Julie Cummins, review of *Hot Air: The (Mostly) True Story of the First Hot-Air Balloon Ride,* p. 1928; September 1, 2005, Jennifer Mattson, review of *The Bake Shop Ghost,* p. 125; February 15, 2008, Jennifer Mattson, review of *This Is the Day!,* p. 84; November 1, 2008, Ilene Cooper, review of *How to Make a Cherry Pie and See the U.S.A.,* p. 46; April 1, 2010, Ilene Cooper, review of *Paris in the Spring with Picasso,* p. 40; July 1, 2010, Ilene Cooper, review of *The Ride: The Legend of Betsy Dowdy,* p. 68.

Bulletin of the Center for Children's Books, February, 1994, review of *How to Make an Apple Pie and See the World,* p. 199.

***Priceman's colorful retro-inspired art adds life to Phillis Gershator's picture-book story in* This Is the Day!** (Illustration copyright © 2007 by Marjorie Priceman. Reprinted by permission of Houghton Mifflin Harcourt Publishing Company. All rights reserved.)

Priceman's art is a perfect fit for Joan Yolleck's picture-book story in **Paris in the Spring with Picasso.** (Illustration copyright © 2010 by Marjorie Priceman. Reproduced by permission of Random House Children's Books, a division of Random House, Inc.)

Horn Book, November-December, 1993, review of *A. Nonny Mouse Writes Again!: Poems,* p. 750; May, 1999, review of *Emeline at the Circus,* p. 320; July, 2001, review of *It's Me, Marva!: A Story about Color and Optical Illusions,* p. 443; September-October, 2004, Roger Sutton, review of *Hot Air,* p. 567: November-December, 2008, Joanna Rudge Long, review of *How to Make a Cherry Pie and See the U.S.A.,* p. 964.

Kirkus Reviews, July 15, 2005, review of *The Bake Shop Ghost,* p. 795; September 1, 2007, review of *This Is the Day!;* September 15, 2008, review of *How to Make a Cherry Pie and See the U.S.A.;* February 15, 2010, review of *Paris in the Spring with Picasso.*

Publishers Weekly, December 22, 1989, "Flying Starts: New Faces of 1989," pp. 26-32; February 19, 1996, review of *Cousin Ruth's Tooth,* p. 215; June 16, 1997, review of *When Zaydeh Danced on Eldridge Street,* p. 59; August 10, 1998, review of *My Nine Lives,* p. 386; March 8, 1999, review of *Emeline at the Circus,* p. 68; July 5, 1999, review of *Serefina under the Circumstances,* p. 20; March 20, 2000, review of *Froggie Went a-Courting,* p. 91; June 4, 2001, review of *It's Me, Marva!,* p. 80; July 23, 2001, review of *Little Red Riding Hood,* p. 75; August 12, 2002, review of *Princess Picky,* p. 299; June 15, 2005, review of *Hot Air,* p. 689; September 19, 2005, review of *The Bake Shop*

Ghost, p. 64; October 29, 2007, review of *This Is the Day!,* p. 54; September 15, 2008, review of *How to Make a Cherry Pie and See the U.S.A.,* p. 66; February 8, 2010, review of *Paris in the Spring with Picasso,* p. 49; July 12, 2010, review of *The Ride,* p. 46.

School Library Journal, July, 1989, Marcia Hupp, review of *Friend or Frog,* p. 75; May, 1996, Anne Parker, review of *Cousin Ruth's Tooth,* p. 94, and Sabrina L. Faunfetter, review of *For Laughing out Louder: More Poems to Tickle Your Funnybone,* p. 107; December, 1996, Barbara Kiefer, review of *What Zeesie Saw on Delancey Street,* pp. 103-104; October, 1997, Susan Scheps, review of *When Zaydeh Danced on Eldridge Street,* p. 108; September, 1999, Miriam Lang Budin, review of *Serefina under the Circumstances,* p. 207; November, 1999, Veronica Schwartz, review of *Zin! Zin! Zin!,* p. 59; May, 2000, Linda R. Skeele, review of *My Nine Lives,* p. 64; June, 2000, Faith Brautigam, review of *Froggie Went a-Courting,* p. 135; February, 2001, Martha Topol, review of *The Brand New Kid,* p. 93; July, 2001, Carol Ann Wilson, review of *It's Me, Marva!,* p. 87; December, 2002, Marian Creamer, review of *Princess Picky,* p. 106; October, 2005, Elaine Lesh Morgan, review of *The Bake Shop Ghost,* p. 123; November, 2007, Martha Simpson, review of *This Is the Day!,* p. 106; November, 2008, Marilyn Taniguchi, review of *How to Make a Cherry Pie and*

See the U.S.A., p. 98; February, 2010, Lisa Glasscock, review of *Paris in the Spring with Picasso,* p. 98; August, 2010, Grace Oliff, review of *The Ride,* p. 76.

ONLINE

Bulletin of the Center for Children's Books Online, http://bccb.lis.uiuc.edu/ (July, 1999), Deborah Stevenson, "Marjorie Priceman."

StorybookArt.com, http://www.storybookart.com/ (February 24, 2006), "Marjorie Priceman."

Teachers at Random/Random House Web site, http://www. randomhouse.com/teachers/authors/ (October 15, 2011), "Marjorie Priceman."*

*   *   *

PRIGMORE, Shane 1977-

Personal

Born 1977. *Education:* California Institute of the Arts, B.F.A. (film animation), 1999.

Addresses

Home—Southern CA.

Career

Illustrator and animator. Dreamworks Studio, Hollywood, CA, animator and designer, beginning c. 2007, currently head of feature animation. Film work includes: (character development and animator) *The Iron Giant,* 1998; (animator) *Lord of the Rings: The Two Towers,* 2002; (character designer) *Curious George,* 2005; (designer and writer) *Foster's Home for Imaginary Friends;* (designer) *How to Train Your Dragon; Coraline,* 2007; (designer) *Crood Awakenings;* (codirector and co-creator) *Project Gilroy;* and (creative consultant) *Dinner for Schmucks.* California Institute of the Arts, teacher of animation, c. 2010. Theme-park designer.

Awards, Honors

Annie Award for character design in a feature film production, 2009, for *Coraline.*

Illustrator

"SPACEHEADZ" GRAPHIC-NOVEL SERIES

Jon Scieszka and Francesco Sedita, *Spaceheadz, Book One!,* Simon & Schuster Books for Young Readers (New York, NY), 2010.

Jon Scieszka, *Spaceheadz, Book Two!,* Simon & Schuster Books for Young Readers (New York, NY), 2010.

Jon Scieszka, *Spaceheadz, Book Three!,* Simon & Schuster Books for Young Readers (New York, NY), 2011.

Sidelights

Shane Prigmore is one of the top creative talents at Dreamworks Feature Animation, and he has worked as an animator and designer for a number of top animated films since beginning his career in the late 1990s. Honored with an Annie award for designing character in the 2006 film version of Neil Gaiman's fantasy novel *Coraline,* Prigmore has also joined popular children's author Jon Scieszka to create the companion books in Scieszka's "Spaceheadz" graphic-novel multiplatform series, which pair humorous stories with online activities.

Prigmore did not intend to branch out into print media, but he began to ponder the possibility following a phone call from New York City Simon & Schuster. He signed on after reviewing Scieszka's first "Spaceheadz" manuscript and becoming inspired by the characters and the story's fast pace and silliness. In his illustration for the series, Prigmore alternates illustration styles, a technique that enhances Scieszka's quirky storytelling style.

In *Spaceheadz, Book One!* readers follow Michael K. through his first days as a certified fifth grader. Not only is it a new grade, but it is also a new school. Michael's difficulty in making new friends is enhanced by the fact that his new classmates are all aliens who claim they have come to save Earth, disguised as innocent children and led by a class hamster named Major Fluffy. As the series plays out, Michael and his otherworldly friends Bob and Jennifer, join Major Fluffy's team of Spaceheadz (or SPHDZ) in helping to convince children everywhere to join a pool of brainwaves strong enough to keep Earth online. Foiling the aliens' efforts is Agent Umber, a member of the Anti-Alien Agency that wants to foil Major Fluffy's progress at every turn.

Calling Prigmore's numerous black-and-white cartoon drawings art for the "Spaceheadz" series "a perfect match," a *Kirkus Reviews* contributor added that "artwork and text have rarely worked so well together in this format." "Science-fiction fans with a taste for off-the-wall humor will be eager to join the SPHDZ movement," predicted *School Library Journal* contributor Elaine E. Knight.

Asked by *Character Design* Web log interviewer Randal Sly where he goes for inspiration, Prigmore noted: "I have very creative and talented friends [who] . . . are always pushing me and inspiring me. I have hundreds and hundreds of books. Also I drive to Toys R Us a lot. Sometimes I go to Disneyland to think and watch people. . . . I am also constantly looking for new images and movies and music. But mainly I am lucky enough to work with and be around really, REALLY talented and creative people every day."

"If you're not observing then you're not growing," Prigmore added in his interview. "Always stay curious about everything. Observe everything. Don't just draw one thing, and don't limit yourself to one specific style. Always keep trying new approaches to your work or to a

Shane Prigmore creates the cartoon art for Jon Scieszka's "Spaceheadz" graphic-novel series, which begins with Spaceheadz, Book One! (Illustration copyright © 2010 by Shane Prigmore. Reproduced by permission of Simon & Schuster Books for Young Readers, an imprint of Simon & Schuster Children's Publishing Division.)

subject matter. Be able to adapt to any artistic challenge, and search. Have fun!! This stuff is fun! We draw first and foremost because it is fun!"

Biographical and Critical Sources

PERIODICALS

Booklist, April 1, 2010, Ian Chipman, review of *Spaceheadz, Book One!,* p. 42; October 15, 2010, Todd Morning, review of *Spaceheadz, Book Two!,* p. 52.

Bulletin of the Center for Children's Books, October, 2010, April Spisak, review of *Spaceheadz, Book Two!,* p. 93.

Kirkus Reviews, May 15, 2010, review of *Spaceheadz, Book One!*

New York Times Book Review, November 7, 2010, Sam Grobart, review of *Spaceheadz, Book One!,* p. 28.

Publishers Weekly, May 31, 2010, review of *Spaceheadz, Book One!,* p. 47.

School Library Journal, September, 2010, Elaine E. Knight, review of *Spaceheadz, Book One!,* p. 133; April, 2011, Mara Alpert, review of *Spaceheadz, Book Two!,* p. 153.

ONLINE

Character Design Web log, http://shane-prigmore-interview.blogspot.com/ (July 29, 2011), Randall Sly, interview with Prigmore.

Shane Prigmore Web log, http://shaneprigmore.blogspot.com (October 15, 2011).

* * *

RAYBURN, Tricia (T.R. Burns)

Personal

Born January 23, in Riverhead, NY. *Education:* College degree (American literature); M.F.A. (creative writing).

Addresses

Agent—Rebecca Sherman, Writers House, 21 W. 26th St., New York, NY 10010. *E-mail*—triciarayburn@gmail.com.

Career

Novelist.

Writings

Ruby's Slippers, Aladdin Mix (New York, NY), 2010.
(Under name T.R. Burns) *The Bad Apple* ("Merits of Mischief" series), Aladdin Mix (New York, NY), 2012.

"MAGGIE BEAN" NOVEL SERIES

The Melting of Maggie Bean, Aladdin Mix (New York, NY), 2007.
Maggie Bean Stays Afloat, Aladdin Mix (New York, NY), 2008.
Maggie Bean in Love, Aladdin Mix (New York, NY), 2009.

"SIREN" NOVEL SERIES

Siren, Egmont USA (New York, NY), 2010.
Undercurrent, Egmont USA (New York, NY), 2011.

Author's work has been translated into several languages, including Bulgarian, Chinese, German, Italian, Polish, Portuguese, Russian, and Turkish.

Adaptations

Siren was adapted for audiobook, narrated by Nicola Barber, Brilliance Audio, 2010.

Sidelights

A lifelong reader, Tricia Rayburn completed her first middle-grade novel, *The Melting of Maggie Bean,* completing her graduate degree in creative writing. The act of writing tapped Rayburn's memories of her childhood years and ended up sparking a sequence of novels that includes *Maggie Bean Stays Afloat* and *Maggie Bean in Love.* The author shifts genre in her "Siren" paranormal romance series, which she sets in coastal Maine and gears for older teen readers. In addition, Rayburn has written the standalone novel *Ruby's Slippers,* about a seventh grader who experiences a culture shock after she and her mom leave their home in rural Kansas and move to Florida to care for her elderly grandmother. Dubbing *Ruby's Slippers* a "cheery novel" that "references . . . the classic movie *The Wizard of Oz,*" *Booklist* critic Abby Nolan added that Rayburn's story ends with a "happy ending" that "brings all three generations together."

When readers meet Rayburn's spunky heroine in *The Melting of Maggie Bean,* seventh grader Maggie is shocked to realize that her weight now tops 185 pounds, a result of her habit of dosing on chocolate and candy to combat the problems of early adolescence. Although her problems are real—her father is unemployed and depressed, her mom is worried, and she feels self-conscious due to her weight—Maggie knows that the weight must go, and after her Aunt Violetta takes her to a meeting of the local Pound Patrol, the teen develops a plan to lose thirty pounds and finds the will to follow through. In *Maggie Bean Stays Afloat* and *Maggie Bean in Love* the teen is encouraged by a series of personal successes as she advances from seventh to eighth grade. As a swim teacher and member of the school swim team she is now able to inspire other kids with healthy-eating habits while also winning the admiration of Peter Applewood, a boy she has secretly been crushing on.

Noting that "the strength of the story lies in the character," Amanda MacGregor added in her *Kliatt* review that the star of *The Melting of Maggie Bean* "is a strong, determined, and infinitely likeable girl." In *School Library Journal* Robyn Zaneski praised Rayburn's fiction debut as a "thoughtful coming-of-age novel" that the critic recommended as "empowering . . . for girls try-

ing to overcome any obstacle." "Readers will enjoy following Maggie on her road to self-acceptance," wrote *Booklist* critic Shelle Rosenfeld, in her review of *Maggie Bean Stays Afloat.*

Timid seventeen-year-old Vanessa Sands is the central character of *Sirens* and its sequel, *Undercurrent,* both which tell a darker tale. Vanessa and her sister older Justine have joined their family on vacations to coastal Maine for years, and they have become friends with Caleb and Simon, two brothers who live close by. Justine has always been Vanessa's rock, but then tragedy strikes: Justine rebels against her parents' controlling behavior by leaping off a cliff to her death. After the family returns to their home in Boston to deal with their grief, Vanessa worries that Justine's death was not the suicide it was deemed to be. As she explores her sister's life hidden things surface, including a relationship with the also-missing Caleb. A trip back to Maine and assistance from Caleb's older brother Simon sends Vanessa on the path to the truth, a truth that someone does not want discovered. The mystery continues in *Undercurrent,* as things continue on a supernatural course that pulls Vanessa into a web of suspicion and uncertainty. "Rayburn's writing has an almost cinematic

Cover of Tricia Rayburn's novel Siren, *the first book in her series and the story of two siblings confronting a tragic series of accidents.* (Photograph copyright © 2010 by Maile Roseland. Reproduced by permission of Egmont USA.)

quality," noted Necia Blundy in *School Library Journal,* the critic adding that the "premise" of *Siren* "is fascinating." A *Publishers Weekly* contributor ranked *Sirens* as "a solid supernatural thriller," and while describing the story's pace as slow, a *Kirkus Reviews* writer predicted that diligent readers "will find their patience rewarded with an intriguing twist."

Biographical and Critical Sources

PERIODICALS

Booklist, April 15, 2008, Shelle Rosenfeld, review of *Maggie Bean Stays Afloat,* p. 40; June 1, 2010, Shelle Rosenfeld, review of *Siren,* p. 60, and Abby Nolan, review of *Ruby's Slippers,* p. 78.
Bulletin of the Center for Children's Books, September, 2010, Kate Quealy-Gainer, review of *Siren,* p. 39.
Kirkus Reviews, June 15, 2010, review of *Siren.*
Kliatt, May, 2007, Amanda MacGregor, review of *The Melting of Maggie Bean,* p. 26.
Publishers Weekly, May 31, 2010, review of *Siren,* p. 50.
School Library Journal, July, 2007, Robyn Zaneski, review of *The Melting of Maggie Bean,* p. 109; February, 2011, Necia Blundy, review of *Siren,* p. 118.

ONLINE

Simon & Schuster Web site, http://authors.simonandschuster.com/ (July 29, 2011), "Tricia Rayburn."
Tricia Rayburn Home Page, http://web.me.com/triciarayburn (July 29, 2011).
Tricia Rayburn Web log, http://triciarayburn.blogspot.com (July 29, 2011).*

* * *

RYAN, Candace

Personal

Married; children: one son. *Education:* B.A. (anthropology); Occidental College, M.A.T.

Addresses

Home—Los Angeles, CA. *Agent*—Kelly Sonnack, Andrea Brown Literary Agency, kelly@andreabrownlit.com. *E-mail*—candace_ryan@hotmail.com.

Career

Author of books for children. Teacher of special education at the secondary-school level for nine years. Presenter at schools.

Writings

Animal House, illustrated by Nathan Hale, Walker Books for Young Readers (New York, NY), 2010.

Ribbit Rabbit, illustrated by Mike Lowery, Walker Books for Young Readers (New York, NY), 2011.
Moo Hoo, illustrated by Mike Lowery, Walker Books for Young Readers (New York, NY), 2012.

Sidelights

After earning a degree in anthropology, Candace Ryan made a shift in her career trajectory: she earned a teaching degree and dedicated almost a decade to helping special-needs students at her local secondary school. Then, as the mother of a young son, Ryan was introduced to the world of children's picture books. Her stories, which tap her whimsical side, are paired with illustrations by several talented artists and include *Animal House* as well as the companion picture books *Ribbit Rabbit* and *Moo Hoo.*

Brought to life in Nathan Hale's detailed and colorful acrylic art, *Animal House* tells a humorous story about young Jeremy, who has trouble at school due to his teacher's skepticism. Mrs. Nuddles admonishes the boy when he tells outlandish stories about his home: a gorilla-shaped house that the boy calls a "gorvilla" where he walks on floormingoes, sits in vulchairs and reads by the light of lampreys or watches manatee-vees. Finally, the flustered teacher makes a trip to Jeremy's boy to speak to his mother . . . and finds herself sitting in a vulchair with her head resting on an armapillow! "Outrageous in its tone," according to a *Children's Bookwatch* contributor, *Animal House* "will be greatly enjoyed by kids age 5 and up."

In *Ribbit Rabbit* and *Moo Hoo* Ryan captures the dynamic nature of childhood friendships. Bunny and Frog are always together, but sometimes they argue and sometimes they really fight. Fortunately, making up comes naturally and brings with it more chances for fun. Cow and Owl, another pair of best friends, exhibit the same closeness in *Moo Hoo,* but here the problem is what to do when someone new enters the scene. Fortunately, Roo shares Cow and Owl's interest in music, and it is an easy shift from duo to trio. "What makes Ryan's text unique is its simplicity," asserted Amy Lilien-Harper in her *School Library Journal* review of *Ribbit Rabbit,* the critic going on to praise Mike Lowery's "simple, childlike" cartoon art for effectively combining with the "minimalist text." Praising Frog and Bunny as "disarming characters," a *Kirkus Reviews* writer added that the "rhythmic, onomatopoeic text" in *Ribbit Rabbit* mixes with "childlike" soft-toned art in "a mingling of the ridiculous with the sublime for a spellbinding effect."

Biographical and Critical Sources

PERIODICALS

Bulletin of the Center for Children's Books, February, 2011, Hope Morrison, review of *Ribbit Rabbit,* p. 295.

Children's Bookwatch, October, 2010, review of *Animal House.*

Kirkus Reviews, December 15, 2010, review of *Ribbit Rabbit.*

Publishers Weekly, December 6, 2010, review of *Ribbit Rabbit,* p. 45.

School Library Journal, August, 2010, Jasmine L. Precopio, review of *Animal House,* p. 85; March, 2011, Amy Lilien-Harper, review of *Ribbit Rabbit,* p. 133.

ONLINE

Candace Ryan Home Page, http://www.candaceryanbooks. com (October 1, 2011).

Michelle Markel Web log, http://michellemarkel.blogspot. com/ (July, 2010), interview with Ryan.*

* * *

SALISBURY, Graham 1944-

Personal

Born April 11, 1944, in Philadelphia, PA; son of Henry Forester Graham (an officer in the U.S. Navy) and Barbara Twigg-Smith; married second wife, Robyn Kay Cowan, October 26, 1988; children: Sandi Weston, Miles, Ashley, Melanie, Alex, Keenan, Zachary, Annie Rose (adopted). *Education:* California State University at Northridge, B.A. (magna cum laude), 1974; Vermont College of Norwich University, M.F.A., 1990. *Hobbies and other interests:* Boating and fishing, biking, running.

Addresses

Home—Portland, OR. *Agent*—Barry Goldblatt, Barry Goldblatt Literary, 320 7th Ave., No. 266, Brooklyn, NY 11215.

Career

Writer. Worked variously as a deckhand, glass-bottom-boat skipper, singer/songwriter, graphic artist, and teacher; manager of historic office-buildings in downtown Portland, OR.

Member

Society of Children's Book Writers and Illustrators, American Library Association, Hawaiian Mission Children's Society, National Council of Teachers of English.

Awards, Honors

Parents' Choice Award, Bank Street College Child Study Children's Book Award, Judy Lopez Memorial Award for Children's Literature, Women's National Book Association, Best Books for Young Adults designation, and American Library Association (ALA), all 1992, Notable Trade Book in the Language Arts selection, National Council of Teachers of English (NCTE), and Oregon Book Award, both 1993, all for *Blue Skin of the Sea;* PEN/Norma Klein Award, 1992; Parents' Choice Honor designation, Scott O'Dell Award, and ALA Best Books for Young Adults and Notable Children's Books designations, all 1994, Teacher's Choice, International Reading Association, Notable Children's Trade Book in the Field of Social Studies selection, National Council for the Social Studies/Children's Book Council (NCSS/CBC), Notable Children's Books selection, Library of Congress, New York Public Library Books for the Teen Age selection, Hawai'i Nene Award, California Young Reader Medal, and Oregon Book Award, all 1995, all for *Under the Blood-Red Sun;* Oregon Book Award, 1998, and Parents' Choice Honor Award, both for *Shark Bait;* New York Public Library Books for the Teen Age selection, and ALA Best Books for Young Adults designation, both 1999, both for *Jungle Dogs;* Parents' Choice Gold Award, Capitol Choices selection, and New York Public Library Title for Reading and Sharing, all 2001, *Riverbank Review* Children's Book of Distinction finalist, *Boston Globe/Horn Book* award, and ALA Best Book for Young Adults, all 2002, and Cooperative Children's Book Center Best of the Year selection, all for *Lord of the Deep;* New York Public Library Books for the Teen Age selection, and Chicago Public Library Best of the Best designation, both 2003, both for *Island Boyz;* John Unterecker Award for Fiction, Chaminade University/Hawai'i Literary Arts Council, for body of work; Notable Children's Trade Book in the Field of Social Studies designation, New York Public Library Books for the Teen Age selection, ALA Best Books for Young Adults designation, and PEN USA Literary Award finalist, all 2006, all for *Eyes of the Emperor;* New York Public Library Books for the Teen Age selection, ALA Notable Book selection, and Outstanding Merit citation, Bank Street College of Education, all 2007, all for *House of the Red Fish;* New York Public Library 100 Titles for Reading and Sharing selection, 2007, Best Children's Book of the Year designation, Bank Street College of Education, Notable Children's Trade Book in the Field of Social Studies designation, and New York Public Library Books for the Teen Age inclusion, all 2008, all for *Night of the Howling Dogs.*

Writings

Blue Skin of the Sea, Delacorte (New York, NY), 1992.

Under the Blood-Red Sun, Delacorte (New York, NY), 1994.

Shark Bait, Delacorte (New York, NY), 1997.

Jungle Dogs, Delacorte (New York, NY), 1998.

Lord of the Deep, Delacorte (New York, NY), 2001.

Island Boyz: Short Stories, Wendy Lamb Books (New York, NY), 2002.

Eyes of the Emperor, Wendy Lamb Books (New York, NY), 2005.

House of the Red Fish, Wendy Lamb Books (New York, NY), 2006.

Night of the Howling Dogs, Wendy Lamb Books (New York, NY), 2007.

"CALVIN COCONUT" CHAPTER-BOOK SERIES; ILLUSTRATED BY JACQUELINE ROGERS

Trouble Magnet, Wendy Lamb Books (New York, NY), 2009.

The Zippy Fix, Wendy Lamb Books (New York, NY), 2009.

Dog Heaven, Wendy Lamb Books (New York, NY), 2010.

Zoo Breath, Wendy Lamb Books (New York, NY), 2010.

Hero of Hawai'i, Wendy Lamb Books (New York, NY), 2011.

Kung Fooey, Wendy Lamb Books (New York, NY), 2011.

Man Trip, Wendy Lamb Books (New York, NY), 2012.

Contributor to anthologies, including *Ultimate Sports: Short Stories by Outstanding Writers for Young Adults,* edited by Donald R. Gallo, Delacorte (New York, NY), 1995; *Going Where I'm Coming From: Memoirs of American Youth,* edited by Anne Mazer, Persea, 1995; *No Easy Answers: Short Stories about Teenagers Making Tough Decisions,* edited by Gallo, Delacorte, 1997; *Working Days: Short Stories about Teenagers at Work,* edited by Anne Mazer, Persea, 1997; *Dirty Laundry: Stories about Family Secrets,* edited by Lisa Rowe Fraustino, Viking (New York, NY), 1998; *Time Capsule: Short Stories about Teenagers throughout the Twentieth Century,* edited by Gallo, Delacorte, 1999, and *Shattered: Stories of Children and War,* edited by Jennifer Armstrong, Knopf (New York, NY) 2002. Contributor to periodicals, including *Bamboo Ridge, Chaminade Literary Review, Hawai'i Pacific Review, Journal of Youth Services in Libraries, Manoa: A Journal of Pacific and International Writing, Northwest, Booklist, ALAN Review, SIGNAL Journal,* and *Hawai'i Library Association Journal.*

Adaptations

A number of Salibury's works were adapted as audiobooks.

Sidelights

Characterizing himself as an author who writes for and about preteen and teenaged boys, Graham Salisbury has published several well-received novels, among them *Blue Skin of the Sea, Jungle Dogs,* and *House of the Red Fish,* as well as the collection *Island Boyz: Short Stories* and the chapter books in his "Calvin Coconut" series. All of Salisbury's books are set on the Hawaiian islands, where he was raised. In addition to their exotic island setting, his fictional coming-of-age tales highlight intricate interpersonal relationships that force young protagonists to take distinct, conscious steps toward maturity. Echoing the qualities many reviewers have cited in Salisbury's works, *School Library Journal*

contributor Alison Follos noted of the short stories in *Island Boyz* that by melding "creative and credible narrative voices" with "difficult situations," the author weaves together tales in which readers will discern "recognizable facts of life."

Although Salisbury was born in Pennsylvania, his family has its roots on the islands of Hawai'i, where his ancestors served as missionaries in the early nineteenth century. His father, an ensign in the U.S. Navy, was at Pearl Harbor during the Japanese attack on December 7, 1941; although he survived that ordeal, the man died a few years later, shot down in his fighter plane on April 11, 1945, his son's first birthday. Young Salisbury and his widowed mother continued to make their home on the islands, and the author's love for this tropical region is reflected in his books.

Unlike many writers, Salisbury was not interested in reading as a child. Because of his father's untimely death, he was raised without a solid male role model to provide guidance, and he spent a lot of time wandering the islands with his friends. Salisbury's mother, immersed in her own problems, was distant both emotionally and physically, leaving her son to seek guidance and approval from other adults in his life, such as friends, relatives, and teachers.

When Salisbury enrolled in boarding school in grade seven, he finally gained the structure and guidance he had missed earlier. However, until his college days at California State University at Northridge, where he graduated with a bachelor's degree in 1974, the idea of being a writer never occurred to him. "I didn't read until I was a little past thirty," Salisbury once confided to *SATA.* "Sure, I . . . read the required *Iliad* and *Odyssey* in high school, but I didn't read of my own choice until my first son was born. Then I read Alex Haley's *Roots,* which changed my life forever." It was *Roots* that inspired Salisbury to become a voracious reader and then to write books of his own. He also earned a master's degree in fine arts at Vermont College of Norwich University in 1990.

Published in 1992, Salisbury's first novel, *Blue Skin of the Sea,* is composed of a series of eleven interlinking short stories that centers on Sonny Mendoza and his cousin Keo. The boys are growing up in Hawai'i during the 1950s and 1960s, at a time when the old island ways are fading due to the increasing influx of tourists and other newcomers. Keo is fearless, while Sonny, whose mother died when he was very young, is more thoughtful and introspective. Still, as friends, the two cousins balance one another. Throughout the novel, the boys learn to deal with the school bully, try to cope with their growing attraction to girls, figure out ways to earn spending money, and jump other hurdles of everyday teen life. Along the way they meet up with a Hollywood film crew that is filming actor Spencer Tracy in *The Old Man and the Sea.* The boys, thinking that the props make the action look unrealistic, decide to educate the veteran actor in how to deal with real, rather than fake sharks.

A *New York Times Book Review* critic termed *Blue Skin of the Sea* an "impressive debut," while *Five Owls* contributor Gary D. Schmidt deemed the novel "entertaining, moving, and poignant," adding praise for Salisbury's realistic depiction of island life, with all its "pressures and tensions and loves and fears." *Blue Skin of the Sea* won several awards and was chosen one of the American Library Association's Best Books for Young Adults.

Reflecting upon his father's experiences during and after the bombing raid at Pearl Harbor, Salisbury began a new novel in which he imagined what it would be like to be there, as a boy, during the bombing and its aftermath. *Under the Blood-Red Sun* is the story of Japanese-American eighth-grader Tomikazu "Tomi" Nakaji, whose parents had left Japan to find a better life in the United States and now live on the island of Oahu. Tomi's life is radically altered after the Japanese attack on Pearl Harbor, an action that prompted the U.S. government to enter World War II. Where baseball, school assignments, and a local bully once occupied his thoughts, young Tomi now must worry about battling the increased tensions between Japanese immigrants and native islanders. One real difficulty is toning down his elderly grandfather's proud display of his Japanese heritage, a heritage that is now viewed with suspicion by the Nakajis' American neighbors. Praising Salisbury for "subtly reveal[ing] the natural suspicions of the Americans and the equally natural bewilderment of the Japanese immigrants," *Booklist* contributor Frances Bradburn wrote of *Under the Blood-Red Sun* that it is "a tribute to the writer's craft that, though there are no easy answers in the story, there is empathy for both cultures." *Voice of Youth Advocates* reviewer John R. Lord also praised *Under the Blood-Red Sun,* noting that, "in a time when positive co-existence is being touted in our schools, this novel is an outstanding example of thought-provoking—and at the same time eerily entertaining—prose for the YA reader."

House of the Red Fish, a sequel to *Under the Blood-Red Sun,* "conveys a sense of community that cuts across race and generations," noted *Booklist* contributor Hazel Rochman. Set in 1943, the work concerns Tomi's efforts to raise and restore his father's fishing boat, which has been sunk by the U.S. Army. With both his father and grandfather imprisoned in internment camps, Tomi relies on his friends and neighbors to help with the rescue effort, despite threats from a vigilante gang. Connie Tyrrell Burns praised *Under the Blood-Red Sun* in *School Library Journal,* stating that Salisbury "writes with balance of the ways in which war touches people, creating characters with fully realized motivations."

The world of boyhood is central to Salisbury's writing, and it contains elements that he well remembers, one being what he calls the "Silent Code of Conduct." In

his *ALAN Review* interview, he recalled a scene from his youth, when he and friends were surfing. While sitting on their surfboards, legs dangling knee-deep in the salt water, one of the boys pointed out to a nearby reef and stated, simply: "'Got one shark surfing with us,' as if it were a mullet, or one of those fat hotel-pond carps," Salisbury remembered. "The strength in my arms suddenly felt like jelly," he continued, adding that stories of the infrequent shark attacks around the island of Oahu immediately reeled through his mind. "None of us moved. None of us started paddling in to shore. We just kept sitting there with our legs, from the knee down, dangling underwater," Salisbury recalled. "I sat there with the rest of them, keeping an eye on the shark . . . trying not to look nervous, which I was." Salisbury attributes the young boys' desires to be accepted to "that unspoken 'code' lurking in the corner" of their minds.

In Salisbury's novel *Shark Bait,* that silent code of male conduct weighs heavily on fourteen-year-old protagonist Eric Chock, nicknamed "Mokes" or "tough guy." Mokes is unsure where his loyalties lie when he and his school friends hear through the grapevine that tensions between native kids and U.S. Navy sailors from a de-

Graham Salisbury's novels for young adults include **Jungle Dogs,** *featuring artwork by Cary Austin.* (Jacket copyright © 1998 by Delacorte Press. Reproduced by permission of Delacorte Press, an imprint of Random House Children's Books, a division of Random House, Inc.)

stroyer docked nearby are about to spark a showdown. Mokes's father, the police chief in their small Hawaiian town, attempts to uphold the law and keep the peace by imposing a six-o'clock p.m. curfew, but Mokes's best friend, seventeen-year-old Booley, plans to go to the fight and vows to kill one of the white sailors if offered the chance during the brawl. Mokes wants to obey his father, but he also feels that he should stand by his friend in battle. Things take a sharp turn for the worse when it is discovered that one of the island kids is going to the fight packing a loaded gun.

Praising Salisbury's "surefooted" portrayal of "the teen milieu of fast cars, faster girls, rivalries, and swagger," *Bulletin of the Center for Children's Books* critic Elizabeth Bush commended *Shark Bait* as "a lot more diverting than luaus and ukuleles." While somewhat concerned about Salisbury's casual treatment of alcohol and drug use among the novel's teen protagonists, *School Library Journal* contributor Coop Renner nonetheless deemed *Shark Bait* "a consistently engaging, well-written problem novel in a well-realized setting."

In *Shark Bait* Salisbury's characters speak Pidgin English, a dialect used by many Hawaiians native to the islands. *Booklist* contributor Helen Rosenberg praised the author's use of this dialect, writing that it adds to his "colorful picture of island life, complete with love interests and local superstitions. Along with the local color, there's some riveting action and a [powerful] climax."

Again featuring a Hawaiian setting, *Jungle Dogs* centers on twelve-year-old Boy Regis, who is growing up in a tough neighborhood in which he must learn to conquer his fears and stand up for his convictions. Boy's older brother, who belongs to a gang, believes he must fight all his younger sibling's battles for him, often making things more difficult for Boy. At the same time, Boy's family relies on the income he earns from his paper route—a route requiring that he daily pass a pack of wild jungle dogs on one of the paths to his deliveries. A *Publishers Weekly* reviewer praised the novel as a "tightly drawn drama," noting that Salisbury's "somewhat exotic scenery and dialect are [the] backdrop for sharp characterizations and inventive, subtle plot twists." Janice M. Del Negro noted in the *Bulletin of the Center for Children's Books* that "The lush Hawaii setting adds a physical dimension that strongly colors the action as Boy faces both canine and human packs with tenacity and nerve that will hearten young readers confronting their own demons."

Winner of the *Boston Globe/Horn Book* award, *Lord of the Deep* introduces readers to thirteen-year-old Mickey Donovan, who works alongside his stepfather, Bill, as a deck hand on Bill's charter boat, the *Crystal C.* To Mickey, Bill is not only the boy's mentor and the man who gave his family emotional and financial stability; he is the best skipper on the islands. Bill is also patient with his stepson as Mickey tries hard to learn the ropes,

Cover of Salisbury's novel **Lord of the Deep,** *featuring a Hawaiian setting and cover art by Joel Peter Johnson.* (Jacket cover copyright © 2003 by Laurel-Leaf. Reproduced by permission of Laurel-Leaf, an imprint of Random House Children's Books, a division of Random House, Inc.)

from piloting the boat to swimming under the *Crystal C.* to de-tangle fishing lines. However, the boy watches his idol tarnish when the older man tolerates the mistreatment of two fishing clients, loutish brothers Ernie and Cal, during a three-day fishing charter. When Ernie strong-arms Bill to let him take credit for a huge, world-record-shattering mahi-mahi that Bill actually brought in by offering the captain money, Mickey is crushed to see his stepfather agree to go along with the lie. Although his first reaction is raw anger, the boy eventually realizes that, all along, his stepfather has been exhibiting the most important attributes of adulthood: patience and the strength to forgive.

In *Horn Book* a contributor deemed *Lord of the Deep* a "masterpiece of subtlety," while *School Library Journal* reviewer Caroline Ward praised it as "a winning combination of riveting deep-sea fishing action, a sensitive depiction of family relationships, and an intriguing exploration of the fine line between lying and telling the truth." While the novel "vividly conveys the pace and dangers of sport fishing," according to *Booklist* contributor John Peters, the overlying plot hinges on the "ethical conundrum" of Salisbury's young protagonist, revealing, as the *Horn Book* contributor noted, "the perilous undercurrents that can lie beneath even the best of human relationships."

Based on actual events, *Eyes of the Emperor* centers on Eddy Okubo, a sixteen-year-old Japanese American who doctors his birth certificate so he can serve in the U.S. Army with his friends. Just weeks after Eddy enlists, Pearl Harbor is attacked and the United States enters World War II; Eddy and his comrades find themselves segregated from their unit because of their Japanese ancestry. Dispatched to Cat Island, Mississippi, Eddy and twenty-five other Japanese-American soldiers are used as "bait" to train attack dogs that will hunt the enemy in the Pacific. "The shameful way Japanese American soldiers were treated will be eye-opening to most readers," noted *Kliatt* reviewer Paula Rohrlick, "and the scenes on Cat Island are dramatic and horrifying." According to a *Publishers Weekly* reviewer, *Eyes of the Emperor* "is a valuable and gripping addition to the canon of WW II historical fiction from a perspective young readers rarely see."

In *Night of the Howling Dogs*, Salisbury offers a fictional account of a natural disaster that occurred in Hawai'i in 1975. Narrated by Dylan, a Boy Scout patrol leader, the work describes a camping trip that threatens to end in disaster when an earthquake hits the area, followed by a violent tsunami. Along with Louie, a troubled member of the scout troop, Dylan mounts a rescue effort that involves an arduous trek along the coastline. "A strong sense of place informs the plot as well as the setting of this convincing story," Carolyn Phelan remarked in *Booklist,* and *School Library Journal* critic Joel Shoemaker observed that "Salisbury's tale of courage, strength, and survival is appealing, exciting, and insightful."

Salisbury returns to his Hawaiian roots in his "Calvin Coconut" chapter-book series, which are all set at Kailua Elementary School, where the author himself was once a student. Illustrated by Jacqueline Rogers, the series includes *Trouble Magnet, The Zippy Fix, Dog Heaven, Zoo Breath, Hero of Hawai'i, Kung Fooey,* and *Man Trip. Trouble Magnet* introduces the nine-year-old hero of the series, who is burdened with his unusual name because his show-biz dad legally changed the family name before abandoning the family. Beginning fourth grade, the boy had one problem after another, while at home he loses his bedroom when the daughter of a family friend comes to visit. That daughter officially joins the family in *The Zippy Fix,* which means that Calvin is actually living with his naggy babysitter, but their relationship strengthens after one of the boy's practical jokes backfires. In *Dog Heaven* Calvin's oft-articulated wish for a dog is answered when a mutt named Streak joins the family, while *Zoo Breath* finds

Mom perplexed over the doggy smell that is now pervading the household. Salisbury's Hawaiian setting takes center stage in *Hero of Hawai'i*, as Calvin's life-saving skills are tested during a tropical storm that sweeps his friend into the ocean, and a new kid with a quirky fashion sense joins Calvin's fourth-grade class in *Kung Fooey.*

"Salisbury's buoyant look into growing up in Hawai'i will be revealing to many stateside readers," predicted Ian Chipman in his *Booklist* review of *The Zippy Fix,* while a *Kirkus Reviews* writer cited the "believable, funny characters" in *Trouble Magnet*. "Supportive adult characters encourage Calvin as he juggles classroom expectations with family relationships," noted *School Library Journal* contributor Meg Smith, and in *Horn Book* Jennifer M. Brabander concluded that Salisbury's "Calvin Coconut" series benefits from "a real boy-like protagonist, funny stories, plenty of illustrations, and both a unique setting and family."

Focusing again on older teen readers, *Island Boyz* contains ten stories (five previously unpublished) that examine the lives of young men in Hawai'i. "Mrs. Noonan" centers on a boarding student's obsession with a faculty member's wife, and "Angel-Baby" tells a story of first love. Critics especially praised "Waiting for the War," which describes a soldier's gesture of kindness before he is shipped off to battle, and "Hat of Clouds," a tale of two brothers whose relationship changes after one is wounded in Vietnam. Calling *Island Boyz* "memorable," Gillian Engberg added in *Booklist* that each story pairs the island's "tropical setting with vivid, tangible details that electrify each boy's drama."

"The important thing for me to understand as a writer for young readers is that, though the world has changed, the basic needs of young people haven't," Salisbury

Salisbury's "Calvin Coconut" series features artwork by Jacqueline Rogers and includes the book Trouble Magnet. (Illustration copyright © 2009 by Jacqueline Rogers. Reproduced by permission of Wendy Lamb Books, an imprint of Random House Children's Books, a division of Random House, Inc.)

once told *SATA*. "There are many, many kids out there with holes in their lives that they desperately want to fill. I can write about those holes. I can do this because I am human and have suffered and soared myself. Strange as it sounds to say, as a writer I consider myself lucky, indeed, to have all the holes I have in my own life. Because when I write, I remember, I understand, I empathize, and I feel a need to explore those holes and maybe even fill a couple of them—for myself and for any reader with a similar need who happens to stumble onto my work."

Biographical and Critical Sources

BOOKS

Gill, David Macinnis, *Graham Salisbury: Island Boy,* Scarecrow Press (Lanham, MD), 2005.

PERIODICALS

ALAN Review, fall, 1994, Graham Salisbury, "A Leaf on the Sea," pp. 11-14; winter, 1997, Janet Benton, "'Writing My Way Home': An Interview with Salisbury."

Booklist, October 15, 1994, Frances Bradburn, review of *Under the Blood-Red Sun,* p. 425; September 1, 1997, Helen Rosenberg, review of *Shark Bait,* p. 107; September 15, 1998, Hazel Rochman, review of *Jungle Dogs,* p. 110; March 1, 2001, Anna Rich, review of *Jungle Dogs,* p. 1295; August, 2001, John Peters, review of *Lord of the Deep,* p. 2108; April 15, 2002, Gillian Engberg, review of *Island Boyz: Short Stories,* p. 1399; May 15, 2005, Hazel Rochman, review of *Eyes of the Emperor,* p. 1669; April 15, 2006, Hazel Rochman, review of *House of the Red Fish,* p. 64; August, 2007, Carolyn Phelan, review of *Night of the Howling Dogs,* p. 70; January 1, 2009, Ian Chipman, review of *Trouble Magnet,* p. 82; September 1, 2009, Ian Chipman, review of *The Zippy Fix,* p. 86.

Bulletin of the Center for Children's Books, December, 1997, Elizabeth Bush, review of *Shark Bait,* pp. 138-139; February, 1999, Janice M. Del Negro, review of *Jungle Dogs,* p. 216.

Five Owls, May-June, 1992, Gary D. Schmidt, review of *Blue Skin of the Sea,* p. 66.

Horn Book, September-October, 1998, Susan P. Bloom, review of *Jungle Dogs,* p. 614; September, 2001, Peter D. Sieruta, review of *Lord of the Deep,* p. 595; March-April, 2002, Peter D. Sieruta, review of *Island Boyz,* p. 219; January-February, 2003, Graham Salisbury, "E Komo Mai" (award acceptance speech), p. 39; July-August, 2005, Peter D. Sieruta, review of *Eyes of the Emperor,* p. 480; September-October, 2007, Betty Carter, review of *Night of the Howling Dogs,* p. 589; March-April. 2011, Jennifer M. Brabander, review of *Hero of Hawai'i,* p. 124.

Journal of Adolescence and Adult Literacy, November, 2002, James Blasingame, review of *Lord of the Deep,* p. 267.

Kirkus Reviews, March 15, 2002, review of *Island Boyz,* p. 425; February 15, 2009, review of *Trouble Magnet*; August 15, 2009, review of *The Zippy Fix*; February 15, 2010, review of *Dog Heaven.*

Kliatt, July, 2002, Jean Palmer, review of *Lord of the Deep,* p. 53; May, 2003, Paula Rohrlick, review of *Lord of the Deep,* p. 20; March, 2004, Olivia Durant, review of *Island Boyz,* p. 28; July, 2005, Paula Rohrlick, review of *Eyes of the Emperor,* p. 16; July, 2006, Paula Rohrlick, review of *House of the Red Fish,* p. 14.

New York Times Book Review, May 2, 1993, review of *Blue Skin of the Sea,* p. 24.

Publishers Weekly, July 13, 1998, review of *Jungle Dogs,* p. 78; July 30, 2001, review of *Lord of the Deep,* p. 86; September 5, 2005, review of *Eyes of the Emperor,* p. 64; March 16, 2009, review of *Trouble Magnet,* p. 61.

School Library Journal, September, 1997, Coop Renner, review of *Shark Bait,* p. 225; October, 2000, Todd Dunkelberg, review of *Jungle Dogs,* p. 94; August, 2001, Caroline Ward, review of *Lord of the Deep,* p. 188; March, 2002, Alison Follos, review of *Island Boyz,* p. 238; August, 2001, Caroline Ward, review of *Lord of the Deep,* p. 188; September, 2005, Carol A. Edwards, review of *Eyes of the Emperor,* p. 213; August, 2006, Connie Tyrell Burns, review of *House of the Red Fish,* p. 128; August, 2007, Joel Shoemaker, review of *Night of the Howling Dogs,* p. 125; May, 2009, Marie Orlando, review of *Trouble Magnet,* p. 88; September, 2009, Alyson Low, review of *The Zippy Fix,* p. 132; February, 2010, Christine Johanson, review of *Dog Heaven,* p. 94; December, 2010, Meg Smith, review of *Zoo Breath,* p. 88; April, 2011, Amy Holland, review of *Hero of Hawai'i,* p. 152.

Voice of Youth Advocates, October, 1994, John R. Lord, review of *Under the Blood-Red Sun,* p. 216.

ONLINE

Graham Salisbury Home Page, http://www.grahamsalisbury.com (October 21, 2011).

Random House Web site, http://www.randomhouse.com/ (October 21, 2011), "Graham Salisbury."*

*   *   *

SHECTER, Vicky Alvear 1961-

Personal

Born February 24, 1961, in Hollywood, FL. *Education:* Florida State University, B.A. (English).

Addresses

Home—Avondale Estates, GA. *E-mail*—valvearshecter@gmail.com.

Career

Writer and novelist. Worked for a financial publisher; freelance writer; worked in advertising and marketing in Atlanta, GA; novelist. Michael C. Carlos Museum of Art at Emory University, Atlanta, docent. Presenter at workshops, festivals, and conferences.

Member

Society of Children's Book Writers and Illustrators.

Awards, Honors

Honor selection for nonfiction, *Voice of Youth Advocates,* 2006, for *Alexander the Great Rocks the World.*

Writings

(With Michael Alvear; as Vicky A. Shecter) *Alexander the Fabulous: The Man Who Brought the World to Its Knees,* Advocate Books (Los Angeles, CA), 2004.

Alexander the Great Rocks the World, illustrated by Terry Naughton, Darby Creek (Plain City, OH), 2006.

Cleopatra Rules!: The Amazing Life of the Original Teen Queen, Boyds Mills Press (Honesdale, PA), 2010.

Cleopatra's Moon, Arthur A. Levine Books (New York, NY), 2011.

Contributor to *Huffington Post.*

Sidelights

Vicky Alvear Shecter began her writing career doing financial writing as well as creating copy for advertising and marketing projects in her native Georgia. Eventually she found the time to follow another passion—her interest in the ancient world—and she became a docent at the Michael C. Carlos Museum of Antiquities on the campus of Atlanta's Emory University, where she introduced school groups to the museum's collection of Egyptian, Greek, Roman, Mesopotamian, and American antiquities. This job inspired Shecter consider ways of combining her talent for writing with her wide-ranging knowledge of ancient history and culture, and her nonfiction books *Alexander the Great Rocks the World* and *Cleopatra Rules!: The Amazing Life of the Original Teen Queen,* as well as her young-adult novel *Cleopatra's Moon,* are the result.

In her nonfiction books, Shecter is careful to show the relevance of ancient history to modern life, whether it be the stratification of society by class, race, or gender, conflicts among cultures or tactical challenges during wartime. In *Alexander the Great Rocks the World* she relates the story of one of ancient Greece's most famous characters, using kid-friendly slang to describe Alexander of Macedon's education by Aristotle and his succession to the Macedonian throne at age twenty. During the next ten years he was given command of the Greek army and led invasion forces from Persia to India, creating the largest empire of the ancient world. In addition to the kid appeal gained through Terry Naugh-

ton's cartoon illustrations for *Alexander the Great Rocks the World,* the "smart-aleck tone" of Shecter's text is balanced by her in-depth research, according to *School Library Journal* contributor Coop Renner. Clearly noting where historians disagree on facets of Alexander's life, she also describes her subject's complex character, which Renner noted ranged between "episodes of arrogance" and militarism and exhibiting his "respect for women, his courage, and his generosity." While Todd Morning recommended the work due to its "extensive notes" and comprehensive bibliography, he added in his *Booklist* review of *Alexander the Great Rocks the World* that "kids will like the irreverent approach."

Shecter takes a similarly upbeat approach in writing *Cleopatra Rules!,* including in her text "puns, informal language, and contemporary metaphors," according to *Booklist* critic Carolyn Phelan. Beginning with Cleopatra VII's childhood, the author follows Egypt's final pharaoh from her childhood as the daughter of Ptolemy XII through her marriage to her brother and surviving ruler of her land. During a reign of less than four years, she married Julius Caesar and then allied herself romantically with Roman general Mark Antony following Caesar's assassination. After Cleopatra's suicide at age thirty-nine, Egypt fell under the rule of Rome. "Shecter's solid research is evident in her account of events," noted Phelan, and *School Library Journal* contributor

Cover of Vicky Alvear Shecter's teen-friendly biography **Cleopatra Rules!***, which describes the life of the most powerful woman of the ancient world.* (Photograph copyright © 2010 by Elizabeth Salib. Reproduced by permission of Boyds Mills Press.)

Paula Willey noted that the author "addresses and questions preconceptions about Cleopatra that have proliferated throughout Western culture since Plutarch." While Lynn Evarts questioned whether "a serious researcher may be put off by the phrasing and word choice" in *Cleopatra Rocks!*, she added in her *Voice of Youth Advocates* appraisal that Schecter's approach will be useful to students reluctant "to read nonfiction or biography."

Contemporary information on Cleopatra is scarce; the surviving historical record is told from a Roman point of view and is therefore biased against the Egyptian queen. During her exploration of the history that has sprung up about the enigmatic Egyptian queen over the centuries, Shecter became fascinated by her subject. "It never occurred to me to write fiction until I came across a fact that grabbed me by the throat and wouldn't let go," the author noted in a post for the *Cynsations* Web log. After she learned that Cleopatra was mother to three children in addition to having a son, Caesarion, with Julius Caesar, she began to wonder what it would have been like for the queen's surviving daughter, Cleopatra Selene.

Shecter explores the possibilities in her novel *Cleopatra's Moon,* which follows the young woman's story after her father and mother both commit suicide. At age seven Cleopatra Selene is taken to Rome and reared in the home of Gaius Julius Caesar Octavinus, along with her two brothers. Living under Roman law, she continues to worship the Egyptian deities and secretly plans for the day when she will reclaim her mother's throne as pharaoh over the land of the Nile. Noting the tragedies in Selene's life, Krista Hutley wrote in her *Booklist* review that *Cleopatra's Moon* "brings ancient Egypt and Rome to life with vivid period details and a fascinating take on a neglected historical figure." "The sadistic family plotting in Octavianus's compound makes for intriguing storytelling," asserted a *Kirkus Reviews* writer, and in *Publishers Weekly* a critic deemed *Cleopatra's Moon* a "fascinating historical novel" in which both the "atmospheric setting and romantic intrigue are highly memorable."

Biographical and Critical Sources

PERIODICALS

Booklist, January 1, 2007, Todd Morning, review of *Alexander the Great Rocks the World,* p. 90; October 1, 2010, Carolyn Phelan, review of *Cleopatra Rules!: The Amazing Life of the Original Teen Queen,* p. 43; August 1, 2011, Krista Hutley, review of *Cleopatra's Moon,* p. 46.
Bulletin of the Center for Children's Books, September, 2010, Elizabeth Bush, review of *Cleopatra Rules!,* p. 42.
Publishers Weekly, July 11, 2011, review of *Cleopatra's Moon,* p. 59.

Kirkus Reviews, July 15, 2011, review of *Cleopatra's Moon.*
School Library Journal, December, 2006, Coop Renner, review of *Alexander the Great Rocks the World,* p. 169; October, 2010, Paula Willey, review of *Cleopatra Rules,* p. 133.
Voice of Youth Advocates, December, 2006, Jennifer Rummel, review of *Alexander the Great Rocks the World,* p. 461; December, 2010, Lynn Evarts, review of *Cleopatra Rules!,* p. 483.

ONLINE

Cynsations Web log, http://cynthialeitichsmith.blogspot.com/ (September 20, 2011), Vicky Alvear Shecter, "Tips for Writing Historical Fiction."
Vicky Alvear Shecter Home Page, http://www.vickyalvearshecter.com (October 1, 2011).
Vicky Alvear Shecter Web log, http://historywithatwist.blogspot.com (October 1, 2011).
Georgia Center for the Book Web site, http://www.georgiacenterforthebook.org (October 1, 2011), "Vicky Alvear Shecter."*

* * *

SIEGEL, Randolph
See SIEGEL, Randy

* * *

SIEGEL, Randy
(Randolph Siegel)

Personal

Married; children: one son, one daughter. *Education:* Wesleyan University, B.A.; Yale University, M.B.A.

Addresses

Home—NY. *Office*—Local Digital Strategy for Advance Publications, 4 Times Square, 11th Fl., New York, NY 10036. *Agent*—Adams Literary, info@adamsliterary.com. *E-mail*—rsiegel@advance.net.

Career

Publisher and author. Marketing executive for *Newsweek* and *Washington Post; Cleveland Free Times,* Cleveland, OH, former publisher and editor; BrasRing (recruitment agency), executive vice president, 1999-2000; Parade Publications, executive vice president beginning 2001, and publisher, 2003-10; Local Digital Strategy Advance Publications, president, 2010—. Founder, Newspaper Project (industry think tank). Member of board of trustees, CURE Epilepsy, beginning 2006; member of advisory board, Committee to Protect Journalists.

Member

National Conference of Editorial Writers, Society of Children's Book Writers and Illustrators.

Writings

Grandma's Smile, illustrated by DyAnne DiSalvo, Roaring Brook Press (New York, NY), 2010.

My Snake Blake, illustrated by Serge Bloch, Roaring Book Press (New York, NY), 2012.

Contributor to periodicals, including *Advertising Age, Chicago Tribune, Media Week, Newsweek, New York Times, USA Today, Wall Street Journal, USA Today,* and the *Washington Post.* Contributing editorial writer, *Providence Journal.*

Sidelights

Randy Siegel has devoted his career to publishing, spending a decade as editor of *Parade,* one of the most widely read magazines in the United States, before leaving to start his own company. In addition to working as an editor, Siegel contributed articles and editorials to a wide range of periodicals. He has also authored the picture books *Grandma's Smile* and *My Snake Blake,* the latter a story about a boy and a pet with an unusual talent that features cartoon drawings by French artist Serge Bloch. In addition to his professional and writing life, Siegel works with Citizens United for Research in Epilepsy (CURE) to increase public awareness about epilepsy, his efforts inspired by a daughter who has the condition.

Illustrated with mixed-media art by DyAnne DiSalvo, *Grandma's Smile* follows the journey of a six-year-old boy as he is given a mission: to travel the many miles that separate him from his doting Grandma Iris and help her find her smile. His mother is there to help: she helps the boy travel to the airport, and fly to Grandma's home town where the smile resurfaces as soon as the extended family is reunited. Paired with detailed illustrations that "capture the child's experience with emotional warmth," according to *Booklist* critic Carolyn Phelan, Siegel's story will help children anticipate the realities of modern-day air travel, which includes a lot of waiting. *Grandma's Smile* treats storytime audiences to a narrative featuring "the delightful voice of a precocious six-year-old who is sure that what he is doing is important," wrote Donna Cardon in a *School Library Journal* review, and a *Publishers Weekly* contributor praised Siegel's picture book as "a wry and contemporary reality check on the going-to-Grandma's genre."

Biographical and Critical Sources

PERIODICALS

Booklist, July 1, 2010, Carolyn Phelan, review of *Grandma's Smile,* p. 66.

Columbia Journalism Review, February 6, 2009, Megan Garber, interview with Siegel.

Publishers Weekly, August 9, 2010, review of *Grandma's Smile,* p. 49.

School Library Journal, November, 2010, Donna Cardon, review of *Grandma's Smile,* p. 83.

ONLINE

Randy Siegel Home Page, http://www.randolphsiegel.com (October 1, 2011).*

* * *

SINGER, Marilyn 1948-

Personal

Born October 3, 1948, in New York, NY; daughter of Abraham (a photoengraver) and Shirley Singer; married Steven Aronson (a financial manager), July 31, 1971. *Education:* Attended University of Reading, 1967-68; Queens College of the City University of New York, B.A. (English; cum laude), 1969; New York University, M.A. (communications), 1979. *Hobbies and other interests:* Dog obedience and agility, reading, hiking, theater, film, bird watching and caring for animals, gardening, meditation, computer adventure games.

Addresses

Home and office—42 Berkeley Pl., Brooklyn, NY 11217. *E-mail*—marilyn@marilynsinger.net.

Career

Poet, author, and educator. Daniel S. Mead Literary Agency, New York, NY, editor, 1967; *Where* (magazine), New York, NY, assistant editor, 1969; New York City Public High Schools, New York, NY, teacher of English and speech, 1969-74; writer, 1974—.

Member

Society of Children's Book Writers and Illustrators, Authors Guild, American Library Association, Dog Writers Association of America, PEN American Center, Nature Conservancy, North American Dog Agility Council, New York Zoological Society, Staten Island Companion Dog Training Club, Phi Beta Kappa.

Awards, Honors

Children's Choice Award, International Reading Association, 1977, for *The Dog Who Insisted He Wasn't,* 1979, for *It Can't Hurt Forever,* 1988, for *Ghost Host,* and 1991, for *Nine o'Clock Lullaby;* Maud Hart Lovelace Award, Friends of the Minnesota Valley Regional Library, 1983, for *It Can't Hurt Forever;* American Library Association (ALA) Best Book for Young Adults citation, 1983, for *The Course of True Love Never Did*

Marilyn Singer (Photograph copyright © 2010 by Steve Aronson. Courtesy of Marilyn Singer.)

Run Smooth; Parents' Choice Award, Parents' Choice Foundation, 1983, for *The Fido Frame-Up,* and 2001, for *A Pair of Wings; New York Times* Best Illustrated Children's Book citation, and *Time* Best Children's Book citation, both 1989, Notable Trade Book in the Language Arts designation, National Council of Teachers of English (NCTE), 1990, and Texas Bluebonnet Award nomination, 1992, all for *Turtle in July;* South Carolina Book Award nomination, 1992-93, for *Twenty Ways to Lose Your Best Friend;* Iowa Teen Award nomination, 1993, for *Charmed;* Notable Children's Trade Book in the Field of Social Studies, National Council for the Social Studies/Children's Book Council (CBC), 1995, for *Family Reunion,* and 2000, for *On the Same Day in March;* Washington Children's Choice Picture Book Award nomination, 1996, for *Chester the Out-of-Work Dog;* Dorothy Canfield Fisher Award nomination, 1997-98, for *All We Needed to Say;* Society of School Librarians International Best Books designation, 1997-98, for *Deal with a Ghost,* 1998-99, for *Bottoms Up,* and 2001, for *Tough Beginnings;* Best Books for the Teen Age selection, New York Public Library, 1998, for *Stay True,* 2001, for *I Believe in Water,* 2005, for *Face Relations,* 2006, for *Make Me Over;* Edgar Allan Poe Award nominee, Mystery Writers of America 1998, for *Deal with a Ghost;* Popular Paperbacks for Young Adults selection, Young Adult Library Services Association, 2000, for *Stay True;* Animal Behavior Society Award, 2002, for *A Pair of Wings;* Canadian Children's Book Centre Our Choice designation, 2002, for *Didi and Daddy on the Promenade;* Outstanding Science Trade Book for Students, National Science Teachers Association/CBC, 2002, for *Tough Beginnings;* Children's Book of Distinction honor, *Riverbank Review,* 2003, for *Footprints on the Roof;* Lee Bennett Hopkins Poetry Award Honor Book designation, 2005, for *Creature Carnival;* ALA Honor Book designation, 2005, for *Central Heating; Time* magazine Top Ten Children's Books designation, 2007, for *City Lullaby;* Bank Street College of Education Best Children's Book designation, 2007, for *Let's Build a Clubhouse;* Orbis Pictus Honor

Book designation, 2008, for *Venom;* Chicago Public Library Best of the Best designation, 2009, for *First Food Fight This Fall, and Other Poems about School;* CYBILS Award for Poetry, ALA Notable Book designation, NCTE Notable Book designation, and Capitol Choice selection, all 2011, all for *Mirror Mirror.*

Writings

PICTURE BOOKS

The Dog Who Insisted He Wasn't, illustrated by Kelly Oechsli, Dutton (New York, NY), 1976.
The Pickle Plan, illustrated by Steven Kellogg, Dutton (New York, NY), 1978.
Will You Take Me to Town on Strawberry Day?, illustrated by Trinka Hakes Noble, Harper (New York, NY), 1981.
Archer Armadillo's Secret Room, illustrated by Beth Lee Weiner, Macmillan (New York, NY), 1985.
Minnie's Yom Kippur Birthday, illustrated by Ruth Rosner, Harper (New York, NY), 1989.
Nine o'Clock Lullaby, illustrated by Frané Lessac, HarperCollins (New York, NY), 1991.
The Golden Heart of Winter, illustrated by Robert Rayevsky, Morrow (New York, NY), 1991.
Chester the Out-of-Work Dog, illustrated by Cat Bowman Smith, Holt (New York, NY), 1992.
The Painted Fan, illustrated by Wenhai Ma, Morrow (New York, NY), 1994.
The Maiden on the Moor, illustrated by Troy Howell, Morrow (New York, NY), 1995.
In the Palace of the Ocean King, illustrated by Ted Rand, Atheneum (New York, NY), 1995.
Good Day, Good Night, illustrated by Ponder Goembel, Marshall Cavendish (New York, NY), 1998.
Solomon Sneezes, illustrated by Brian Floca, HarperFestival (New York, NY), 1999.
On the Same Day in March: A Tour of the World's Weather, illustrated by Frané Lessac, HarperCollins (New York, NY), 2000.
The One and Only Me, illustrated by Nicole Rubel, HarperFestival (New York, NY), 2000.
Fred's Bed, illustrated by JoAnn Adinolfi, HarperFestival (New York, NY), 2001.
Didi and Daddy on the Promenade, illustrated by Marie-Louise Gay, Clarion (New York, NY), 2001.
Boo-Hoo, Boo-Boo!, illustrated by Elivia Savadier, HarperFestival (New York, NY), 2002.
Quiet Night, illustrated by John Manders, Clarion (New York, NY), 2002.
Block Party Today!, illustrated by Stephanie Roth, Knopf (New York, NY), 2004.
So Many Kinds of Kisses, illustrated by Emily Arnold McCully, Atheneum (New York, NY), 2004.
Monday on the Mississippi, illustrated by Frané Lessac, Holt (New York, NY), 2005.
What Stinks?, Darby Creek Publishing (Plain City, OH), 2006.

City Lullaby, illustrated by Carll Cneut, Clarion Books (New York, NY), 2007.

Shoe Bop!, illustrated by Hiroe Nakata, Dutton Children's Books (New York, NY), 2008.

I'm Getting a Checkup, illustrated by David Milgrim, Clarion Books (New York, NY), 2009.

I'm Your Bus, illustrated by Evan Polenghi, Scholastic Press (New York, NY), 2009.

Tallulah's Tutu, illustrated by Alexandra Boiger, Clarion Books (Boston, MA), 2011.

What Is Your Dog Doing?, illustrated by Kathleen Habbley, Atheneum Books for Young Readers (New York, NY), 2011.

The Boy Who Cried Alien!, illustrated by Brian Biggs, Disney/Hyperion (New York, NY), 2012.

CHILDREN'S FICTION

It Can't Hurt Forever, illustrated by Leigh Grant, Harper (New York, NY), 1978.

Tarantulas on the Brain, illustrated by Leigh Grant, Harper (New York, NY), 1982.

Lizzie Silver of Sherwood Forest (sequel to *Tarantulas on the Brain*), illustrated by Miriam Nerlove, Harper (New York, NY), 1986.

The Lightey Club, illustrated by Kathryn Brown, Four Winds (New York, NY), 1987.

Mitzi Meyer, Fearless Warrior Queen, Scholastic (New York, NY), 1987.

Charmed (fantasy), Atheneum (New York, NY), 1990.

Twenty Ways to Lose Your Best Friend, illustrated by Jeffrey Lindberg, Harper (New York, NY), 1990.

California Demon, Hyperion (New York, NY), 1992.

Big Wheel, Hyperion (New York, NY), 1993.

Josie to the Rescue, illustrated by S.D. Schindler, Scholastic (New York, NY), 1999.

The Circus Lunicus, Holt (New York, NY), 2000.

Let's Build a Clubhouse, illustrated by Timothy Bush, Clarion Books (New York, NY), 2006

CHILDREN'S POETRY

Turtle in July, illustrated by Jerry Pinkney, Macmillan (New York, NY), 1989.

In My Tent, illustrated by Emily Arnold McCully, Macmillan (New York, NY), 1992.

It's Hard to Read a Map with a Beagle on Your Lap, illustrated by Clement Oubrerie, Holt (New York, NY), 1993.

Sky Words, illustrated by Deborah K. Ray, Macmillan (New York, NY), 1994.

Family Reunion, illustrated by R.W. Alley, Macmillan (New York, NY), 1994.

Please Don't Squeeze Your Boa, Noah!, illustrated by Clement Oubrerie, Holt (New York, NY), 1995.

The Morgans Dream, illustrated by Gary Drake, Holt (New York, NY), 1995.

All That We Needed to Say: Poems about School from Tanya and Sophie, photographs by Lorna Clark, Atheneum (New York, NY), 1996.

Monster Museum, illustrated by Chris Grimly, Hyperion (New York, NY), 2001.

Footprints on the Roof: Poems about the Earth, illustrated by Meilo So, Random House (New York, NY), 2002.

The Company of Crows, illustrated by Linda Saport, Clarion (New York, NY), 2002.

How to Cross a Pond: Poems about Water, illustrated by Meilo So, Knopf (New York, NY), 2003.

Fireflies at Midnight, illustrated by Ken Robbins, Atheneum (New York, NY), 2003.

Creature Carnival, illustrated by Gris Grimley, Hyperion (New York, NY), 2004.

Central Heating: Poems about Fire and Warmth, illustrated by Meilo So, Alfred A. Knopf (New York, NY), 2005.

First Food Fight This Fall, and Other School Poems, illustrated by Sachiko Yoshikawa, Sterling (New York, NY), 2008.

Mirror Mirror: A Book of Reversible Verse, illustrated by Josée Massee, Dutton Children's Books (New York, NY), 2010.

Nose to Nose, Tail to Tail: Love Poems from the Animal Kingdom, illustrated by Lee Wildish, Alfred A. Knopf (New York, NY), 2010.

A Full Moon Is Rising: Poems, illustrated by Julia Cairns, Lee & Low Books (New York, NY), 2011.

Twosomes: Love Poems from the Animal Kingdom, illustrated by Lee Wildish, Alfred A. Knopf (New York, NY), 2011.

A Stick Is an Excellent Thing: Poems Celebrating Outdoor Play, illustrated by LeUyen Pham, Clarion Books (New York, NY), 2012.

Every Day's a Dog's Day, illustrated by Miki Sakamoto, Dutton (New York, NY), 2012.

The Superheroes Employment Agency, illustrated by Noah Z. Jones, Clarion (New York, NY), 2012.

"SAM AND DAVE" MYSTERY SERIES

Leroy Is Missing, illustrated by Judy Glasser, Harper (New York, NY), 1984.

The Case of the Sabotaged School Play, illustrated by Judy Glasser, Harper (New York, NY), 1984.

A Clue in Code, illustrated by Judy Glasser, Harper (New York, NY), 1985.

The Case of the Cackling Car, illustrated by Judy Glasser, Harper (New York, NY), 1985.

The Case of the Fixed Election, illustrated by Richard Williams, Harper (New York, NY), 1989.

The Hoax on You, illustrated by Richard Williams, Harper (New York, NY), 1989.

"SAMANTHA SPAYED" MYSTERY SERIES

The Fido Frame-Up, illustrated by Andrew Glass, Warne (New York, NY), 1983.

A Nose for Trouble, illustrated by Andrew Glass, Holt (New York, NY), 1985.

Where There's a Will, There's a Wag, illustrated by Andrew Glass, Holt (New York, NY), 1986.

YOUNG-ADULT FICTION

No Applause, Please, Dutton (New York, NY), 1977.
The First Few Friends, Harper (New York, NY), 1981.
The Course of True Love Never Did Run Smooth, Harper (New York, NY), 1983.
Horsemaster (fantasy), Atheneum (New York, NY), 1985.
Ghost Host, Harper (New York, NY), 1987.
Several Kinds of Silence, Harper (New York, NY), 1988.
Storm Rising, Scholastic (New York, NY), 1989.
Deal with a Ghost, Holt (New York, NY), 1997.

JUVENILE NONFICTION

Exotic Birds, illustrated by James Needham, Doubleday (New York, NY), 1990.
A Wasp Is Not a Bee, illustrated by Patrick O'Brien, Holt (New York, NY), 1995.
Bottoms Up!, illustrated by Patrick O'Brien, Holt (New York, NY), 1998.
Prairie Dogs Kiss and Lobsters Wave, illustrated by Normand Chartier, Holt (New York, NY), 1998.
A Dog's Gotta Do What a Dog's Gotta Do: Dogs at Work, Holt (New York, NY), 2000.
A Pair of Wings, illustrated by Anne Wertheim, Holiday House, 2001.
Tough Beginnings: How Baby Animals Survive, illustrated by Anna Vojtech, Holt (New York, NY), 2001.
Cats to the Rescue: True Tales of Heroic Felines, illustrated by Jean Cassels, Henry Holt (New York, NY), 2006
Venom, Darby Creek Publishing (Plain City, OH), 2007.
Eggs, illustrated by Emma Stevenson, Holiday House (New York, NY), 2008.
Caterpillars, Early Light Books, 2008.

OTHER

(Editor and author of introduction) *A History of Avant-Garde Cinema,* American Federation of Arts, 1976.
(Editor and contributor) *New American Filmmakers,* American Federation of Arts, 1976.
The Fanatic's Ecstatic, Aromatic Guide to Onions, Garlic, Shallots and Leeks, illustrated by Marian Perry, Prentice-Hall (Englewood Cliffs, NJ), 1981.
(Editor) *Stay True: Short Stories for Strong Girls,* Scholastic (New York, NY), 1998.
(Editor) *I Believe in Water: Twelve Brushes with Religion* (short stories), HarperCollins (New York, NY), 2000.
(Editor) *Face Relations: Eleven Stories about Seeing beyond Color* (short stories), Simon & Schuster (New York, NY), 2004.
(Editor) *Make Me Over: Eleven Stories about Transforming Ourselves* (short stories), Dutton (New York, NY), 2005.

Also author of teacher's guides, catalogs, and program notes on films and filmstrips, including Jacob Bronowski's *The Ascent of Man* and David Attenborough's *The Tribal Eye.* Writer of television scripts for *The Electric Company.* Contributor to books, including *Children's Writers and Illustrators Market,* 2003. Contributor of short stories to books, including *Shattered,* edited by Jennifer Armstrong, Knopf; and *Sport Shorts: Eight Stories about Sports,* edited by Tanya Dean, Darby Creek Publishing. Contributor of poetry to books, including *Food Fight,* edited by Michael J. Rosen; and *Book of Valentine Hearts: Holiday Poetry* and *Oh, No! Where Are My Pants? and Other Disasters: Poems,* both edited by Lee Bennett Hopkins. Contributor to periodicals, including *American Kennel Club Gazette, Archer, Click, Corduroy, Encore, Gyre, Storyworks, Tamesis,* and *Yes.*

Sidelights

Marilyn Singer is a distinguished author of children's books in a wide variety of genres, including fiction and nonfiction picture books, juvenile novels and mysteries, young-adult fantasies, and poetry. Among her many characters are a dog who insists that he is not a dog, an armadillo, a young heart-surgery patient, obsessive Lizzie Silver, Stryker the poltergeist, twin detectives Sam and Dave, and a clever canine detective. Singer's ability to write for so many different audiences has won her critical acclaim as well as a large collection of awards and honors, among them Children's Choice awards, Edgar Allan Poe award nominations for her mysteries, and a Lee Bennett Hopkins Honor designation.

Singer began her writing career creating teaching guides on film and filmstrips. Although she enjoyed the work, she was not entirely satisfied and decided to shift to magazine writing, where some of her poetry was published. Then came a major turning point. Singer was sitting in the Brooklyn Botanic Garden with a pad of paper and a pen in case she was inspired to write a new poem, when she suddenly found herself writing a story instead. With her husband's encouragment, Singer wrote a number of children's stories featuring animals and mailed them off to various publishers. In the meantime, she joined a workshop for unpublished children's authors at Bank Street College and continued writing. A letter from Dutton informing her that they wanted to publish one of her books—*The Dog Who Insisted He Wasn't*—marked the beginning of Singer's career as a children's author.

In *The Dog Who Insisted He Wasn't* Singer tells the story of Konrad, a dog who is absolutely positive that he is not a dog but a person. He is lucky enough to find Abigail, who convinces her family to go along with Konrad's whim and treat him as if he were a human. Konrad sits at the table to eat, takes regular baths in the tub, and even goes to school. When the other dogs in the neighborhood decide that they too want to be treated like people, all chaos breaks loose. A reviewer for the *Bulletin of the Center for Children's Books* praised Singer's portrayal of conversations between animals and humans in *The Dog Who Insisted He Wasn't* and further observed that "the adult-child relationships are exemplary."

Singer often features dogs in her work, including the nonfiction book *A Dog's Gotta Do What a Dog's Gotta Do: Dogs at Work* and the poetry collection *It's Hard to Read a Map with a Beagle on Your Lap.* In another dog-based title, *Chester the Out-of-Work Dog,* a border collie loses his job when he and his family move from their farm to the city. Writing in *Booklist,* Ilene Cooper noted that *Chester the out-of-Work Dog* "has it all—slapstick comedy, a touch of pathos, and an actual story with a beginning, a middle, and an end." Just to balance the scales, Singer also addresses felines in *Cats to the Rescue: True Tales of Heroic Felines,* a picture book illustrated by Jean Cassels that relates several stories about cats who have led exemplary lives—such as a mouser who has kept a Scottish distiller free of an estimated 30,000 rodents. "Written with affection and a bit of amazement," *Cats to the Rescue* "is a pleasure to read," concluded Cooper of the picture book.

Singer's writing for younger children also addresses people and places throughout the world. In *Nine o'Clock Lullaby* she explores what children around the world are doing at the same hour a child in Brooklyn is getting ready for bed. Complemented by the illustrations of Frané Lessac, the book provides a simple introduction to time zones and children of other cultures, as well as serving as a "rhythmic, pleasing lullaby," according to a *Publishers Weekly* critic. Patricia Dooley, writing in *School Library Journal,* praised the way *Nine o'Clock Lullaby* demonstrates "the connectedness of the inhabitants of our global village."

Singer and Lessac again team up for *On the Same Day in March,* a picture-book look at weather in seventeen locations around the globe. For each location, "Singer

Singer introduces young readers to the real-life experiences of young animals in her picture book **Tough Beginnings,** *illustrated by Anna Vojtech.* (Illustration copyright © 2001 by Anna Vojtech. Reproduced by permission.)

provides a few lines of lyrical text that vividly create the climate," noted *Booklist* reviewer Michael Cart, the critic concluding that *On the Same Day in March* "doubles as a delightfully agreeable introduction to both climatology and geography." Jody McCoy, writing in *School Library Journal,* called the same title a "useful and engaging addition." Another collaboration between Singer and Lessac, *Monday on the Mississippi,* takes readers on a trip down the fabled Mississippi river from its source at Lake Itasca, Minnesota, to the Gulf of Mexico.

Young readers are drawn into the land of myth in *The Golden Heart of Winter,* Singer's original folktale about three sons who set off to bring back a prize for their aging father. "The rich prose and haunting illustrations of this original story give it the texture of a folktale," wrote Miriam Martinez in her review for *Language Arts.* In *The Painted Fan* readers are transported to ancient China where a cruel ruler destroys all the fans in the kingdom after a soothsayer tells him a painted fan will be his undoing. Here Singer's story is told with "simplicity and dignity," according to Carolyn Phelan in *Booklist.*

Medieval England serves as the setting of *Maiden on the Moor,* a story about two shepherd brothers who find a young maiden lost on a snowy moor. Donna L. Scanlon, reviewing the picture book in *School Library Journal,* predicted that the tale will "spark imaginations as it transcends ordinary fairy-tale conventions." Scanlon also noted that Singer "knows how to distill words into images, and she conveys the bleak beauty of the setting with clarity and precision." Singer presents another original fairy tale in *The Palace of the Ocean King,* in which traditional roles are reversed: this time it is the maiden who must save the imprisoned young prince.

Young readers enter the bustling streets of multicultural Brooklyn in the pages of *Didi and Daddy on the Promenade,* as an eager preschooler joins her father on a Sunday-morning outing. In contrast, *City Lullaby* brings to life the many layers of sounds that fade from the urban landscape with the coming of night. Shelle Rosenfeld, writing in *Booklist,* commented of *Didi and Daddy on the Promenade* that both young and adult readers will "recognize and enjoy Didi's humorous enthusiasm (and Daddy's good-natured participation) as the walk brings anticipated joys and unexpected surprises." Noting Singer's use of onomatopoeia in *City Lullaby,* Engberg added that the author "writes in infectious, rhyming poetry that scans smoothly to a rapid beat." Also set in Brooklyn, *Block Party Today!* finds a girl letting go of her anger at being left out by her friends in order to enjoy the fun of a neighborhood gathering. "Both text and art beautifully catch the excitement of an event that transforms ho-hum surroundings into a playground," wrote Jennifer Mattson in her review of *Block Party Today!* for *Booklist,* and in *School Library Journal* Genevieve Gallagher deemed Singer's picture book "a fun choice for welcoming summer or for exploring friendships."

A determined young dreamer with high aspirations is the star of Singer's picture book *Tallulah's Tutu.* Tallulah wants to become a ballerina when she grows up, but dance lessons do not get her to her goal fast enough. What she really wants is a tutu, and she wants it now. With the help of her dance teacher, Tallulah learns that valuable things, such as tutus and toe shoes, gain their value because they must be earned. Singer's story captures "the transformative power of discovering a true calling," according to a *Publishers Weekly* contributor, the critic also praising Alexandra Boiger's "sunny" watercolor illustrations. In *School Library Journal* Kris Hickey cited the mix of "rich vocabulary" and "muted, rosy" artwork in *Tallulah's Tutu,* predicting that young readers "will love Tallulah's tenacity and vivaciousness."

From a spunky young dancer, Singer shifts her focus to a freewheeling yellow school bus in *I'm Your Bus.* Illustrated in digital art by Evan Polenghi that combines heavy black, free-drawn lines with splashes of bright color, *I'm Your Bus* follows a busy school bus on its daily rounds, collecting children on its route to school, then patiently waiting until it is time to open its doors outside the school building and retrieve them when the closing bell rings. Singer captures the thoughts and feelings of the bus in "short lines that read with the rhythm and bounce of a chant," explained Engberg, making *I'm Your Bus* a good choice for storyhour sharing. In *Kirkus Reviews* a contributor recommended Singer's upbeat story as a "top-notch" "reassurance for newly minted kindergartners" who are nervous about their first school-bus ride.

Another worry-producing element of childhood, the trip to the doctor, is addressed in *I'm Getting a Checkup,* as Singer's reassuring rhymes are paired with illustrations by David Milgrim. Presenting what *School Library Journal* contributor Lynn K. Vanca characterized as a "clear, informative" explanation about those dreaded visits to the pediatrician, *I'm Getting a Checkup* also features additional text that describes well-child exams in reassuring detail. "Prescribe this child-centered offering to all nervous young patients," suggested a *Kirkus*

Ken Robbins creates the luminous and detailed artwork for Singer's nature-themed picture book Fireflies at Midnight. (Illustration copyright © 2003 by Ken Robbins. Reproduced by permission of Atheneum Books for Young Readers, an imprint of Simon & Schuster Children's Publishing Division.)

Reviews writer, the critic adding that the smiling characters in Milgrim's cartoon paintings—along with a playful group of rabbits—"add comfort and warmth to the potentially anxiety-producing subject."

In addition to picture books, Singer has also produced a wide array of nonfiction works for young readers. In *Exotic Birds* she provides a "fact-filled but readable introduction" to the subject, according to *Booklist* contributor Leone McDermott. Ellen Dibner, reviewing the same title in *School Library Journal,* concluded that *Exotic Birds* is a "most satisfying book for browsing, general information, and exotic bird watching." Other flying creatures are dealt with in *A Wasp Is Not a Bee* and *A Pair of Wings,* while bird growth is the subject of the simply titled *Eggs.* Illustrated with color photographs, *Venom* introduces children to the many creatures that release poison when they sting, stab, bite, or spit—and some that release poison when a predator bites them. Describing *Eggs* as "handsome" due to its artwork by Emma Stevenson, Phelan added that Singer's "smoothly written . . . text creates an even, almost conversational flow from page to page." Moving close to the ground, *Venom* ranges from pond to forest, profiling spiders, snakes, and other creatures that defend and attack using poisons. "Browsers . . . will enthusiastically dig their teeth into this substantial survey," concluded John Peters in his review of Singer's detailed look at the darker side of nature.

Some of Singer's nonfiction titles came about because she was annoyed: "When I heard one too many folks call a wasp a 'bee,' a gorilla a 'monkey,' and even a heron a 'duck,' I got bugged enough to write *A Wasp Is Not a Bee,*" she explained in an article for *School Library Journal.* "Then there was the time at the Prospect Park Zoo when a little boy asked his mom why baboons have such big red butts. Despite a series of placards explaining the reason for these simian endowments, the mother loudly replied, 'Because they're sick.' Instead of howling at her, I came up with *Bottoms Up!: A Book about Rear Ends.*" Focusing on animal anatomy, *Bottoms Up!* was described as a "cheerful book about behinds and their uses" by *Booklist* reviewer Ilene Cooper. In *Prairie Dogs Kiss and Lobsters Wave,* Singer shows how animals greet one another. The book, according to *Booklist* contributor Hazel Rochman, is noteworthy for its "friendly, immediate text and active, colorful pictures."

Of her several poetry books for young readers, Singer's personal favorite is the award-winning *Turtle in July,* "a lovely picture book of poetry that moves through the seasons," according to Janet Hickman in *Language Arts.* Nancy Vasilakis, reviewing *Turtle in July* for *Horn Book,* reported that Singer and noted illustrator Jerry Pinkney create a "vivid picture book that is visually as well as auditorily pleasing," and that Singer's use of the first person "captures the essence of each animal."

Fireflies at Midnight has been considered a companion title to *Turtle in July* by several critics. Set over the course of a single day, *Fireflies at Midnight* features poems on the various animals that live near a pond, beginning with the robin who wakes earliest in the morning, stopping to visit a lordly frog, and continuing on until midnight when the fireflies are encountered. *Fireflies at Midnight* "is well suited for storytime," advised Marge Loch-Wouters in *School Library Journal,* and *Booklist* reviewer Gillian Engberg commented that "Singer clearly imagines the voices and personalities of familiar animals in exuberant lines." A *Kirkus Reviews* critic cited the book for featuring "luminous poems that will stand the test of time."

With Meilo So as her illustrator, Singer has produced three inter-related poetry collections: *Footprints on the Roof: Poems about Earth, How to Cross a Pond: Poems about Water,* and *Central Heating: Poems about Fire and Warmth. Footprints on the Roof* features nineteen poems dealing with various topics about the Earth, from volcanoes and mud to burrows and trees. Although So's illustrations make the collection accessible for a younger audience, Engberg recommended the title to "middle-school and teen writers," and Kathleen Whalin called *Footprints on the Roof* "a welcome addition to nature-poetry collections." *How to Cross a Pond* focuses on watery topics ranging from oceans to tears, discussing how dearly water is valued when it is hard to get in poems such as "Wells." Hazel Rochman reviewed the collection for *Booklist* and wrote that, "never pretentious, [Singer] . . . celebrates the physical joy of splashing . . . as well as the wonder of the rain forest." *Central Heating* covers birthday candles, marshmallow roasts, and a fire that destroys an old, abandoned house. "Its engaging design will surely entice readers to open and read," noted a contributor in appraising *Central Heating* for *Kirkus Reviews.*

Unlike Singer's environmentally focused verse collections, *Creature Carnival* covers animals that are anything but natural. Featuring monsters and other creatures from myth, legend, and popular movies, the poet introduces new readers to famous monsters such as the Pegasus of Greek mythology and Godzilla of monster-movie fame. "The poems will bring appreciative smiles from readers who know the stories," assured Kathleen Whalin in *School Library Journal,* noting that unfamiliar readers can use a glossary in the back of *Creature Carnival* to identify each monster. Although Engberg cautioned in *Booklist* that, even with the glossary, some references "may fly over kids' heads," she concluded that the book serves up "a playful collection of shivery delights." A *Kirkus Reviews* critic predicted that Singer's "attention-getting menagerie will have readers and listeners sitting on the edges—and probably falling out—of their seats." *Creature Carnival* was named a Lee Bennett Hopkins Poetry Award honor book.

In *Mirror Mirror: A Book of Reversible Verse* Singer introduces readers to an intriguing poetic form of her own invention: a "reversos," in which one meaning is derived by reading from the top of the page to the bottom, while another is gleaned from reading from the bottom of the page to the top. Each of the book's fourteen

Singer's award-winning poetry collection **Mirror Mirror** *features colorful, stylized artwork by Josée Masse.* (Illustration copyright © 2010 by Josee Masse. Reproduced by permission of Dutton Children's Books, a division of Penguin Young Readers Group, a member of Penguin Group (USA) Inc., 345 Hudson Street, New York, NY 10014. All rights reserved.)

reversos is inspired by a fairy story—from "Goldilocks" to "Cinderella" to Hans Christian Andersen's "The Ugly Duckling"—and is accompanied by a colorful illustration by artist Josée Masse. Dubbing the format "ingenious," Patricia Austin added in *Booklist* that readers are also encouraged "to write their own reversos on any topic," and Joan Kindig praised *Mirror Mirror* as "a remarkably clever and versatile book" that would be a perfect fit for language-arts curricula in the upper elementary grades. In *A Stick Is an Excellent Thing: Poems Celebrating Outdoor Play,* illustrated by LeUyen

Pham, the poet continues to explore the many uses for verse, this time creating poems that capture the fun of simple childhood games. Illustrator Miki Sakamoto creates the canine-filled art that brings to life Singer's engaging poems in yet another poetry collection, *Every Day's a Dog's Day.*

Singer's first middle-grade novel, *It Can't Hurt Forever,* recounts a trauma she experienced as a child. In this fictionalized version of her experience, Ellie Simon is to enter the hospital for corrective heart surgery. Unlike Singer, however, Ellie is told what is going to happen to her, with the exception of the catheterization she must undergo. When she learns about it, she argues with the doctors and her parents, just as Singer wished she had done. Singer "provides an honest and thorough look at pre-and post-operative care and at the concerns of a girl facing a major trauma," pointed out Karen Harris in *School Library Journal*. A *Kirkus Reviews* contributor concluded that *It Can't Hurt Forever* is "sharp, fast, funny, genuinely serious, and helpfully informative."

Singer's other books for middle-grade children include two novels about the obsessions of a young girl named Lizzie Silver. *Tarantulas on the Brain* has ten-year-old Lizzie doing everything she can to earn enough money to buy a pet tarantula. She tries having a junk sale and even works as a magician's assistant to get the necessary money, lying to her mother about what she is doing. In the end, her secret desire and activities are discovered and everyone is much more sympathetic than Lizzie imagined they would be. The pace of *Tarantulas on the Brain* "is fast and exciting; the characters are sufficiently quirky to keep the readers engrossed and narrator Lizzie Silver . . . wins their affections," asserted a *Publishers Weekly* reviewer. In the sequel to *Tarantulas on the Brain*, *Lizzie Silver of Sherwood Forest*, Lizzie's new preoccupations include her desires to be one of Robin Hood's merry followers and to learn how to play the harp so she can attend the same music school as her best friend. *Lizzie Silver of Sherwood Forest* is a "funny, touching sequel," stated another *Publishers Weekly* contributor, adding: "This is an adroitly balanced and enjoyable tale about a naive and eager girl."

A fantasy novel for younger readers, *Charmed* introduces Miranda, a twelve year old with an active imagination. The girl travels to worlds around the galaxy in a quest to collect the "Correct Combination": a group of characters who must unite to destroy an evil being known as the Charmer. Besides Miranda and a humanoid named Iron Dog, the group includes Bastable, Miranda's invisible feline friend; Rattus, a clever rodent; and the wise cobra-goddess Naja the Ever-Changing. The fact that these characters manage to work together even though some of them represent animals that are natural enemies was appreciated by *Voice of Youth Advocates* contributor Jennifer Langlois, who stated that the plot of *Charmed* is "a good way to show young people that just because someone is different doesn't mean they are bad." Sally Estes declared in *Booklist* that in *Charmed* "the various worlds created by Singer are fascinating," and *School Library Journal* reviewer Susan L. Rogers lauded the fantasy's "somewhat surprising and quite satisfying conclusion."

Other middle-grade and juvenile novels by Singer include *Twenty Ways to Lose Your Best Friend, California Demon, Big Wheel, Josie to the Rescue,* and *The Circus Lunicus.* Rosie Rivera opens up the wrong bottle in her mother's magic shop and unleashes a genie in *California Demon,* a book in which "humor keeps the story buoyant, magic gives it sparkle," according to Kathryn Jennings in *Bulletin of the Center for Children's Books.* Wheel Wiggins, a leader of a gang, is trying to organize a Fourth of July Carnival, but is running into problems from a rival in *Big Wheel,* a "surefire story from a popular author," as a writer for *Kirkus Reviews* noted.

More magic and fantasy is served up in *The Circus Lunicus* when young Solly's toy lizard turns into a fairy godmother and helps teach him some home truths about himself, his supposedly dead mother, and his evil stepmother and siblings. "This loony, fast-paced mystery-fantasy . . . is full of surprises and clever plot twists," observed Cart in *Booklist,* "and it's as much fun as a three-ring circus." A *Kirkus Reviews* critic described *The Circus Lunicus* as "luminous and humorous."

Mysteries and young-adult fantasy novels are also among Singer's writings. Her "Sam and Dave" series stars a pair of twins who solve mysteries, some set in school, some further afield. *A Clue in Code* has the young detectives in search of the thief who stole the class trip money. When the obvious suspect insists that he is innocent, Sam and Dave embark on an investigation. "Singer's ability to subtly incorporate the necessary facts of the case into the narrative demonstrates her respect for young readers eager for satisfying mysteries they can solve on their own," pointed out a *Booklist* reviewer.

Elements of the supernatural are introduced into Singer's young-adult novel *Ghost Host.* Bart Hawkins seems to have an ideal life—he is the quarterback of the high school football team and dates Lisa, the captain of the cheerleading squad. Bart secretly loves to read, though, and he fears that if this gets out he will be labeled a nerd. When he discovers that his new house is haunted by a nasty spirit, his life is thrown into chaos and he must enlist the help of a friendly ghost and the class brain to pacify the poltergeist. Ghosts are also at the center of *Deal with a Ghost* as fifteen-year-old Delia thinks she is terribly sophisticated until she comes face to face with a spectre who knows her name. "*Ghost Host* is above all else fun to read," maintained Randy Brough in *Voice of Youth Advocates,* while in *Booklist* critic Chris Sherman described *Deal with a Ghost* as "fast-paced" and "engrossing."

Singer also addresses older teen readers in *Several Kinds of Silence,* which tackles the theme of prejudice when young Franny falls in love with a Japanese boy. Another novel, *Storm Rising,* tells an inter-generational tale of lonely Storm, who finds comfort with an older woman who possesses unusual powers. In *The Course of True Love Never Did Run Smooth* the author focuses on longtime friends Becky and Nemi as their costarring roles in a high-school production of *A Midsummer Night's Dream* transform their relationship into one that is more sexually charged. "Singer neatly uses Shakespeare's comedic mix-up as a foil for the tangled web woven by her teenage protagonists," noted Estes in a *Booklist* review of the novel. Highlighting Singer's writing style, *Bulletin of the Center for Children's Book* reviewer Zena Sutherland found much merit in *The Course of True Love Never Did Run Smooth*, noting that "the minor characters are sharply defined [and] the familial relations are strongly drawn, with perceptive treatment of the dynamics of the acting group and especially of its gay members."

In addition to her many book-length works, Singer has edited several volumes of short stories for young-adult readers, including *Stay True: Short Stories for Young Girls, I Believe in Water: Twelve Brushes with Religion,* and *Make Me Over: Eleven Original Stories about Transforming Ourselves.* Calling Singer "an experienced anthologist," *Booklist* contributor Cindy Dobrez characterized *Make Me Over* as a "diverse, solid group of stories" featuring young people who use adolescence as a time to recreate some aspect of their life to change their future. "Every story is a winner," asserted a *Kirkus Reviews* writer, the critic praising Singer for choosing contributors on the order of Margaret Peterson Haddix and Joyce Sweeney.

Reflecting her own desire for social change, Singer also donated the proceeds from the sale of her anthology *Face Relations: Eleven Stories about Seeing beyond Color* to the Southern Poverty Law Center's Teaching Tolerance project. Featuring stories by such well-known authors as M.E. Kerr, Rita Williams-Garcia, Jess Mowry, and Naomi Shihab Nye, *Face Relations* focuses on young people striving to overcome racial differences while building a relationship with another. While commenting that some pieces in the collection are stronger than others, a critic for *Kirkus Reviews* commented that the best stories "will engage teens point blank, though all will be appreciated in a classroom setting." Kathleen Isaacs, in her *School Library Journal* review, also commented on the educational value of *Face Relations*, noting that the stories "raise questions that could lead to good classroom discussion." According to a *Publishers Weekly* reviewer, the stories offer "upbeat conclusions and an even balance of funny and sad moments" and produce a book that is "as much about appreciating color as it is about looking beyond it."

Biographical and Critical Sources

BOOKS

Authors of Books for Young People, 3rd edition, edited by Martha E. Ward, Scarecrow Press (Metuchen, NJ), 1990.

Children's Literature Review, Volume 48, Gale (Detroit, MI), 1998.

St. James Guide to Young Adult Writers, 2nd edition, edited by Tom Pendergast and Sara Pendergast, St. James (Detroit, MI), 1999.

PERIODICALS

Booklist, May 15, 1983, Sally Estes, review of *The Course of True Love Never Did Run Smooth,* p. 1197; September 15, 1985, review of *A Clue in Code,* p. 140; January 1, 1991, Sally Estes, review of *Charmed,* p. 922; February 1, 1991, Leone McDermott, review of *Exotic Birds,* pp. 1126-1127; October 15, 1992, Ilene Cooper, review of *Chester the Out-of-Work Dog,* p. 425; May 1, 1994, Carolyn Phelan, review of *The Painted Fan,* p. 1609; June 1, 1997, Chris Sherman, review of *Deal with a Ghost,* pp. 1686-1687; March 15, 1998, Ilene Cooper, review of *Bottoms Up!,* pp. 1242-1243; December 1, 1998, Hazel Rochman, review of *Prairie Dogs Kiss and Lobsters Wave,* p. 681; February 15, 2000, Michael Cart, review of *On the Same Day in March: A Tour of the World's Weather,* p. 1116; December 1, 2000, Michael Cart, review of *The Circus Lunicus,* p. 708; April 1, 2001, Shelle Rosenfeld, review of *Didi and Daddy on the Promenade,* p. 1480; March 15, 2002, Gillian Engberg, review of *Footprints on the Roof: Poems about the Earth,* p. 1250, Stephanie Zvirin, review of *Quiet Night,* p. 1264; November 15, 2002, John Peters, review of *The Company of Crows: A Book of Poems,* p. 606; April 1, 2003, Gillian Engberg, review of *Fireflies at Midnight,* p. 1408; August, 2003, Hazel Rochman, review of *How to Cross a Pond: Poems about Water,* pp. 1975-1976; April 1, 2004, Gillian Engberg, review of *Creature Carnival,* p. 1367; May 15, 2004, Jennifer Mattson, review of *Block Party Today!,* p. 1627; December 1, 2004, Hazel Rochman, review of *Central Heating: Poems about Fire and Warmth,* p. 650; September 15, 2005, Cindy Dobrez, review of *Make Me Over: Eleven Original Stories about Transforming Ourselves,* p. 60; September 15, 2006, Ilene Cooper, review of *Cats to the Rescue: True Tales of Heroic Felines,* p. 62; December 15, 2006, Carolyn Phelan, review of *Let's Build a Clubhouse,* p. 52; October 1, 2007, John Peters, review of *Venom,* p. 58; October 15, 2007, Gillian Engberg, review of *City Lullaby,* p. 51; April 1, 2008, Carolyn Phelan, review of *Eggs,* p. 52; October 15, 2008, Randall Enos, review of *First Food Fight This Fall and Other School Poems,* p. 45; July 1, 2009, Gillian Engberg, review of *I'm Your Bus,* p. 66; January 1, 2010, Patricia Austin, review of *Mirror Mirror: A Book of Reversible Verse,* p. 81; February 15, 2011, Carolyn Phelan, review of *Tallulah's Tutu,* p. 79.

Bulletin of the Center for Children's Books, January, 1977, review of *The Dog Who Insisted He Wasn't,* p. 82; May, 1983, Zena Sutherland, review of *The Course of True Love Never Did Run Smooth,* p. 179; February, 1993, Kathryn Jennings, review of *California Demon,* p. 191.

Horn Book, January-February, 1990, Nancy Vasilakis, review of *Turtle in July,* pp. 82-83; January-February, 2008, Sarah Ellis, review of *City Lullaby,* p. 79; May-

June, 2008, Danielle J. Ford, review of *Eggs,* p. 341; March-April, 2010, Roger Sutton, review of *Mirror Mirror,* p. 79.

Kirkus Reviews, October 15, 1978, review of *It Can't Hurt Forever,* p. 1140; December 1, 1993, review of *Big Wheel,* p. 1529; September 15, 2000, review of *The Circus Lunicus;* January 15, 2002, review of *Footprints on the Roof,* p. 110; April 1, 2002, reviews of *Quiet Night,* pp. 498-499, and *Boo Hoo Boo-Boo,* p. 579; August 15, 2002, review of *The Company of Crows,* p. 1237; March 15, 2003, review of *Fireflies at Midnight,* p. 479; July 1, 2003, review of *How to Cross a Pond,* p. 915; February 15, 2004, review of *Creature Carnival,* p. 185; April 15, 2004, review of *Block Party Today!,* p. 401; May 1, 2004, review of *Face Relations,* p. 449; December 15, 2004, review of *Central Heating,* p. 1207; March 15, 2005, review of *Monday on the Mississippi,* p. 358; August 15, 2005, review of *Make Me Over,* p. 922; September 15, 2007, review of *Venom;* June 1, 2009, review of *I'm Your Bus;* August 1, 2009, review of *I'm Getting a Checkup.*

Language Arts, April, 1990, Janet Hickman, review of *Turtle in July,* pp. 430-431; January, 1992, Miriam Martinez, review of *The Golden Heart of Winter,* p. 67.

Publishers Weekly, July 9, 1982, review of *Tarantulas on the Brain,* p. 49; June 27, 1986, review of *Lizzie Silver of Sherwood Forest,* pp. 91-92; March 1, 1991, review of *Nine o'Clock Lullaby,* p. 72; January 24, 2000, review of *On the Same Day in March,* p. 311; February 25, 2002, review of *Quiet Night,* p. 64; August 19, 2002, review of *The Company of Crows,* p. 89; July 12, 2004, review of *Face Relations,* p. 65; November 12, 2007, review of *City Lullaby,* p. 54; June 9, 2008, review of *Shoe Bop!,* p. 50; November 8, 2010, review of *Mirror Mirror,* p. 31; January 10, 2011, review of *Tallulah's Tutu,* p. 49.

School Library Journal, September, 1978, Karen Harris, review of *It Can't Hurt Forever,* p. 149; August, 1983, Joan McGrath, review of *The Course of True Love Never Did Run Smooth,* p. 80; December, 1990, Susan L. Rogers, review of *Charmed,* p. 111; June, 1991, Ellen Dibner, review of *Exotic Birds,* p. 120; July, 1991, Patricia Dooley, review of *Nine o'Clock Lullaby,* p. 64; April, 1995, Donna L. Scanlon, review of *The Maiden on the Moor,* p. 146; April, 2000, Jody McCoy, review of *On the Same Day in March,* p. 126; July, 2000, p. 87; March, 2002, Catherine Threadgill, review of *Quiet Night,* p. 204; May, 2002, Kathleen Whalin, review of *Footprints on the Roof,* p. 144; January, 2003, Marilyn Singer, "Nurturing Wonder," pp. 42-43; May, 2003, Marge Loch-Wouters, review of *Fireflies at Midnight,* p. 142; August, 2003, Sally R. Dow, review of *How to Cross a Pond,* p. 152; April, 2004, Kathleen Whalin, review of *Creature Carnival,* p. 142; May, 2004, Genevieve Gallagher, review of *Block Party Today!,* p. 124; June, 2004, Kathleen Isaacs, review of *Face Relations,* p. 150; September, 2004, Marilyn Singer, "A Blast of Poetry," pp. 41-42; January, 2005, Lee Bock, review of *Central Heating,* p. 156; November, 2006, Kara Schaff Dean, review of *Cats to the Rescue,* p. 164; December, 2006, Nancy Silverrod, review of *Let's Build a Clubhouse,* p. 116;

July, 2008, Kathleen Kelly MacMillan, review of *Shoe Bop!,* p. 92; October, 2008, Sally R. Dow, review of *First Food Fight This Fall and Other School Poems,* p. 137; November, 2009, Lynn K. Singer, review of *I'm Getting a Checkup,* p. 97; January, 2010, Joan Kindig, review of *Mirror Mirror,* p. 90; March, 2011, Kris Hickey, review of *Tallulah's Tutu,* p. 134; April, 2011, Lauralyn Persson, review of *Twosomes: Love Poems from the Animal Kingdom,* p. 164.

Voice of Youth Advocates, June, 1987, Randy Brough, review of *Ghost Host,* p. 83; December, 1990, Jennifer Langlois, review of *Charmed,* p. 32.

ONLINE

Marilyn Singer Home Page, http://www.marilynsinger.net (October 21, 2011).*

*　　　*　　　*

SKINNER, Daphne
See SPINNER, Stephanie

*　　　*　　　*

SMITH, Wendy
See FRENCH, Wendy

*　　　*　　　*

SPINNER, Stephanie 1943-
(Daphne Skinner)

Personal

Born November 16, 1943, in Davenport, IA; daughter of Ralph (in business) and Edna Spinner. *Education:* Bennington College, B.A., 1964. *Hobbies and other interests:* Horses, painting, traveling.

Addresses

Home—Sherman, CT.

Career

Writer and editor. Former children's book editor in New York, NY; worked as a thangka painter for several years.

Member

Authors Guild.

Awards, Honors

Texas Bluebonnet Award, 1991, for *Aliens for Breakfast;* Sydney Taylor Award Notable Book designation, Association of Jewish Libraries, and Notable Social Studies Trade Books for Young People selection, National Council for the Social Studies/Children's Book Council, both c. 2003, both for *It's a Miracle!*

Writings

Water Skiing and Surfboarding, Golden Press (New York, NY), 1968.

First Aid, Golden Press (New York, NY), 1968.

(Adaptor) *Popeye: The Storybook Based on the Movie,* Random House (New York, NY), 1980.

(Adaptor) *Dracula,* illustrated by Jim Spence, Random House (New York, NY), 1982, reprinted, 2005.

Raggedy Ann and Andy and How Raggedy Ann Was Born, Bobbs-Merrill (Indianapolis, IN), 1982.

(Adaptor) Carlo Lorenzini, *The Adventures of Pinocchio,* illustrated by Diane Goode, Random House (New York, NY), 1983.

The Mummy's Tomb, Bantam (New York, NY), 1985.

(With Jonathan Etra) *Aliens for Breakfast,* illustrated by Steve Björkman, Random House (New York, NY), 1988.

(With Jonathan Etra) *Aliens for Lunch,* illustrated by Steve Björkman, Random House (New York, NY), 1991.

Little Sure Shot: The Story of Annie Oakley, illustrated by Jose Miralles, Random House (New York, NY), 1993.

Aliens for Dinner, Random House (New York, NY), 1994.

(With Ellen Weiss) *Gerbilitis,* illustrated by Steve Björkman, HarperCollins (New York, NY), 1996.

(With Ellen Weiss) *Sing, Elvis, Sing,* illustrated by Steve Björkman, HarperCollins (New York, NY), 1996.

(With Ellen Weiss) *Born to Be Wild,* illustrated by Steve Björkman, HarperCollins (New York, NY), 1997.

(With Ellen Weiss) *Bright Lights, Little Gerbil,* illustrated by Steve Björkman, HarperCollins (New York, NY), 1997.

(With Ellen Weiss) *The Bird Is the Word,* illustrated by Steve Björkman, HarperCollins (New York, NY), 1997.

(With Ellen Weiss) *We're Off to See the Lizard,* illustrated by Steve Björkman, HarperCollins (New York, NY), 1998.

Snake Hair: The Story of Medusa, illustrated by Susan Swan, Grosset & Dunlap (New York, NY), 1999.

The Magic of Merlin, illustrated by Valerie Sokolova, Golden Books (New York, NY), 2000.

(With Terry Bisson) *Be First in the Universe,* Delacorte (New York, NY), 2000.

(Adaptor) Margaret Landon, *Anna and the King,* illustrated by Margaret Ayer, HarperTrophy (New York, NY), 2000.

Monster in the Maze: The Story of the Minotaur, illustrated by Susan Swan, Grosset & Dunlap (New York, NY), 2000.

(With Terry Bisson) *Expiration Date: Never,* Delacorte (New York, NY), 2001.

King Arthur's Courage, illustrated by Valerie Sokolova, Golden Books (New York, NY), 2002.

Who Was Annie Oakley?, Penguin Putnam (New York, NY), 2002.

Quiver, Knopf (New York, NY), 2002.

It's a Miracle!: A Hanukkah Storybook, illustrated by Jill McElmurry, Atheneum (New York, NY), 2003.

Quicksilver, Knopf (New York, NY), 2005.

Damosel: In Which the Lady of the Lake Renders a Frank and Often Startling Account of Her Wondrous Life and Times, Knopf (New York, NY), 2008.

Uno: Blue-ribbon Beagle, Grosset & Dunlap (New York, NY), 2008.

(Reteller) *The Nutcracker* (included audio CD), illustrated by Peter Malone, Knopf (New York, NY), 2008.

Paddywack, illustrated by Daniel Howarth, Random House (New York, NY), 2010.

Alex the Parrot, illustrated by Meile So, Knopf (New York, NY), 2012.

EDITOR

Rock Is Beautiful: An Anthology of American Lyrics, 1953-1968, Dell (New York, NY), 1969.

Feminine Plural: Stories by Women about Growing Up, Macmillan (New York, NY), 1972.

Live and Learn: Stories about Students and Their Teachers, Macmillan (New York, NY), 1973.

Motherlove: Stories by Women about Motherhood, Dell (New York, NY), 1978.

UNDER NAME DAPHNE SKINNER

Raggedy Ann Gets Lost, illustrated by Cathy Beylon, Random House (New York, NY), 1987.

Jim Henson's Muppets in I'm Sorry!: A Book about Apologizing, illustrated by Joel Schick, Grolier (Danbury, CT), 1993.

(Adaptor) *Tim Burton's Nightmare before Christmas* (novelization of film), Hyperion (New York, NY), 1993.

(Adaptor) *The Santa Clause* (novelization of film), Hyperion (New York, NY), 1994.

(Adaptor) *The Aventures of Stuart Little* (novelization of film), HarperTrophy (New York, NY), 1999.

Tightwad Tod, illustrated by John Nez, Kane Press (New York, NY), 2001.

Henry Keeps Score, illustrated by Page Eastburn O'Rourke, Kane Press (New York, NY), 2001.

Almost Invisible Irene, illustrated by Jerry Smath, Kane Press (New York, NY), 2003.

Palapalooza, illustrated by Jerry Smath, Kane Press (New York, NY), 2006.

All Aboard!, illustrated by Jerry Smath, Kane Press (New York, NY), 2007.

"MY SIDE OF THE STORY" SERIES; UNDER NAME DAPHNE SKINNER

Cinderella/Lady Tremaine, Disney Press (New York, NY), 2003.

Snow White/The Queen, Disney Press (New York, NY), 2003.

The Little Mermaid/Ursula, Disney Press (New York, NY), 2004.

101 Dalmatians/Cruella de Vil, Disney Press (New York, NY), 2005.

Sidelights

A talented and versatile writer, Stephanie Spinner is the author of *Be First in the Universe, Quicksilver,* and *It's a Miracle!: A Hanukkah Storybook.* Spinner, a former children's book editor who has worked with such notables as Robin McKinley, and Garth Nix, first gained recognition for her popular "Aliens" series of chapter books, coauthored with Jonathan Etra. *Aliens for Breakfast* centers on Richard Bickerstaff, a youngster who discovers Aric, a creature from the planet Ganoob, in his cereal. "The plot is simple but satisfying," Sharron McElmeel observed in *School Library Journal.* The adventures of Richard and Aric continue in *Aliens for Lunch* and *Aliens for Dinner.*

Spinner's success with the "Aliens" trilogy led to a collaborative project with Ellen Weiss about a clever gerbil named Weebie. The "Weebie Zone" books began in 1996 with *Gerbilitis* and followed the travails of Weebie, the third-grade classroom pet who is taken home for the summer by a boy named Garth. Angered one day when he feels that Garth is neglecting him, Weebie

Stephanie Spinner chooses a perennially popular subject among young girls—horses—for **Paddywack,** *a story featuring artwork by Daniel Howarth.* (Illustration copyright © 2010 by Daniel Howarth. Reproduced by permission of Random House Children's Books, a division of Random House, Inc.)

bites the boy on the hand, and the injury gives Garth the ability to communicate with Weebie. Even Garth's cat, who wants to eat Weebie, joins in on their conversations. During that summer, when Garth's family goes camping, he is able to talk to a friendly bear that he meets in the woods. Stressed because of his parents' squabbles, Garth acquiesces to Weebie's idea: the bear will "attack" the campsite, which works in reconciling the parents.

Garth's ability to talk with animals continues in *Sing, Elvis, Sing.* This story involves a dog named Elvis, which is owned by Garth's aunt, and his dreams of achieving stardom for his ability to "sing" the national anthem. "Readers will delight in the light-hearted humor in *Sing, Elvis, Sing,* noted *Booklist* critic Shelley Townsend-Hudson. The "Weebie Zone" series continues through several more titles, including *Born to Be Wild,* which finds Weebie going along on another family vacation, this one in Maine, where he and Garth must rescue Ding Dong, a rabbit who has run away from its adoring owner. *School Library Journal* critic Jody McCoy called Spinner and Weiss's story "an entertaining, quick read."

Spinner teamed up with noted author Terry Bisson for *Be First in the Universe,* a comic science-fiction tale about the adventures of twins Tessa and Todd. One day, they visit their local mall on an errand and by walking backwards find a mysterious new store. "Gemini Jack's U Rent All" sells fascinating gadgets, such as the Fib Muncher, which beeps when someone tells a lie. Readers learn that Jack is really an alien and has set up shop on Earth in order to steal a DNA sample from human twins. Tessa and Todd are not ruthless enough for his needs, however, but when the twins take Jack's electronic pet to school, it is stolen. Their sleuthing leads them to the Gneiss twins, who are suitably unsound enough for Jack's purpose. They deliver the necessary DNA and in turn are injected with something that makes them nicer. A *Kirkus Reviews* contributor termed *Be First in the Universe* "an amusing, satisfying caper."

Spinner and Bisson reunited to write a sequel, *Expiration Date: Never,* which finds Tessa and Todd again working with Jack. At the mall, the twins meet Nigel Throbber, a famous rock drummer who claims that he is desperate for some peace from his fans. When Jack sprays "Fame Ban" on Nigel, it makes him anonymous, but Nigel then becomes depressed. A secondary plot involves the mysterious behavior of some goats belonging to Tessa and Todd's hippie grandparents. Critiquing *Expiration Date: Never* in *Booklist,* GraceAnne A. DeCandido stated that "a daft and deft mixture of mall culture, [science-fiction] tropes, and flower-child references bedazzle." "The characters are zany, yet believable; real, yet surreal," wrote *School Library Journal* critic Kay Bowes in her review of the same novel.

In *Snake Hair: The Story of Medusa* Spinner retells the Greek myth about a woman who was frightening in appearance because of her tresses, which were made of serpents. Here the author "does an excellent job," noted *Booklist* critic Ilene Cooper, the reviewer praising Spinner for translating the tale and "keeping all its exciting moments." In *Quiver,* Spinner offers her version of the legend of Atalanta. Abandoned as an infant by her father, King Iasus, Atalanta is rescued by Artemis, goddess of the hunt, and she develops into a skilled archer and swift runner. When the dying king demands that Atalanta marry and produce an heir to the throne, she instead offers a challenge: she will only wed the suitor who can outrun her, and those who fail will be put to death. "Spinner comes to this ancient story with respect for the traditional tales and with a somber language that seems fitting," Claire Rosser observed in *Kliatt,* and Angela J. Reynolds, commenting in *School Library Journal* that the novel's "setting is well done, putting readers easily into the ancient world, and the language is refreshingly unmodern."

Spinner retells the myth of Persephone and Demeter, Perseus's battle with Medusa, and several stories from the Trojan War in *Quicksilver,* a tale narrated by Hermes, the messenger god also known as Mercury. "Spinner gives these ancient tales a lively spin without inventing major new events or characters for them," a contributor noted in *Kirkus Reviews.* Other reviewers complimented the author's use of an engaging narrator to recount the myths. "Teens will connect with Hermes' immediate, often very funny voice," predicted Gillian Engberg in *Booklist,* and *Horn Book* reviewer Deirdre F. Baker similarly noted that "smart-aleck irony mixed with charm makes the god's account a memorable, entertaining avenue into Greek mythology."

Spinner explores Arthurian legend in *Damosel: In Which the Lady of the Lake Renders a Frank and Often Startling Account of Her Wondrous Life and Times.* A gifted metalworker, Damosel creates the sword Excalibur for Arthur, the future king, at the request of the magician Merlin. Damosel also agrees to serve as Arthur's protector, although this task grows complicated when she falls in love with Sir Pelleas. Interspersed with Damosel's narrative is the story of Twixt, Arthur's jester, "who offers a more intimate and gritty picture of court life," according to Beth L. Meister in *School Library Journal. Booklist* contributor Anne O'Malley offered praise for *Damosel,* remarking that Spinner's "strong characterizations, energetic dialogue, and lively plot combine in a memorable, accessible novel."

Spinner has also written several books for younger children. *It's a Miracle!* focuses on six-year-old Owen, who serves as his family's O.C.L (Official Candle Lighter) during the holiday season. Each night, as he performs his task, Owen is treated to a humorous story featuring a cast of intriguing characters who sound suspiciously like his relatives. In her *School Library Journal* review fo the book, Mara Alpert reported that "children will enjoy the silliness of Grandma's fanciful, zany family stories." In *The Nutcracker* Spinner presents a retelling of E.T.A. Hoffmann's classic 1816 tale,

offering a detailed summary of the plot of the beloved ballet. Her "smoothly written story introduces all the major characters and dancers," according to a contributor in *Kirkus Reviews.*

Biographical and Critical Sources

PERIODICALS

Booklist, February 1, 1994, Ilene Cooper, review of *Little Sure Shot: The Story of Annie Oakley,* p. 1013; January 1, 1997, Shelley Townsend-Hudson, reviews of *Gerbilitis* and *Sing, Elvis, Sing!,* both p. 862; December 1, 1999, Ilene Cooper, review of *Snake Hair: The Story of Medusa,* p. 716; August, 2001, GraceAnne A. DeCandido, review of *Expiration Date: Never,* p. 2122; January 1, 2003, Gillian Engberg, review of *Quiver,* p. 870; September 1, 2003, Ilene Cooper, review of *It's a Miracle!: A Hanukkah Storybook,* p. 136; April 15, 2005, Gillian Engberg, review of *Quicksilver,* p. 1450; October 1, 2008, Anne O'Malley, review of *Damosel: In Which the Lady of the Lake Renders a Frank and Often Startling Account of Her Wondrous Life and Times,* p. 36.
Horn Book, March-April, 2005, Deirdre F. Baker, review of *Quicksilver,* p. 207; November-December, 2008, Lolly Robinson, review of *The Nutcracker,* p. 653.
Kirkus Reviews, January 1, 1997, review of *Born to Be Wild,* p. 68; December 1, 1999, review of *Be First in the Universe,* p. 1891; September 1, 2002, review of *Quiver,* p. 1320; November 1, 2003, review of *It's a Miracle!,* p. 1320; April 1, 2005, review of *Quicksilver,* p. 426; September 1, 2008, review of *Damosel;* November 1, 2008, review of *The Nutcracker.*
Kliatt, November, 2002, Claire Rosser, review of *Quiver,* p. 16; March, 2005, Claire Rosser, review of *Quicksilver,* p. 16.
New Yorker, December 5, 1983, Faith McNulty, review of *The Adventures of Pinocchio,* p. 204.
Publishers Weekly, November 25, 1988, review of *Aliens for Breakfast,* pp. 66-67; July 29, 1996, review of *Gerbilitis,* p. 89; January 31, 2000, review of *Be First in the Universe,* p. 107; November 4, 2002, review of *Quiver,* p. 86; September 22, 2003, review of *It's a Miracle!,* p.66.
School Library Journal, April, 1985, Drew Stevenson, review of *The Mummy's Tomb,* p. 103; March, 1989, Sharron McElmeel, review of *Aliens for Breakfast,* p. 156; December, 1992, Elizabeth C. Fiene, "Step-up to Classic Chillers," p. 59; February, 1994, Sharron McElmeel, review of *Little Sure Shot,* p. 98; November, 1996, Charlyn Lyons, reviews of *Gerbilitis* and *Sing, Elvis, Sing!,* both pp. 110A-110B; February, 1997, Jody McCoy, review of *Born to Be Wild,* pp. 84-85; July, 1997, Elizabeth Trotter, review of *Bright Lights, Little Gerbil,* p. 76; February, 2000, Beth Wright, review of *Be First in the Universe,* p. 104; July, 2001, Kay Bowes, review of *Expiration Date,* p. 89; May, 2002, Anne Chapman Callaghan, review of *Who Was Annie Oakley?,* p. 144; October, 2002, An-

gela J. Reynolds, review of *Quiver,* p. 173; October, 2003, Mara Alpert, review of *It's a Miracle!,* p. 68; September, 2005, Coop Renner, review of *Quicksilver,* p. 214; October, 2008, Virginia Walter, review of *The Nutcracker,* p. 98; December, 2008, Beth L. Meister, review of *Damosel,* p. 138; June, 2010, Gloria Koster, review of *Paddywack,* p. 84.

ONLINE

Random House Web site, http://www.randomhouse.com/ (September 15, 2011), "Stephanie Spinner."

Stephanie Spinner Home Page, http://www.stephanie spinner.com (September 15, 2011).*

* * *

STEPHENS, Helen 1972-

Personal

Born 1972, in England; married; husband named Gerry; children: Frieda. *Education:* Attended art school.

Addresses

Home—Northumberland, England. *Agent*—Hilary Delamere, The Agency, hdelamere@theagency.co.uk. *E-mail*—helenstephens1@yahoo.co.uk.

Career

Author and illustrator of books for children. Presenter at schools.

Awards, Honors

Sainsbury Baby Book Award shortlist, 2002, for *Twinkly Night;* Dundee Picture Book Award, Sheffield Picture Book Award Commended selection, and Silver Star award, Norfolk (UK) Libraries Children's Book Award, all c. 2008, all for *Fleabag;* White Ravens International Library selection, and Booktrust Early Years Award, both 2010, both for *The Night Iceberg.*

Writings

SELF-ILLUSTRATED

I'm Too Busy, DK Pub. (New York, NY), 1999.
What about Me?, DK Pub. (New York, NY), 1999.
Ruby and the Muddy Dog, Kingfisher (New York, NY), 2000.
Ruby and the Noisy Hippo, Kingfisher (New York, NY), 2000.
Blue Horse and Tilly, Doubleday (London, England), 2001, published as *Blue Horse,* Scholastic Press (New York, NY), 2003.

Poochie-poo, David Fickling Books (London, England), 2002, David Fickling Books (New York, NY), 2003.
Ahoyty-toyty!, David Fickling (Oxford, England), 2003, David Fickling Books (New York, NY), 2004.
Fleabag, Alison Green (London, England), 2008, Henry Holt (New York, NY), 2010.
Witchety Sticks, Simon & Schuster UK (London, England), 2010.
The Night Iceberg, Alison Green Books (London, England), 2010.
The Big Adventure of the Smalls, Egmont (London, England), 2012.

Author's books have been translated into several languages.

SELF-ILLUSTRATED; "BABY DAZZLERS" BOARD-BOOK SERIES

Glittery Garden, Campbell (London, England), 2002, Little, Brown (New York, NY), 2003.
Shiny Seaside, Campbell (London, England), 2002, Little, Brown (New York, NY), 2003.
Sparkly Day, Campbell (London, England), 2002, Little, Brown (New York, NY), 2003.
Twinkly Night, Campbell (London, England), 2002, Little, Brown (New York, NY), 2003.

SELF-ILLUSTRATED; "RATTLE BUGGY BUDDIES" BOARD-BOOK SERIES

Farm, Campbell (London, England), 2004.
Pets, Campbell (London, England), 2004.
Jungle, Campbell (London, England), 2004.
Safari, Campbell (London, England), 2004.

SELF-ILLUSTRATED; "RAG TAGS" BOOK SERIES

Coco Crocodile, Campbell (London, England), 2005.
Zaza Zebra, Campbell (London, England), 2005.
Effie Elephant, Campbell (London, England), 2005.

SELF-ILLUSTRATED; "MAGIC MOVERS" INTERACTIVE BOOK SERIES

Lucy Loves Shapes, Campbell (London, England), 2008.
Archie's Animal Friends, Campbell (London, England), 2008.
Clara's Counting Tea Party, Campbell (London, England), 2008.

ILLUSTRATOR

Margaret Mayo, editor, *Plum Pudding,* Orchard Books (London, England), 2000.
Sophie Hannah, *The Box Room,* Orchard (London, England), 2001.
Poetry by Heart (poetry anthology), Chicken House, 2001.

Margaret Mayo, editor, *Hoddley Poddley,* Orchard Books (London, England), 2001.

Roger McGough, *The Bee's Knees,* Puffin (London, England), 2003.

ILLUSTRATOR; "QUIGLEYS" CHAPTER-BOOK SERIES BY SIMON MASON

The Quigleys, David Fickling Books (New York, NY), 2002.

The Quigleys at Large, David Fickling Books (New York, NY), 2003.

The Quigleys Not for Sale, David Fickling Books (New York, NY), 2004.

The Quigleys in a Spin, David Fickling Books (New York, NY), 2005.

Sidelights

When Helen Stephens completed her art degree, she knew that wherever her career path took her, it would incorporate drawing, which was her favorite creative outlet. Fortunately for legions of picture-book fans, the British-born Stephens eventually found the perfect vocation: crafting and illustrating picture books. In addition to creating artwork for stories by authors such as Margaret Mayo, Simon Mason, and Sophie Hannah, she has also produced numerous original, self-illustrated texts, among them toddler concept books in the "Magic Movers,""Rag Tag," and "Rattle Buggy Buddies" series as well as standalone picture books that include *Blue Horse and Tilly, Fleabag, Poochie-poo,* and *The Big Adventure of the Smalls.* Reviewing Stephens' artwork for Mason's four-volume "Quigleys" chapter-book series, a *Kirkus Reviews* contributor praised the "hilarious cartoon illustrations" in *The Quigleys at Large,* while Jean Gaffney predicted in *School Library Journal* that the book's "frequent line drawings will help attract children bridging into" more sophisticated reading.

Growing up in a quiet home where she often found herself alone, Stephens quickly found that art and making things happily filled her free time. Art school became her goal in secondary school, although she never really viewed art as a path toward an adult career. In her mid-twenties, Stephens created her first books for children, *I'm Too Busy* and *What about Me?,* which ultimately jump-started her career.

Drawing ideas from her surroundings, as well as from her experiences raising her own daughter, Stephens has since gained recognition for stories that pair a light-hearted, childlike perspective with color-enhanced line drawings. Several of her picture books have even been recognized by prestigious book-award juries, among them *Fleabag, Blue Horse and Tilly,* and *The Night Iceberg.* In *Fleabag,* which tells the story of a scruffy, homeless pup and a lonely little boy, Stephens marries a poignant but happy ending with "paint-and-pencil artwork [that] nicely muddles the messy gray areas of a gritty city" while "beautifully evolk[ing]" the story's

underlying sentiment, according to *Booklist* contributor Daniel Kraus. Also recommending the book's art, which is "bright and happy," Judith Constantinides added in her *School Library Journal* review that *Fleabag* presents "an enjoyable story" that will find equal favor among youngsters, whether used "for groups or bedtime sharing."

Stephens introduces readers to another likeable pup in *Ahoyty-toyty!* and its companion volume, *Poochie-poo.* Victor, a small white terrier, has mastered dog obedience and endeavors to please his well-heeled owner, Miss Loopy, while Butch prefers to skirt the line between "Good Dog" and "Bad Dog." When the two pups accompany their owners on a cruise, they make friends with the captain's dog, Lord Laa-Di-Dah. When only Butch is invited to join Lord Laa-Di-Dah at the captain's table, he realizes that upscale friends are not always the best mannered. Victor and Butch return in *Poochie-Poo,* as the white dog is nudged by Butch into committing an act of badness, even though his good manners ultimately kick in. Although the very young may miss Stephens' "tongue-in-cheek wordplay," Wanda Meyers-Hines added in her *School Library Journal* review that the "vibrantly colored" illustrations in *Ahoyty-toyty!* "effortlessly convey the [story's] meaning." Praising *Poochi-Poo* in the same periodical, Maryann H. Owen predicted that the author/artist's "trademark bright, clear illustrations will appeal to preschoolers."

Published in the United States as *Blue Horse, Blue Horse and Tilly* introduces a shy young girl as she adjusts to a move to a new town and a new school. Although Tilly is unwilling to join the children busy on the playground, she manages to make a companion of her stuffed blue horse, using her imagination to shape the toy into a playmate and confidante. When she spots another girl playing alone on the playground, Tilly and Blue Horse go together to make their introductions, forging fast friendships in the process. Stephens' "warmly reassuring" and "empathetic tale" in *Blue Horse and Tilly* "compassionately addresses the trials of bashfulness," noted a *Kirkus Reviews* writer, "and models simple coping strategies that are appropriate for small fry." Stephens' story is captured in what *Booklist* contributor Carolyn Phelan described as "naive artwork [that] is large in scale, bold in color, and fresh in every way." These naif illustrations mix "bold swatches of color and an exuberant informality," asserted Marge Loch-Wouters in *School Library Journal,* and readers who number imaginary friends among their acquaintances "will find a kindred spirit in Tilly."

Biographical and Critical Sources

PERIODICALS

Booklist, July, 2002, Ilene Cooper, review of *The Quigleys,* p. 1848; March 15, 2003, Carolyn Phelan, review of *Blue Horse,* p. 1334; December 1, 2003, Ed

Sullivan, review of *The Quigleys at Large,* p. 667; December, 2004, Carolyn Phelan, review of *The Quigleys Not for Sale,* p. 653; January 1, 2006, Carolyn Phelan, review of *The Quigleys in a Spin,* p. 88; April 15, 2010, Daniel Kraus, review of *Fleabag,* p. 50.

Horn Book, July-August, 2002, Martha V. Parravano, review of *The Quigleys,* p. 468; September-October, 2003, Martha V. Parravano, review of *The Quigleys at Large,* p. 615; March-April, 2006, Martha V. Parravano, review of *The Quigleys in a Spin,* p. 193.

Kirkus Reviews, May 1, 2002, review of *The Quigleys,* p. 661; January 15, 2003, review of *Blue Horse,* p. 148; September 15, 2003, review of *The Quigleys at Large,* p. 1178; March 15, 2004, review of *Ahoyty-toyty!,* p. 277; November 1, 2004, review of *The Quigleys Not for Sale,* p. 1045; January 15, 2006, review of *The Quigleys in a Spin,* p. 87.

Publishers Weekly, April 15, 2002, review of *The Quigleys,* p. 64; February 17, 2003, review of *Blue Horse,* p. 73.

School Library Journal, June, 2002, Susan Hepler, review of *The Quigleys,* p. 104; March, 2003, Marge Loch-Wouters, review of *Blue Horse,* p. 208; December, 2003, Jean Gaffney, review of *The Quigleys at Large,* p. 120, and Maryann H. Owen, review of *Poochie-Poo,* p. 128; June, 2004, Wanda Meyers-Hines, review of *Ahoyty-toyty!,* p. 120; December, 2004, Edith Ching, review of *The Quigleys Not for Sale,* p. 113; April, 2006, Cheryl Ashton, review of *The Quigleys in a Spin,* p. 112; July, 2010, Judith Constantinides, review of *Fleabag,* p. 69.

ONLINE

Helen Stephens Home Page, http://www.helenstephens.com (October 4, 2011).

Helen Stephens Web log, http://ohifortottosay.blogspot.com (October 4, 2011).

Scholastic U.K. Web site, http://www5.scholastic.co.uk/ (October 4, 2011), "Helen Stephens."*

*   *   *

STUBER, Barbara 1951-

Personal

Born 1951; married; children: six. *Hobbies and other interests:* Running.

Addresses

Home—Mission Hills, KS. *Agent*—Ginger Knowlton, Curtis Brown Ltd., 10 Astor Pl., New York, NY 10003. *E-mail*—barbarajstuber@gmail.com.

Career

Author. Nelson-Atkins Museum of Art, Kansas City, MO, docent. Presenter at schools and libraries.

Member

Heartland Writers for Kids and Teens, Society of Children's Book Writers and Illustrators.

Awards, Honors

William C. Morris Award finalist, 2010, and Writers' League of Texas Book Award finalist, Thorpe Menn Award finalist, YALSA Best Fiction for Young Adults selection, and Kansas Notable Book selection, all 2011, all for *Crossing the Tracks.*

Writings

Crossing the Tracks, Margaret K. McElderry Books (New York, NY), 2010.

Contributor to periodicals, including *Cricket.*

Sidelights

Barbara Stuber takes readers back to 1920s Missouri in her award-winning debut young-adult historical novel *Crossing the Tracks.* In Stuber's novel readers meet fifteen-year-old Iris Baldwin. With her mother long dead, Iris shares a house with her busy businessman father but she has never felt part of a home or a family. Now that a new girlfriend and an expanding retail business demand more and more of her father's time, he hires Iris out as a housekeeper and companion to the elderly mother of a doctor in a rural part of the state. Iris feels cast out, a hobo of sorts with no home, no real family, and no plan. Slowly, however, Dr. Nesbitt's house begins to feel like home to her, and the girl builds a strong and caring friendship with her elderly charge. As Iris becomes emotionally invested in her new home, the abuse of a neighbor's young daughter sparks her anger. In standing up to this local injustice she overcomes her self-doubt and discovers that she is not as helpless—or as hopeless—as she once belived. In the span of one dusty summer, Iris learns to trust, hope, and, ultimately, love.

Praising *Crossing the Tracks* as "a moving and heartwarming piece of historical fiction," *Voice of Youth Advocates* critic Victoria Vogel added that Stuber's "poetic and charming" text "does an excellent job of making the readers feel at home with her characters." In *Booklist* Michael Cart found the novel to be quiet in its pacing as well as "richly atmospheric in its setting and . . . successful in its character development." *Crossing the Tracks* treats teens to a "thought-provoking and tenderhearted" story, asserted Debra Banna in *School Library Journal,* the critic adding that Stuber's novel also benefits from "an engaging" teen heroine who "faces life with courage and common sense."

In addition to writing, Stuber works as a docent at the Nelson-Atkins Museum of Art in Kansas City. "Many parallels exist between composing a book and composing a painting," the author told *SATA.* "I often steal inspiration for my writing from the museum. Portraits open their mouths and become characters, and landscapes and interior scenes become settings."

Biographical and Critical Sources

PERIODICALS

Booklist, July 1, 2010, Michael Cart, review of *Crossing the Tracks,* p. 50.

Bulletin of the Center for Children's Books, September, 2010, Deborah Stevenson, review of *Crossing the Tracks,* p. 45.

School Library Journal, August, 2010, Debra Banna, review of *Crossing the Tracks,* p. 114.

Voice of Youth Advocates, October, 2010, Victoria Vogel, review of *Crossing the Tracks,* p. 359.

ONLINE

Barbara Stuber Home Page, http://www.barbarastuber.com (October 1, 2011).

Barbara Stuber Web log, http://barbarastuber.wordpress.com (October 1, 2011).

Heartland Writers Web site, http://heartlandwriters.com/ (October 1, 2011), "Barbara Stuber."

Simon & Schuster Web site, http://authors.simonandschuster.com/ (August 4, 2011), "Barbara Stuber."

*   *   *

STUTSON, Caroline 1940-

Personal

Born September 14, 1940; daughter of Malcolm (a purchasing agent) and Randolph (a librarian) MacLachlan; married Al Stutson (a wood carver), September 5, 1964; children: A.C., Christine. *Education:* Metro State College, certificate in early education, 1978; attended College of William & Mary, 1958-60; University of Denver, B.A., 1962. *Hobbies and other interests:* Hiking, puppetry, gardening, reading, stitchery.

Addresses

Home—Littleton, CO. *E-mail*—astutson@aol.com.

Career

Writer and educator. Bemis Public Library, Littleton, CO, children's librarian, 1961-65; kindergarten teacher and special reading teacher in Littleton. Highlands Ranch Library, Highlands Ranch, CO, part-time storyteller and puppeteer.

Member

Society of Children's Book Writers and Illustrators, Authors Guild, Colorado Author's League, Pikes Peak Writers.

Awards, Honors

Teacher of Excellence, Colorado Association for Childhood Education, 1991.

Caroline Stutson (Reproduced by permission.)

Writings

By the Light of the Halloween Moon, illustrated by Kevin Hawkes, Lothrop, Lee & Shepard (New York, NY), 1993.

On the River ABC, illustrated by Anna-Maria Crum, Roberts Rinehart (Boulder, CO), 1993.

Mountain Meadow 1, 2, 3, illustrated by Anna-Maria Crum, Roberts Rinehart (Boulder, CO), 1995.

Prairie Primer A to Z, illustrated by Susan Condie Lamb, Dutton (New York, NY), 1996.

Star Comes Home, illustrated by Rick Reason, The Benefactory/Humane Society of the United States, 1999.

Cowpokes, illustrated by Daniel San Souci, Lothrop, Lee & Shepard (New York, NY), 1999.

Night Train, illustrated by Katherine Tillotson, Roaring Brook Press (Brookfield, CT), 2002.

Mama Loves You, illustrated by John Segal, Scholastic (New York, NY), 2005.

Pirate Pup, illustrated by Robert Rayevsky, Chronicle Books (San Francisco, CA), 2005.

By the Light of the Halloween Moon, illustrated by Kevin Hawkes, Marshall Cavendish Children (Tarrytown, NY), 2009.

Cats' Night Out, illustrated by J. Klassen, Simon & Schuster Books for Young Readers (New York, NY), 2010.

Contributor of poetry to magazines, including *Children's Playmate, Highlights for Children, On the Line,* and *Spider.*

Adaptations

By the Light of the Halloween Moon was adapted for video by Weston Woods Studios, 1997.

Sidelights

A former teacher and librarian, Caroline Stutson is the author of the children's books *Night Train* and *Cats' Night Out,* both which feature poetic narratives. "I write in verse because I have Rhyming Disease," Stutson admitted on her home page. "It's not catching, but it is very difficult to cure."

Stutson's fast-paced debut poem, *By the Light of the Halloween Moon,* holds a "toe" up for grabs. The toe belongs to a little girl who dangles her legs over a footbridge while playing a fiddle on Halloween night. A cat, a witch, a bat, a graveyard ghoul, a ghost, and a sprite all stream through this boisterous tale, and each

character, more pleasurably gruesome than the one before, aims to grab the tempting toe. A *Kirkus Reviews* critic called Stutson's poem a "catchy, lilting cumulative tale," and Ilene Cooper declared in *Booklist* that this "rousing" tale with its "bouncy text" would make a "terrific choice for holiday story hours." In *Horn Book* Ann A. Flowers also praised *By the Light of the Halloween Moon,* describing the book as "rhythmically bouncy and appealing."

In *On the River ABC* an ant floats down the river sitting on a leaf. As he drifts, wildlife species from A to Z pass alongside his makeshift vessel. Stutson ends her book with factual information about each animal, all which live in the western regions of the United States. *School Library Journal* contributor Kathy Piehl commented favorably on the lyrical quality of Stutson's writing in *On the River ABC,* noting that the author "does not fall into the trap of singsong regularity." Piehl encourages teachers to use this picture book as a springboard for "children to create similar alphabet books based on trips in their own environment."

With *Prairie Primer A to Z* Stutson once again presents a rhyming ABC book, this time evoking the daily life of a Midwestern farm family in the early 1900s. Each letter helps to explore life on a farm of long ago; from

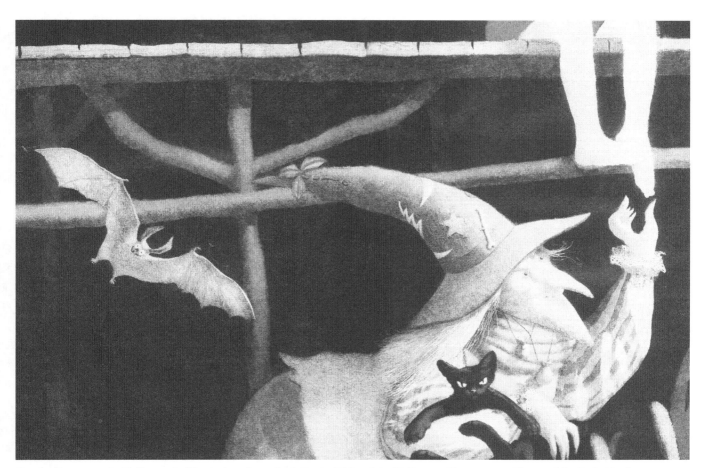

Stutson focuses on the Halloween holiday in her picture book **By the Light of the Halloween Moon,** *a story illustrated by Kevin Hawkes.* (Illustration copyright © 1993 by Kevin Hawkes. All rights reserved. Reproduced by permission of Marshall Cavendish Corporation.)

churning butter to illustrating the uses of whirligigs and velocipedes. Although a critic for *Kirkus Reviews* suggested that Stutson's book might be too "old-fashioned" for today's "rough-and-ready preschool set," *School Library Journal* critic Paula A. Kiely called *Prairie Primer A to Z* a "pleasant step back in time," pointing out that "young children will enjoy trying to pronounce" these forgotten words. Carolyn Phelan, writing in *Booklist,* suggested that the primer be used to introduce "today's young children to another time, another place."

In *Cowpokes,* illustrated by Daniel San Souci, Stutson chronicles a day in the life of Tex, Curly, Slim, and their comrades on the open range. According to *Booklist* reviewer John Peters, "Stutson hangs her cadenced, very brief text on rhymes and partial rhymes." A young boy revels in the excitement of an overnight train ride with his father in *Night Train,* a work featuring Stutson's "poetic text in rhyming couplets with evocative language," observed a contributor in *Kirkus Reviews. Night Train* follows the boy as he boards a gleaming passenger train and begins his journey through the countryside to visit his grandmother's home in the city. According to Gillian Engberg in *Booklist,* Stutson's spare narrative "captures the feel and noise of the train," and a *Publishers Weekly* critic applauded the author's focus on the smallest of details, such as the child's enjoyment of a meal in the dining car, noting that *Night Train* "offers evidence that, when it comes to the romance of train travel, a child's love is here to stay," the critic added.

Stutson's *Pirate Pup* concerns a group of canine buccaneers that set off aboard their ship, the *Rover,* to locate buried treasure before their rivals, a crew of unruly cats, finds the booty. "This rowdy, rousing yarn will be a real treasure for any pirate enthusiast or young adventurer," predicted a contributor in *Kirkus Reviews.* In *Cats' Night Out,* illustrated by J. Klassen, a bevy of furry creatures samba, fox-trot, and tango their way through the alleys and along the rooftops of their urban home. As the night beckons, feline couples join together in a dazzling display of fancy footwork, at least until their sleep-deprived neighbors finally raise their objections to the revelry. "Stutson's syncopated rhymes sport fun flourishes of dance and fashion vocabulary," Kristen McKulski reported in *Booklist,* and Elizabeth Bird, in a *Fuse #8 Production* review that the "rhymes and wordplay" in *Cats' Night Out* "are delightful." A *Publishers Weekly* critic applauded Klassen's art for the book, stating that the "dependable rhythms of Stutson's . . . verse are reflected in the faces of the dancers."

Stutson once told *SATA:* "Looking back at one's life is an interesting process. If enough time has passed, you can see the pieces fitting neatly together. Yet, on a day to day basis, so much seems haphazard and iffy.

"One of the few things I know for sure about my life is that I've always loved books. Shortly before I was born, longer ago than I'll publicly admit, my mother worked

Four frisky kitties take advantage of an evening of freedom in Stutson's **Cats' Night Out,** *featuring J. Klassen.* (Illustration copyright © 2010 by J. Klassen. Reproduced by permission of Simon & Schuster for Young Readers, an imprint of Simon & Schuster Children's Publishing Division.)

as a librarian at the Brooklyn Public Library in New York. I was lucky to have lots of early links with literature, from my mother's reading out loud to me, to a friend of hers who sent me copies of book reviews she wrote for a parenting magazine.

"In addition to listening to and reading books, I always enjoyed playing pretend. My best friend and I were careful to note where our adventure left off when it was time to go home. That way we knew where our chosen characters would begin the next day. Writing for children still lets me play pretend. All those 'what ifs' are great fun, and you get to create your own universe with a happy ending to boot.

"My writing began in kindergarten. I didn't know how to write words then, but every day after school I drew pictures and made up stories to go with the drawings. Later when we had writing assignments, I struggled with the spelling. I still struggle with spelling, but it doesn't stop me from writing any more. I just circle the troublesome words and look up how to spell them later.

"Today, things are so much better for the students I meet when I visit schools promoting my books. Some of their writing involves choice. They get to write about things that really matter to them, and they get to share their work with each other. They also get to respond to the literature they are reading. I can't help feeling a little envious."

Biographical and Critical Sources

PERIODICALS

Booklist, July, 1993, Ilene Cooper, review of *By the Light of the Halloween Moon,* p. 1977; October 15, 1996, Carolyn Phelan, review of *Prairie Primer A to Z,* p. 437; September 15, 1999, John Peters, review of *Cowpokes,* p. 270; May 1, 2002, Gillian Engberg, review of *Night Train,* p. 1536; February 15, 2010, Kristen McKulski, review of *Cats' Night Out,* p. 79.

Horn Book, November-December, 1993, Ann A. Flowers, review of *By the Light of the Halloween Moon,* p. 728.

Kirkus Reviews, July 15, 1993, review of *By the Light of the Halloween Moon,* pp. 942-943; September 15, 1996, review of *Prairie Primer A to Z,* p. 1408; March 1, 2002, review of *Night Train,* p. 346; September 15, 2005, review of *Pirate Pup,* p. 1035; February 15, 2010, review of *Cats' Night Out.*

New York Times Book Review, August 15, 2010, Julie Just, review of *Cats' Night Out,* p. 13.

Publishers Weekly, March 18, 2002, review of *Night Train,* p. 102; February 8, 2010, review of *Cats' Night Out,* p. 48.

School Library Journal, September, 1993, Kathy Piehl, review of *On the River ABC,* p. 220; October, 1996, Paula A. Kiely, review of *Prairie Primer A to Z,* p. 107; May, 2002, Wanda Meyers-Hines, review of *Night Train,* p. 128; February, 2010, Marilyn Taniguchi, review of *Cats' Night Out,* p. 96.

ONLINE

Caroline Stutson Home Page, http://carolinestutson.com (September 1, 2011).

Fuse #8 Production Web log, http://blog.schoollibrary journal.com/afuse8production/ (May 6, 2010), Elizabeth Bird, review of *Cats' Night Out.*

University of Denver Magazine Online, http://www.du. edu/ (September 1, 2010), Greg Glasgow, "Caroline Stutson Keeps Kids Counting with Latest Picture Book."*

T

TASHJIAN, Jake 1994-

Personal
Born 1994, in MA; son of Jake and Janet (an author) Tashjian.

Addresses
Home—Worcester, MA.

Career
Student and illustrator.

Illustrator
Janet Tashjian, *My Life as a Book,* Henry Holt (New York, NY), 2010.
Janet Tashjian, *My Life as a Stuntboy,* Henry Holt (New York, NY), 2011.

Biographical and Critical Sources

PERIODICALS

Booklist, August 1, 2010, Ilene Cooper, review of *My Life as a Book,* p. 54.
Bulletin of the Center for Children's Books, September, 2010, Kate Quealy-Gainer, review of *My Life as a Book,* p. 46.
Horn Book, July-August, 2010, Betty Carter, review of *My Life as a Book,* p. 124.
Publishers Weekly, June 28, 2010, review of *My Life as a Book,* p. 129.
School Library Journal, August, 2010, Helen Foster James, review of *My Life as a Book,* p. 114.

ONLINE

Macmillan Web site, http://us.macmillan.com/author/ (August 4, 2011), "Jake Tashjian."*

TAXALI, Gary 1968-

Personal
Born 1968, in Chandigarh, India; immigrated to Canada, 1969. *Education:* Ontario College of Art, degree, 1991.

Addresses
Home—Toronto, Ontario, Canada. *E-mail*—info@taxali. com.

Career
Illustrator, author, and toy designer. Chump Toys (toy company), Toronto, Ontario, Canada, founder, c. 2006. Lecturer at schools, including Art Center College of Design, Pasadena, CA; Texas State University, San Marcos; Fachhochschule Mainz, Mainz, Germany; Ontario College of Art and Design, Toronto; Dankmarks Designskole, Copenhagen, Denmark; and Istituto Europeo di Design, Rome, Italy; presenter at schools. Member of advisory board, *3x3: The Magazine of Contemporary Illustration.* Also works as a DJ. *Exhibitions:* Work exhibited at galleries and shows in North America and Europe, including 450 Broadway Gallery, New York, NY; Anno Domini Gallery, San Jose, CA; La Luz de Jesus Gallery, Los Angeles, CA; Tin Man Alley, Philadelphia, PA; Victoria & Albert Museum, London, England; Froden Gallery, Los Angeles; Jonathan Le-Vine Gallery, New York, NY; L'Autre Galerie, Montreal, Quebec, Canada; Toy Tokyo, New York, NY; Whitney Museum of American Art, New York, NY; Hemphill Fine Arts, Washington, DC; Iguapop Gallery, Barcelona, Spain; Outsiders Gallery, London; and Narwhal Art Projects, Toronto, Ontario, Canada.

Member
Illustrators' Partnership of America (founding member).

Awards, Honors
Gold Medal, Society of Illustrators; awards from Chicago Creative Club, Advertising and Design Club of

Canada, and Society of Publication Designers; Gold Medal, National Magazine Awards; National Gold Addy award; Cannes Lion award shortlist.

Writings

SELF-ILLUSTRATED

Orange, Piggy Toes Press (Los Angeles, CA), 2003.
Red, Piggy Toes Press (Los Angeles, CA), 2003.
Yellow, Piggy Toes Press (Los Angeles, CA), 2003.
This Is Silly!, Scholastic Press (New York, NY), 2010.
(With Aimee Mann and Shepard Fairey) *Gary Taxali: I Love You, Ok?*, TeNeues (New York, NY), 2011.

Artwork published in professional journals, including *American Illustration* and *Communication Arts*. Contributor to periodicals, including *Business Week, Entertainment Weekly, Esquire, Fast Company, Fortune, Gentleman's Quarterly, Newsweek, Readers' Digest, Rolling Stone, Time*, and *Toronto Life*.

Sidelights

An Indian-born artist and teacher who now makes his home in Canada, Gary Taxali draws on the retro graphic style popular during the 1930s as well as the inspiration of pop artist Andy Warhol. Evoking the pixilated "Funnies" of a past age, his illustrations have appeared in graphic advertising and numerous periodicals, as well as in children's books that include his original, self-illustrated *This Is Silly!* In 2005 Taxali moved into toy design, inspired by a vinyl toy monkey he had designed

Gary Taxali is inspired by the art of the first half of the twentieth century in his quirk This Is Silly!, *a picture book that lives up to its title.*
(Copyright © 2010 by Gary Taxali. Reproduced by permission of Scholastic, Inc.)

and marketed through the Whitney Museum of American Art. Called Chump Toys, his Toronto-based company produces old-fashioned wooden toys. "I want to give kids a license to be crazy and encourage them to be ultra-imaginative," Taxali explained to *National Post* writer Ben Kaplan in discussing his creative career, "especially when the school system's not equipped to handle children like I was, who don't think in the traditional way."

This Is Silly! features a story about a boy named Silly Sol who falls down a hole and winds up in a land of cartoon characters. Taxali's "rhyming text is not plot-driven but revels in phonemic silliness," according to Sarah Townsend, the *School Library Journal* critic adding that the book's mix of "vibrant" art and "rollicking rhymes will engage young readers and art buffs alike." Colored in faded pastel tones, Taxali's "aesthetically pleasing" images resonate with "faded nostalgia," according to *Quill & Quire* contributor Ian Daffern, the critic adding that *This Is Silly!* closes with a kid-magnet: "a shiny mirror in which kids can make their own silly faces." In *Publishers Weekly* a contributor described the author/illustrator as "channeling candy wrapper script, amusement park funhouse art, and comic books," and predicted that readers would find *This Is Silly!* both silly and "strangely compelling."

Biographical and Critical Sources

PERIODICALS

Communicating Arts, February 27, 2008, interview with Taxali.
National Post, September 22, 2010, Ben Kaplan, "Gary Taxali's New Children's Book 'An Idea I've Had My Entire Life.'"
Publishers Weekly, July 5, 2010, review of *This Is Silly!*, p. 40.
Quill & Quire, December, 2010, Ian Daffern, review of *This Is Silly!*
School Library Journal, July, 2010, Sarah Townsend, review of *This Is Silly!*, p. 70.

ONLINE

Excerpt Web site, http://theexcerpt.com/ (September, 2010), interview with Taxali.
Gary Taxali Home Page, http://www.garytaxali.com (August 4, 2011).*

*   *   *

TENNAPEL, Doug 1966-

Personal

Born July 10, 1966, in Norwalk, CA; married, 1990; wife's name Angie; children: Ahmi, Edward. Olivia, John. *Education:* Point Loma Nazarene University, B.A. (art), 1988. *Religion:* Christian.

Addresses

Home—Glendale, CA. *E-mail*—dougt@tennapel.com.

Career

Artist, animator, musician, and author. Animator and creator of characters for video games, c. 1990s; creator/producer of films, including *Kog-Head and Meatus* (short), 2000, *Mothman,* 2000, and *Sockbaby* (short), 2004; consulting producer for television series *Push, Nevada;* creator and executive producer of television series *Catscratch,* 2005-06, *Random! Cartoons,* 2007-08, *Ape Escape,* 2008, and *Go Sukashi!* Lead singer of band Truck.

Awards, Honors

Eisner Award.

Writings

"STRANGE KIDS CHRONICLES" SERIES; ILLUSTRATED BY MIKE KOELSCH

Mighty Monday Madness, Scholastic (New York, NY), 1997.
Tuna Fish Tuesday, Scholastic (New York, NY), 1997.
Wisenheimer Wednesday, Scholastic (New York, NY), 1998.
Just Thursday, illustrated by Michael Koelsch, Scholastic (New York, NY), 1998.
Fateful Friday, Scholastic (New York, NY), 1998.

GRAPHIC NOVELS

Gear (originally published in comic-book form), Fire Man Press, 1999.
Creature Tech, Top Shelf Productions (Marietta, GA), 2002, new edition, 2010.
Tommysaurus Rex, Image Comics (Berkeley, CA), 2004.
Earthboy Jacobus, Image Comics (Berkeley, CA), 2005.
Iron West, Image Comics (Berkeley, CA), 2006.
Black Cherry, Image Comics (Berkeley, CA), 2007.
Flink, Image Comics (Berkeley, CA), 2007.
Monster Zoo, Image Comics (Berkeley, CA), 2008.
Power Up, Image Comics (Berkeley, CA), 2009.
Ghostopolis, Scholastic/Graphix (New York, NY), 2010.
Bad Island, Scholastic/Graphix (New York, NY), 2011.

Contributor to graphic novels, including *Parable,* 2010.

OTHER

Contributor to comic-book series, including "Bart Simpson's Treehouse of Horror," "Scud," "Fractured Fables," "Chumble Spuzz," and "Flight." Writer for animated television series, including *Catscratch* and *Random! Cartoons.* Author of Web comics "Ratfist," 2010-11, and "Bigfoot for Hire."

Adaptations

Creature Tech was produced as a motion picture by Twentieth Century-Fox; *Ghostopolis* was optioned for film by Disney, 2009.

Sidelights

Doug TenNapel is the creator of the cartoon character "Earthworm Jim," which appeared in a video game in the mid-1990s and eventually wormed his way into a television series. Although much of TenNapel's work has been in film, he has also produced a number of books for children, among them the "Strange Kids Chronicles" as well as the comic-book series "Gear," "Earthboy Jacobus," "Flink," and "Ghostopolis," all which have been collected and bound as graphic-novel anthologies.

Raised in Denair, California, TenNapel studied at Point Loma Nazarene University. He began his professional life as an animator, then moved to video games where he worked on projects for Sega Genesis. He created Earthworm Jim, who eventually starred in a video game and a cartoon series in addition to being memorialized in a line of children's toys. Other video games by Ten-

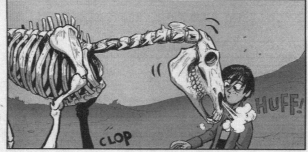

Doug TenNapel's popular graphic novels include the imaginative and highly acclaimed Ghostopolis. (Copyright © 2010 by Doug TenNapel. Reproduced by permission of Scholastic, Inc.)

Napel included *The Neverhood, Skullmonkeys,* and *Boombots.* TenNapel's work in film included several shorts as well as *Mothman,* and among his television projects were creating the cartoon series *Project G.e. e.K.* and helping to produce a television series, *Push, Nevada.*

TenNapel's first graphic novel, *Gear,* was originally published in comic-book form and stars his own four cats as they marshal a giant killer robot in their war against stray dogs. The adventures stray even further into the bizarre in *Creature Tech,* which finds an undead scientist infiltrating a top-secret installation in order to acquire the strange biological specimens that will allow him to wreak vengeance on mankind . . . unless he can be stopped by the brilliant teenaged Dr. Michael Ong. A plane crash into a remote area starts the action in *Flink,* as the lone survivor, a boy, is befriended by a Bigfoot-like creature. A man finds the key to wealth, power, and immortality in a video-game console in *Power Up,* while an average American family finds more trouble than its members would like while wandering through in a creature-infested region in *Bad Island.*

TenNapel's "goofy, kinetic [cartooning] style makes a winner out of this crazed romp," asserted *Booklist* critic Ray Olson in a review of *Creature Tech,* and Steve Raiteri noted in *Library Journal* that the cartoonist's "black-and-white art . . . combines cartooniness with complexity" in a "freewheeling story" with "unexpected depth." The author/illustrator's "creativity and attention to detail fill this book with pleasant surprises and entertaining twists," wrote a *Publishers Weekly* critic, the reviewer adding that the sequential art in *Creature Tech* is "dynamic, comic and often startlingly touching." Dubbing TenNapel a "quirky cartoonist," *Booklist* contributor Jesse Karp ranked the creatures of *Bad Island* high in the "ick" factor, concluding that the "clever, old-fashioned adventure . . . is not to be missed."

One of TenNapel's most popular books, *Ghostopolis* was originally published in 2003 and reappeared in a new edition seven years later. Described by *Booklist* contributor Ian Chipman as a "ghost-driven graphic novel," *Ghostopolis* was inspired by the author's desire to frame the concept of the afterlife in a way that would not disturb or frighten younger children. In the story, the government-run Supernatural Immigration Task Force manages the transportation of paranormal beings out of the realm of the living, and Officer Frank Gallows works for this agency. During the course of one paranormal transport, Gallows transports determined but sickly Garth Hale into the spirit world by mistake. Since the physical laws of the afterlife are different from those of the living, Garth stands out: he exhibits

human powers unknown in this strange realm and this makes him a target of the afterlife's power-hungry ruler. Fortunately, Garth will not battle this evil alone: the preteen ghost of his deceased grandfather Cecil becomes his guide until Gallows arrives to try and fix his mistake. "TenNapel mixes emotional epiphanies with humor in a way that will appeal to a broad audience," wrote Andrea Lipinski in her *School Library Journal* review of the new edition of *Ghostopolis,* and his "colorful illustrations are filled with energy and life." Chipman praised the book's story as "a good blend of creepy, grotesque, and wacky," while in *Publishers Weekly* a contributor lauded *Ghostopolis* for its "likeable" hero, "energetic drawings," and "a host of smart-talking characters [that] make the story fun."

"I . . . find a great a great deal of joy in the creation process," TenNapel told *Comic Book Resources* online interviewer Alex Dueben. "It's a unique part of this medium that lets me create worlds and characters. This is what I've always been doing in my imagination, since I can remember. I love to look at a blank page and start pushing and pulling ideas until there is something so real that someone else can enjoy it."

Biographical and Critical Sources

PERIODICALS

Booklist, November 1, 2002, Ray Olson, review of *Creature Tech,* p. 467; March 15, 2010, Ian Chipman, review of *Ghostopolis,* p. 60; March 15, 2011, Jesse Karp, review of *Bad Island,* p. 38.
Library Journal, January, 2003, Steve Raiteri, review of *Creature Tech,* p. 85.
Publishers Weekly, May 26, 2003, review of *Creature Tech,* p. 50; March 1, 2010, review of *Ghostopolis,* p. 54.
School Library Journal, July, 2010, Andrea Lipinski, review of *Ghostopolis,* p. 108.
Teacher Librarian, April, 2008, Joe Sutliff Sanders, review of *Flink,* p. 59.

ONLINE

Alternative Magazine Online, http://alternativemagazine online.co.uk/ (September 4, 2010), interview with TenNapel.
Comic Book Resources Web site, http://www.comicbook resources.com/ (August 4, 2011), Alex Dueben, "Exploring the Afterlife in TenNapel's 'Ghostopolis.'"
Douglas TenNapel Home Page, http://tennapel.com (October 14, 2011).
Doug TenNapel Web log, http://tennapel.wordpress.com (October 14, 2011).

WATTS, Sarah 1986-

Personal

Born 1986, in Kennesaw, GA. *Education:* Marchman Technical Education Center, certificate (graphic arts), 2002-04; Illustration Academy, certificate, 2007; Ringling School of Art and Design, B.F.A. (illustration), 2008. *Hobbies and other interests:* Antique shopping.

Addresses

Home—GA. *Agent*—Abi Samoun, Red Fox Literary, abigailsamoun@gmail.com. *E-mail*—wattsalot@me.com.

Career

Illustrator, hand-letterer, and designer. Carter's, designer and artist, 2008-10; designer for International Greetings USA, 2010-11. Ringling College of Art and Design, trustee. *Exhibitions:* Work exhibited at Ringling School of Art and Design and by Society of Illustrators.

Awards, Honors

Silver medal, ADDY Awards.

Writings

Tom Llewellyn, *The Tilting House,* Tricycle Press (Berkeley, CA), 2010.

Sidelights

Sarah Watts is a Georgia-based artist and designer whose inky line drawings and gouache-and-acrylic paintings evoke the work of nineteenth-century illustrators like Aubrey Beardsley and Will Bradley, but with a touch of the macabre. In addition to advertising design and works of original art, Watts has also created the illustrations that appear alongside Tom Llewellyn's story in the unusual young-adult novel *The Tilting House.*

A native of northern Georgia, Watts moved south with her family and spent her teen years in Florida. After deciding to pursue a degree in art, she enrolled at the Ringling College of Art and Design and earned her B.F.A. in illustration. As a freelance artist now based in Atlanta, she has worked as a designer for children's clothing manufacturer Carters as well as International Greetings.

Llewellyn's *The Tilting House* was an apt choice for Watts's first illustration assignment. The story centers on Josh Peshik, who has just moved with his family to an old house in Tacoma, Washington, where everything seems a little "off." With handwriting and mathematical equations covering the walls, and floors canted differently than ceilings, the house serves as a surreal setting for Josh's adventures, which involve a family of taciturn talking rats, threatening neighbors, a mad scientist, and local legends about a body buried somewhere under the squeaky floorboards of the front porch. The author's "decidedly nonlinear" plot "ranges from exaggerated humor to Gothic horror to downright grotesque," noted *School Library Journal* contributor Eliane E. Knight, and Watts's line-drawn spot art heads each chapter, "help[ing to] set the tone for each episode" in Josh's adventures. In *Publishers Weekly* a reviewer remarked on the "quick pace" and unusual storyline of *The Tilting House,* adding that "Watts's shadowy woodblock-style illustrations . . . will keep readers attentive."

Biographical and Critical Sources

PERIODICALS

Booklist, August 1, 2010, Ian Chipman, review of *The Tilting House,* p. 56.
Kirkus Reviews, May 15, 2010, review of *The Tilting House.*
Publishers Weekly, June 21, 2010, review of *The Tilting House,* p. 46.

School Library Journal, June, 2010, Elaine E. Knight, review of *The Tilting House,* p. 110.

ONLINE

Sarah Watts Home Page, http://wattsalot.com (October 10, 2011).
Sarah Watts Web log, http://wattsalot.blogspot.com (October 10, 2011).

* * *

WEBER, Dennis J. 1951-

Personal
Born 1951, in Prince Albert, Saskatchewan, Canada; married; wife's name Sharon. *Ethnicity:* "Native American/Métis." *Education:* Attended Alberta College of Art.

Addresses
Home—Kelowna, British Columbia, Canada. *E-mail*—dsweb@shaw.ca.

Career
Fine-art painter and illustrator. Teacher of portraiture; teacher at schools and workshops. Métis Community Services Society of British Columbia, youth mentor. *Exhibitions:* Work included in invitational shows, group and solo exhibitions, and at Kelowna Museum, Kelowna, British Columbia, Canada, 2007; Moonstone Gallery, Calgary, Alberta, Canada; and Turtle Island Gallery, Kelowna. Work represented in private collections.

Member
Federation of Canadian Artists, Canadian Institute of Portrait Artists.

Writings

David Bouchard, *The Secret of Your Name: Proud to Be Métis/Kiimooch ka shinikashooyen: aen kishchitaymook aen li Michif iwik,* Red Deer Press (Calgary, Alberta, Canada), 2010.

Texts featuring Weber's illustrations have been translated into French.

Biographical and Critical Sources

PERIODICALS

Artists Magazine, March, 2001, profile of Weber.

Dennis J. Weber (Self-portrait in pencil and charcoal. Reproduced by permission.)

Canadian Review of Materials, February 26, 2010, Gregory Bryan, review of *The Secret of Your Name: Proud to Be Métis/Kiimooch ka shinikashooyen: aen kishchitaymook aen li Michif iwik.*
Children's Bookwatch, July, 2010, review of *The Secret of Your Name.*
Kirkus Reviews, May 15, 2010, review of *The Secret of Your Name.*

ONLINE

Art in Canada Web site, http://artincanada.com/ (September 29, 2011), "Dennis Weber."
Dennis Weber Home Page, http://www.webergallery.com (September 29, 2011).*

* * *

WELSH, C.E.L.
(Chris Welsh)

Personal
Married; wife's name Tiffany; children: two.

Addresses
Home—TX. *E-mail*—celwelsh@gmail.com.

Career
Comics and fiction writer.

Writings

GRAPHIC NOVELS

Harry Houdini, illustrated by Lalit Kumar Singh, Campfire Comics/Kalyani Navyug Media (New Delhi, India), 2010.

(Adaptor) Robert Louis Stevenson, *The Strange Case of Dr. Jekyll and Mr. Hyde,* illustrated by Lalit Kumar Singh, Campfire Comics/Kalyani Navyug Media (New Delhi, India), 2010.

(Adaptor) H. Rider Haggard, *King Solomon's Mines,* illustrated by Bhupendra Ahluwalia, Campfire Comics/ Kalyani Navyug Media (New Delhi, India), 2010.

Space Race, illustrated by K.I. Jones, Campfire Comics/ Kalyani Navyug Media (New Delhi, India), 2011.

Also author of stories published by Amazon Digital, including *A.I. Trigger, Tubifex, Shiver,* and *Coffeyville,* all 2011.

Biographical and Critical Sources

PERIODICALS

School Librarian, autumn, 2010, Mary Crawford, review of *Harry Houdini,* p. 172.

ONLINE

C.E.L. Welsh Web log, http://www.celwelsh.com (August 4, 2011).

Comics Career Web site, http://www.comicscareer.com/ (February 5, 2009), interview with Welsh.*

* * *

WELSH, Chris
See WELSH, C.E.L.

* * *

WHITE, Kathryn 1956-
(K.I. White, Kathryn Ivy White)

Personal

Born 1956, in Bradford-on-Avon, England; married; husband's name David; children: five.

Addresses

Home—Wells, Somerset, England. *E-mail*—kwauthor@ gmail.com.

Career

Author of books for children. Works for H.M.P. Service. Presenter at schools, libraries, workshops, and conferences.

Kathryn White (Reproduced by permission.)

Member

British Society of Authors.

Awards, Honors

Nottingham Children's Book Award shortlist, and Sheffield Book Award shortlist, both 2005, both for *Here Comes the Crocodile.*

Writings

PICTURE BOOKS

Good Day, Bad Day, illustrated by Cliff Wright, Oxford University Press (Oxford, England), 2000, published as *When They Fight,* Winslow Press (Delray Beach, FL), 2000.

Here Comes the Crocodile, illustrated by Michael Terry, Little Tiger Press (London, England), 2004.

The Nutty Nut Chase, illustrated by Vanessa Cabban, Good Books (Intercourse, PA), 2004.

Snowshoe the Hare, illustrated by Ruth Rivers, Egmont (London, England), 2005, Crabtree (New York, NY), 2006.

Click Clack Crocodile's Back, illustrated by Joélle Dreidemy, Little Tiger Press (London, England), 2009.

Sleepy Time, illustrated by Sanja Rešĉek, Caterpillar Books, 2009.

Cheese Hunt, illustrated by Debbie Tarbett, Caterpillar Books, 2010.

Ruby's School Walk, illustrated by Miriam Latimer, Barefoot Books (Cambridge, MA), 2010.

The Very Noisy Jungle, illustrated by Gill Guile, Good Books (Intercourse, PA), 2011.

When Will It Snow?, illustrated by Alison Edgson, Little Tiger Press (London, England), 2011.

Author's works have been translated into several languages, including Chinese, Danish, Dutch, Finnish, French, German, Japanese, Polish, Slovenian, and Swedish.

READERS

The Hunt, Heinemann (London, England), 2002.

Girls Watch, Heinemann (London, England), 2002.

The Tupilak, Heinemann (London, England), 2002.

Heads or Tails, Heinemann (London, England), 2004.

(Under name K.I. White) *Splitzaroni,* illustrated by Paul Savage, Badger Books (London, England), 2004, Stone Arch Books (Mankato, MN), 2006.

Pitch Pond Curse, Heinemann (London, England), 2005.

(With Ruskin Bond) *Eye of the Eagle,* Heinemann (London, England), 2005.

The Gift, Ginn (Oxford, England), 2005.

Ghost Thief, Heinemann (London, England), 2005.

(With Evelyne Duverne) *Carving the Sea Path,* Evans Bros. (London, England), 2009.

Sharks on the Loose!, illustrated by Andy Elkerton, Oxford University Press (Oxford, England), 2009.

Beast Hunter, A. & C. Black (London, England), 2011.

Contributor of poems and stories to anthologies, including *Lines in the Sand,* Frances Lincoln, 2004, and *Wow! 366.*

Sidelights

Kathryn White began her career as a children's writer after her own children were grown and she had time to reflect on her experiences as both a parent and a child. White's first book, *Good Day, Bad Day,* draws on her difficulties growing up in an anger-filled home, and it resonated with readers so much that it was also published in the United States under the title *When They Fight.* With this encouraging start, White quickly found her niche writing both picture-book texts and easy-reading stories for slightly older bookworms, such as *Splitzaroni, The Gift,* and the Arctic-themed reader *Carving the Sea Path.* White's stories have been paired with colorful illustrations by talented artists who include Cliff Wright, Vanessa Cabban, Joélle Dreidemy, and Michael Terry.

White often casts animals in children's roles in her stories for the very young. In *When They Fight* a young badger is the child stand-in as the sounds of his parents' arguments are transformed into battling monsters

and buffeting storms in his imagination. Fortunately, there are sunny, serene times as well, in a story that *Booklist* critic Hazel Rochman characterized as "the opposite of [Maurice] Sendak's classic *Where the Wild Things Are.*" Recommending White's story for children dealing with difficult family situations, Marianne Saccardi added in *School Library Journal* that the badger characters in *When They Fight* will help "make the situation easier to face and talk about."

Another story for young children, *Snowshoe the Hare,* finds a gullible Arctic hare worried by Otter's stories about the changing seasons and nervous that he will melt like the winter snow. Two squirrels fighting over a large brown nut that suddenly pops out of the earth are sent on a surprising jaunt in *The Nutty Nut Chase,* which Maryann H. Owen described in her *School Library Journal* review as "an endearing romp" featuring Cabban's appealing watercolor art.

A little girl named Ruby stars in *Ruby's School Walk,* a story illustrated with animation-style artwork by Miriam Latimer. In Williams' story, the child's first walk to school reveals a set of worries which play out in her active imagination as encounters with a sharp-toothed tiger, fording a sea of crocodiles, and walking past a haunted house. Fortunately, White's rhyming text also reveals that Ruby's mother is there to hold her hand, especially when the girl faces her greatest challenge: entering the classroom and meeting her new teacher. White's "energetic" and "repetitive lines will encourage lively, interactive read-alouds," according to *Booklist* contributor Gillian Engberg.

Ruby's School Walk **pairs White's eye-popping Halloween story with Miriam Latimer's colorful stylized art.** (Illustration copyright © 2010 by Miriam Latimer. Reproduced by permission of Barefoot Books.)

Biographical and Critical Sources

PERIODICALS

Booklist, April 15, 2000, Hazel Rochman, review of *When They Fight,* p. 1554; September 1, 2010, Gillian Engberg, review of *Ruby's School Walk,* p. 114.

School Library Journal, June, 2000, Marianne Saccardi, review of *When They Fight,* p. 127; January, 2005, Maryann H. Owen, review of *The Nutty Nut Chase,* p. 100; December, 2010, Ieva Bates, review of *Ruby's School Walk,* p. 90.

ONLINE

Kathryn White Home Page, http://www.kathrynwhite.net (October 14, 2011).

*   *   *

WHITE, Kathryn Ivy
See WHITE, Kathryn

*   *   *

WHITE, K.I.
See WHITE, Kathryn

*   *   *

WILKINS, Ebony Joy

Personal

Female. *Education:* Purdue University, B.A. (communications); Purdue University-Purdue University at Indianapolis, M.S. (education); New School University, M.F.A. (creative writing); postgraduate work toward Ph.D. (education) at University of Illinois Chicago. *Hobbies and other interests:* Reading, travel, visiting family.

Addresses

Home—Chicago, IL. *E-mail*—ebonybooks@yahoo.com.

Career

Educator and writer. Former education journalist; teacher for ten years. Presenter at schools.

Writings

Sellout, Scholastic Press (New York, NY), 2010.
(Coauthor) Dorene Lewis, *Someone to Hear Me,* Lulu. com, 2011.

The Will to Dance: Based on the Life Story of How Dorene Lewis Has Overcome, Lulu.com, 2011.

Sidelights

Ebony Joy Wilkins began writing as a child growing up in the Midwest, her efforts encouraged by her parents and enjoyed by the friends she read her stories to. Wilkins' first novel, *Sellout,* had its start in a class assignment as part of her master's degree at New School University, and it was completed as her thesis project. The manuscript found an enthusiastic publisher when its author sent it to one of her former teachers, Scholastic editor and Y.A. novelist David Levithan. Although Wilkins was hoping for constructive feedback, Levithan decided that *Sellout* was worth publishing and instead of suggestions for revisions the young author received a book contract.

Based on its authors own experiences moving from a multiracial community to the predominately white suburbs, *Sellout* introduces NaTasha Jennings, a high-school freshman who has moved with her parents to an all-white school district where it is hoped that she will benefit from the area's increased academic and social opportunities. Although NaTasha tries to remake herself

Cover of Ebony Joy Wilkins' young-adult novel Sellout, *which finds an African-American teen reevaluating her cultural influences.* (Photograph copyright © 2010 by Michael Frost. Reproduced by permission of Scholastic, Inc.)

and jump the many cultural hurdles blocking her path toward acceptance by her classmates, she cannot change who she really is. Fortunately, Tilly, the teen's feisty grandmother, recognizes NaTasha's difficulties and allows the girl to spend the summer at her home in Harlem. As she makes new friends and helps Tilly in her volunteer efforts at a local teen crisis center, where several of the tougher girls dismiss her as a sellout to her race, NaTasha begins to really understand who she is and recognize that a person's character is measured by more than superficial things.

Wilkins' fiction debut was described by Megan Honig in *School Library Journal* as a "novel about race, fitting in, and finding oneself" in which "the message of staying true to oneself shines through." Also reviewing *Sellout*, a *Publishers Weekly* critic noted that the author effectively "explores the building of confidence, morals, and survival skills," while *Booklist* critic Karen Cruze concluded that "NaTasha's budding realization that appearances and expectations often mask a person's true nature . . . signals an important adolescent journey."

"I believe children relate to the characters they see on the page," wrote Wilkins in an interview with blogger Amy Bowlan on the *School Library Journal* Web site. "When I was a younger reader there were not many books with African-American central characters that I could relate to. As I read more and more, I began searching desperately for characters who told my own story. In my professional experience, I have found that the best way to find these stories was to pick up a pen and write the story myself. I encourage everyone to read, research, and write their own stories."

Biographical and Critical Sources

PERIODICALS

Booklist, September 1, 2010, Karen Cruze, review of *Sellout*, p. 100.
Publishers Weekly, July 12, 2010, review of *Sellout*, p. 48.
School Library Journal, August, 2010, Megan Honig, review of *Sellout*, p. 116.

ONLINE

Ebony Joy Wilkins Home Page, http://www.ebonyjoywilkins.com (October 10, 2011).
Ebony Joy Wilkins Web site, http://ebonyjoywilkins.blogspot.com (October 10, 2011).
School Library Journal Web site, http://blog.schoollibraryjournal.com/bowllandsblog/ (November 10, 2009), Amy Bolland, interview with Wilkins.
Teen Writers Bloc Web site, http://www.teenwritersbloc.com/ (February 14, 2011), Dhonielle Clayton, interview with Wilkins.

WILLIAMS, Richard Treat
See WILLIAMS, Treat

*   *   *

WILLIAMS, Treat 1951-
(Richard Treat Williams)

Personal

Born Richard Treat Williams, December 1, 1951, in Rowayton (some sources cite Stamford), CT; son of Richard Norman (a corporate executive) and Marion (an antiques dealer) Williams; married Pamela Van Sant (a dancer and actress), June, 1988; children: Gil, Elinor Claire. *Education:* Attended Franklin and Marshall College.

Addresses

Home—Park City, UT. *Agent*—United Talent Agency, 9560 Wilshire Blvd., 5th Fl., Beverly Hills, CA 90212.

Career

Actor, producer, director, and writer. Actor in plays, including *Grease*, 1973; *The Pirates of Penzance*, 1981-82; *The Glass Menagerie*, 1986; *Oleanna*, 1993-94; *Captains Courageous*, 1999; *Stephen Sondheim's Follies*, 2001; and *War Letters: Extraordinary Correspondence from American Wars*, 2002. Actor in motion pictures, including *Deadly Hero*, 1976; *The Eagle Has Landed*, 1976; *Hair*, 1979; *The Pursuit of D.B. Cooper*, 1981; *Prince of the City*, 1981; *Once upon a Time in America*, 1984; *The Men's Club*, 1986; *Heart of Dixie*, 1989; *Things to Do in Denver When You're Dead*, 1995; *Mulholland Falls*, 1996; *The Devil's Own*, 1997; *Deep End of the Ocean*, 1999; *Critical Mass*, 2000; *Miss Congeniality 2: Armed and Fabulous*, 2005; and *127 Hours*, 2010. Actor in television movies, including *Dempsey*, 1983; *A Streetcar Named Desire*, 1984; *J. Edgar Hoover*, 1987; *The Water Engine*, 1992; *Road to Avonlea*, 1993; *The Late Shift*, 1996; *The Substitute 2: School's Out*, 1998; *The Substitute 3: Winner Takes All*, 1999; *The Staircase Murders*, 2007; and *Boston's Finest*, 2010. Actor in television miniseries, including *Echoes in the Darkness*, 1987; *Drug Wars: The Camarena Story*, 1990; *Deadly Matrimony*, 1992; *Journey to the Center of the Earth*, 1999; and *Guilty Hearts*, 2002. Actor in television series, including *Eddie Dodd*, 1991; *Good Advice*, 1993-94; *Everwood*, 2002-06; *Brothers and Sisters*, 2006; *Heartland*, 2007; and *Against the Wall*, 2011—. Producer of *Bonds of Love* (television movie), 1993; director of *Texan* (television movie), 1994.

Member

Screen Actors Guild.

Treat Williams (AP/Wide World Photos. Reproduced by permission.)

Awards, Honors

Golden Globe Award nomination for New Star of the Year in a Motion Picture—Male, 1980, for *Hair;* Golden Globe Award nomination for Best Motion Picture Actor—Drama, 1982, for *Prince of the City;* Golden Globe Award nomination for Best Performance by an Actor in a Mini-Series or Motion Picture Made for TV, 1985, for *A Streetcar Named Desire;* Independent Spirit Award nomination for Best Male Lead, 1986, for *Smooth Talk;* best new director honor, Aspen Short Film Festival, and best short film honor, Fort Lauderdale Film Festival, both 1994, both for *Texan;* Emmy Award nomination for Outstanding Supporting Actor in a Miniseries or a Special, 1996, for *The Late Shift;* Drama League Award for best performer in a Broadway production, 1998, for *Captains Courageous,* 2001, for *Stephen Sondheim's Follies;* Family Television Award for best actor in a TV show, 2003, and Screen Actors Guild Award nominations for Outstanding Performance by a Male Actor in a Drama Series, 2003, 2004, all for *Everwood.*

Writings

Air Show!, illustrated by Robert Neubecker, Hyperion (New York, NY), 2010.

Sidelights

A respected stage, film, and television actor who has garnered a host of Emmy and Golden Globe award nominations, Treat Williams made his literary debut in 2010 with *Air Show!,* a children's book featuring illustrations by Robert Neubecker. The work, which focuses on two siblings who journey aboard their father's plane to watch him perform in an air show, had its origins in an experience from Williams' own life. A certified flight instructor, Williams once traveled to an air show with Neubecker, a friend and neighbor who shared his love of airplanes. "Air shows are huge in the aviation culture," Williams told *Publishers Weekly* interviewer Sally Lodge. "We spent three days there enjoying the show, and Robert took pictures and lots of notes. So that planted the seeds of the book, and we then tossed around ideas about the best way to accommodate his wonderful art work into a story."

Air Show! concerns Ellie, a spirited girl who longs for a ride in a stunt plane, and Ellie's younger brother Gill, who possesses an encyclopedic knowledge of the various types of aircraft. As the children take to the sky with their dad, readers are treated to "a backseat tour of a flight, from last-minute fueling to landing," a critic in *Kirkus Reviews* stated. Writing in *School Library Journal,* Kathleen Kelly MacMillan remarked that *Air Show!* "will resonate with young transportation lovers," and a *Publishers Weekly* reviewer predicted that Williams' tale is "certain to capture the imaginations of young airplane aficionados." Neubecker's contributions also drew praise. "With different angles and perspectives, both aerial and terrestrial," Andrew Medlar commented in *Booklist,* "the standout art makes this well worth the ride."

Williams told Lodge that creating a book is, in many ways, similar to making a film. "It wasn't a process that was unnatural to me, since what I do as an actor involves working with a director and many other people," he explained. "I came to realize that this was like an ensemble, a group effort, with input from a lot of people. I realized that everyone's ideas and suggestions were making the book better and better. It was a fun process and very exciting."

Biographical and Critical Sources

BOOKS

Newsmakers, Issue 3, Gale (Detroit, MI), 2004.

PERIODICALS

Booklist, June 1, 2010, Andrew Medlar, review of *Air Show!,* p. 87.
Horn Book, September-October, 2010, Tany D. Auger, review of *Air Show!,* p. 68.
Kirkus Reviews, May 15, 2010, review of *Air Show!*
Publishers Weekly, May 17, 2010, review of *Air Show!,* p. 47.
School Library Journal, July, 2010, Kathleen Kelly MacMillan, review of *Air Show!,* p. 72.

Williams teams up with friend and artist Robert Neubecker to create the picture book **Air Show!** (Illustration copyright © 2010 by Robert Neubecker. Reproduced by permission of Disney-Hyperion, an imprint of Disney Book Group LLC. All rights reserved.)

ONLINE

Publishers Weekly Online, http://www.publishersweekly. com/ (June 4, 2010), Sally Lodge, interview with Williams.*

*   *   *

WISNEWSKI, Andrea

Personal
Born in MD; married Chris Butler (a graphic designer and digital prepress expert); children: Allison. *Education:* Attended Portland (ME) School of Art; University of Connecticut, B.F.A., 1985.

Addresses
Home—Storrs, CT.

Career
Cut-paper artist, illustrator, and author of children's books. *Hartford Courant,* Hartford, CT, former staff illustrator; Running Rabbit Press, CT, founder and producer of art prints and greeting cards. 1989.

Awards, Honors
Best of Category, New England Book Show, 2007, for *Little Red Riding Hood.*

Writings

SELF-ILLUSTRATED

A Cottage Garden Alphabet, David R. Godine (Boston, MA), 2002.
(Reteller) *Little Red Riding Hood,* David R. Godine (Boston, MA), 2006.

ILLUSTRATOR

Crescent Dragonwagon, *The Cornbread Gospels,* Workman Publishing (New York, NY), 2007.
C.M. Millen, *The Ink Garden of Brother Theophane,* Charlesbridge (Watertown, MA), 2010.

Contributor to periodicals, including *Babybug, Business Week, Cleveland Plain Dealer, Cricket, Newsweek, New York Times, Wall Street Journal, Washington Post,* and *Weekly Reader.*

Sidelights
The founder of Running Rabbit Press, Andrea Wisnewski grew up on a farm in Connecticut, and she draws on her love of rural life in her illustrations and printmaking. In addition to creating her own self-illustrated *A Cottage Garden Alphabet,* Wisnewski retells a traditional and well-loved story in *Little Red Riding Hood,* which highlights her unique art form: a

combination of traditional old-world cut-paper techniques and metal-plate printing that is hand-tinted with water color.

Wisnewski moved to southern New England to attend the University of Connecticut and developed her interest in papercutting while working for the region's major daily newspaper, the *Hartford Courant,* as a staff artist. Constantly dealing with quick deadlines, she wanted to find a way to achieve the look of a block print in a relatively short amount of time, and she did so by cutting paper rather than carving reliefs into a wood or linoleum block. Wisnewski begins with a drawing and then transfers it to a piece of clay-coated paper. An X-Acto knife and a steady hand are necessary to make the detailed cuts. Black-and-white images gain color either through the introduction of colored-paper elements or by burning the image on a metal plate, printing it on her husband's wooden press, and then adding watercolor accents by hand.

Wisnewski's first book for children, *A Cottage Garden Alphabet,* takes children on a tour of backyard gardens from Apple to Zucchini, including fruits and vegetables as well as herbs and flowers. Noting that her "detailed pictures . . . invite inspection," Ilene Cooper added in her *Booklist* review that *A Cottage Garden Alphabet* stands out as "a beautiful piece of bookmaking."

In *Little Red Riding Hood* the artist pairs her unique folk-style art with an original version of a well-known story in which her "retelling is straightforward and the language has a comfortable, folksy cadence," according to *School Library Journal* critic Joy Fleishhacker. Observing that Wisnewski sets her story in a well-known New England living-history museum, Old Sturbridge Village, Fleishhacker suggested that this version of *Little Red Riding Hood* would make "an eyecatching addition" to school and library collections. The book showcases "effective compositions, the restrained use of color, and the distinctive look of Wisnewski's artwork," maintained *Booklist* critic Carolyn Phelan, and in *Publishers Weekly* a critic lauded the author/illustrator's retelling as "adorn[ed] . . . with graceful illustrations that emulate woodcuts, washed with saturated watercolors, and brimming with details."

As an illustrator, Wisnewski has also created the art for Crescent Dragonwagon's cookbook *The Cornbread Gospels* and C.M. Millen's picture book *The Ink Garden of Brother Theophane.* Set in a remote monastery during medieval times, Millen's story focuses on a monk who devised a range of colorful inks for use in illuminating manuscripts. Reviewing *The Ink Garden of Brother Theophane* in *School Library Journal,* Susan Scheps cited the book's "exquisitely detailed illustrations," and a *Publishers Weekly* contributor asserted that "Wisnewski's intricate, woodblock-like portraits of Irish monastery life are this book's principal charm."

Biographical and Critical Sources

PERIODICALS

Booklist, February 15, 2003, Ilene Cooper, review of *A Cottage Garden Alphabet,* p. 1071; January 1, 2007, Carolyn Phelan, review of *Little Red Riding Hood,* p. 118; July 1, 2010, Carolyn Phelan, review of *The Ink Garden of Brother Theophane,* p. 60.

Kirkus Reviews, December 15, 2006, review of *Little Red Riding Hood,* p. 1274.

Library Journal, January 1, 2008, Pauline Baughman, review of *The Cornbread Gospels,* p. 126.

Publishers Weekly, December 23, 2002, review of *A Cottage Garden Alphabet,* p. 73; January 8, 2007, review of *Little Red Riding Hood,* p. 51; July 5, 2010, review of *The Ink Garden of Brother Theophane,* p. 42.

School Library Journal, May, 2003, Lauralyn Persson, review of *A Cottage Garden Alphabet,* p. 143; June, 2007, Joy Fleishhacker, review of *Little Red Riding Hood,* p. 137; August, 2010, Susan Scheps, review of *The Ink Garden of Brother Theophane,* p. 80.

Tribune Books (Chicago, IL), January 14, 2007, Mary Harris Russell, review of *Little Red Riding Hood,* p. 7.

ONLINE

Andrea Wisnewski Home Page, http://www.runningrabbit. biz (August 4, 2011).

Andrea Wisnewski's illustration projects include C.M. Millen's history-themed picture book **The Ink Garden of Brother Theophane.** (Illustration copyright © 2010 by Andrea Wisnewski. Reproduced by permission of Charlesbridge Publishing, Inc. All rights reserved.)

University of Connecticut Library Web site, http://www.lib.uconn.edu/ (October 15, 2011), "The Cutting Edge: Papercut Illustrations by Andrea Wisnewski."*

* * *

WOOD, Douglas 1951-
(Douglas Eric Wood)

Personal

Born December 10, 1951, in New York, NY; son of James H. (a college professor) and Joyce (a college professor) Wood; married Kathryn Sokolowski (a teacher and singer), May 26, 1973; children: Eric, Bryan. *Education:* Morningside College (IA), B.Ed., 1973; attended St. Cloud State University, 1984. *Hobbies and other interests:* Canoeing and wilderness trips, tennis, fishing, reading.

Addresses

Home and office—3835 Pine Point Rd., Sartell, MN 56377. *E-mail*—doug@douglaswood.com.

Career

Writer and musician. Music teacher in Iowa and Minnesota, 1973-77; naturalist and wilderness guide in northern MN, beginning 1977; host of weekly radio show, *Wood's Lore,* St. Cloud, MN, 1984-91; recording artist and performer in musical groups, including Wild Spirit Band.

Awards, Honors

Named among Ten Outstanding Young Minnesotans by Minnesota Jaycees, 1991; Minnesota Book Award for younger children, 1992, and Book of the Year Award (children's division), American Booksellers Association, International Reading Association Children's Book Award, and Midwest Publishers Award, all 1993, all for *Old Turtle;* Minnesota Book Award nomination and North East Minnesota Book Award nomination, both 1995, both for *Minnesota: The Spirit of the Land*; Christopher Medal, 1999, for *Grandad's Prayers of the Earth.*

Writings

FOR CHILDREN

Old Turtle, illustrated by Cheng-Khee Chee, Pfeifer-Hamilton (Duluth, MN), 1992, reprinted, Scholastic (New York, NY), 2007.
Northwoods Cradle Song: From a Menominee Lullaby, illustrated by Lisa Desimini, Simon & Schuster (New York, NY), 1996.
The Windigo's Return: A North Woods Story, illustrated by Greg Couch, Simon & Schuster (New York, NY), 1996.

Rabbit and the Moon, illustrated by Leslie Baker, Simon & Schuster (New York, NY), 1998.
Making the World, illustrated by Yoshi and Hibiki Miyazaki, Simon & Schuster (New York, NY), 1998.
Grandad's Prayers of the Earth, illustrated by P.J. Lynch, Candlewick Press (Cambridge, MA), 1999.
What Dads Can't Do, illustrated by Doug Cushman, Simon & Schuster (New York, NY), 2000.
What Moms Can't Do, illustrated by Doug Cushman, Simon & Schuster (New York, NY), 2001.
A Quiet Place, illustrated by Dan Andreasen, Simon & Schuster (New York, NY), 2001.
What Teachers Can't Do, illustrated by Doug Cushman, Simon & Schuster (New York, NY), 2002.
Old Turtle and the Broken Truth, illustrated by Jon J. Muth, Scholastic (New York, NY), 2003.
What Santa Can't Do, illustrated by Doug Cushman, Simon & Schuster (New York, NY), 2003.
The Secret of Saying Thanks, illustrated by Greg Shed, Simon & Schuster (New York, NY), 2005.
What Grandmas Can't Do, illustrated by Doug Cushman, Simon & Schuster (New York, NY), 2005.
Nothing to Do, illustrated by Wendy Anderson Halperin, Dutton (New York, NY), 2006.
When Mama Mirabelle Comes Home, illustrated by Andy Wagner, National Geographic Society (Washington, DC), 2007.
Miss Little's Gift, illustrated by Jim Burke, Candlewick Press (Somerville, MA), 2009.
Aunt Mary's Rose, illustrated by LeUyen Pham, Candlewick Press (Cambridge, MA), 2010.
Franklin and Winston: A Christmas That Changed the World, Candlewick Press (Cambridge, MA), 2010.
No One but You, Candlewick Press (Somerville, MA), 2010.
Where the Sunrise Begins, illustrated by K. Wendy Popp, Simon & Schuster Books for Young Readers (New York, NY), 2010.

OTHER

(And illustrator) *Paddle Whispers* (adult nonfiction), Pfeifer-Hamilton (Duluth, MN), 1993.
Minnesota, Naturally (adult nonfiction), Voyageur Press (Stillwater, MN), 1995.
Minnesota: The Spirit of the Land, Voyageur Press (Stillwater, MN), 1995.
(And illustrator) *Fawn Island,* University of Minnesota Press (Minneapolis, MN), 2001.

Lyricist on musical recordings, including *Solitary Shores,* EarthSong, 1980; *EarthSong,* NorthWord Press, 1985; *Northwoods Nights,* EarthSong, 1986; and *Wilderness Daydreams,* Pfeifer-Hamilton, 1988. Contributor of essays to *NorthWriters,* University of Minnesota Press, 1991, ant of articles to magazines.

Adaptations

Several of Wood's books were adapted as audiobooks.

Sidelights

Douglas Wood became well known for his very first children's book, *Old Turtle*, which was called "a New Age fable" by *School Library Journal* contributor Shirley Wilton. From its modest first printing, the book eventually tapped a national audience and earned several prestigious awards, prompting Wood—a bluegrass musician, wilderness guide, and naturalist—to embark on a new career as a children's book author. In the years since, he has produced many other nature-themed stories, among them *Grandad's Prayers of the Earth, A Quiet Place, The Secret of Saying Thanks,* and *Where the Sunrise Begins.*

"I never set out to write a children's book," Wood once told *SATA,* discussing *Old Turtle* in an interview. "And I sure never thought that it would touch so many people across the nation and the world. Clearly there is a resonance at work—it reaches both adults and children." Part of that resonance comes from the book's text, which is deceptively simple, like good song lyrics. Wood, who has been writing and performing music for years, is no amateur in this area. "My whole family is involved in music," he said. "My parents were both music instructors at the college level, and my two brothers are professional musicians. [In my family] music was kind of like breathing."

Trained in the piano and violin, Wood started playing guitar after he graduated from high school. While he continued to study the violin and majored in music at college, he was increasingly drawn to the simple yet eloquent themes of folk music. At the same time, he was plagued by a tension between his two loves. "I was always frustrated with music as a kid," Wood said, "because I didn't like to practice. I liked to be outdoors."

Music and nature continue to be the two themes of Wood's life. Although raised in Sioux City, Iowa, he loved spending time with his grandparents in Minnesota's boreal forests, and in 1975, fresh out of college and after briefly teaching music, he and his wife relocated to his favorite state. Inspired by the naturalist writings of Minnesotan Sigurd Olson, with whom he also corresponded, Wood combined his twin loves by writing songs about nature and supported his family by working as a wilderness guide and establishing himself as a professional musician. From working in local bars, he eventually built the following needed to support a concert career performing original folk music with his guitar and baritone vocals. In addition to recording his music on his own EarthSong label, Wood also contributed reflective nature essays to outdoor magazines, hosted a nature-themed radio program, *Wood's Lore,* and participated in artist-in-residence programs in the Minnesota public schools.

Douglas Wood mines Native American legend in **Old Turtle,** *a picture-book celebration of the natural world that features Cheng-Khee Chee's luminous paintings.* (Scholastic Press, 2001. Illustration © 1992 by Cheng-Khee Chee. Reproduced by permission of Scholastic, Inc.)

It was during one such public-school stint that Wood was inspired to write *Old Turtle*. "I'd been working all day with these kids, with their energy and love for creativity, and I was driving back to my parents' home, where I was visiting," he later recalled. "Suddenly the idea for *Old Turtle* popped into my mind, all of a piece. I knew exactly what I wanted to say, exactly where the story would take me. I got to my parents' house, said 'Hi,' and went upstairs and set to work. In a half an hour I had the basic text." After several months of polishing, he showed the manuscript to an editor at Pfeifer-Hamilton and the publisher paired Wood's text with watercolor illustrations by Cheng-Khee Chee to create the soon-to-be-popular picture book *Old Turtle*.

Essentially a teaching book in the manner of Sufi or other religious texts, *Old Turtle* is set in a mythic time when all living and inanimate things could communicate. During one such discussion, discord results during a conversation regarding the forms that God takes: over knowing who or what God is. A cacophony ensues which Old Turtle stops with sage words. To remind the world of God's presence, humans are sent to Earth. However, they soon forget the message of love that they themselves are meant to convey and begin to destroy the planet. Old Turtle once again has to remind all creatures that God exists in all things. Wood tells his story "in lyrical prose and pictures that delight the eye," Wilton wrote in her *School Library Journal* review of *Old Turtle,* and a *Publishers Weekly* critic cited the "lilting cadence of the poetic text" in Wood's "enchanting book." Merry Mattson, writing in the *Wilson Library Bulletin,* called *Old Turtle* a "marvelous fable" that deals with the concept of God, the planet Earth, and the "interconnectedness" of all creatures.

A sequel to *Old Turtle, The Old Turtle and the Broken Truth,* continues Wood's theme of tolerance. Here he describes how a core truth is broken in two pieces upon its fall to earth, thus causing undue suffering until a child reunites the truth's two halves. As GraceAnne A. DeCandido noted in *Booklist, Old Turtle and the Broken Truth* benefits from John J. Muth's "gorgeous, shimmering" pen-and-ink and watercolor art, while *School Library Journal* reviewer Marianne Saccardi predicted that Wood's "beautiful text" will "spark discussion among older [elementary-grade] students."

Wood followed up *Old Turtle* with *Paddle Whispers,* a collection of reflections on nature and humanity's part in it. Written and illustrated by Wood for adult readers, *Paddle Whispers* follows a metaphoric canoe voyage that mirrors a person's journey through life. Although he has gone on to write several other books for adults, Wood has primarily focused on younger audiences. In addition to adapting Native-American folk tales in *The Windigo Returns: A North Woods Story* and *Northwoods Cradle Song: From a Menominee Lullaby,* he shares his personal beliefs in books such as *A Quiet Place, Nothing to Do, The Secret of Saying Thanks,* and *Grandad's Prayers of the Earth.*

In *The Windigo Returns* members of an Ojibwe tribe notice that some of their people are missing and the terrifying Windigo is blamed. A pit is dug, and when the Windigo is tricked into falling into it, the creature is set on fire. His dying threat—that he will return to eat the tribe and all succeeding generations—is considered to come true the next summer in the stinging bite of the mosquito. "The changing seasons flow through this story like a slow river, linking the plot to nature's calendar," remarked a contributor to *Kirkus Reviews* of Wood's porquois tale. Karen Morgan, writing in *Booklist,* considered the story's blend of horror and humor to be utterly successful, citing the transformation of the monster's ashes into the ubiquitous and annoying mosquito. In *The Windigo Returns* Wood offers readers "a blending of humor and spookiness that children will surely love," Morgan concluded.

Northwoods Cradle Song is an adaptation of a Menominee lullaby that finds a Native-American woman rocking her child and pointing out the ways in which other creatures in nature are also preparing to go to sleep. "The tender tone and quiet, respectful references to nature beautifully convey the timeless sense of night and lullaby," remarked Margaret A. Bush in *Horn Book,* while a *Publishers Weekly* contributor concluded that in *Northwoods Cradle Song* "Wood has crafted an image-rich, eminently musical lullaby."

Featuring Leslie Baker's luminous art, Wood's picture book **Rabbit and the Moon** *is based on a Cree trickster tale.* (Aladdin Paperbacks, 1988. Illustration copyright © by 1998 Leslie Baker. Reprinted with the permission of Simon & Schuster Books for Young Readers, an imprint of Simon & Schuster Children's Publishing Division.)

In *Rabbit and the Moon* Wood crafts another Native-American folktale which, like *The Windigo Returns,* contains a porquois element. Rabbit wishes he could ride on the moon and convinces Crane to fly him up to the sky. Holding onto the bird's legs so tightly that they bleed, and patting the bird in thanks upon his arrival, Rabbit thus gives Crane its distinctive red legs and crown.

Like *Old Turtle,* the message of *Making the World* drives the story, as artists Yoshi and Hibiki Miyazaki join Wood to journey from continent to continent, observing how the world is continually altered by its interactions with wind and sun, animals, and humans. "This ambitious, philosophical picture book, with its lyrical, simple prose, attempts to show how everything and everyone has a significant effect upon life and the landscape," Shelle Rosenfeld observed in *Booklist.* For Diane Nunn, writing in *School Library Journal,* the collaboration between illustration and text in *Making the World* "broadens a young child's awareness of our planet, its beauty, and everyone's ability to affect change."

In *Grandad's Prayers of the Earth* a young boy asks his father about prayer and receives an answer that encompasses all the creatures on earth. When the grandfather dies, the boy loses his ability to pray for a long time, until one day, when he returns to the forest where Grandad consulted him. With its evocative paintings by P.J. Lynch, *Grandad's Prayers of the Earth* "is a depiction of the spiritual that is without reference to a particular faith or tradition, and that doesn't lapse into greeting-card platitudes," observed a contributor to *Kirkus Reviews.* By centering his story on the loving relationship between a grandson and grandfather, and through extensive use of tangible metaphors, Wood makes "a difficult religious concept somewhat more concrete for children," remarked a contributor to *Publishers Weekly.* Likewise, Shelley Townsend-Hudson concluded in *Booklist* that in *Grandad's Prayers of the Earth* "Wood presents the subjects of prayer and death in a way that stirs the imagination and offers hope."

Wood and Lynch team up again in *No One but You,* which focuses on the uniqueness of every person's path through life. Whether standing in a summer rain, tasting the first strawberry of the season, or engaging in any other simple sensory activity that connects one with Nature, everyone will perceive the moment differently and weave it into a different tapestry.

In *A Quiet Place* Wood "hearkens back to a simpler time," according to a *Kirkus Reviews* writer. Enhanced by acrylic paintings by Dan Andreasen that evoke what *Booklist* reviewer Hazel Rochman dubbed an "old-fashioned *Saturday Evening Post*" nostalgia, the simple story follows a boy as he uses his imagination to expand his experiences beyond what he sees, ultimately finding the greatest serenity inside himself. Although several reviewers remarked that Wood's ode to solitude may appeal more to adults than to children, Rochman

maintained that "many children will welcome the change of pace," and that "the imaginary adventures" contained in Andreasen's paintings "are elemental." Citing a text "saturated with simile and metaphor," a *Publishers Weekly* reviewer called *A Quiet Place* "a vivid romp through a child's imagination," while a *Kirkus Reviews* contributor characteruzed the picture book as "solid soul guidance for a media-saturated society."

Similar in theme to *A Quiet Place, Nothing to Do* is a "picture-book celebration of the joys to be found in all-too-rare unscheduled time," according to a *Publishers Weekly* writer. Another reflective picture book, *The Secret of Saying Thanks,* focuses on acknowledging and appreciating the simple things in life. Employing a "gentle, assured tone and graceful phrasing," in the opinion of a *Publishers Weekly* contributor, Wood's message in *The Secret of Saying Thanks* is filtered through many faiths and reflected in Greg Shed's detailed paintings about a girl and her dog. The book serves as "a quiet, reflective piece on the importance of a grateful attitude," noted *School Library Journal* contributor Roxanne Burg, and its focus extending to "the wonders of nature as well as the comforts of home and family," according to a *Kirkus Reviews* writer.

Wood celebrates the reflection and creativity that solitude provides in **A Quiet Place,** *a picture book featuring Dan Andreasen's detailed and evocative paintings.* (Aladdin Paperbacks, 2002. Illustration copyright © 2002 by Dan Andreasen. All rights reserved. Reprinted with the permission of Simon & Schuster Books for Young Readers, an imprint of Simon & Schuster Children's Publishing Division.)

Wood honors an important teacher who helped him combat his difficulty in learning to read in *Miss Little's Gift.* As a new student in Miss Little's second-grade class, Douglas has trouble sitting still and concentrating during reading lessons. Recognizing that the boy's distractibility and need to fidget required a special approach to teaching, Miss Little keeps Douglas after school and finds books featuring illustrations that will capture his interest and lead him slowly to the point where he can tackle the accompanying sea of letters. Brought to life in Jim Burke's oil paintings, *Miss Little's Gift* serves as "a tribute to those unsung teacher heroes whose dedication . . . and native intuition about children have changed lives," according to *School Library Journal* critic Grace Oliff. Wood's story "shows that the magic of books is how much fun they are to read," asserted a *Kirkus Reviews* writer, while a *Publishers Weekly* critic predicted that *Miss Little's Gift* "will resonate with those who struggle with reading."

Wood continues to team up with talented artists in picture books such as *Aunt Mary's Rose* and *Where the Sunrise Begins.* Set during the 1950s and illustrated in sepia-toned water-color art by LeUyen Pham, *Aunt Mary's Rose* introduces a woman who cherishes a rosebush growing at her family's homestead. Talking to her young nephew, Douglas, Aunt Mary explains that the plant is linked to his family: planted by his grandfather and his father, the rose also carries a part of the boy as its gnarled roots weave together these many generations.

Praising *Aunt Mary's Rose* as "a gentle slice of the past," a *Kirkus Reviews* writer predicted that young readers "will enjoy asking their grandparents about their lives after reading about Douglas's extended family." In *School Librarian,* Elizabeth Baskeyfield wrote that the book's "gentle, soothing pace . . . is complimented by the subtle illustrations of Pham." *Where the Sunrise Begins* features artwork by K. Wendy Popp and prompts young children to ponder where a circle begins and ends as it describes the sun's orbit around the earth and the moment its light lightens the night sky to begin dawn in different regions. "The collaboration of author and illustrator is near perfection as the text and artwork build on one another," asserted Lisa Glasscock in her *School Library Journal* review of *Where the Sunrise Begins,* and a *Publishers Weekly* critic asserted that Wood's "noble sentiment" is expressed here in "prayer-like prose that even less spiritually oriented [readers] . . . will be drawn to."

Wood is also the author of several humorous picture books featuring dinosaurs as main characters. In *What Dads Can't Do* and *What Moms Can't Do,* a young dinosaur narrator recounts the many things his parents cannot seem to get right without his help, from picking out clothes to sleeping in on Saturday mornings. At the end of each book, however, the young dinosaur concludes that one thing parents always know how to do is love their children. A similar format extends to books on the limitations of grandmas, grandpas, teachers, and

The value of family traditions are captured by Wood in his picture book **Aunt Mary's Rose,** *featuring artwork by LeUyen Pham.* (Illustration copyright © 2010 by LeUyen Phan. Reproduced by permission of Candlewick Press, Somerville, MA.)

even Santa. "This amusing picture book will tickle youngsters' funny bones and make every parent and child smile with recognition," predicted Wanda Meyers-Hines in her review of *What Dads Can't Do* for *School Library Journal.*

"I love writing for children," Wood once told *SATA.* "It is clearly different than writing for adults, which is not to say that one is less important. It's the focus I take that is different. I write for children in a pure way. It's idea-oriented, and my number-one priority is to find one good and meaningful idea. In that way, it's not so different than writing a good song. All my years spent song writing prepared me very well for writing children's books. That experience enabled me to hear and listen for the rhythm of a sentence. I'll spend two hours on a sentence getting the rhythm right. I'm always using my ear when I write."

As for his impact on young readers, Wood explained: "I came to a decision long ago that I was not going to be topical or political in my work. And I am not a scientist. What I am is a poet. I want to try to capture in my words and music the meanings of nature. And if by those words and that music I can help someone else fall in love with the Earth, then I've done my job, because they will find a way to become connected in it and to help re-establish a connectedness with others. To me, the natural world is inside us all as well as outside. We're all a part of one big thing called nature, and when we forget that, that's when bad things happen."

Biographical and Critical Sources

PERIODICALS

Audubon, November-December, 2001, Christopher Camuto, review of *Grandad's Prayers of the Earth,* p. 86.

Booklist, August, 1992, Julie Corsaro, review of *Old Turtle,* p. 2016; September 15, 1996, Karen Morgan, review of *The Windigo's Return: A North Woods Story,* p. 235; February 15, 1998, Elizabeth Drennan, review of *Rabbit and the Moon,* p. 1016; July, 1998, Shelle Rosenfeld, review of *Making the World,* p. 1892; December 1, 1999, Shelley Townsend-Hudson, review of *Grandad's Prayers of the Earth,* p. 715; April 15, 2001, Amy Brandt, review of *What Moms Can't Do,* p. 1567; February 15, 2002, Hazel Rochman, review of *A Quiet Place,* p. 1023; August, 2002, Connie Fletcher, review of *What Teachers Can't Do,* p. 1777; November 15, 2003, GraceAnne A. DeCandido, review of *The Old Turtle and the Broken Truth,* p. 604; May 1, 2006, Gillian Engberg, review of *Nothing to Do,* p. 94; February 15, 2010, Julie Cummins, review of *Aunt Mary's Rose,* p. 79.

Bulletin of the Center for Children's Books, November, 1996, Betsy Hearne, review of *The Windigo's Return,* p. 112.

Horn Book, May-June, 1996, Margaret A. Bush, review of *Northwood's Cradle Song: From a Menominee Lullaby,* p. 331.

Kirkus Reviews, July 15, 1996, review of *The Windigo's Return,* pp. 1057-1058; January 15, 1998, review of *Rabbit and the Moon,* p. 120; November 1, 1999, review of *Grandad's Prayers of the Earth,* p. 1750; March 15, 2002, review of *A Quiet Place,* p. 429; June 1, 2002, review of *What Teachers Can't Do,* p. 814; October 1, 2005, review of *The Secret of Saying Thanks,* p. 1092; April 15, 2006, review of *Nothing to Do,* p. 419; July 15, 2009, review of *Miss Little's Gift;* February 15, 2010, review of *Aunt Mary's Rose.*

Los Angeles Times, August 29, 1992, Lynne Heffley, "Naturalist Sings, Writes of Love of Earth," pp. F5, F7.

Publishers Weekly, January 1, 1992, review of *Old Turtle,* p. 55; April 15, 1996, review of *Northwoods Cradle Song,* p. 67; September 16, 1996, review of *The Windigo's Return,* p. 82; February 23, 1998, review of *Rabbit and the Moon,* p. 75; August 10, 1998, review of *Making the World,* p. 386; September 27, 1999, review of *Grandad's Prayers of the Earth,* p. 97; May 15, 2000, review of *What Dads Can't Do,* p. 115; July 2, 2001, review of *Rabbit and the Moon,* p. 78; February 4, 2002, review of *A Quiet Place,* p. 75; September 22, 2003, review of *What Santa Can't Do,* p. 69; October 27, 2003, review of *Old Turtle and the Broken Truth,* p. 68; August 29, 2005, review of *The Secret of Saying Thanks,* p. 60; May 29, 2006, review of *Nothing to Do,* p. 57; August 10, 2009, review of *Miss Little's Gift,* p. 53; April 26, 2010, review of *Where the Sunrise Begins,* p. 105; March 28, 2011, review of *No One but You,* p. 57.

School Librarian, autumn, 2010, Elizabeth Baskeyfield, review of *Aunt Mary's Rose,* p. 160.

School Library Journal, June, 1992, Shirley Wilton, review of *Old Turtle,* p. 105; May, 1996, Ruth K. MacDonald, review of *Northwoods Cradle Song,* p. 109; November, 1996, Ellen Fader, review of *The Windigo's Return,* p. 102; July, 1998, Adele Greenlee, review of *Rabbit and the Moon,* p. 91; August, 1998, Diane Nunn, review of *Making the World,* pp. 147-148; January, 2000, Patricia Pearl Dole, review of *Grandad's Prayers of the Earth,* p. 114; May, 2000, Wanda Meyers-Hines, review of *What Dads Can't Do,* p. 159; March, 2001, Sally R. Dow, review of *What Moms Can't Do,* p. 224; July, 2002, Jody McCoy, review of *A Quiet Place,* p. 102; October, 2002, Louise L. Sherman, review of *What Teachers Can't Do,* p. 136; October, 2003, Linda Israelson, review of *What Santa Can't Do,* p. 69; December, 2003, Marianne Saccardi, review of *Old Turtle and the Broken Truth,* p. 162; July, 2005, Kathleen Whalin, review of *What Grandmas Can't Do,* p. 85: October, 2005, Roxanne Burg, review of *The Secret of Saying Thanks,* p. 134; May, 2006, Maryann H. Owen, review of *Nothing to Do,* p. 106; August, 2009, Grace Oliff, review of *Miss Little's Gift,* p. 93; April, 2010, Susan Scheps, review of *Aunt Mary's Rose,* p. 149; June, 2010, Lisa Glasscock, review of *Where the Sunrise Begins,* p. 86; April, 2011, Heidi Estrin, review of *No One but You,* p. 157.

Wilson Library Bulletin, December, 1993, Merry Mattson, review of *Old Turtle,* p. 31.

ONLINE

Douglas Wood Home Page, http://www.douglaswood.com (October 15, 2011).*

*   *   *

WOOD, Douglas Eric
See WOOD, Douglas